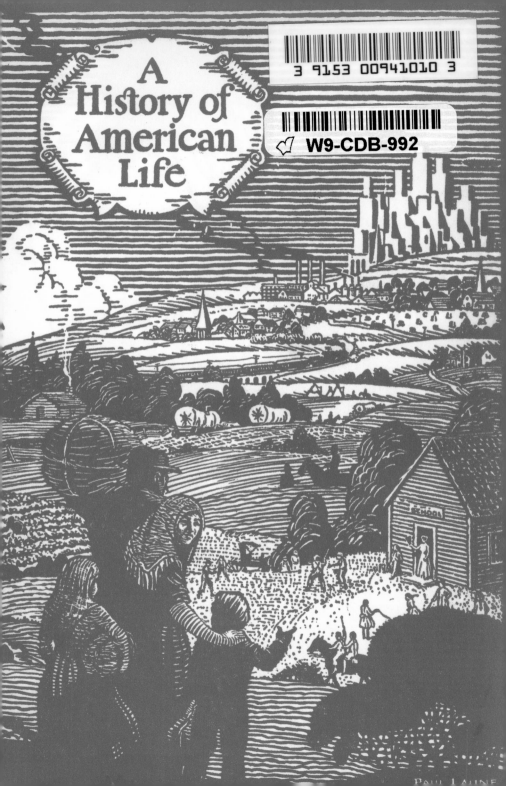

A
History of
American
Life

3 9153 00941010 3

☑ W9-CDB-992

PAUL LAUNE

A HISTORY OF AMERICAN LIFE

IN

THIRTEEN VOLUMES

ARTHUR M. SCHLESINGER
DIXON RYAN FOX

Editors

A HISTORY OF AMERICAN LIFE

Toasting the Champion.

A HISTORY OF AMERICAN LIFE
Volume XIII

THE AGE OF THE GREAT DEPRESSION
1929-1941

BY

DIXON WECTER
CHAIRMAN OF THE RESEARCH GROUP, HUNTINGTON LIBRARY

New York

THE MACMILLAN COMPANY

Everything nailed down is comin' loose.

The Angel Gabriel in MARC CONNELLY, *The Green Pastures* (1930).

It does not follow, because our difficulties are stupendous, because there are some souls timorous enough to doubt the validity and effectiveness of our ideals and our system, that we must turn to a State-controlled or State-directed social or economic system in order to cure our troubles. That is not liberalism; it is tyranny.

HERBERT HOOVER, in acceptance of renomination, August 11, 1932, *Campaign Speeches of 1932* (N. Y., 1933), 8-9.

History proves that dictatorships do not grow out of strong and successful governments, but out of weak and helpless ones. If by democratic methods people get a government strong enough to protect them from fear and starvation, their democracy succeeds; but if they do not, they grow impatient. Therefore, the only sure bulwark of continuing liberty is a government strong enough to protect the interests of the people, and a people strong enough and well enough informed to maintain its sovereign control over its government. We are a rich Nation; we can afford to pay for security and prosperity without having to sacrifice our liberties in the bargain.

FRANKLIN D. ROOSEVELT, Fireside Chat of April 14, 1938, *Public Papers and Addresses* (S. I. Rosenman, ed., N. Y., 1938-1941), VII, 242-243.

CONTENTS

ILLUSTRATIONS

EDITORS' FOREWORD

THE writing of contemporary history lends itself to the danger of biased interpretation. The Age of the Great Depression, however, lies much farther away from the present than the mere lapse of years would signify. The Second World War, with the still unsettled problems of taming the unforeseen forces it engendered, has conferred a curious sense of distance and remoteness upon a chapter of United States history which forms an indelible part of most Americans' lives. Moreover, at the governmental level, the partisan rancors of the time have cooled, encouraging a calmer judgment of events and actions that once tried men's souls. If the signs in today's political heavens are reliable, the nation has accepted as a permanent legacy the innovations of public policy called forth by the Depression.

Professor Wecter, writing from this vantage point, thus swings his historical telescope from new watchtowers. He scans the scene with particular attention to human values— the frustrations, hopes, exertions and idealism of a mighty people afflicted with economic travail such as they had never before known in peace time. This central dilemma he traces in its ramifications through all ranks of society, through government, economics and the varied aspirations of the human mind and spirit. Not content with the cool abstractions of statistics, he constantly illumines his theme with local incident and circumstance chosen with nice discrimination from the experiences of ordinary men and women as revealed in personal writings, case studies and the surveys of investigative agencies. In like fashion he levies toll upon public-opinion polls in order to depict authoritatively shifting currents in folk attitudes. Probably no better example exists of how the historian can use for his own particular purposes the tools that social workers and political analysts devised for theirs.

The reader lives once more through these tragic and hopeful years and perhaps gains fresh insight into events which once overwhelmed him by their swiftness and complexity. Professor Wecter writes with vividness and spirit but not at the sacrifice of a studied effort at fairness. Believing that the historian's function is to explain and interpret rather than to advocate, he seeks to give a sympathetic portrayal of both the Old Deal and the New. No one will leave his pages without a clearer understanding of this critical period and of its tremendous impact upon all phases of American civilization: the family, the church, work, education, learning, letters, taste, the arts, philanthropy, morals, recreation and the like. A portion of the present work formed the basis for five lectures which the author delivered in July, 1947, at Northwestern University on the Harris Foundation.

The account stands complete in itself, but it is also the thirteenth volume of *A History of American Life,* not contemplated in the original design. While it was still in an early stage of planning, Dixon Ryan Fox, my long-time associate in editing the set, died of a sudden heart attack on January 30, 1945. The loss to historical scholarship as well as to the cause of higher education was immeasurable. Fortunately he had already impressed his ideas and standards upon the series, and Professor Wecter and I have striven to fashion a book that would have equaled his expectations.

A. M. S.

CHAPTER I

FROM RICHES TO RAGS

IN mid-October, 1929, the average middle-class American saw ahead of him an illimitable vista of prosperity. A newly inaugurated president, Herbert Hoover, had announced soberly in the previous year that the conquest of poverty was no longer a mirage: "We have not yet reached the goal, but given a chance to go forward with the policies of the last eight years, and we shall soon with the help of God be within sight of the day when poverty will be banished from the nation." * This was the economic promise interwoven with what a popular historian soon would call the American Dream. More complacently, Irving Fisher and other economists in the confidence of Wall Street assured the citizen that he was dwelling upon "a permanently high plateau" of prosperity.

This upland of plenty—more tangible than the Beulahland dear to the old Protestant hymnal—appeared to be the final triumph of a great industrial development dating from the Civil War. The aftermath of America's latest war had seen the arrival in strength of mass production, to compound the wonders of the new technology. Even now, in this third week of October, 1929, with the president and other notables in attendance, Henry Ford was sponsoring the "Golden Jubilee of Light," honoring Edison and the fiftieth birthday of the incandescent lamp. Motor cars, bathtubs, electric refrigerators, radios, were the touchstones of progress. Keeping up

* Speech accepting the nomination of the Republican party, *N. Y. Times,* Aug. 12, 1928. With omission of "yet" and "soon" and "with the policies of the last eight years," Hoover stoutly repeated these words in the depths of the Depression, in his Madison Square Garden speech of October 31, 1932. Herbert Hoover, *State Papers* (W. S. Myers, ed., N. Y., 1934), II, 426-427.

with the Joneses, under the spur of fashion and advertisement, demanded nothing less than the latest model. Pressures of salesmanship urged even the duplication of luxuries—two cars in every garage—in a consumer's market already displaying symptoms of surfeit, not because all Americans were gorged with worldly goods, but because buying power was unevenly distributed.

The nation's policies and institutions were closely enmeshed with the prosperous middle class. "The suburban community is the dominant American group," one observer wrote in the summer of 1929. The increasing stress upon the solidarity and good fellowship of certain organizations—fraternal orders, business men's luncheon clubs, Legion conventions—and the moral meddlesomeness of others like the Anti-Saloon League bred a regimentation which he feared as foreshadowing "the group from which the Fascisti of the future will be drawn, if there are Fascisti." That Babbitt might ever doff his natty silk shirt for one of brown or black was problematical; but the cult of conformity, in so far as it boosted material success, was in the saddle. Cotton Mather, Ben Franklin, Peter Parley and Horace Greeley would have understood the spirit of the times, even though old maxims of drudgery and penny pinching seemed to have been by-passed for quicker ways to wealth.

Time, liveliest weekly of the decade, in January, 1929, hailed Walter P. Chrysler as "Man of the Year," because during the past twelvemonth he had introduced the public to Plymouth and DeSoto cars, bought out Dodge Brothers for one hundred and sixty million dollars and begun to build "the world's tallest skyscraper, a 68-story colossus." * Now, on the cover of *Time* for October 14, 1929, appeared the face of William Wrigley, jr., to be followed in successive weeks by

---

* As announced in January, 1930, "Man of the Year" was Owen D. Young, author of the Young Plan for the payment of German reparations and also endowed with the glamour of great wealth; but *Time's* choice for the following year, by significant contrast, was Mahatma Gandhi.

Harry F. Guggenheim, Ivar Kreuger, Samuel Insull and Thomas W. Lamont—heroes all. The last issue before the Wall Street crash carried a triple-page announcement of the new magazine *Fortune*, at the "unique price of $10 a year," which proclaimed the "generally accepted commonplace that America's great achievement has been Business." Other large advertisements featured Babson's *Reports* ("Your Dollars—Are They Continuously and Efficiently at Work?"), the Hamilton watch ("Can you tell a successful man by the time he carries?"), Robert I. Warshow's new book *The Story of Wall Street* ("These giants march through its pages . . . like the adventurers of the middle ages . . . Daniel Drew, Jim Fisk, Jay Gould, Vanderbilt, Hill, Harriman . . . and the many others whose exploits have astounded the nation"), and the investment services of a firm to collapse in 1932 leaving millions in defaulted bonds, S. W. Straus & Co. ("He invests his modest earnings in good sound securities"). They represented the stimuli which beat incessantly upon the mind of the average magazine reader.

Masses of Americans who bought their first bonds in the liberty loans of 1918 had lately turned to more speculative issues. Advertisements flaunting high prices instead of bargains—from $45,000 apartments on Park Avenue and bathrooms equipped with "Crane Louis XVI Trianon Fittings Gold-Plated," down to $2.50 lipsticks and razor blades at three for fifty cents—set the sumptuary scale for a generation of easy money. To keep abreast of the traffic in this climb to the highlands of permanent prosperity, the stock market was the obvious vehicle. In 1920 there had been 29,609 stockbrokers in the United States; within ten years they had jumped to 70,950. It was commonly observed that a great many citizens no longer read the front page of their newspaper, but turned hurriedly to the financial columns. Tabloid papers and tip sheets offered investment advice to amateurs. Over the radio flowed the voice of the "Old Counselor," steady as a deacon, intoning the wisdom of Samuel Insull's own brokers.*

Popular interest was growing about the mystery of business cycles. Whether they were ruled by overproduction or underproduction, banking operations, innovations in method, hysterias of hope or panic, or perhaps sun spots, was not clear. Guessing was garbed in the robes of prophecy. Wishfulness took priority over planning. Optimists believed that the old laws of economics had been arrested; others conceded that rainy days might come, but after every storm the skies must clear—if everybody, as the season's most popular song exhorted, would keep his sunny side up. Above all, recession was the abnormal thing. Prosperity needed no explanation. Nor was it the monopoly of so-called leisured classes, or the Republican party, despite their effort to claim all the credit.

> If a man saves $15 a week, and invests in good common stocks, and allows the dividends and rights to accumulate, at the end of twenty years he will have at least $80,000 and an income from investments of around $400 a month. He will be rich. And because income can do that, I am firm in my belief that anyone not only can be rich, but ought to be rich.

So declared John J. Raskob, chairman of the Democratic national committee, in the summer of 1929. Employees were encouraged to invest in the stocks and bonds of their employers—a system regarded somewhat vaguely as the American equivalent of profit sharing, or perhaps social security.

Much of this buying of stocks was on margin, which meant that investors, including the small fry with little cash but big hopes, put up about a fourth of the price. The broker

---

* The identity of this famous character was a minor mystery. While the head of Halsey, Stuart & Co., his sponsors, told a Senate committee that the "Old Counselor" was a University of Chicago professor paid $50 a week to read their script, the president of NBC, M. H. Aylesworth, testified that he was an actor. Ruth Brindze, *Not to Be Broadcast* (N. Y., 1937), 40-41.

advanced the rest by borrowing from banks. This precarious credit structure of brokers' loans had trembled in February, 1929, when the Federal Reserve Board ordered member banks not to lend money for such speculative purposes. But private bankers, led by Charles E. Mitchell, had promptly unlocked their millions for speculation and given a further fillip to the great bull market and the age of confidence upon which it was built. This caused another spasm of activity, unwarranted by any such tangibles as consumer demand, gains in productive efficiency or real earning of the stocks in question. While the rich were growing richer, several million citizens with small incomes were raiding their savings, reducing their immediate purchasing power and mortgaging their future in order to speculate. Ninety per cent of these market transactions in the twenties, it has been estimated, were gambling ventures rather than permanent investments.

Almost imperceptibly a shift had occurred in economic control, from the industrial capitalism of an earlier day to finance capitalism. Exploitation of investors and frequent duplicity in bookkeeping were among the less lovely traits of the new order. The holding company—an avatar which sprang from the slain dragon of the "trusts" late in the previous century—now flourished mightily. It permitted control by a small group of stockholders over a widely scattered empire of interlocking or even loosely related interests, like Samuel Insull's three-billion-dollar domain in utilities. The power exercised by the holding company, particularly in the utility field, was often so disproportionate to its size that Franklin D. Roosevelt as president well described it as "a ninety-six-inch dog being wagged by a four-inch tail."

These concerns were sometimes pyramided one upon another, towers of Babel reaching to the skies and equally tremulous at the base. Not infrequently they were used to mask the true state of corporate finances from the eyes of regulatory authorities or the public. A New York state bank called Bank of United States, in January, 1930—almost a year before its spectacular failure brought down the roof upon nearly half a million depositors—concealed its growing weakness by creating a dummy company, the Bolivar Development Corporation, capitalized at one hundred dollars, to buy and sell the stock of still another dummy conjured by the Bank into making the motions of prosperity. Deceived by this solemn farce, the outsider was slow to suspect that many a façade of granite and marble had become a hollow shell of indebtedness and precarious bookkeeping.

Another development in the pathology of Wall Street was the mushrooming in the latter twenties of so-called investment trusts, whose function was to invest moneys loaned to them and to distribute the net return to their stockholders or beneficiaries. Some were "rigid," *i.e.* confined to a restricted list of securities, but many were "flexible," which meant that the selection of securities for investment was left wide open. In practice they were little better than gambling establishments in which the innocent patron intrusted his stakes not even to a fellow player picked at random but to the croupier —whose main interest, of course, was to represent "the house." Four and a half million Americans, it was reported, handed over part or all their savings to investment trusts, eventually losing about a third of their capital, or a total of three billion dollars.

The overexpansion of credit was a prime cause of the disasters that followed 1929. The First World War began a process which reckless financing continued to accelerate. In the background loomed the huge structure of long-term debt in the United States—a public debt, federal, state and municipal, of thirty-three billion dollars, and corporate and individual debts of one hundred billion—which demanded expanding markets and world prosperity for successful carrying. A relatively small reduction in buying power, or backsliding of prices, could send tremors along the whole length of this mountain chain. The grand operations of credit, a new force of such power that one economist likened it to the prime movers of physics, were still imperfectly understood and recklessly abused. The average American in 1929 had little notion of credit on the imperial scale, such as the growth of international financing dependent upon a constant transfusion of credit from have to have-not nations, nor even the magnitude of eight billion dollars' credit in the form of brokers' loans which Wall Street recorded at its all-time crest of September 3, 1929.

The common man knew more about overexpansion of credit in such homely shapes as installment buying. Intensive campaigns to break down "sales resistance"—often insufficient purchasing power among small citizens—led to new extensions of the time-payment plan for cars, clothes, electric washers, refrigerators, furniture, jewelry. In effect it was a loan from producer to consumer, because the latter lacked cash, and the former, with his urgent need for sales, preferred this method to that of increasing mass purchasing power by cutting prices and boosting wages. By 1929 felicity on the installment plan had lured its tens of millions. In the harsh light of the Great Depression, such aspects of the system as inflated prices and exorbitant carrying charges, along with misrepresentation of the product, would become all too plain. Certain state laws, like those of New York and Kentucky, held a still more pernicious trap, sprung during the early thirties, by which a debtor's entire wages could be attached until the account was cleared.

Meanwhile important business enterprises were being concentrated in fewer hands. The forging of chain stores all over the nation was no less significant than recent big mergers in the automotive industry. Centralized industry made every metropolis the center of a regional web, and each of these networks fitted into a national pattern for making, selling and distributing commodities. The economy of a continent had never been so highly integrated, nor its equilibrium so sensitive. The frontier, the farm, the village and Middletown had at last been engulfed by the rise of the city. As never before, urban industrialism called the tune. In 1870 wage and salary workers had made up about half the working population; now they composed four fifths. An interdependence unknown to old-fashioned America had become the basic economic fact. The fabric of industrial and corporate life, joined to the structure imposed by labor unions and labor legislation, had imperceptibly altered the flexibility of *laissez faire* into something more rigid, less accommodating.

These sweeping changes had hardly entered the consciousness of the average citizen. In his own mind he was never more loyal than in 1929 to the doctrine of individualism and unhampered private enterprise. Clashes between theory and practice, like the potential friction of capital and labor, remained almost inaudible so long as the nation's economic mechanism ran with the oil of prosperity.

Not, indeed, that the prosperity of the twenties was consistently sound. To the later view it resembled a hectic flush rather than the bloom of health. Agriculture still groaned from its dropsical overexpansion in 1917-1918. Along with bituminous coal mining and textiles, it belonged to a clinical ward known as the "sick industries." Great was the industrial turnover; a sense of insecurity about jobs had been rising for several years. Even in 1926 the unemployed were estimated at 1,500,000; by 1929 their number had swelled to upwards of 1,800,000.* Unperceived by the optimists, joblessness and poverty had come to be chronic social problems in the United States—neither a passing crisis nor one readily met by efforts of private charity. The ratio of private to public funds for such purposes was diminishing, as public relief expenditures gradually mounted. Sixteen major cities which

* R. R. Nathan, *Estimates of Unemployment in the United States, 1929-1935* (Geneva, 1936), gives the higher computation of 2,860,000 by March, 1929—a figure accepted by Harry L. Hopkins, *Spending to Save* (N. Y., 1936), 13. Generally speaking, liberals tended to estimate unemployment in the twenties and early thirties at higher figures than did the Hoover administration and the majority of conservatives.

in 1911 had spent $1,500,000 on public charity were by 1928 spending $20,000,000 annually.

Flaws in banking practice might also have been suspected. During the six years prior to the October crash of 1929 bank failures occurred at an average rate of nearly two a day, but since the delinquents were minor institutions, chiefly in small towns, scant publicity resulted. Nor was the output of goods commensurate with the capacity to produce. At least twenty per cent of the country's resources were not being utilized, to the loss of about fifteen billion dollars in national income, or one fourth of the goods and services it was actually producing.

Yet beyond question the major shortcomings of the American economy lay not with production but consumption. Already in the early autumn of 1929 financial pages gloomed over "heaviness" in automobiles and radios, slackening of the building trades, disappointment along the new frontiers of aviation. Much of America's productive effort and income had lately gone into luxuries and durable goods, whose purchase could be postponed without affecting daily needs. At the first storm warnings these goods would pile up in warehouses, causing wheels to stop turning and huge areas of joblessness to appear. This was one reason why the Depression following 1929 was unparalleled for severity and duration.

Even in 1929 the purchasing power of the American people looked ill-balanced, an anomaly soon to be pointed up by quotation of Carlyle's phrase, "poverty in the midst of plenty." Between 1923 and 1928, while the index of speculative gains rose from 100 to 410, the index of wages advanced from 100 to a mere 112. Naturally enough, too little income went for consumer goods in proportion to the torrents that flowed into investment channels and the call-money market, into the making of new capital equipment for future production and into the savings of the well-to-do. Never before had so large a share of the national income been saved and invested as in this decade, nor had current production ever outstripped current consumption so spectacularly. The National Survey of Potential Product Capacity later described the period from 1923 to 1929 as an "orgy of saving" among the rich.

Two thirds of the country's savings were made by families with incomes over $10,000 a year. Those with less than $1500, comprising forty per cent of the population, actually paid out more than they earned. Six million families, one fifth of the nation, fell below even $1000. Making provision for a rainy day seemed less than feasible when one was already drowning. Up to the income bracket of $5000, American families had to spend a disproportionate amount merely to get sufficient food; hence among those nine out of ten families "not in a position to enjoy a liberal diet," substantial savings could hardly be expected.* In presenting the extremes of the economic spectrum a study by the Brookings Institution observed that the twenty-four thousand families which received over $100,000 apiece in 1929 enjoyed a total income three times as great as that of the six million poorest families. In other words, the average income among the top group was six hundred and thirty times that in the bottom one.

Orthodox economists argued that savings led to more capital equipment and superior efficiency and, in turn, to lower production costs, lower prices and greater purchasing power for the masses. It was plain by 1929, however, that this chain of causation had developed weak links. Mass buying power was unable to absorb the nation's output, not alone because wages had advanced comparatively little but because retail prices took virtually no cut between 1922 and 1929. Savings achieved by improved technologies were not being

* Maurice Leven and others, *America's Capacity to Consume* (Wash., 1934), 93, 123. At 1929 prices an adequate diet for the average family was estimated to cost $800; $2000 was reckoned the minimum for basic necessities of living. A summary of statistics on this subject for 1929 and later will be found in S. C. Menefee, "Standard of Living," *Survey*, LXXIII (1937), 281-282.

handed on to the consumer in the form of lower prices. They were diverted into dividends, reserves, bigger salaries and bonuses. Various shapes of monopoly, like trusts in disguise, mergers, combinations in mining and manufacturing, helped keep prices up, even while new machinery, better production methods and services of "efficiency experts" increased the over-all output of American labor by more than a third in the decade after the First World War. In some trades, like automobiles, productive efficiency was reported to have tripled.

But from this plenitude the average consumer gathered only the crumbs, and even the producer reaped merely a shortsighted advantage. To reckon profit not for a day or season, but upon a broad and long-term base of buying power, might have proved wiser. Posterity would probably agree with the retrospective view of Hoover who, after praise for the technologists, remarked:

> When we fully understand the economic history of the 'twenties, we shall find that the débâcle which terminated another apparently highly prosperous period was largely contributed by a failure of industry to pass its improvement (through labor-saving devices) on to the consumer.

Some others were less inclined to praise the engineers than to damn them. Their ingenuity, it was charged, had supplanted men with machines. The effect of invention in upsetting group equilibrium was, of course, no novelty. In the past, management had sometimes shown reluctance to scrap old equipment for new; more often, labor feared the "immigration of iron men." Naturally at the first threat of spreading unemployment the machine was indicted, for this generation was less apt than its forefathers to accept all calamities as mysterious visitations of Providence. Soon, in the wake of apprehensions that technology had done its job too well, came a flock of ideas about social engineering. Could not the same magic which had rid the factory of waste and inefficiency do the same for society? This hope—newer to American life than the invincible faith in applied science—led from Hoover the "Great Engineer" to Technocracy, the National Recovery Administration, the Tennessee Valley Authority, the National Resources Committee and other concepts of a managed economy. Few could have foreseen in 1929 all the paths of this projection. Nevertheless in that year the fundamental balances of a vast industrial civilization were slipping: the precarious relations between wages and prices, production and consumption, machines and man power.

Upon this world of uneasy prosperity the first blow fell in late October. Like the sound of gunshot which starts an Alpine avalanche, a minor panic on the New York Stock Exchange began on the twenty-third among stocks that speculators had pushed to fantastic heights. The next day, "Black Thursday," saw hysteria rampant. Brokers wept and tore off their collars trying to keep abreast selling orders; sight-seers jammed the Wall Street district, ogled the arrival of great bankers in their limousines before the House of Morgan, and under the rumor of mass suicide gathered to watch an ordinary workman on a scaffolding in morbid expectation of his plunge.

At first it appeared that the magicians of finance had arrested disaster, but just as the public cheered them and breathed more easily, another sickening lurch sent the market to new depths, spreading conviction that these wizards had merely propped the falling timbers long enough to get out from under. October 29 set a lurid record for sales, a total of 16,410,000 shares. At the month's close fifteen billion dollars in market value had been wiped out, and before the end of the year losses reached an estimated forty billion.

After the first shock official optimism took over. A generation taught to be "a bull on the United States" was conditioned to respond. Upon feeling the initial jolt, many seemed as incredulous about the real gravity of the situation as the

passengers of a luxury liner ripped below decks by an ice-
berg: the boat listed only a trifle at first while the band
played on. Manhattan's dapper mayor, "Jimmy" Walker,
asked the movies to show nothing but cheerful pictures. The
patient was recommended to try the hair of the dog that bit
him: *True Story Magazine* ran big advertisements in the
newspapers urging wage-earners to buy more luxury items
on credit. "Wall Street may sell stocks, but Main Street is
buying goods," came a cheery assurance from the *Saturday
Evening Post*. A Manhattan jeweler in early November put
on display a "$750,000 pearl necklace," while the Shuberts
revealed plans for a $15,000,000 theater-hotel on Broad-
way. "Forward America, Nothing Can Stop U. S.," shouted
the nation's billboards. And over the radio Julius Klein, assistant secretary of commerce, announced that only four per
cent of the people had been adversely affected. A tuneful hit
called "Happy Days Are Here Again" was copyrighted on
November 7 for one of the new talking pictures appropri-
ately named "Chasing Rainbows"; three years later it would
become the campaign song of the New Deal. And early in
1930, with skies growing blacker, makers of a cheap radio
brought out a "prosperity model."

The solvent of American humor began early to attack the
crisis. Grim jokes arose about the complimentary revolver
given with every share of Goldman Sachs, or the room clerk's
query of every registrant, "For sleeping or jumping?" A
little later, when mass unemployment began to steal the headlines from Wall Street, bravado succeeded flippancy. Billboards began to ask, "Wasn't the Depression Terrible?" The
departing owner of a ruined shop scrawled upon the door
"Opened by mistake" if he were a humorist, or "Busted and
disgusted" if possessed by the blues. Trained in the cult of
the stiff upper lip, of singing in the rain, Americans hated
to admit that things were not as they had always been. The
International Association of Lions Clubs observed the week
of October 19, 1930, as Business Confidence Week. Pros-

perity was just around the corner; perhaps the corner was one already turned.

For a while the momentum of the great bull market carried certain enterprises. The year 1931, for example, saw the opening of the world's finest luxury hotel, the new Waldorf-Astoria in Manhattan, and completion of the tallest of all skyscrapers, the Empire State Building of one hundred and two stories topped by a "mooring mast" for airships—but functionally as useless as the metallic needle surmounting its nearest rival, the new Chrysler Building. Many floors in each of these grandiose business palaces remained spectrally vacant in the times ahead. The same year saw publication of architects' plans for New York's most impressive cluster of buildings, Rockefeller Center, which the next two years consummated. Housing broadcasting studios, ornate movie and music halls, foreign-trade syndicates and other business enterprises upon a scale never before attempted, this group culminated in the austere gray seventy-story shaft of the R. C. A. building.

Some critics of architecture prophesied that these would be the last dinosaurs of America's metropolitan era, convinced that such vainglory had overreached itself, promoting little save congested traffic, overcrowding and colossal debts. Like many other vanities of the century, perhaps the skyscraper too was bankrupt. At any rate, the nation's outlay for new construction fell sixty per cent between 1931 and 1932 as the momentum of prosperity ground to a dead stop. By 1933 architects were doing less than a seventh of the business they had enjoyed in 1928.

Gala openings and soothing statements no longer fitted the temper of the times; the smile of official optimism slowly froze into something that resembled a *risus sardonicus*. In 1931 Edward Angly garnered the more fulsome assurances of Wall Street and Washington into a little book with the derisive title *Oh Yeah!* Early in the following year appeared a new magazine called *Ballyhoo*, its first issue packaged in cellophane as a touch of commercial parody. Within six

months it rocketed to a two-million circulation largely by debunking the specious salesmanship of the twenties.*

The public, seeking a scapegoat for its bitterness, found
one with the help of a shrewd publicist hired by the Democratic party, Charles Michelson. Old newspapers were called
"Hoover blankets," jack rabbits "Hoover hogs" and the
shanties of starvation rising on outskirts of cities "Hoovervilles," A large share of popular odium also fell upon the
shoulders of rich and weary Andrew Mellon, lately toasted
by business as the "greatest secretary of the treasury since
Alexander Hamilton." In February, 1932, Mellon was glad
enough to relinquish his portfolio and be kicked upstairs as
ambassador to Britain.

As President Coolidge had said in the palmy days, the
business of America had indeed been business. But now the
luxuries and amusements, the bustling sense of power which
cloaked life's essential materialism for the prosperous urban
or suburban citizen, were suddenly stripped away. This
greatest of economic reverses gave millions of citizens the jolt
of taking a downward step in the dark when expecting an
upward one. A nation used to regarding prosperity as a habit
found itself startled, then incredulous, more than a little
helpless and finally resentful. It made the situation no easier
that the adversary was invisible, and unlike a domestic or
foreign foe, invulnerable to ridicule, ballots or bullets.

But the reality of this enemy admitted no doubt. His unseen stature could be measured by the two yardsticks of income and employment. The loss of earnings, chiefly paper
profits, had first taken the spotlight. A few moths had singed
their wings; so what? But as early as the spring of 1930,
when the Federal Council of Churches set aside April 27 as
"Unemployment Sunday," the crisis had assumed breadth as

* Its creator was a disillusioned Manhattan editor and artist, Norman
Anthony, but the name which *Ballyhoo* made famous was that of a fictional
high-powered advertising man, one Elmer Zilch. In a chapter called "Jackpot!"
Anthony gave the history of this magazine in *How to Grow Old Disgracefully*
(N. Y., 1946).

well as depth. Soon, lowered income and unemployment were seen in constant interaction, forcing the national economy into a descending spiral. White-collar workers began to take salary cuts, laborers to find discharge slips in pay envelopes. The city felt the shock first. Initial symptoms were not ostentatious: postponement in buying that new car, or breaking ground for a new home; surrender of small apartments by young couples moving in with parents; a drop in pleasure travel and theater attendance; more business for the cleaner, invisible mender, shoe-repair man, less for tailor and haberdasher.

A few grimmer signs appeared early, upon a small scale. In late February, 1930, Seattle, Los Angeles and Chicago witnessed minor demonstrations of the unemployed, in which Communists usually had a hand. In the same month bread lines in the Bowery were drawing two thousand daily. In March Milwaukee opened a municipal soup kitchen. The summer of 1930, as happened seasonally through the Depression, brought a measure of relief. Food was fresher, more plentiful and cheaper; clothing, fuel and shelter offered problems less acute. But the descent of winter in 1930-1931 inaugurated harder times, with New York City appropriating a million dollars for direct relief and Lloyd's of London announcing that for the first time on record they were selling riot and civil-commotion insurance in quantity to American clients.

Outside the city, harbingers of the crisis were less newsworthy. Farmers had known nothing but depression since the Armistice boom burst, and even though their plight continued to worsen, they had the gloomy satisfaction of long conditioning. Smaller industrial cities and towns, however, were reluctant to admit the fact of hard times, which in many citizens' eyes was either a Manhattan gamblers' fiasco or else just a state of mind. They congratulated themselves upon a firmer foundation. Notwithstanding that every fourth factory worker in Muncie, Indiana—the Middletown of sociologists—had lost his job before the end of 1930, men of substance in that community kept insisting to the end of 1931 that the Depression was "mainly something we read about in the newspapers." Still feeding upon the gospel of keeping up appearances, a delegation of local business men in 1932 persuaded General Motors not to board up the windows of its abandoned Muncie plant, which stood in clear view of the passing trains. The philosophy of the peptomists died hard.

As the average citizen could see for himself, working capital and jobs were closely interlocked, and upon their joint scarcity the years of depression hinged. What happened to income may be shown briefly. National income dwindled from eighty-one billion dollars in 1929 to less than sixty-eight in 1930, then cascaded to fifty-three in 1931 and hit bottom in 1932 with forty-one. Correspondingly, the country's estimated wealth over this span shrank from three hundred and sixty-five billion to two hundred and thirty-nine, a loss representing diminished values in real property, capital and commodities. Much of the nation's physical plant, of course, rusted in idleness and disrepair. These three years took a toll of eighty-five thousand business failures with liabilities of four and a half billion dollars and the suspension of five thousand banks. Nine million savings accounts were wiped out, and wage losses upwards of twenty-six billion dollars sustained.

While the debt structure of the American economy remained little changed—only 3.5 per cent less money being paid out in interest in 1932 than in 1929—in other fields deflation proceeded furiously, making long-term debts more crushing than borrowers had anticipated when incurring them. The volume of money paid as salaries dwindled 40 per cent, dividends 56.6 per cent, and wages 60 per cent. Early in the crisis, at the Hoover administration's earnest request, major industries made few cuts in pay rates, but by drastic reduction of working hours and days they contrived to slash pay rolls about 40 per cent between 1929 and September,

1931. Since a workingman's family had to live on the money he brought home, this procedure looked better in the headlines than in private.

For the country at large, per-capita realized income (adjusted to the cost of living) tumbled from $681 in 1929 to $495 in 1933. At the apex of the economic pyramid the number of persons reporting an annual income over a million dollars fell from seventy-five in 1931 to only twenty the next year. Despite repeated assurances from government circles and high finance that the recession had reached bedrock —the "terminal trough," forecasters liked to call it—the general course of business after the Wall Street crash plunged fitfully downward for more than three years.

Many industries and small businesses denied even lip service to the administration's plea for maintenance of wage rates. A growing backwater of unemployment led department stores to pay clerks as little as five or ten dollars weekly. Investigation of a group of working girls in Chicago showed the great majority toiling for less than twenty-five cents an hour, a fourth for less than ten cents. Makers of ready-to-wear dresses, confectionery employees and cannery workers were among the classes exploited most callously. First-class New York stenographers' salaries fell from $35 and $45 a week to $16; domestic servants were obliged to labor for room and board plus ten dollars a month. As usual, unskilled workers had been the shock troops, followed by white-collar workers and technicians. Professional classes felt the jar a little later, as teachers' and ministers' salaries were cut or fell into arrears, and the practice of other groups declined, with fees increasingly hard to collect. Even in 1936 physicians' incomes were still from eighteen to thirty per cent below their 1929 level, lawyers' between eighteen and thirty-eight per cent.

Turning from lowered income and diminished working capital to the other side of the coin, one comes upon the face of total unemployment. In April, 1930, President Hoover

Apple-selling on city streets was one response of the unemployed.

"Hoovervilles" symbolized the plight from which many of them sought escape.

First Blows of the Depression.

Jobless veterans in their hour of need demanded that Congress immediately pay the bonus, which was not due until 1945.

ordered a house-to-house survey of this situation, the first federal census of unemployment in the nation's history. In all, slightly more than three million employables were reported out of work, against forty-five million persons gainfully employed. But the tide was rising fast, and a special census by the department of commerce in January, 1931, based upon sampling, disclosed more than six million unemployed. Before the end of that year almost all appraisers agreed that the ten-million mark had been passed, and 1932 saw the addition of four or five million more. Thanks to seasonal factors and local flurries of advance or retreat, the national picture shifted constantly; unemployment tended also to propagate itself, with wives and older children of idle men now joining in the scramble for any crumbs of odd jobs. Exhaustion of savings and losses in modest investments drove aged folk to participate in the frantic search and be counted.

This cycle brought forth its changing tokens and symbols. If the still cheerful desperation of 1931 was crystallized in the song "Life Is Just a Bowl of Cherries," the grimmer abasement of 1932 was epitomized by "Brother, Can You Spare a Dime?" appealing on behalf of casualties like the jobless war veteran or the discarded builder of an industrial empire. The most memorable symbol of the great unemployment, and of pride in facing it, came to be the apple. In the autumn of 1930 the International Apple Shippers' Association devised a scheme to dispose of surpluses. It offered to sell the fruit on credit to the jobless, to retail at five cents apiece. By early November six thousand apple sellers had taken their stand on the sidewalks of New York, and the idea soon spread elsewhere. In this early phase of the Depression, the stubborn self-reliance of America—the poor as well as the rich—bridled at the notion of direct relief or a dole, as had been practised since the First World War in Britain. But this meager toll upon the passing throng soon lost its novelty. In 1931 Manhattan began to forbid apple selling upon certain streets. By 1932 people were reported to be "sick of apples."

Those who could lift their eyes from this bleak domestic picture to scan the international horizon could draw at least some solace from the proverbial fellowship of misery. President Hoover himself at first was inclined to lay the ultimate blame upon causes outside the United States. In the war of 1914-1918 and its aftermath he saw the wellspring of this bitter draught. Waste and destruction, loss of man power, war debts and taxes, inflation and subsequent devaluation, the greed and imperialism of others, together with the fears and new spending bred by rearmament, were the malign heritage of a struggle "for which our people had no blame." And so far as America was concerned, these complications sprang from the days of Woodrow Wilson, "this war having come on during a Democratic administration." *

If this analysis seemed overcomforting—presenting the American people in the classic rôle of innocents at home and abroad—at least none could deny that the Depression was fast spreading over an economically interdependent world. Nations were seen to be roped together like mountain climbers in the bonds of loans and debts, cartels and tariffs, and quick communication whether of hope or panic. The footing of countries mainly agricultural tended to give way first, with the industrial powers slipping later but more spectacularly. By the spring of 1929 or slightly earlier, Australia, Brazil, the Orient, the Near East, Argentina, Canada and Poland were showing symptoms of decline, while Germany's chronic postwar depression deepened. Later than the United States to feel the shock were Great Britain, France, Czechoslovakia, Switzerland and the Scandinavian countries. A second wave, beginning about 1931 and more severe than the first, likewise affected all these lands, and did not begin to recede until around the spring of 1933.

In most places similar factors had been at work, although

* Hoover, *State Papers*, II, 137, 437. "Without the war, we would have had no such depression," Hoover said flatly at Indianapolis in June, 1931. Myers and Newton, *Hoover Administration*, 90.

the shape and gravity of the crisis varied a good deal. A look at the global picture, however, showed that Americans had not been the only dupes of hit-or-miss prosperity, the Republicans not the sole villains of 1929, nor the Democrats the exclusive heroes of 1933.

Refusal to admit this fact of economic interdependence was never shown more clearly than by the Hawley-Smoot tariff of June, 1930, in itself an aggravation of the crisis. The armistice of 1918 found the United States for the first time in history a great creditor country. At the same time its citizens' private investments abroad were growing so rapidly that from a prewar total of three billion dollars they had swollen to fourteen by 1932. A mighty producing nation, America naïvely construed foreign commerce as the right to sell, with little or no obligation to buy in exchange. Indeed, the nightmare of foreign dumping led both farmers and industrialists to clamor for the highest protective rates yet known and to obtain them in 1930 at an average of forty per cent. President Hoover wished to limit the bill chiefly to a few agricultural commodities, but he was overborne.

Abroad the Hawley-Smoot act was interpreted as a declaration of economic war. It met such prompt retaliatory tariffs, quotas and anti-American embargoes that by 1932 twenty-five governments had joined in the reprisal, thus halving the volume of United States exports. The vicious spiral held another twist. To escape this threat of boycott, American manufacturers during the first two years of the Hawley-Smoot act set up two hundred and fifty-eight separate factories in foreign countries, including seventy-one across the Canadian line.

What the average American thought about these matters depended largely upon his region, politics and business. Southerners had always been taught to regard high tariffs as iniquitous, but in the industrial North and agricultural Midwest "protection" still exercised its charm. No doubt many solid citizens would have echoed an editorial in Middletown's press: "The difference between good times and bad times in the United States, so far as history indicates, is the difference between an adequate protective tariff for the products of our farms and our factories and an inadequate tariff." When regression rather than improvement followed, Middletown's editor stuck doggedly to his line, ridiculing the "mistaken" view that "conditions in Europe have something to do with America's coming out of the depression."

Within the United States the twenties had seen a remarkable increase in the number and influence of trade associations, by which rival producers pooled statistical information, credit standards, cost formulae, and the like, and sought to curb unfair marketing practices. To this extent they were beneficent, and so impressed Hoover as secretary of commerce and as president. But not infrequently they sought by their definition of "fair" and "unfair" price policies to achieve price control while sailing to the leeward of the Sherman antitrust act, and sometimes the effect was to eliminate the small independent operator. Their growth was further indulged by a series of Supreme Court decisions which an earlier progressivism would have eyed with suspicion as entering wedges for native cartels and capitalist syndicalism.*

Although domestic cartels remained illegal under federal law, in the international sphere certain American concerns benefiting by the concentration of economic power—Du Pont, United States Steel, General Electric, Westinghouse, Bendix Aviation, Diamond Match, Anaconda Copper, Standard Oil of New Jersey—entered into agreements in the twenties and the thirties with foreign producers often to restrict production in order to raise prices and increase profits, and still more commonly to divide world markets and exchange patents. In hampering free enterprise cartels tended to constrict the flow of supplies, retard foreign and domestic

* For example, the cracking patents pool in the oil industry (282 U. S., 163, 1931) and the organization of a joint sales agency among major producers in the Appalachian Coals case (288 U. S., 344, 1933).

trade and prevent the introduction of new products and improvements (such, for example, as the "everlasting" match usable many times).

Their effect upon prices may be illustrated by the fact that in 1914 the cost of quinine sulfate was twenty-five cents an ounce, but after Merck joined the international cartel the price rose to seventy-five cents by 1941. The imposition of production quotas is suggested by the fact that, while in 1930 domestic aluminum production exceeded a hundred thousand metric tons and that of Germany was only thirty thousand, in 1934, three years after Alcoa entered the cartel, the American output had fallen to thirty-three thousand tons and the German had risen to thirty-seven.* In the Depression their effect apparently was to aggravate unemployment and underconsumption. Later in the thirties cartels began to attract unfavorable notice from Senate investigating committees and the antitrust division of the justice department because of their alleged threat to the national security.† On the whole, the shapes assumed by the internationalism of Big Business seemed as futile as those of economic nationalism in promoting the greatest good for the greatest number.

Lurking in the background of the ordinary American's insularity remained the old issue of unpaid debts from the

* U. S. *v.* Aluminum Co. of America, 148 Fed. Rep., ser. 2, 416, an action which resulted on March 12, 1945, in a decision adverse to the aluminum interests, holding that they had violated the Sherman act.

† Most notably the cartel under which Standard Oil of New Jersey had promised the German firm, I. G. Farben, "the benefit of all its know-how in the oil and chemical fields." Special Committee Investigating the National Defense Program, *Hearings on Senate Resolution 71,* pt. xi, 4698 (77 Cong., 1 sess., March 1942). Wendell Berge, assistant attorney-general, declared in retrospect: "The good-neighbor policy, which is supposed to govern our relations with Latin America, the reciprocal trade treaties, our alien-property policy, and other basic principles of America's conduct of foreign affairs have in many instances been seriously weakened by the interference of cartel activities." Subcommittee of the Committee on the Judiciary, *U. S. Senate Hearings on S. 11,* 47 (79 Cong., 1 sess., May 1945). Cartels in the Great Depression are discussed by Louis Domeratzky, "Cartels and the Business Crisis," *Foreign Affairs,* X (1931), 34-53.

First World War. Here, he believed, was proof that in dealing with foreigners he and his compatriots always got trimmed. Isolation was best. Other persons saw the urgency of war debts and reparations as strangling the economy of Europe and ultimately harming the creditor as well. President Hoover's decision in June, 1931, to sponsor a moratorium on intergovernmental war debts was hailed in some circles as a great contribution to good will and recovery, by others as a ruse to help the bankers and holders of foreign bonds. By the time of Franklin D. Roosevelt's inauguration, practically all the war debts were in hopeless default. Popular grievance over these unpaid bills did much to feed the pacifism of the mid-thirties and impede the international education of Americans.

The period 1929-1941 began with a domestic débâcle which stemmed from many causes, but perhaps the most basic was selfish blindness to the bond between group welfare and the satisfactions of the individual. Disaster helped Americans to recollect that they were one nation and that only through coöperation could the cart be pulled from the mire. This period closed upon the eve of American participation in a global war which had been bred largely by the equally stubborn refusal of many nations to admit the tie between their security and the good estate of all—the concept of one world. About the commonalty of man and the commonweal of nations revolved the great debates, the most significant activity, of these dozen years. Even in his daily life the average American could not help being profoundly affected by the outcome.

CHAPTER II

New Design for Living

THE impact of this severest and longest depression upon daily life could be observed everywhere. The average woman's world of cooking, mending, sewing and keeping house continued less impaired than that of the average man, that is, so long as there was food to cook, clothing to repair and a roof overhead. One out of five women, however—a total of nearly eleven million—worked outside the home in 1930. Since 1890 their number had increased sixfold. Such women were directly vulnerable to the employment crisis, though at first they tended to fare comparatively well since their lower wages and usually greater docility found favor in employers' eyes.

As the Depression wore on and labor surpluses brought short hours and scant wages for all, this feminine advantage shrank steadily. Women who lost their footing in the undertow of unemployment found jobs hard to regain, and to combat the handicap of gray hair a feminist campaign with the cheery slogan, "Always twenty-eight," was begun early in the decade urging women employers to hire older members of their own sex as counterweight to the masculine partiality for youth and beauty.

Even in the teaching profession they met growing discrimination. In 1931 the National Education Association reported that more than three quarters of all cities had banned employment of wives. This policy meant more rapid turnover, delayed marriages and removal from the schoolroom of many mothers whose interest in children had often aided their professional success. Women workers, in whatever field, were assumed to be filching some male breadwinner's job for

25

the sake of pin money or to augment the family's sumptuary margin.*

In the home, hard times caused many urban families quickly to give up domestic help.† In small towns and rural districts the onset of adversity sometimes added another burden to already busy wives by reviving half-forgotten crafts of an earlier day. Taught perhaps by the grandmother, many a household embarked upon soapmaking, fruit drying, pickling, preserving, bread baking, curing in smokehouses and storage in root cellars, brewing medicine from herbs, cleaning, dyeing and clothmaking. In 1931 sales of glass jars exceeded any in the previous eleven years, while the demand for canned goods dwindled.

But this revival was short-lived, hardly lasting through the times of greatest stringency, for even the rural family had little abiding interest in those skills still cherished by Old World peasants. Drastic cuts in income deprived poorer households of amenities like newspapers, magazines, movies, and often such commodities as toilet paper, coffee, tea and sugar. Observers tended to speak brightly of "the live-at-home movement"; farm families with few illusions sourly called it "wooden shoes." Frequently the wife improved finances at the cost of her own energy by such means as taking in laundry or sewing, baking cakes and pies for sale, or accommodating boarders or tourists. Individuals with a little capital might open motor camps, wayside stands, beauty parlors, novelty stores.

---

* In the wake of the Depression, a survey early in 1937 by the National Federation of Business and Professional Women's Clubs yielded, however, a somewhat different picture. Of more than twelve thousand female employees, 48 per cent had dependents, while 17.4 per cent carried the sole responsibility for households ranging from two to eight persons. Furthermore, while average earnings fell appreciably between 1930 and 1936, the number of dependents per woman increased. *Why Women Work* (*Public Affairs Pamphlet*, no. 17, 1938), 3, 30.

† By the end of the decade, despite partial recovery, probably 95 per cent of American homes were being run by the housewife with no outside aid. J. C. Furnas and others, *How America Lives* (N. Y., 1941), 330.

The spate of gadgets which industry had poured into the American home since the First World War—electric toasters, egg beaters, grills, waffle irons, percolators, washing machines, electric stoves—abruptly slackened in the early thirties, along with sales of furniture and sewing machines. On the other hand, electric refrigerators, meeting a still unsatisfied market with their new efficiency and convenience, continued to sell briskly. Condensed milk, rayon and radios were other commodities which the public refused to yield. Gasoline and automobile-accessory sales also persisted, but the purchase of new cars dropped like a plummet, now that driving yesteryear's model was no longer a social stigma. Manhattan cab drivers saw their revenues decline from seven dollars a day to two or three.

A more revealing index of retrenchment in New York City was the loss of some forty thousand telephones between 1930 and 1931 and the quadrupling of the cheap dinners served by Childs restaurants. The cigarette, boomed by the war nerves of 1917-1918, proved an equal solace to the depression jitters of the thirties, production rising from a hundred and twenty-three billion in 1930 to a hundred and fifty-eight by 1936. The single standard in smoking continued to win its way, restaurant service for women in a typical middle-sized town now including an ash tray.

Conditions in Middletown afford a close-up picture. Between 1929 and 1933, while the number of filling stations almost doubled, sales fell only four per cent, for most families regarded their automobile as indispensable. At the other extreme, jewelry stores showed the heaviest decline of custom, eighty-five per cent of their dollar volume. Trade in lumber and building materials fell almost as much, while furniture stores and candy shops lost seventy per cent of their patronage. Commercial eating places saw their business reduced sixty-three per cent, with surrender of the family luxury of "eating out for a change." It should be added, however, that this was no permanent reversal, for with the first symptom of better times cooking resumed its interrupted flight from the home, and before the end of the decade the number of restaurants was multiplying faster than the number of families.

Everywhere clothing offered a natural province for economy. Men's attire was more sensitive to depression than women's, for even the most elemental sense of chivalry recognized the superior importance of fashion for the wife and daughter. As early as 1930, when the output of women's and children's dresses fell only thirteen per cent below the previous year, men's suits dropped twenty-five and in the next year sank thirty-two per cent under the 1929 level. For the sake of both economy and convenience, more males began to abandon stiff collars, hats, garters, undershirts, vests and the tops of bathing suits.

In women's clothes the early thirties saw the large-scale copying of smart frocks with cheaper materials and workmanship. Also, under pinch of need, the average girl tended as never before to make her own dresses and hats. "An accompanying return to statelier morals and manners" was forecast by a fashion report in September, 1930, concerning the longer skirts and more feminine modes which had begun to repudiate the boyish angularity of the jazz-age flapper. Ruffles, bows and curvaceous lines heralded the rediscovery late in 1931 of Empress Eugènie hats and other styles. Bravado at small cost found expression in brightly painted fingernails, introduced in Paris in 1929, which within the next two years spread from Park Avenue to the sales girl and typist.

Meanwhile the débutante slouch yielded to better fashions in posture, with a tendency to "tuck in and walk tall." Bobbed hair scored an apparently lasting triumph, although the close-cropped extremes of the jazz age grew rarer, and after the middle years of the period the page-boy or curled bob reaching to the shoulder dallied with the old-fashioned idea of crowning glory and comported with a passing vogue for bows in the hair and "little girl" costumes seen wherever dancers followed the rhythms of "swing." Loose, athletic clothing was so clearly the modern preference that by the mid-thirties skirts began to rise again—almost an index of national confidence—while the informality of Florida and California introduced beach pajamas, slacks and shorts to the rest of the country, under protest in many staid communities. Sandals for street and evening wear prepared the way in the latter thirties for the open-toed shoe.

So long as the Depression was paramount, people had to face retrenchment not only in food and clothing, but often in lodgings as well. While economy among the rich might involve closing or selling at a loss a "cottage" at Newport, Bar Harbor, Palm Beach or Santa Barbara, or relinquishing a villa in the South of France, middle-class folk might have to give up a rented house at the shore or vacation spot in the mountains and, quite commonly, move to a less expensive house or apartment in town. "Doubling up" with parents, in-laws and employed children occurred countless times. A survey of sixty-four cities in January, 1934, revealed that, among all sorts and conditions, the number of "extra families" varied from two to fifteen per cent of the total, with the highest proportion in the South. South Carolina's population increased a sixth during the Depression, Georgia's nearly as much.

Youths who had left dour and slovenly surroundings to win independence or better their chances, contribute support to the old folks, or enroll in training school on borrowed funds, now returned stone-broke and crestfallen, acquiescing in Robert Frost's well-known definition of home as "the place where, when you have to go there, they have to take you in." Everywhere tension between father and son seemed to increase if the latter came back jobless after a period of self-support. A wage-earning parent was prone to reassert his authority, as if the youth had never been his own boss. In the city the crowding of families into small apartments and tenements unquestionably aggravated tempers and the general mood of defeat. Relief recipients in their constant search for cheaper quarters tended to move oftener than did others, though in so far as possible they clung to the old familiar neighborhood.

Yet jobless men and their families often kept to themselves —shabbily dressed children hiding from visitors, adults sullenly refusing hospitality from still employed friends because of the hardship of repaying an evening at cards over sandwiches and coffee. The more sensitive just wanted to be let alone. In this way contact between the haves and have-nots, along with the old comradeship of American life in fat times and lean, tended through pride to be broken.* Some families, determined to keep up appearances at all costs, went their accustomed pace until disaster broke their spirit; others arrived at the same pass from a carefree outlook upon life or from unwillingness to lower certain standards of living. Still others battled the Depression with resourcefulness and pluck, sometimes making a game of penny pinching and savoring to the full their rare extravagances in recreation.

Within the family circle were likely to dwell such specters as unpaid bills, sickness, need of eye and dental care, loss of a nest egg for youth's education or age's security. Such cumulative worries often warped normal relations in the home, causing hitherto loyal wives to scold job-seeking husbands returning late for meals, or hurl the taunt—picked up all too easily from lips of the affluent—that "anybody can find work if he wants it." The discredited breadwinner was apt to lose his spunk, the household its initiative. With old work habits gone and laziness no longer grounds for reproach the family often stayed up late listening aimlessly to the radio

* Among two hundred workless families questioned in New Haven, two thirds in former days had practised neighborly visiting, but now only a little more than a quarter continued the habit, while participation in parties fell from twenty per cent to three. E. W. Bakke, *Citizens without Work* (New Haven, 1940), 7-8. For a similar report, see Lilian Brandt, *An Impressionistic View of the Winter of 1930-1931 in New York City* (N. Y., 1932), 16-17.

or just sitting, and slept far into the morning. Restiveness sometimes led to a craving for drink or the excitement of gambling, if any funds lay at hand, and an aftermath of self-reproach or the blues.

In homes where the stern dictatorship of husband and father was traditional, such as immigrant families from Continental Europe or rural households, the breadwinner's loss of prestige or even abdication of authority proved striking. Elder children contributing to family support gained new prestige as members of the inner council. If the wife became chief money-maker, she usually assumed greater family command, with the jobless husband turning to domestic chores. Frequently, however, in the urban home no stern male dominion had ever been asserted. Here in gloomy times the wife often tried to cheer up and pamper the workless husband, even as he had been prone to spoil her in the days of their prosperity. Also the constant presence of an unemployed father at home was likely to heighten his companionship with the younger children, promoting play and intimacy.

Many observers tried to find a silver lining in this stronger *esprit de corps* of the clan. Secretary Ray Lyman Wilbur told the National Conference of Social Workers in May, 1932, that delegated responsibility for children had ended: "In adversity the home takes its normal place. There is no substitute for intelligent parental care exercised through the day, at meal times, and in controlling proper sleeping conditions at night." Applying accurately enough to abodes where the nursemaid had been discharged, these words were hardly realistic in respect to homes where wage-earners' wives were driven forth to earn an extra dollar, food was meager, children too shabby to attend school. In similar vein Middletown boosters liked editorials cheerily avowing that "many a family that has lost its car has found its soul," thanks to sounder nerves, rested bodies, better digestion and more sober Sabbath observance. Nor were such utterances merely the revised Protestant version of old Puritan gospel, for the Reverend John

F. O'Hara, president of Notre Dame University, added his assurance that "as a result of the Depression a great portion of the American public rediscovered the Home, rediscovered fireside joys, rediscovered the things of the spirit."

Such optimism held a grain of truth but also much chaff. Husband and wife, for example, almost certainly spent more time together, sharing inexpensive pastimes like listening to the radio, playing cards or reading aloud. Declining attendance at amusement places chiefly for men, such as pool halls, bowling alleys, baseball games, prize fights, bore negative proof of the change. But if some couples were drawn together anew in the bonds of misfortune and enforced propinquity, others grew embittered by want, insecurity and each partner's futile reproaches. A collector of many case histories in a big industrial city found that among the married unemployed "sex life decreased, if it was affected at all," from fear of pregnancy, feminine loss of respect for an economic failure and a general atmosphere of repressive anxiety.

Bewilderment, hesitation, apathy, loss of self-confidence, were the commonest marks of protracted unemployment. A man no longer cared how he looked. Unkempt hair and swarthy stubble, shoulders a-droop, a slow dragging walk, were external signs of inner defeat, often aggravated by malnutrition. Joblessness proved a wasting disease. What social workers called "unemployment shock" affected some men as if they were in the grip of panic, driving them to frenzied search for work by day, sleepless worry at night. To a few persons joblessness apparently brought a sense of personal importance—of being part of a national crisis, a front-page problem—but more universal was a mood of lost self-esteem, perplexity, or bitterness toward old employers and life in general.

The sum of these effects upon the former breadwinner added up to weaker morale, by a vicious cycle making him still more unemployable. A survey of idle engineers reported in 1933 that three out of every four showed morale inferior to that of the average job holder. A physical counterpart of these losses revealed itself in flabby muscles, faulty coördination and lack of stamina when work was resumed. As with an inactive plant, rust had taken its toll. In 1933 when a group of forty long-unemployed stenographers were set to work in a New York office, all quickly showed signs of nervous fatigue under the old routine and several grew hysterical. More than two thirds needed from two to three weeks' readjustment before they could take dictation without breaking down.

Those who still clung to jobs or oscillated between spells of work and idleness were haunted by the same bogey of insecurity. Dogged resolve to hold on to what one had, along with fear of exchanging poor but steady wages for better-paying jobs with greater risks, blunted the American sense of enterprise. Enthusiasm for work and loyalty to the concern also tended to dim. Many agreed that it "didn't pay to work too hard, because employers will only take advantage of you." The success legend, whose brightness for generations had hypnotized youth, now began visibly to tarnish, along with those kindred Puritan virtues of diligence and frugality. The trusty old formulas seemed to have failed. "We realize that honesty, integrity, and industry don't get you to the top any more," said a collegian at Thomas Jefferson's university in the mid-thirties.

Such misgivings were not confined to youth. "It ain't any good starting saving again," said old folks who had seen banks close one after another and hoarded funds eaten by the years of the locust. "We've got in so deep I guess we'll never try to get out." Among a group of nearly four hundred jobless men, half agreed that "luck" or "pull" determined success more than did ability; a little less than half accepted the traditions of "rugged individualism" in business, although three fourths of a similar group of employed men still indorsed that time-hallowed philosophy. For many this disaster impeached the gospel of thrift. Some decided that the apostles

of saving—the bankers and self-made industrialists—were
largely responsible for what had happened. Still others reflected philosophically that "you can't take it with you"—
an old saying caught up by the refrain of a song hit in 1931
and echoed five years later in one of the decade's favorite
plays, a comedy by George S. Kaufman and Moss Hart about
a happy-go-lucky family who picnic through life. Why
worry? Those still able to buy books made Edmund Jacob-
son's *You Must Relax* a best seller in 1934, and a little later
took up the self-help manuals of Marjorie Hillis, *Live Alone
and Like It* (1936) and *Orchids on Your Budget* (1937),
mingling gay insouciance with doctrines which her father, a
once famous Congregational preacher, in his day had set
forth in all their pristine strenuousness.

Too deep for the average citizen to fathom, the floods of
disaster had rolled in to erase ancient tide marks and tug at
the moorings of inherited wisdom. This era brought a ques-
tioning into American life deeper than any other since the
Civil War. Stereotypes of thought, traditional saws, the
tribal wisdom of the elders, all were challenged in books,
magazines and private talk. Perhaps, after all, the promise
of American life would turn out merely to be propaganda,
the tyranny of words or the folklore of capitalism. But while
youth was prone to rebel, middle age and senescence often
clung all the more stoutly to old loyalties, particularly if they
had a personal stake in the *status quo*—leaping to the defense of verities like hard work, thrift and individual enterprise, and opposing change in those concepts of law and government which they associated with happier days. Yet even
among this group the threat of poverty wrought its effect,
as the Townsend crusade demonstrated.

For, after the passage of two or three years, unemployment had entered into the grain of American life. Its severity
and apparent hopelessness were without parallel. Panics and
bank failures, rainy days and lean years, flood and drought,
had come and gone many times since the first settlers carved

out a civilization in the howling wilderness. This crisis, it seemed, had no precedent. Poverty was everywhere; cornered by it, the jobless man now felt something resembling claustrophobia.

A case history from the files of the California State Unemployment Commission in 1932 will illustrate the difference. This octogenarian had struck many ups and downs since that day in 1873 when, as he recalled, he was working in New York City and

> the bank of Jay Cooke and Company broke and my boss closed up and I was thrown out of work and I became a tramp. . . . At that time the whole West was open to homesteaders. At that time the mountains were honeycombed with new homes, and new mines that were being opened. At that time railroads had been building all over the country.

From a tramp he became a section hand, and after that employment was steady, first as a coal miner and later a grocer, until by 1890 he found himself "a fairly well-to-do business man." But the Panic of 1893 cleaned him out, and once more he took to the road as a wanderer until in 1895 he succumbed to the lure of California and managed to raise enough cash to grubstake him in ranching. Life again became easier as he accumulated another competence. Now in old age he had lost everything, and in his bones he knew this was worse and different. "There isn't an acre of decent land to be had for homesteading. There isn't a railroad to be built anywhere," he reflected. "Years ago Horace Greeley made a statement, 'Young man, go West and grow up with the country.' Were he living today, he would make the statement, 'Go West, young man, and drown yourself in the Pacific Ocean,' like the lemmings do in Norway." There was no farther range.

An idle man seeking to rationalize his plight was apt to follow one of several roads. If he saw it as the result of machines supplanting men, he might take it all pretty calmly since no one could get very angry with a machine. If he blamed himself or his hard luck, he slid down the path of defeat. If he laid the responsibility upon society or the economic system, he chose the fork of radicalism. The steps of an undetermined number veered toward the left. One careful study found that unemployment made men a good deal more radical than it made women. Nearly a quarter of the idle, or about four times as many as among job holders, agreed that "a revolution might be a very good thing for this country," though practically all reacted strongly against concepts like "communism" and "alien radicals" and affirmed that "a man should be willing to fight for his country."

Such radicalism as existed was mainly homespun, doctrinally naïve and, at bottom, the plain man's instinctive resentment of poverty surrounded by shops bursting with food and farms smothered under their own productive surplus. "Thinking is dangerous these days," said one down-and outer to a social worker in 1932. "Please leave me alone." A newspaperman going through the towns and backwoods of North Carolina in this same year—amid the ruin wrought by five-cent cotton, stagnant mills, bank failures, foreclosures and other evils conveniently saddled upon the Yankees of Wall Street—heard murmurs of the word "revolution." A Michigan villager early in the New Deal told a Federal Emergency Relief official:

> I don't believe you realize how bad things were getting before this set-up started. . . . They all said that if things got any worse and something didn't happen pretty soon, they'd go down Main Street and crash the windows and take what they needed. They wouldn't pick on the little stores. They'd go after the big stores first . . . no man is going to let his wife and children starve to death.

Did not Daniel Willard, president of the Baltimore and Ohio Railroad, to the scandal of some people, say in a speech at the Wharton School of Finance in 1931 that capitalism was out of joint, adding doughtily, "I would steal before I would starve"?

Spring of the next year saw hunger marches far and wide over the country and a serious unemployment riot at Dearborn, Michigan, with the shedding of blood. The nearest approach to widespread mass action was the "Bonus Army." "Adjusted compensation" certificates for veterans of the First World War, authorized by Congress in 1924, had been made payable in 1945. Early in 1931 the administrator of veterans' affairs reported to Hoover that about two hundred and seventy-two thousand men stood in need of relief. A cash loan upon these certificates was soon provided, over the president's veto, but shortly thereafter the Patman bill proposed immediate payment of the balance.

To lobby for this measure some twelve to fifteen thousand homeless veterans, following the lead of an Oregon band shepherded by a jobless cannery manager, Walter Waters, converged from all quarters upon Washington in the late spring of 1932. They took shelter in empty federal buildings or pitched tents on mud flats across the Potomac. The administration stressed infiltration of their group by a sprinkling of Communists and persons with criminal records. In fact, however, known "Bolshies" were given the bum's rush; and when on June 16 the Senate overwhelmingly rejected the Patman bill, veterans keeping vigil on the Capitol steps swallowed their disappointment and rousingly sang "America."

When Congress early in July voted to pay the passage home of impoverished marchers, about five thousand left town; later in the month, with Congress adjourned, the president ordered General Douglas MacArthur, chief of staff, to evacuate the rest. A riot between the men and Washington police brought death to two veterans. With tear gas and fixed bayonets the troops quickly scattered the laggards, who retreated whence they came or joined the migratory flux of the dispossessed along roads and railways. At all events, the talk heard in some excitable circles that ex-servicemen would follow the precedent set abroad and become the spearhead of revolution—whether to the right or the left—proved silly.*

Against the spread of doctrinaire Marxism, even in the darkest days of 1932, stood the strong American faith in democratic processes, the people's habit of hopefulness and their distrust of "foreign" agitators. To the ballot box rather than the soapbox most citizens looked when they wanted a change. Here and there, in a few industrial centers, discontent simmered beneath the lid: Seattle, for example, with its syndicalist background and the activities in 1932 of its Unemployed Citizens League, or Detroit after the city's credit reached exhaustion and Father Charles E. Coughlin began to fish in the troubled waters. But equally bad conditions elsewhere were accepted with fortitude.

In New York City homeless men were sleeping in subway stations; and in the hollow of an abandoned reservoir in Central Park flourished a locally famous settlement of 1932 called "Hoover Valley," whose inhabitants, feeding on stale bread and the refuse of markets, gazed listlessly at Manhattan's skyline ringed with half-empty skyscrapers. In Youngstown, Ohio, where open-hearth furnaces lately glowed with the enterprise of a major American industry, derelicts by the hundreds huddled for warmth in the structure housing the municipal incinerator. Through the nation men were dwelling in abandoned factories, freight cars on sidings or shacks made of waste lumber and flattened tin cans. With their women and children the uprooted tended to congregate on the outskirts of town, living from hand to mouth. These

---

* One side of the story is given by Walter Waters, *B.E.F.: the Whole Story of the Bonus Army* (N. Y., 1933); another by Herbert Hoover, *State Papers* (W. S. Myers, ed., N. Y., 1934), II, 242, 274-275, and T. G. Joslin, *Hoover Off the Record* (N. Y., 1934), 269-275. Spurred by the powerful Legion lobby Congress in January, 1936, overrode President Roosevelt's veto and ordered immediate payment of the bonus. Needy veterans also received special assistance from several New Deal agencies, including the Civilian Conservation Corps and the Works Progress Administration.

were the consumers without buying power. By the summer of 1932 many communities were turning over tracts of public land to the unemployed for cultivation as small farms or vegetable gardens. In Gary, Indiana, for example, twenty thousand families raised their own provender on land lent by the city.

Despite repeated official assurance that nobody would be allowed to starve, in New York City at least twenty-nine persons are known to have died from starvation in 1933, while one hundred and ten such fatalities, chiefly children, were reported for the nation at large prior to 1934. Far more numerous were those victims of disease, accident and general collapse to whose death hunger was largely contributory. Philadelphia's community health center experienced a rise of about sixty per cent in its malnutrition diagnoses between 1928 and 1932, markedly in the age group between six and sixteen. A sharp decline in the consumption of milk, eggs and fresh fruit showed all too clear a correlation with an increase of rickets, scurvy, pellagra. In one New York City health center the National Organization for Public Health Nursing reported a growth of malnutrition patients from eighteen per cent of total admissions in 1928 to the startling figure of sixty per cent by 1931.

"Hog 'n' hominy," so long the bane of Southern poor whites, was now matched in inadequacy by the diet of the new poor in other regions, living on bread, potatoes and beans, with cabbage once a week as a treat. To be sure, restaurant managers often contributed leftovers, bakers their stale bread, and wholesale fruit and vegetable dealers their overripe produce. Truck drivers were known to spill an occasional crate of oranges from their vehicles on the Lower East Side and pretend to ignore the scattered fruit. The acme of degradation was garbage eating, practised in many cities. Investigators of the Chicago slums in 1932 pictured a scene: "Around the truck which was unloading garbage and other refuse were about thirty-five men, women and children. As soon as the truck pulled away from the pile, all of them started digging with sticks, some with their hands, grabbing bits of food and vegetables."

Upon a minority the worries and struggles of the Depression bore with intolerable effect. The annual rate of increase in admissions to state hospitals for the insane between 1930 and 1932 rose to almost triple that from 1922 to 1930. Inability to take care of mental cases in private homes or private hospitals must, of course, have contributed largely to this growth. But the number of insane per hundred thousand population in New York state registered an abrupt jump in 1932-1933.*

An expected sensational increase in the suicide rate following the stock-market crash was not, however, borne out by the facts. In October and November, 1929, New York City reported only 219 suicides, as against 223 for the corresponding period in 1928; but the annual national rate, of 14 per hundred thousand in 1929, rose steadily to a record high of 17.4 in 1932, then gradually ebbed to 14.2 in 1936.

It was apparent that men felt the brunt of economic failure much more than did their wives, that suicide predominated at both extremes of the financial scale but especially the upper, and that change from high to low estate provoked self-destruction more often than did poverty in itself. As a final index of desperation, it might be remarked that the number of deaths necessitating burial at public expense doubled in 1931 over 1929, to reach a ratio of about one in ten, while in rural districts the number of homemade coffins increased.

* C. J. Enzler, *Some Socia. Aspects or the Depression* (Wash., 1939), 171. In harmony with previous years, a slow steady increase took place from 439.2 insane per hundred thousand in 1929 to 447.6 in 1931, thence a sudden rise to 458.3 in 1932, and 472.3 in 1933. The next year showed a slight loss in rate of acceleration, but a general increase continued through the decade. *World Almanac for 1943*, 883.

CHAPTER III

CHANGE OF COMMAND

IN his battle against the Depression, Herbert Hoover assumed greater responsibilities than any predecessor had done in a similar plight. Van Buren in the crisis of 1837, Grant in 1873 and Cleveland in 1893 had approved monetary measures intended to cushion the shock. Theodore Roosevelt in 1907 had sent Congress a peppery message which evoked a temporary law to give greater flexibility to the currency in periods of emergency. In 1921 Harding called a President's Conference on Unemployment, whose purpose was firmly to hand the problem back to local charity. But after 1929 unprecedented disaster demanded unprecedented action. In attempting federal interposition in the workings of the economic cycle Hoover willingly took several steps, and was forced by circumstance and a Democratic House into taking still others, which broke with tradition.

In the past, economic recovery had come about from seemingly natural causes. Slackened output led to the absorption of surplus goods, while reduced capital charges and cheaper raw materials lowered the unit cost of new production. Both consumption and employment were thus stimulated, and industry began to expand again. Not only the continental frontier but the foreign export market had in former times invited such renewal, as did the steady multiplication of consumers due to the high birth rate and immigration. Now the whole world lay under the same blight, and American industrial expansion appeared to be near its limit. The nation was ill not from a single malady but from a mixed infection, and years of easy living had helped sap its innate powers of resistance. Could the patient recover by himself, without using

41

up all his reserves in a long debilitating fight? Would old-fashioned remedies like patience, hard work, a little monetary tinkering and much hope suffice to cure him?

Herbert Hoover, who believed in social planning and abhorred waste and inefficiency, answered these questions in the negative. Yet this doctor was largely the product of what his successor would blithely call horse-and-buggy days, for Hoover held firmly to a belief in modified *laissez faire*, the gold standard, individual enterprise and the profit motive as mainsprings of progress, and in savings and self-denial as the essence of economic security. In a campaign speech in 1928 he had distilled his doctrine into the phrase "rugged individualism," which the years of crisis would see under constant attack, derision, or parody as "ragged individualism." Replying to his critics in 1934 Hoover wrote,

> While I can make no claim for having introduced the term "rugged individualism," I should be proud to have invented it. It has been used by American leaders for over a half-century in eulogy of those God-fearing men and women of honesty whose stamina and character and fearless assertion of rights led them to make their own way in life. It is they who have borne the burdens and given leadership in their communities.

Such an attitude went hand in hand with deep distrust of state paternalism, use of the tax power to reduce inequalities between haves and have-nots, and free federal spending which reckoned not with repayment. It was therefore plain that this physician, while faced with new and alarming symptoms, would dole out his medicines cautiously and look askance at major surgery, even though the patient himself was increasingly in the mood for experiment.

Indeed the nation, before falling upon evil days, had been partially conditioned to those ideas of greater governmental responsibility which seemed everywhere to be in the drift of modern times. The First World War had inducted even Americans into the necessity for federal control in crises. Still more deeply, the development of an urban industrial order almost imperceptibly had interwoven government with business, the state with the individual's daily life. Some citizens thought of government as an economic balance wheel among the forces of private enterprise, others as the supreme source of action in times of war, mass misery or panic, and still others—apparently the majority—as a shield for the average man against corporate greed and exploitation. Those who remembered the progressivism of Theodore Roosevelt, Taft and Wilson had seen a demonstration of the third attitude. And invocation of any of these rôles was sufficient to inject federal power into the desperate *impasse* which followed 1929. Furthermore, the citizen who in the early 1930's turned his gaze abroad perceived that governments in Britain, France, Germany, Japan and other lands were undertaking huge responsibilities, often applying measures more drastic than anything witnessed in the United States in this decade.

Like most of his countrymen, Hoover in the autumn of 1929 failed to gauge either the gravity or duration of the crisis. Seeing the market crash as a paper débâcle that could be checked by intelligent coöperation at the top, he called industrial, financial and labor leaders to the White House repeatedly in November and December, 1929. He gained promises of increased spending from railroads, the telephone and steel companies, and pledges of sustained wage rates from major industries. Most of these commitments were honored half-heartedly or evasively, if at all. Hoover's basic faith in the self-recuperative power and socially coöperative spirit of business was doomed to disappointment again and again through the next three years. Meanwhile he sought to banish "unjustified fear" and restore confidence by utterances resembling a coach's pep talk. "Ninety per cent of our difficulty in depressions is caused by fear," he told his secretary, in words prophetic of his successor's ringing inaugural declaration: "The only thing we have to fear is fear itself . . . ." *

After his hectic activity in the closing weeks of 1929 Hoover desisted, believing that the brakes would hold, the spell of optimism work and the self-help of business come into play. He was slow to give up his expectations, and as the months passed, a mood of impatience arose not only among the needy unemployed but also among men of property, well-nigh as eager to invoke the government's intercession in the "flat-wallet era" as they had been to protest its interference in flush times. The year 1930 saw minor skirmishes fought against the Depression, such as federal assistance to drought victims, aid to the farmer to feed his cattle though not his children, and a program of public works including a half-billion dollars for federal buildings and sixty-five million for the construction of Boulder (later rechristened Hoover) Dam. These latter enterprises continued for several years to play a part in relieving local unemployment, but under the rising mood of desperation they seemed timid and half-hearted. The cry everywhere was for action.

From the time of the moratorium in June, 1931, Hoover tacitly admitted the full magnitude of the crisis and concentrated his energies fiercely upon it. A hard worker, dogged and sincere, he was nevertheless unable to dramatize his battle with the Depression in a way to kindle popular imagination or rally the nation's morale. He was blamed for a disaster whose seeds had been sown long before his accession to office and which undoubtedly would have come had his opponent triumphed in 1928.

But Hoover lent himself unhappily to the rôle of scapegoat. For all his abilities, he lacked the gifts which his successor possessed in such abundance—political camaraderie, communicable personal warmth, a comprehensive program, thrilling leadership. With the aid of a "smear campaign"

---

* As early as January, 1932, an editorial on the Depression in the *Ladies' Home Journal* had declared: "There is nothing to fear—except fear."

Hoover was made to appear dour and taciturn and, quite un-
fairly, callous to the people's plight. An oft-repeated wise-
crack observed that the Great Engineer had quickly drained,
ditched and dammed the country. His career illustrates the
ironies of a public man's reputation. In the First World War
his entry into the American home and kitchen as the counselor
of conservation had made him a symbol of friendly efficiency,
thrift and the homely precepts of "hooverizing." Meanwhile
in 1916 and again in 1919 his labors in feeding the starving
millions of Europe had invested him with the magic of the
hero as provider. When the Great Depression came, he was
expected somehow to duplicate this miracle of social engineering, although there was no longer an outside source from
which largess could be tapped for a distressed people. These
earlier experiences, however, had confirmed Hoover in his
faith that voluntary coöperation and community effort were
the answer to all emergencies. With such schooling and his
temperament of a Manchester liberal, Hoover worked long
and late over the puzzle of the economic collapse.

The most acute problem was relief. Traditional American
ideas about relief sprang not from modern Britain, with its
"soul-destroying dole," but from English poor laws dating
back at least to Queen Elizabeth. It was commonly believed
that charity pauperizes those who receive it, that public relief and politics are inseparable and, above all, that such dis-
bursements are "something for nothing." Aid to the indigent
thus tended to become a local responsibility, given as grudgingly and humiliatingly as possible in order to discourage
spongers and point up the disgrace of poverty. The bleak
horror of the poorhouse was thought to be salutary.

In a virgin and agrarian nation local relief had not worked
too badly; it was cushioned by the neighborliness which
Americans liked to think was a national trait. Later, private
philanthropy through the channels of charity-organization
societies and the Red Cross had tempered the harshness of
municipal relief. It was natural for the president to turn to

them in a crisis which at first looked hardly different from a San Francisco earthquake or Mississippi River flood. "The sense of voluntary organization and community service in the American people has not vanished . . . has been strong enough to cope with the problem for the past year," Hoover told the press in October, 1930, upon appointing an Emergency Committee for Employment headed by an ex-police commissioner of New York, Colonel Arthur Woods. Indeed, donations to community chests for charitable purposes had been rising since 1925, reaching a peak in the autumn of 1931 and the spring of 1932; in the following year, whether from exhaustion of funds or the fact that public agencies had entered the field in strength, they dropped to a low unmatched since 1924.

Hoover believed that the obligation for relief and reëmployment began with the individual. Failing there, the effort might then call upon private organizations like the Red Cross, thence turn to municipal and state governments and, finally, as a last resort to the federal government—whose succor, in this ultimate extremity, should take the form of loans rather than gifts. Slowly and reluctantly Hoover was driven back trench after trench in what he conceived to be his defense of the public treasury.

Though citizens' committees did sporadic good work in 1930-1931, in the larger view it fell short of the need. The Woods Committee failed to create enough new jobs to build even a footbridge across the growing chasm of unemployment, and in August, 1931, Hoover supplanted it with the Organization on Unemployment Relief, headed by the industrialist Walter S. Gifford and later by Wilson's secretary of war, Newton D. Baker. The purpose of this committee—in itself an admission of the deepening gravity of the situation —was to coördinate the activities of local organizations, while exhorting each community and state to care for its own. "Spread the Work" was its slogan for industry.

In January, 1932, the American Legion opened a drive to

obtain a million jobs under a six-hour day and five-day week program. Employers who agreed were entitled to display a sign, "We have enlisted." Early that spring New York City launched its block-aid campaign, pledging weekly contributions up to a dollar from employed dwellers in each block to help the workless. J. P. Morgan, breaking an almost impenetrable reserve, took to the radio to praise the movement. Meanwhile the Red Cross aided approximately a million persons during the grim winter of 1931-1932.

For all the valor of private charity it was not enough. And when the swelling throng of the needy turned to municipal governments, they found the cupboard bare by reason of dwindling tax collections and the drain of two depression years. For a few weeks or months in that winter, states made grants to local authorities to meet relief costs until these sources, too, ran dry, and the eyes of hunger were lifted ever more importunately toward Washington. In March Congress voted to distribute forty million bushels of Farm Board wheat through the Red Cross to feed the unemployed, and four months later it released forty-five million bushels more and half a million bales of cotton from the same stores, the latter under Red Cross direction being made into clothing. These measures, utilizing for relief federally owned commodities—even though channeled through private philanthropy—marked an innovation. Hoover opposed appropriation of federal funds for distribution by the Red Cross, and upon this point Congress sustained him.

The ultimate stage, against which the president held out so long, was reached in July, 1932, when the Reconstruction Finance Corporation was empowered to lend needy states sums from the national Treasury. The RFC, most important of the new agencies which the Roosevelt régime would inherit from Hoover, had been set up in January, 1932, after the ill success of a scheme called the National Credit Corporation, which Hoover had promoted in the hope that strong banks would voluntarily form a credit pool to help the weak.

Like many of his assumptions it counted too heavily upon the enlightened self-interest of business. The strong showed scant zeal for aiding the weak, and so the whole burden fell upon the government in Washington.

Thus the RFC came into being, created by Congress to lend two billion dollars to banks, insurance companies, building and loan associations, agricultural credit organizations, railroads and similar enterprises. Hostile critics led by Congressman Fiorello La Guardia promptly called it the millionaires' dole. Hoover believed, however, that buttressing the nation's credit structure would indirectly benefit everybody. Resignation of the first head of the RFC, General Charles G. Dawes, on June 6, 1932, three weeks before his Chicago bank received a ninety-million-dollar loan from the Corporation, led to clamor for full publicity of its lending activities and for the use of federal bounty for starving individuals as well as embarrassed banks.

In the summer of 1932 not merely the bonus marchers but masses of distressed citizens, together with local and state governments, were stretching empty hands toward Capitol Hill and the Treasury of the world's richest nation. Democrat John N. Garner, speaker of the House and political wiseacre, demanded federal loans to needy men and women. The American Federation of Labor favored appropriations to pay teachers in bankrupt cities. Many voices urged revival of the federal employment service, defunct since the last war, and the creation of a national system of unemployment insurance. Though looking coldly upon all these proposals, President Hoover in July, 1932, felt obliged to accept a relief bill levying $2,122,000,000 upon the Treasury, of which $1,-800,000,000 could be lent by the RFC to states and municipalities for relief and public works, with the remainder earmarked for federal construction. This measure, like the earlier distribution of federal wheat and cotton, set a precedent for the New Deal. Under the Roosevelt administration, demand for repayment of these sums was abandoned, thus converting the loans into gifts.*

True to his conservative lights, President Hoover was wary of increased taxes and of all federal grants save loans for self-liquidating enterprises. He disliked "non-productive public works," such as city halls and state capitols, highways, streets, river and harbor improvements, military and naval construction beyond the usual volume, but approved "income-producing works" like toll bridges, toll tunnels, waterworks, docks and other projects whose steady earning capacity promised repayment. Largely through his efforts, the relief act of July, 1932, favored the latter to the extent of a billion and a half as against some three hundred million dollars for the former.

The president's attack upon still another problem, that of the distressed homeowner, showed in different guise his financial caution and determination to deal with destitute institutions rather than directly with individuals. The catastrophic effect of the Depression upon the building trades has already been remarked. Most spectacularly of all, between 1928 and 1933 construction of residential property fell ninety-five per cent, while expenditures for repairs dropped from half a billion to fifty million dollars. Still more grave was the fact that in 1932 some two hundred and seventy-three thousand homeowners lost their property by foreclosure, until by early 1933 about a thousand homes a day were falling into the hands of mortgage holders. After some months of urging, President Hoover in July, 1932, induced Congress to establish Federal Home Loan Banks, twelve in number, in order to allow funds to be borrowed by building and loan associations, banks and insurance companies whose credit had been

---

* While federal loans for relief were a novelty, the use of local funds for such purposes was not. In the Panic of 1893, for example, many cities appropriated public funds both for direct relief and for municipal works like streets and sewers. See Leah H. Feder, *Unemployment Relief in Periods of Depression* (N. Y., 1936), chaps. iv-vii, and bibliography in A. M. Schlesinger, *The Rise of the City* (*A History of American Life*, X), 429 n.

sorely strained by loans to residential and farm owners. This procedure helped to keep certain mortgage-lending institutions afloat, but its effect in removing the incubus of worry and loss from the backs of individual homeowners proved disappointingly small.

Meanwhile, the anxious summer of 1932 witnessed Hoover's renomination for president by the Republican party and the nomination by the Democrats of New York's popular governor, Franklin Delano Roosevelt. His promising youthful career, first as state senator and later assistant secretary of the navy under Wilson, had seemingly been blighted when in 1920 he went down to defeat as vice-presidential candidate of the Democrats and shortly afterwards was stricken with infantile paralysis. But with great courage he mastered the strategy of living in a crippled body, and in 1928 was persuaded to reënter politics by his friend "Al" Smith—to whom Roosevelt had attached a famous sobriquet that seemed still better to fit his own temperament, the "Happy Warrior."

A landslide reëlection to the governorship in 1930, a vigorous state program of social welfare and the political fence-building of Roosevelt's devoted lieutenants, James A. Farley and Louis McHenry Howe, made him the preconvention favorite. His flight by plane to Chicago to receive the nomination not only shattered precedent but gave the country a foretaste of his innate gift of drama, his summary sense of action. Yet as Ernest K. Lindley, Roosevelt's favorite newspaperman, has said, he was "no great popular idol during the Presidential campaign of 1932." He seemed too urbane to be a voice crying in the wilderness. Often quoted was Walter Lippmann's famous description of him on January 8, 1932, as "no tribune of the people . . . no enemy of entrenched privilege . . . a pleasant man who, without any important qualification for the office, would very much like to be President." The country nevertheless warmed to this tireless campaigner, sometimes making as many as sixteen speeches a

President Roosevelt returning with Mrs. Roosevelt from his Second Inauguration.

Conservative Fears of the New Deal.

day, hearty, self-confident and smiling. Of his real quality, however, it had little conception.

The platforms and campaigns of the two parties were naturally at variance about the Depression. The Republicans, following Hoover's lead, stressed its international roots, while the liberal Democrats and Roosevelt pointed up its domestic causes. Regarding its cure, their thoughts were also divided. To the former, recovery was the *summum bonum* and reform secondary; the latter accepted recovery as important, but demanded reform as an indispensable element for recovery and insurance against another collapse, invoking old-age and unemployment insurance, control of crop surpluses, more federal credit to states for unemployment relief and reciprocal trade agreements with other nations. "The removal of government from all fields of private enterprise" was promised "except where necessary to develop public works and natural resources in the common interest."

Hoover still clung to his faith in the spirit of local self-help, whether for recovery or relief—relief being generally regarded as the most urgent of the three R's—and he believed that all would eventually be well if the credit structure of business continued to be underpropped by federal loans. He also stood by the gold standard, so that "the dollar should ring true on every counter in the world," and upheld the high tariff, solemnly warning that "the grass will grow in streets of a hundred cities, a thousand towns; the weeds overrun the fields of millions of farms if that protection is taken away." Republicans hailed a mild upsurge of improvement in the late summer and early autumn of 1932, as the RFC retarded the rate of bank failures, gold began to return to the United States after its recent flight, the stock market rallied and the business index climbed a little. But the average citizen, looking at his meager pay envelope, the soup kitchens and bread lines, felt hardly better and yearned for a change. "I'll tell you what our trouble is," acknowledged Hoover to his secretary on election eve. "We are opposed by six million unemployed, ten thousand bonus marchers, and ten-cent corn."

Among the masses of dissatisfied voters, Roosevelt's promise of action was fortifying, along with his assurance that "failure is not an American habit." "It is common sense to take a method and try it," he said at Oglethorpe University, Georgia. "If it fails, admit it frankly and try another. But above all, try something. The millions who are in want will not stand by silently forever while the things to satisfy their needs are within easy reach." His early utterances made little mention of explicit means, but as the campaign developed, they grew more definite, including reform of holding companies and protection of the investor against fraudulent claims, reciprocal tariff agreements, federal power projects on the Tennessee and Columbia rivers, the easing of farm mortgage burdens, and social security.

He told San Francisco's Commonwealth Club that "private economic power is . . . a public trust," and often invoked the progressivism of Theodore Roosevelt and Wilson whose momentum had been so unhappily lost in the twenties. At other times the Democratic candidate seemed eager to reassure and please almost everybody. He paid tribute to "sound money" without pausing to define it, scolded Hoover's "reckless and extravagant past" which had raised the cost of government from two billion in 1927 to three in 1931, yet he stood ready to assume vastly augmented responsibilities for the federal authority.

The campaign brought significant new labels into political life. In an early radio speech on April 7, 1932, Roosevelt crystallized his solicitude for the underprivileged in a phrase: "the forgotten man at the bottom of the economic pyramid." Ironically, its source was that bluff individualist William Graham Sumner, the Yale economist whose Darwinian social philosophy had denied "the absurd attempt to make the world over," arguing that "the survival of the unfittest" as advocated by sentimental reformers was an affront to industry and frugality.* Plucked out of its context, "the forgotten man" had been offered to the candidate by Professor Raymond Moley of Columbia, best-known member of that intimate advisory circle which a journalist later dubbed "the brains trust," soon popularized as "brain trust." † Shortly after the election Roosevelt defined his great objective for the American people as "a more abundant life," his own political position as "slightly to the left of the center."

All these phrases would be recalled repeatedly, but the most indispensable was the "New Deal." "I pledge you, I pledge myself," said Roosevelt in accepting his nomination, "to a new deal for the American people." With the implication of social justice a "new deal" had been invoked by Mark Twain's Connecticut Yankee; at the end of August following Roosevelt's declaration, a book by Stuart Chase appeared with that title.‡ Within a short time, the candidate and his public were speaking definitively of *the* New Deal, a label recalling both the "Square Deal" advocated by Roosevelt's fifth

* F. D. Roosevelt, *Public Papers and Addresses* (S. I. Rosenman, ed., N. Y., 1938-1941), I, 625. Sumner's lecture title "The Forgotten Man," first used in 1883, had in view not the underprivileged but the mass of average middle-class citizens who "just work and save and pay" the cost of political inefficiency and social quackery. See H. E. Starr, *William Graham Sumner* (N. Y., 1925), 287.

† The author was James M. Kieran of the *New York Times*, not to be confused with John F., later a performer on the radio program "Information Please." See E. K. Lindley, *The Roosevelt Revolution* (N. Y., 1933), 26 *n*. The assumption in some quarters that Roosevelt was the first to invoke "professors" as governmental advisers was of course absurd: Wilson had used many during the First World War, for example, and Hoover had his fiscal counselor in Professor E. W. Kemmerer of Princeton. But such became the fame of Messrs. Moley, Tugwell and Berle of Columbia that the hostile cartoonist's figure of "the New Dealer" was inevitably garbed in cap and gown.

‡ For Roosevelt's account of its adoption, see *Public Papers*, II, 4-5. Raymond Moley, *After Seven Years* (N. Y., 1939), 23 *n*., claims its initial use in this campaign and opposite page 146 offers a facsimile of his first memorandum employing it. In an interview early in his first term Roosevelt acknowledged indebtedness to the Connecticut Yankee's remark that, when six men out of a thousand crack the whip over their fellows' backs, "it seemed to me that what the nine hundred and ninety-four other dupes needed was a new deal." "Mark Twain's New Deal," *Sat. Rev. of Lit.*, X, 352 (Dec. 16, 1933).

cousin Theodore and the "New Freedom" espoused by the last Democratic president, Wilson. Whether for praise or blame, it quickly became the most universal political tag of the era.

Hoover closed the campaign by radio from Elko, Nevada, with the declaration: "We are a nation of progressives. We wish to see our Nation march forward. We differ strongly as to the method to progress. . . . I feel deeply that the Republican Party has been the party of progress in our history from the day of Abraham Lincoln," and he warned the voters not to be "led astray by false gods arrayed in the rainbow colors of promises." Roosevelt made his last address in Madison Square Garden, saying,

> The next Administration must represent not a fraction of the United States, but all of the United States. No resource of mind or heart or organization can be excluded in the fight against what is, after all, our real enemy. Our real enemies are hunger, want, insecurity, poverty and fear.

The verdict lay with the people. By almost twenty-three million votes to less than sixteen Roosevelt was elected, carrying all the states but six, of which four were in New England. The Democratic party also swept both houses of Congress. William Allen White, veteran progressive of an earlier Roosevelt's crusade, who had shrewdly watched the world spin for forty years from his Kansas newspaper office, viewed the landslide as registering "a new attitude in American life . . . a firm desire on the part of the American people to use government as an agency for human welfare."

The summer and autumn of 1932 had indeed seen the nation at one of the vital crossroads of its history: two very different temperaments and political philosophies had appealed to the electorate. In the retrospective light of 1935 Lippmann would declare that "most of President Roosevelt's recovery program is an evolution from President Hoover's" —an assertion calculated to please neither Republicans in their resolve to see the New Deal as a wicked apostasy, nor Democrats zealous to claim its beneficent originality.

Yet the statement held a grain of truth. Both leaders took unprecedented responsibility for lifting the nation's economic mechanism back onto the track of prosperity by attempting to raise farm prices and underpin wages, create jobs and "prime the pump" by public works, spread employment by fostering shorter hours, and regulate the value of the dollar (though, while Hoover undertook to bolster its internal value by expanding the credit base through open-market operations in the Federal Reserve system, Roosevelt addressed himself to its external value as well and took the country off gold). Both Hoover's RFC and his Home Loan Banks continued through the New Deal; and although the Republican president nipped the idea of a Tennessee Valley Authority with a frosty veto in March, 1931—"I am firmly opposed to the Government entering into any business the major purpose of which is competition with our citizens"—yet it could be argued that he promoted the St. Lawrence seaway as a competitor of the railroads. And while Hoover's trade associations foreshadowed one facet of the national recovery act, the Norris-La Guardia anti-injunction act approved by him adumbrated another.

Such, briefly, is the case for Hoover as the unacknowledged sire of the New Deal. Like most piquant paradoxes it ignores a number of things, beginning with the necessary resemblance between certain acts of two social planners engaged in fighting the same disaster. It also overlooks the distinction between Hoover's reluctant caution in adopting some of these measures and Roosevelt's zest for experiment and innovation. While Hoover shivered on the brink, Roosevelt gleefully took the plunge and invited the nation to follow. Still more vitally the comparison dismisses the difference between Hoover's temporary expedients and Roosevelt's permanent blueprints for reform as well as recovery, between the former's basic reliance upon industrial self-government and the latter's growing resort to legal compulsion.

Hoover termed the campaign of 1932 "a contest between two philosophies of government," individualism against regimentation. Roosevelt saw it as a dilemma between two theories of prosperity: one which sought to make the rich richer in the hope that some benefit would trickle down to the common man, the other "that if we make the average of mankind comfortable and secure, their prosperity will rise upward, just as yeast rises up, through the ranks." In practice, as the future would demonstrate, this largely meant that government should regulate wealth more firmly, taxing profits and income while spending more freely for the common man's benefit. Was it the business of government to do these things? Herein lay the essence of their disagreement.

A liberal aristocrat whose roots belonged to agrarian rather than industrial America, Roosevelt in the approved tradition of Thomas Jefferson, Charles Pinckney and Edward Livingston joined the obligations of public service to a deepening concern for the less fortunate—as if his own physical handicap had given him the key of intuitive sympathy for all disadvantaged. A lover of fair play and a humanitarian, he believed passionately in decent treatment for all human beings. The pinch of poverty and the grind of exploitation he had never known save from the lips of others, such as the little band of enthusiastic organizers in the Women's Trade Union League whose visits to him in his convalescent days may largely have molded his attitude toward labor and its problems of health and wages. His qualities of heart and imagination transcended those of cool intellectual analysis.

On the other hand, his opponents never tired of pointing out that Roosevelt, born with a silver spoon in his mouth, was prone to assume an aristocrat's attitude toward money very unlike that of Hoover, the self-made Iowa farm boy. As private citizen and as governor of New York Roosevelt was manifestly an easy spender, to whom the disbursement of funds to promote human happiness appealed more strongly than did budget balancing and meticulous economy; and he held the lords of Wall Street in no such veneration as did Coolidge and Hoover. Most of his information on economics Roosevelt gained by his characteristically quick, though necessarily superficial, absorption from those he met.

As a "country squire" he had an interest as keen as Jefferson's in the problems of farming, particularly that of conservation, for to him the waste of the nation's human and natural resources seemed far more real and grave than the fiscal extravagance which scandalized most of his critics. In simplifying and dramatizing the aspirations of liberalism for ready popular assimilation, he proved a consummate master. His sense of direction was usually superior to his logical prevision. Often tacking and veering, always able to utilize prevailing winds and currents to the full, Roosevelt was a born navigator.

What was the promise of the New Deal? It was of a piece with the oldest aspirations of the Republic, beginning with "life, liberty, and the pursuit of happiness," an experiment in promoting the greatest good of the greatest number. To some extent, this quest for perfectibility had shifted during the last century from the individual to the social order, from isolated clusters of utopian communities to regulation of the national economy. Ever since the 1880's federal legislation had addressed itself to interstate commerce and the railroads in particular, while still other forms of supervision, for example over money and foreign trade, dated back to the cradle of the Republic. Conservation of natural resources along with curbs upon "malefactors of great wealth" had been keynotes of the first Roosevelt, and agricultural relief dated from a rural-credits law under Wilson and the grain-and-commodities-exchange acts under Harding and Coolidge. Progressive states like Wisconsin, New York, Massachusetts and Kansas had made independent strides in such matters as farm relief, water-power regulation, unemployment insurance and old-age pensions.

Nevertheless, the easier conditions of life in the United States and the traditions glorified as "rugged individualism" had retarded developments in government regulation and social security such as European countries like Sweden and Britain adopted long before the Depression, not to mention the extremes of collectivism which for the majority of Americans meant Soviet Russia, the one nation their country refused to recognize until late in 1933. Even so, this world-wide drift toward socialization had not failed to register its effect upon American life. In January, 1929, for example, the Commission on the Social Studies of the American Historical Association, representing various points of view, set to work upon a sweeping inquiry under the conviction that trends of deep import were stirring in the nation's social and educational system, the majority holding that the American people were moving toward greater democracy and collectivism.

As Herbert Croly had said two decades earlier in *The Promise of American Life,* the pledges of democracy could no longer be taken as inevitable, but must now be regarded as goals to be won only through planning and controls. Roosevelt and his advisers—mostly young men trained by Justice Oliver Wendell Holmes and Professor Felix Frankfurter, or reared in the school of practical social work developed in New York City and New York state under the governorship of Roosevelt—envisaged the New Deal as attempting precisely that. They conceived of it as a system of checks and balances between management and labor, Big Business and small independent concerns, producer and consumer, agriculture and industry, domestic and foreign markets, fat times and lean. They held, however, that certain interests, hitherto neglected, stood in particular need of government support and encouragement, also that even the good estate of Big Business depended vitally upon the economic health of the whole nation, including laborer and farmer, white-collar worker and middle-class consumer.

Above all, in the immediate crisis the federal government must assume a more drastic and vigorous generalship in directing relief and recovery. To a *laissez-faire* economist arguing that natural causes be allowed to work their will, Roosevelt "with a gray look of horror on his face" is said to have replied, "People aren't cattle, you know!" As for ways and means of encompassing these ends, the New Deal was not an explicit program drafted under Roosevelt's direction in 1932 or even fully conceived at his inauguration, but rather a general attitude toward government for the people, later embodied in action and shaped by the urgency of circumstance.

Certain broad theories, however, could be detected interwoven with the New Deal from its early stages. The British economist John M. Keynes, whose ideas were gaining wide acceptance among social planners in the thirties, argued the desirability of compensatory spending in times of depression, "deficit financing" and a managed currency. Taxation and relief, indeed the regulation of the whole social system, should be so contrived that less money flowed into the coffers of the rich, who saved it, and more into the hands of the poor, who spent it, thus quickening monetary circulation and mass consumption. Large fortunes, it was said, came not merely from individual but from community effort as well, and therefore could justly be taxed heavily for the sake of the whole people. It was argued that returns from production should go more and more to consumer and wage-earner, less and less to investor and speculator.

The New Deal, under the sway of this logic, early set its sights upon a living wage, reasonable leisure, economic security for the masses and curtailment of great wealth and power for a few, although its pace was too slow to suit the more extreme Keynsians like Senator Robert M. La Follette, jr. If opponents objected that this theory discouraged initiative and penalized success, while keeping investment funds frozen from a sense of insecurity, many liberals pronounced it the only way by which a nation could live up to its old boast as the land of opportunity. A new vision thus swam into the ken of the American people. Whether it would turn out to be Utopia or myopia, only the future could tell.

According to its friends, the New Deal proposed to apply legislation to those fields where private enterprise had failed to accept proper responsibility for the social consequences of its acts. Roosevelt later cited a precedent in Lincoln's words, that "the legitimate object of government is to do for the community of people whatever they need to have done, but cannot do at all, or cannot do so well, for themselves, in their separate and individual capacities." The mechanism of Keynsian economics might remain a debatable issue, but the grand strategy of Roosevelt the humanitarian never lacked clarity. And if this was the rising tide of revolution, a nation which had witnessed the "revolutions" of Jefferson and Jackson could still recognize most of the old landmarks.

CHAPTER IV

THE HUNDRED DAYS

ALTHOUGH the people had signified their desire for change, an interval of four months filled with uncertainty and party bickering passed before the mandate became effective. Such was the slow majestic tempo decreed by the Constitution, an interregnum when it seemed as if the strength of the American eagle had yielded momentarily to the tragi-comic impotence of the lame duck. This was destined to be the last such interlude in American history, for the Twentieth Amendment, proposed on March 2, 1932, and declared ratified on February 6, 1933, was preparing henceforth mercifully to end the life of an expiring Congress on the third day of January, the term of a retiring president on the twentieth.

Autumn and winter had long since withered the few sprouts of revival which summer had brought forth. In October, with markets for commodities and securities slumping again, the Democrats blamed Hoover's "fear campaign"; when this ebb tide persisted after election and through the winter, the Republicans retorted by ascribing it to the dread of Roosevelt's accession. An obsolete Congress refused to undertake major responsibilities with their successors crowding impatiently on the threshold. Roosevelt declined to collaborate with Hoover on joint statements about war debts and "sound" money, playing his cards close to his chest and refusing to sacrifice future freedom of action to please his predecessor. Political recrimination flew thick and fast, while bread lines lengthened, the bottom of the relief barrel was scraped again and again, and the nation's banking system began its final nose dive toward disaster.

From the beginning of 1930 to the end of 1932 a total of 773 national banks involving deposits of more than seven hundred million dollars had failed, along with 3604 state banks—those still weaker links in the fiscal chain—with deposits exceeding two billion. It was not unusual during these years to see armored cars rushing to threatened banks and their moneybags unloaded by guards with guns.

Depositors throughout the nation were in an uneasy mood. Aggravating bad banking practices of old and the absence of adequate federal supervision, the depression jitters and rumors of impending failure caused wave after wave of withdrawals. Hosts of panicky citizens, taking their cash in hand, resorted to hoarding and hiding—in safety-deposit vaults, trunks, tin boxes and even holes in the backyard—or perhaps sent sums abroad. As a result, Hoover early in 1932 had launched a nation-wide campaign against hoarding. Yet circulating money continued so scarce that before the year's end several cities in the South like Richmond, Knoxville and Atlanta—where secessionist ways of thought tended in crisis to come uppermost—began to print their own currency. It served to pay municipal employees and to keep the unemployed alive by providing some kind of money to buy farmers' surpluses. During Hoover's last fortnight in office the Treasury estimated that some $1,212,000,000 was withdrawn from circulation, orthodox Republicans taking a dismal view of "the flight of the dollar" and of Senator Carter Glass's refusal to serve as Roosevelt's secretary of the treasury.

The first clear symptom of universal collapse occurred as early as October 31, 1932, when the lieutenant governor of Nevada proclaimed a twelve-day banking holiday to save a chain of local banks. In the late winter matters swiftly reached a head. On February 4, 1933, the state of Louisiana embarked upon what was in effect a bank suspension. Ten days later Michigan's governor proclaimed a similar breathing spell, and by the first of March, Alabama, California,

Idaho, Kentucky, Mississippi and Tennessee had followed suit. Savings banks, after enjoying phenomenal popularity during early stages of the Depression, now suffered devastating runs. One institution after another called its balance on the New York money market. Early in the morning of inauguration day, Saturday, the fourth of March, Governor Herbert H. Lehman closed the New York banks, and the rest of the country quickly knuckled under. In the fell clutch of circumstance the president, who had battled the crisis valiantly if sometimes clumsily for three long years, saw the nation's banking system during his last hours crash completely about his ears.

That week-end and the week which followed witnessed strange sights. Visitors to the inauguration were stranded without cash. In Salt Lake City the Mormons prepared to issue paper negotiable locally for goods and services. In Pasadena a luxury hotel printed scrip for its penniless guests. In Detroit a prosperous citizen, unable to change a ten-dollar bill anywhere, at last obtained a nickel from an apple seller to telephone his wife. Stamps, telephone slugs, Mexican and Canadian dollars and personal IOU's became media of circulation. With everybody in the same boat, empty pockets had ceased to be invidious; neighborliness and an air of jaunty desperation prevailed.

All eyes were fastened upon the nation's president-elect who, a story of the time rumored, might well be its last president. At Miami little more than a fortnight before his inauguration he had barely missed an assassin's bullet which instead killed Mayor Anton J. Cermak of Chicago. The country, sensing that its destiny rested upon the shoulders of Franklin Roosevelt, was reassured by his cool courage in the face of death. On March 4 a hundred thousand spectators, in an atmosphere of almost tremulous tension, filled forty acres of lawn and pavement before the east front of the Capitol, while millions more gathered about their radios. Hoover's grave and downcast face seemed in striking contrast to the vibrant self-confidence of his successor, who stood without hat or overcoat in the chill wind, speaking for twenty minutes with firm voice and almost defiant chin.

"This is a day of national consecration," he began, adding that "these dark days will be worth all they cost us if they teach us that our true destiny is not to be ministered unto but to minister to ourselves and to our fellow men." On the domestic front he spoke of treating unemployment "as we would treat the emergency of war," of helping to save homes from foreclosure and farmers from bankruptcy. "This Nation asks for action, and action now." His words about foreign affairs and "the policy of the good neighbor" would often be recalled in years ahead, but at the moment the majority of Americans probably listened most attentively to Roosevelt's utterances about the banking system, his demand for "an end to speculation with other people's money, and . . . provision for an adequate but sound currency." "The money changers," he declared, "have fled from their high seats in the temple of our civilization. We may now restore that temple to the ancient truths. The measure of that restoration lies in the extent to which we apply social values more noble than mere monetary profit."

As he entered his open car to return to the White House, Roosevelt responded to cheering by vigorously shaking his hands over his head in the manner of the prize ring. To many Americans it seemed as if the Champion had at last arrived. The war upon the Depression had shifted from defense to attack. Whenever Hoover had uttered words of optimism, he was invariably charged with wishfulness or complacency; when at last he admitted the full gravity of the situation, he became "the distinguished pessimist, who never would be missed," satirized several years later in "The Swing Mikado." But a leader inheriting national disaster from his predecessor—America's Roosevelt in 1933, like Britain's Churchill in 1940—could boldly face the situation in all its blackness, needing no personal apologia, as he summoned mass effort and the tonic sense of sacrifice to master a crisis which had given him the mandate of power.

Action came thick and fast. On Sunday the fifth Roosevelt called Congress into special session. The next day he forbade the export of gold and all dealings in foreign exchange, and proclaimed a national bank holiday to permit examination of the soundness of individual banks before their gradual reopening. After Glass's refusal the Treasury portfolio had gone to William H. Woodin, whose former traditions of Union League Republicanism seemed to harmonize as little with his new rôle as did his career of successful railway-equipment manufacturer comport with his appearance. But there he sat under a gray toupee, with china-blue eyes and a puckish little smile, dispensing puns and whimsy while he steered the nation's eighteen thousand banks past the rocks, with nonpartisan help from Hoover appointees lingering at Roosevelt's behest.

On March 9 the Congress of the Hundred Days met to indorse overwhelmingly all the president had done, calling upon the RFC for new capital to reorganize the banks and authorizing the issue of more currency. Unfreezing of the banks had already begun for such essentials as cash for medicines, relief funds and pay rolls. In the face of new penalties hoarders began to bring back their gold to deposit windows and turn in their gold certificates. Louisiana's bumptious Senator Huey Long offered an amendment to bring every bank in the land under the mantle of the Federal Reserve system, while leftists grieved that Roosevelt was letting slip an unparalleled opportunity to nationalize credit.

A moderate at heart, the president serenely went his way. In a broadcast on Sunday, March 12, the first of what the press called his "fireside chats," he explained in simple words just what had been done and invited coöperation: "Let us unite in banishing fear." The average citizen warmed to this appeal, and the most successful medium of publicity for the New Deal had been discovered, with the voice of a stellar radio personality behind it. Meanwhile the worst of the crisis had been weathered. Solvent banks began to reopen the next day all over the nation.*

More permanent banking reforms commenced with the Glass-Steagall act of June 16, 1933. It divorced commercial from investment banking, provided for deposit insurance and gave the Federal Reserve Board power to prevent loans for speculation. The Senate banking committee's investigation of Wall Street in the winter and spring of 1933, and the grilling administered by inquisitor Ferdinand Pecora, did much to topple the idols of the market place. J. P. Morgan suffered the minor indignity of holding a midget on his knee —placed there by a circus publicity agent—but the wizard of the National City Bank, Charles E. Mitchell, was so discredited ethically that he joined Samuel Insull, lately dethroned utilities tycoon, on the shysters' bench. The financier's gambit of selling stock at a loss to some member of his own family in order to reduce his income tax, only to buy it back next year, was one disclosure of the Pecora committee that lingered long in the small taxpayer's aggrieved mind. The tall silk hat, once the *ne plus ultra* of success, had itself become a symbol of comic derision.†

To the satiric political gossip of books in the vein of

* The bank crisis of early March, 1933, may be regarded as the long-expected "terminal trough" of the Depression. Among forty important measurements of economic activity, twelve reached bottom in the second half of 1932, and twenty-four around March, 1933; unlike the pattern set by recovery from earlier and milder crises, revival first affected consumer goods rather than durable ones. W. C. Mitchell and A. F. Burns, *Production during the American Business Cycle of 1927-1933* (Natl. Bur. of Econ. Research, *Bull.*, no. 61, 1936), 2. H. G. Moulton and others, *The Recovery Problem* (Wash., 1936), 74, favor July, 1932, as the nadir, because at that time the production index, measured from a level of 100 in 1929, sank to a record low of 48.7.

† Thanks largely to the public notice given in the winter of 1932-1933 to Postmaster-General Walter Brown's requisition of a new limousine to accommodate his top hat. J. A. Farley, *Behind the Ballots* (N. Y., 1938), 201. For its serving as a butt of rustic parody, see *These Are Our Lives* (Chapel Hill, 1939), 286. The best account of the banking investigation is Ferdinand Pecora, *Wall Street under Oath* (N. Y., 1939).

Washington Merry-Go-Round (1931) and the gay irreverence of musical shows like "Of Thee I Sing" (1931), now were joined debunking biographies of the titans of business, like Jonathan N. Leonard's *The Tragedy of Henry Ford* (1932), John T. Flynn's *God's Gold: the Story of Rockefeller and His Times* (1932), Harvey O'Connor's *Mellon's Millions* (1933), Matthew Josephson's *The Robber Barons* (1934) and, a little later, Ferdinand Lundberg's *America's Sixty Families* (1937). Many Americans were disenchanted with the supermen of wealth and power who had once ruled the skies of New York and Washington, and for months after the March crisis the nation's great bankers seemed too chastened to lift the voice of self-assertion.

They also knew that Roosevelt, at least temporarily, was irresistible. "The house is burning down, and the President of the United States says this is the way to put out the fire," Bertrand Snell, Republican whip in Congress, had declared when the emergency banking bill came up for debate. Playing with the same image, Will Rogers wrote of the chief executive, "The whole country is with him. Even if what he does is wrong they are with him. Just so he does something. If he burned down the Capitol, we would cheer and say, 'Well, we at least got a fire started anyhow.'"

The new temper of the country was shown by Congress's passage of the securities act in late March, 1933, the securities-exchange act in 1934 and the public-utility-holding-company act in 1935. This network of legislation placed a limit on bank credit for speculative purposes, set up safeguards against manipulation of stocks, decreed full information for the buyer of securities, created the Securities and Exchange Commission as overseer and passed a "death sentence" against all utility holding companies after the end of 1937 save those composing a "geographically and economically integrated system." All these measures, though hotly opposed in business circles, promised greater security to the depositor and small investor and won widespread popular approval.

In 1940, as supplementary safeguards, came the investment-company act and the investment advisers' law.

Less widely indorsed were certain monetary ventures of the New Deal, which showed the president in his not unusual rôle of experimentalist, seeking to raise prices. It was his special concern to increase agricultural prices relative to nonagricultural ones, and since prices like those of wheat and cotton were highly sensitive to international demand, it was believed with considerable justification that devaluation of the dollar would prove efficacious. In April, 1933, the government announced that it had gone off the gold standard. From Congress Roosevelt obtained permissive authority to inflate the currency in any of five stipulated ways. In June, 1933, the world monetary and economic conference met in London with hopes of achieving currency stabilization; but it came to naught, thanks on the one hand to the self-seeking of France and her gold-bloc satellites and, on the other, to President Roosevelt's sudden fear lest such stabilization check a groundswell of rising prices just beginning at home. His wireless message of July 3 was widely blamed for having "torpedoed" the conference. The net result was to foster hostility to the United States abroad, and on this side of the water to confirm the average citizen's isolationism. Not until September, 1936, did Britain, France and the United States finally reach agreement to prevent sharp fluctuations and competitive devaluation.

The most dubious monetary essay of the New Deal came in the autumn of 1933 after the honeymoon of early recovery had waned. The president ventured to try the commodity-dollar theory of Professor George F. Warren of Cornell, called by Republicans the "rubber-dollar program" and by Al Smith the "baloney dollar." Forced devaluation of the dollar to slightly less than sixty per cent of its former gold content was expected to advance prices generally and specifically to improve the position of American exports. A slight improvement in foreign trade followed, but the chief visible effect came when the higher prices paid for gold—set arbitrarily each morning over the president's breakfast tray in consultation with Warren, Farm Credit Administrator Henry Morgenthau, jr., and Jesse Jones of the RFC—promptly began to siphon gold, ultimately to the amount of over fourteen billion dollars, from many lands into the vaults of Fort Knox, Kentucky. This gold-purchase plan, operative from October 25, 1933, through January, 1934, failed appreciably to lift the domestic commodity price level, while the variations it decreed from day to day proved unsettling to confidence and stability.

The silver-purchase act of June 19, 1934, forced through Congress by the silver bloc after agreement with the president, was also inflationary in intent. Its most tangible result was not only to boost domestic silver but to acquire a billion dollars of foreign silver at prices well above market value, and to deposit the bullion largely in the vaults at West Point. But while the nation bade fair to become a cemetery for the world's precious metals, the effect of these manipulations upon prices was hardly the moderate reflation for which the planners prayed, nor certainly the uncontrolled inflation which Wall Street foretold. Reflected in such monetary policies, however, was that not uncommon blend of unrealism, gay extemporizing and shrewd politics enmeshed with so much of the honest, sincere and often eminently practical humanitarianism of the New Deal. A president who tried everything was bound to make mistakes.

Underlying most federal activities of these early months was the assumption that money and credit, the price and profit system, had broken down under the buffetings of depression, and that to let nature take its course would be both slow and ruinous. The flow of money must be invigorated by government spending, the track toward prosperity smoothed for worker and consumer. Since virtually every consumer is a producer and every producer a consumer, it was argued that four interlocking processes would benefit the whole nation: the creation of government-financed work; an increase of employment and wage rates under a system of codes for industry; the bolstering of farm income by raising market prices through crop restriction plus direct benefit payments; and the lifting of the general price level through currency manipulation, aided by federal support and regulation of credit institutions. To win these objectives an enormous program was launched, in part by legislative act, in part through the newly increased powers of the executive. Congress stood ready to acquiesce in the vast authority which the president sought, and soon found itself signing checks for huge sums whose allocation and spending it tendered into his hands.

The New Deal had begun on a note of retrenchment, with Roosevelt's stern warning in his inaugural week that "for three long years the Federal Government has been on the road to bankruptcy," followed by Congress's passage of the economy bill authorizing reductions in federal pay rolls and veterans' compensation by more than four hundred million dollars in that year. The powerful Legion lobby and all the traditions of American politics were set at defiance. But Roosevelt began almost immediately by executive order to restore the cuts bit by bit and, with the president himself soon leading the procession of spending—requesting billions for relief, pump-priming and running costs for a host of new federal agencies—Congress on March 28, 1934, under the goad of an election year kicked over the traces of economy and, defeating Roosevelt's veto, completed the restoration. Henceforth all pretense of keeping the budget in balance was dropped.

The month of March, 1933, which beheld so much drama, innovation and reviving hope, saw the return of 3.2 per-cent beer as almost an anticlimax, but it was at least the welcome portent of another break with recent tradition. At the opening of the decade prohibition had been the hottest issue under national debate; in a poll on "paramount problems of the United States" taken in January, 1930, and again in January, 1931, the supposedly intelligent and civic-minded members of the National Economic League ranked prohibition first, with unemployment trailing far behind. President Hoover's support of national prohibition—"a great social and economic experiment, noble in motive and far-reaching in purpose"—failed to stem the rising tide of its violation and the growing impotence of federal enforcement. In 1931 the report of the Wickersham commission appointed by Hoover merely confirmed the breakdown of popular sentiment in its favor. Farmers' needs to sell their grain and sugar, plus the fabulous revenues expected from a federal liquor tax —funds currently going into the pockets of an underworld which prohibition had helped to spawn—were other factors making for repeal.

The Republican platform of 1932 hedged on this issue, but the Democrats and Roosevelt called emphatically for repeal. Speedily the lame-duck Congress in February, 1933, proposed a constitutional amendment for repeal, and the final decision went to the states. Return of beer in the next month was a foretaste of things to come. Ratifications from state conventions soon began pouring in. Old strongholds of the drys like Indiana, Iowa and Alabama joined the parade; the *Dallas News,* from the heart of Baptist suzerainty, spoke of "the utter rout of preacherdom." On December 5, 1933, Utah became the thirty-sixth state to support the Twenty-first Amendment, and the "experiment" was written off as a failure.

In that momentous spring of 1933, however, the most urgent problem, once the banking crisis eased, was the stark one of relief. Upwards of fifteen million unemployed and nearly six million persons on state and municipal charity rolls clamored for attention. In a message to Congress on March 21 the president proposed three types of remedial legislation: grants to states largely for direct relief to feed and clothe the destitute; enrollment of workers by the federal government in enterprises which could be swiftly launched and would not interfere with private industry; and a program of durable public works.

The second and third of these desiderata, containing the germ of the Civilian Conservation Corps and the Public Works Administration respectively, came to fruition more slowly than the first, the seed from which the Federal Emergency Relief Administration sprang. This agency was the special care of Harry L. Hopkins, frail and earnest social worker from Iowa who had served as chairman of state relief in New York during Roosevelt's governorship. Under his direction the FERA, admittedly a makeshift because of the urgency of the crisis, was set up by Congress on May 12, 1933, to help the needy chiefly with money for direct relief administered through established channels of state and municipal welfare. Beginning with funds of half a billion dollars, it spent eventually about three billion.

Local agencies were expected to share the load according to their ability, but no rigorous matching was required. For the nation as a whole, in the final accounting, Washington supplied over seventy cents of each relief dollar, the states thirteen and the municipalities sixteen. Relatively rich commonwealths like Massachusetts contributed vastly more than did impoverished ones like South Carolina, with New Englanders grumbling audibly about the decay of self-reliance. In the South objectors deprecated filling the pockets of Negroes and poor whites with cash. Many states, looking upon the FERA as a "gravy train," aspired to give as little and get as much as possible. Federal and state administrators not infrequently had to crack down upon the stingier counties, threatening to cut off contributions unless local purse strings were loosened.

Hopkins's thinking drifted steadily away from direct help —the quickest, cheapest and most inclusive type—toward "made work" paid for according to need and, finally, toward a systematic work program at minimum wage rates, which would utilize idle skills. Once he had the immediate crisis under control, he looked about for employment that might foster morale, for the usefulness of the task raised the doer's self-respect and kept his hand in. Hopkins's ideas, however, did not meet with universal agreement. While organized labor feared the effect of low pay for relief work on wages in private industry, many conservatives objected to such relief on quite other grounds. They favored the dole as cheaper, and argued that a public-works program would divert funds from the money market, sometimes undermining existing values (as in the low-cost housing field), and would saddle the nation with huge debts, which in themselves would further retard recovery.

That the mass of people, however, indorsed Hopkins's choice admitted little doubt. After four years of the New Deal, a Gallup poll in May, 1937, reported that four persons out of five approved relief through public works; and later in that year, with the start of a new recession, a Roper poll found that work relief easily outstripped all other proposed solutions, though by a wider margin among the poor than among the rich and among city dwellers more than farm folk. A story popular in the early days of the program concerned an elderly man who, after his relief checks began to arrive, went out unasked and began to sweep the streets of his little town, saying, "I want to do something in return for what I get."

In the summer of 1933 the FERA was already fostering the idea of work relief, however improvised and trivial—like picking up papers in the park, raking leaves, counting automobiles at intersections for local traffic records. By a ruling of August 1 unskilled labor was paid a minimum wage of thirty cents an hour. Except in the South and a few isolated industries such pay offered no serious competition with wages in private occupations, which the National Recovery Administration was trying to stabilize, nor with the man-power needs of management, which the newly revived United

States Employment Service was broadcasting among the job-less.

This shift from the dole to work relief proceeded so far in later phases of the FERA that in 1935, during the last months of its existence, the agency counted nearly half of its beneficiaries as workers, a total of two and a half million during the peak month of January in that year. The previous winter, however, that of 1933-1934, had witnessed the widest expansion of the FERA and of relief rolls in the Great Depression, with nearly eight million households, representing almost twenty-eight million persons, on the lists in February, 1934.

That enormous dilation was due to the fleeting development of a special work-relief branch called the Civil Works Administration, which operated straight from Washington through regional subdivisions, thus avoiding local red tape. It went into action in November, 1933, to meet the onset of cold weather and a flagging in mass optimism which began to tell against the initial spurt of the New Deal. The CWA speedily put four million to work, about half drawn from the regular rolls of the FERA and the remainder from the nonrelief unemployed. It set up a thirty-hour week for manual labor and thirty-nine hours for clerical and professional skills, with a fairly high wage and favorable working conditions which sometimes made the CWA a serious competitor with the lower-paid ranks of private employment. In all, it spent about nine hundred million dollars, mostly on road mending, repair of schoolhouses, parks and playgrounds, swimming pools, pest and erosion control and work on municipally owned utilities. Under spur of the emergency, made work of a flimsy or picayune kind was almost inevitable, and probably no New Deal agency was more vulnerable than the CWA to charges of "boondoggling"—an old pioneer term for handicrafts, introduced to the nation and the delight of hostile critics early in 1935 by a "training specialist," Robert

Marshall, when testifying before a New York aldermanic inquiry.

If the usefulness of certain CWA projects was dubious, their general effect was to demonstrate the psychological value of job relief. A Michigan county administrator, observing that "the joy of the men at having even this brief opportunity to earn a decent living wage knew no bounds," saw some leave her office "weeping for sheer happiness." With their initial pay checks many went straight to the barber for their first professional haircut in months, and during the weeks that followed their appearance mirrored further stages in the recovery of self-respect. Naturally the barber himself, along with the grocer, druggist and clothier, also benefited. True, not every relief worker took so blithe an attitude. For the man who had come down in the scale from a professional or technical career to the ranks of crude labor, a certain bitterness was apt to rankle against the whole system. A mechanical engineer, the forty-one-year-old father of seven children, after toiling a few weeks for the CWA wrote ironically about "the idea that ditch-digging is a noble occupation." * This agency reached the end of its allotted span in the spring of 1934, its uncompleted projects being taken over by the general FERA program.

On the whole, the FERA raised the tone of state and municipal relief and supported only a small minority of spongers, probably never exceeding ten per cent. Against the stubborn pride of many of the newly poor it sought to lend a certain dignity to the acceptance of aid. As more persons went on relief and treatment grew more liberal, the stigma became less and additional border-line cases capitulated, their savings drained to the last dollar. Furthermore, millions of young people coming of age could find no jobs, while parents and grandparents reached years of retirement with no means of

* "The biggest thing to learn about ditch-digging is to bring your mind down to the ditch. You must forget about chickens in pots and polished cars in garages." "In the Ditch," *New Outlook*, CLXIII (Feb. 1934), 35-36.

support. Individuals, of course, began to accept poverty with complacence, deducing that Uncle Sam owed them a living, and under prolonged idleness some of the unemployed came at length to be the unemployable. Local authorities often indulgently retained on federal rolls doubtful cases and ne'er-do-wells who would have been quickly cashiered from county or municipal relief.

When, within the limits of seasonal fluctuation, it grew clear that New Deal policies were not reducing but apparently augmenting the number on relief, the administration decided to scrap the FERA, returning direct relief wholly to local governments and devoting the federal outlay to able-bodied clients and projects of more durable value. December, 1935, saw the demise of the FERA. The story of its successor, the Works Progress Administration, belongs, however, to the New Deal's later phases rather than to legislation set up by the Congress of the Hundred Days and its immediate chain of consequences.

The defects of the FERA and its short-lived offshoot, the CWA, appeared striking beside the record of another venture, the Public Works Administration, organized on June 16, 1933, with an appropriation of $3,300,000,000. The PWA was designed to stimulate heavy industry by fostering public works that required huge quantities of material. President Roosevelt placed it in the hands of cautious, hard-headed Harold L. Ickes, secretary of the interior and self-styled "curmudgeon," whose aversion to using federal funds "to hire grown men to chase tumbleweeds on windy days" colored the whole doctrine of the PWA. Where, however, circumstances compelled Hopkins to build his program largely upon relief labor, with all its nondescript ineptitudes, Ickes faced no such requirement; PWA work was done under contract with private concerns. The PWA insisted upon careful inspection of projects before lending or giving funds (ranging from a third to nearly half the total construction cost) to states and municipalities. Others it undertook independently in the national interest and ultimately, in 1938, these became its sole concern.

The PWA was conceived by New Dealers as the pump-priming agency best calculated to stimulate private employment, upon the Keynsian theory of compensatory spending. This figure of speech was suggested by the old-fashioned pump, into which water sometimes had to be poured to swell the leather valve before it drew properly.* Whether Uncle Sam by priming could coax the pump of industry into efficient operation, or whether he got out of the pump merely the water he had poured into it, occasioned much dispute. Although the PWA was mistrusted by those fearful of a planned economy, it seems early to have had a stimulating effect upon private business. Not adapted primarily to succor the unemployed, the PWA nevertheless kept an average of half a million men steadily at work through the year 1934 under a thirty-hour week. By the time it began liquidation in the early forties, it had spent over four billion dollars upon more than thirty-four thousand projects.

Their social usefulness admitted no question. PWA allotments brought Boulder (later called Hoover) Dam to completion by day-and-night shifts two and a half years ahead of schedule. Under the same sponsorship a variety of other irrigation and reclamation projects began, of which the Tennessee Valley Authority was the most famous. New York City's Triborough Bridge, left unfinished in 1932 through dearth of municipal funds, resumed construction under the PWA, drawing upon the steel mills of Pennsylvania, the cement of the Mississippi Valley and the giant forests of the Pacific slope. In 1936 the bridge stood an accomplished fact —with the federal government making a million and a half profit on the sale of bonds which bankers in 1933 had re-

---

* "Sensible people will give a bucket of water to a dry pump, that they may afterward get from it all they have occasion for," wrote Benjamin Franklin to his sister, Sept. 20, 1787. *Autobiographical Writings* (Carl Van Doren, ed., N. Y., 1945), 684.

fused at any price. Sewage systems, turning basins, water-supply works, civic auditoriums, school and university buildings, slum clearance and model housing, farm-to-market roads and school-bus roads were other favored enterprises. This agency provided 121,760 beds in hospitals whose completion cost more than a third of a billion dollars—the equivalent of five years' normal growth.

Of special significance for the future, the PWA between 1933 and 1935 financed the building of more than fifty military airports, helped the army lay out seventy-four thousand miles of strategic highways, built a wind tunnel for plane designers, employed ten million dollars in renovating ordnance and improving arsenals, and under navy supervision used two hundred thirty-seven million dollars in constructing warships. In 1935, however, persuaded by the spirit of pacifism and clamor from the Nye committee, Congress forbade spending public-works and relief funds "for munitions, warships, or military or naval material," and most phases of this activity ceased. The PWA had gone slowly into action—in the face of considerable local impatience on the one side, suspicion on the other—but in retrospect its diverse achievements would look impressive.

The Congress which on the first of its hundred days had broached bank-reform legislation, on its last passed the national industrial recovery act, inaugurating not only the PWA but also placing a large segment of the nation's private industry under centralized direction. In the interval it had taken steps of vital importance to the farmer, the distressed homeowner, impoverished youth and the hillbilly of the Tennessee Valley. The articulation of these policies, their shapes and adaptations through the middle years of the New Deal, will be traced in later chapters, but from their conception in these crucial times they sprang with a heritage which experience and the shifting pattern of the national economy would modify merely in detail.

Great changes swept over American life during the latter months of 1932 and still more during the first half of 1933 after the steady pressure of three depression years and subtle alterations in public opinion finally buckled the barriers of resistance. A reshuffling of group values unmistakably occurred. The primacy of Big Business, the glamour of material success, the sanctity of the gold standard, the nobility of prohibition and the sufficiency of self-help had all been challenged sharply and in large measure scrapped.

A new spirit was in the air, a promise of leadership which millions found thrilling, a minority viewed with alarm. It was no coincidence that 1933 saw the reprinting of Edward Bellamy's utopian classic, *Looking Backward,* while in that year the first book by Franklin D. Roosevelt as president bore the title *Looking Forward.* "We are on our way," he told the nation, and after long incertitude no words could have been more welcome. In this honeymoon of the New Deal it was a true love match between the president and the people, possibly a little irrational on both sides with its trust in mutual infallibility—but love, after all, transcends logic.

Further decisions of moment were pending. Some were frank experiments, within which certain contradictions seemed to be at war—the short-term economics of scarcity against long-range economics of abundance, higher wages and farm prices without much rise in the cost of living, suspension of the antitrust laws cheek by jowl with new solicitude for the little business man. The philosophy behind these actions was more consistent than the policies themselves, and upon his intuition of that trend the average citizen was content to pillow his head. Points of strength and weakness in the New Deal, successes and failures, would grow clearer as time passed, along with the fact that Roosevelt's talent for brilliant improvisation tended to exceed his grasp of steady objectives. Probably the fairest judgment which could be reached, while the dust of controversy still hung thick in the air, was that of a British economist near the close of the first term: "Mr. Roosevelt may have given the wrong answers to many of his problems. But he is at least the first President of modern America who has asked the right questions."

CHAPTER V

THE CITIZEN AND HIS GOVERNMENT

JEFFERSON'S conviction molded by a simple agrarian nation, that the best government is that which governs least, had long been cherished by his countrymen. The federal sphere, in particular, seemed traditionally vague and remote from the citizen's daily life and needs, though, of course, he looked to Washington for services like national defense, the postal system and patent laws and, increasingly with the growth of scientific knowledge, for protection along the frontiers of sanitation and public health.

True, some Americans upon occasion had invoked federal aid when the job was too big, unprofitable or impossible for individuals, whether in developing turnpikes and canals, setting up protective tariffs, abolishing slavery, curbing trusts or prohibiting the sale of liquor. But to regard the national government in the rôle of a beneficent friend, a mighty arm against insecurity and an employer to serve—this attitude, prior to the New Deal, was as unfamiliar to certain classes of citizens as to others was the contrary one of seeing in the government an enemy whose power of regulation and taxation grew steadily more inimical. By the close of this era the word "government," alluding almost always to the administration in Washington, held for men of all classes meanings and emotional overtones rare in 1929.

Under the New Deal, Capitol Hill and the White House replaced Manhattan and Wall Street as the nation's cerebral cortex. The government began to impinge upon the life of the citizen as never before—taxing, lending, spending, building, setting quotas in agriculture and conditions of employment in industry, erecting new controls over the highways of interstate commerce. Washington offered itself to private industry sometimes as partner, sometimes as competitor. Eventually the budding of administrative agencies to fit new concepts of government created a complexity that sometimes hampered efficiency. To house these bodies, a vast new architecture, largely limestone and marble, arose along the Mall, Pennsylvania Avenue and Constitution Avenue. Some of the older agencies, like the department of labor and the Federal Trade Commission, moved into handsome new quarters, while others, like the interior and agriculture, overflowed into adjacent structures of immense size. Correspondingly occurred an increase, unprecedented in peace time, in the number of federal employees, from 588,000 civilians in 1931 to 1,370,000 in 1941.*

Awareness of this new relationship of government to the daily life of the citizen dawned for many with the advent early in the summer of 1933 of the National Recovery Administration. It was President Roosevelt's chief prescription for recovery—a tonic, with an incidental purgative of reform, designed to stimulate buying and selling, get idle men back on private pay rolls, quicken consumption, shorten hours, raise wages, abolish child labor, strengthen collective bargaining, reduce competitive waste and put a floor under prices. In signing the act Roosevelt foretold that history would record it as "the most important and far-reaching legislation ever enacted by the American Congress." If these words were too sanguine, they sprang doubtless from the enthusiasm of the hour, the hope that the same morale could be maintained after recovery began and that a single agency

* H. C. Mansfield, "Government," *Am. Journ. of Sociology*, XLVII, 959. The number of jobs outside the merit system doubled during Roosevelt's first term until it embraced two fifths of the whole system. Foes assailed the "new spoils system" and "Farleyism," while friends saw it as an emergency development, also remarking the many experts and high-minded citizens lately drawn into public service. Countermeasures began in 1938, when Congress placed 15,000 first, second and third-class postmasters under the merit plan, and Roosevelt himself sought unsuccessfully to extend its spread to all federal employees save those expressly exempt by statute.

Atlanta Slums give way to Techwood Homes, a PWA project.

Example of Human Erosion: a Sharecropper's Family.

for economic planning could meet the manifold needs and desires of all citizens.

Conceived as an experiment in industrial self-government under mild federal supervision, it was not without precedent. Trade associations, which Hoover had encouraged to adopt codes of fair practice and price-fixing agreements, were now invited to do these things directly under the eye of the government. Representatives of the United States Chamber of Commerce, who had been advocating stabilization of prices to prevent drastic cutting, helped frame the act of June, 1933. In effect, industry agreed to increase wages and shorten hours in exchange for federal aid in regulating prices. Each code proposed by the leaders of an industry was submitted for criticism to advisory committees representing labor, employers and consumers; then the administrator held public hearings, and after weighing the indorsements and objections took the amended code to the chief executive for final sanction.

Behind these NRA codes lay still another *quid pro quo* between management and government, the latter again representing the interests of labor. The step which business was permitted to take away from the antitrust laws through price fixing and regulation of competition—almost as if the trusts "busted" by the first Roosevelt were being invited back by the second—was paid for by industry's conceding to labor a similar right to consolidate, namely, the guarantee of collective bargaining pledged by Section 7A of the act.

The NRA went into action with all the fanfare, parades and oratory of a liberty-bond drive fifteen years before. All employers of more than two persons (save professional folk and farmers) were urged to sign up under the Blue Eagle, symbol of the NRA bearing the slogan: "We Do Our Part." More than two and a quarter million firms promptly enrolled, involving over sixteen million employees; ultimately the scope embraced twenty-two million persons. A blanket agreement serving as an interim policy assured white-collar workers minimum wages of from twelve to fifteen dollars for a forty-hour week and factory workers a minimum of forty cents an hour for a thirty-five-hour week, which for a seasonal interval might rise to forty hours.

Meanwhile, representatives of nearly eight hundred groups of fabricators and distributors of goods and services—from iron and steel magnates to beeswax bleachers, from rock-crusher manufacturers to private home-study schoolmasters —thronged into Washington to get codes of their own. In the great stampede it seemed as if no industry wanted to be left out, whether its practices needed codification or not. Many of these nearly eight hundred codes were drawn up in haste after consultation between harried federal officials and industrialists who knew better what they wanted than what was best for the nation, and were approved with scant tarrying for review.

The NRA diminished child labor and the sweatshop, brought a measure of improvement into business practices and working conditions, tended to set a single standard for black and white wage-earners in the South, and by shortening the work week caused the rehiring of nearly two million workers out of thirteen million unemployed. Perhaps most important of all its immediate effects was the restoration of confidence. For the first time, millions felt that something big and universally coöperative was being done to battle the Depression. The leadership of General Hugh Johnson, picturesque soldier and author of juvenile fiction, who as first NRA administrator blustered to conceal his misgivings and ruled the agency with a velvet hand in an iron glove, at first proved as potent as adrenalin—then, like most stimulants, began to lose its effect. Administrative intricacy, poor teamwork with other federal authorities and the outcries of certain business men over "unfair competition"—signifying that others were making more money than they—increased the din of confusion. Prices tended to rise faster than wages despite the General's expostulation with a group of merchants in January, 1934: "Keep prices down—for God's sake, keep prices down. That and that alone is the royal road to recovery."

In regions and occupations of traditionally low wages, as among Southern mill towns, the employers' answer to the NRA was often to utilize the stretch-out and speed-up in order to achieve the same output without additions to the pay roll.* Furthermore, its fixing of wages solely on a man-hour basis rather than by production units discriminated against the smaller and less mechanized industries. In consequence the NRA often lifted manufacturing costs by half or more, or else encouraged the scrapping of hand processes and obsolescent equipment to speed the cycle of technological unemployment.

Violation of codes by those displaying the Blue Eagle became so manifold that after a few months the public began to wax cynical. In vain did General Johnson storm against "chiselers" and threaten a "crackdown." Policing, half-hearted and ill-financed, soon grew as lax as under national prohibition in its dying days; violent spasms of enforcement bore results equally demoralizing. "Little NRA" laws passed by certain emulous states multiplied the chaos. When a small tailor in Jersey City was jailed for pressing suits at less than the state code price, foes of the NRA seized upon the incident to damn the federal system, though it was in no direct way involved. The most conspicuous rebel to defy the Blue Eagle, rugged old Henry Ford, suffered no apparent loss in sales; indeed, under the swelling outcry against the NRA, he came to be hailed in conservative circles as a hero.

So many curses, merited and unmerited, rained upon the

* For a North Carolina mill worker's complaint on this point, see *These Are Our Lives* (Chapel Hill, 1939), 209-210. Yet, like so many of the rank and file, he discriminated between the errors of the NRA and the leader of the New Deal, adding: "I do think that Roosevelt is the biggest-hearted man we ever had in the White House. . . . It's the first time in my ricollection that a president ever got up and said, 'I'm interested in and aim to do somethin' for the workin' man.'"

agency, so unwieldy did its code revision and enforcement grow, that New Dealers might well have heaved a sigh of relief when on May 27, 1935—even as Congress was debating an extension of its original two-year lease of life—the Supreme Court invalidated it and, in the caustic words of the president, relegated the nation "to the horse-and-buggy definition of interstate commerce." The government, contending that local poultry markets ramified into interstate commerce, had prosecuted a Brooklyn wholesale poultry firm for selling an "unfit chicken" in defiance of the live-poultry code. Ruling that Congress had exceeded its authority in empowering the president to set up codes over enterprises only "indirectly" involved in interstate commerce, the Court stingingly rebuked a "completely centralized government" for its alleged meddling in local affairs.

Big Business, having found the yoke of regulation it once helped to fit about its neck increasingly galling, hailed the decision with glee. Wags observed that the nine justices had converted the Blue Eagle into an unfit chicken. Its demise was almost instantaneous, with the dismissal of more than four hundred similar cases by which the government had hoped to stem violation of the codes. As an agency for voluntary agreements the NRA lingered almost a year longer, a ghost of its former self.

That the NRA had helped along the summer boomlet of 1933, improved working conditions and the position of labor nobody could well deny. But, as concluded by a Brookings Institute report, in the longer uphill pull toward prosperity, increased manufacturing costs and prices attributable to the NRA slowed rather than speeded the effort. In other words, the NRA despite its name largely failed as a recovery measure, but succeeded as one of reform. This lesson was not lost upon the president and his advisers, who from 1935 onward bent their energies in the latter direction.

In retrospect it appeared also that the NRA tried to do too much too quickly and that the practice frequently violated the theory. New Dealers had favored the plan from conviction that the operations of Big Business were a public service and should therefore be controlled in the common interest; in practice, however, there was little doubt that the NRA, through regulation of both prices and output, furthered monopoly in many instances. When the NRA authorities during the second year attempted modifications at the instance of consumers and small business, the great industrialists were rapidly alienated.

Was it possible that Roosevelt had repeated Hoover's mistake in pinning too much faith upon the enlightened and unselfish coöperation of business? New Dealers at any rate drifted toward that conclusion. The liberal lawyer Donald R. Richberg, who had inherited the limelight of the NRA when, behind the curtain of a reorganization late in 1934, General Johnson departed under a rain of "dead cats," wrote some years later in reviewing the débâcle:

> The most tragic result was an unhappy demonstration that businessmen as a whole had not learned either the need or the essential principles of a positive regulation of business for the very purpose of preserving free enterprise.

Less partisan opinion inclined to see the Blue Eagle as neither flesh nor fowl, lacking on the one hand the dispersion of authority implicit in free competition and on the other the ruthless efficiency supposed to reside in the corporative state. Its taste of bureaucracy was just enough to offend many American palates. The NRA's best features were probably salvaged by the Robinson-Patman act of 1937 curbing discriminatory trade practices and by a series of beneficent labor laws passed between 1935 and 1938. Roosevelt himself was nettled by the Court's disapproval, taking it as a personal affront, but among citizens at large regrets seemed few.

Two years of bickering over the NRA, in terms of "planned economy" versus "rugged individualism," set the national stage for a debate which continued with almost monotonous iteration through the lifetime of the New Deal. The chief mouthpiece for criticism of the president's policies was the press, and the genesis of its hostility to Roosevelt is worth remark. An acrimonious dispute over the newspaper publishing code—with NRA officials seeking, among other things, to prohibit child labor among news vendors—early antagonized the owners of the press. Certain publishers never tired of pointing to the barefoot newsboy as the sacred symbol of self-help despite Warden Lewis E. Lawes's testimony that seven out of ten inmates of Sing Sing had sold papers in their youth. In respect to staff employees as well, the NRA's proposals concerning working hours, wages and fair practices proved unacceptable to the American Newspaper Publishers Association. Late in 1933 this group submitted a code providing neither minimum wages nor shorter hours, claiming that imposition of a more rigid policy would hamper freedom of the press and the discharge of those civic services which (they argued) set journalism apart from ordinary businesses. Eventually, in February, 1934, a compromise code was signed that appeared to satisfy nobody.

As another by-product of the collective-bargaining guarantees under the Blue Eagle, a group of newsmen with vivid memories of the steep salary cuts and dismissals of 1929-1933 organized the American Newspaper Guild in December, 1933. The first national union of its kind, it owed much to the leadership of that bluff, crusading columnist Heywood Broun and gained some twenty thousand members within the decade. With fair success it helped to raise the meager salaries of reporters, but even at the close of this era had failed to win for them any real contractual security. Meanwhile, publishers loudly lamented the decline of self-reliance in the ranks and of the old romantic ideas of individualism, blaming it all on the officiousness of the New Deal.

Besides these contested points, the identification of great newspaper corporations with other forms of Big Business tended to swing editorial opinion considerably to the right of center. Even before the NRA was well started, William Randolph Hearst, whose chain had backed Roosevelt and Garner in 1932, turned against the administration, thereby joining Colonel Robert R. McCormick of the *Chicago Tribune* and Frank E. Gannett, owner of a chain mainly in upstate New York, who had been foes from the start. Paradoxically, while Roosevelt himself was winning unparalleled popularity among Washington correspondents, the press back home was solidifying against him. By the time of his second election approximately two newspapers out of every three fought his candidacy. The opposition journals, however, generally printed the president's speeches and, save for the bitterest diehards, reported Washington news with fairer objectivity than that of the anti-Jefferson press of 1800 or the anti-Lincoln press in 1860. Hence, as one friend of the New Deal observed, it was evident that "the people voted with the news columns and against the editorials."

Among persons in the higher-income brackets hostility to the New Deal arose as the bank crisis passed, the honeymoon period waned and the NRA disappointed its business sponsors. The anxieties and industrial jitters of 1933 gave way by the next spring to "open undisguised indignation and anger at Washington," as a Kiplinger newsletter of March 31, 1934, reported after polling its patrons. Among the prime causes were "the confusions and inconsistencies of NRA and AAA," the stock-exchange bill, labor policies and fears of Communist infiltration of government.

In August the American Liberty League was formed under an executive board of millionaires to oppose "the caprice of bureaucracy" and "the tyranny of autocratic power." Such persons regarded the New Deal as a plot to use hard times as a springboard to socialism. The more vindictive concentrated their hate upon the president, "that Man," "a traitor to his class," who symbolized the threat of change. One of Peter Arno's best-known cartoons, appearing in September, 1936, in *The New Yorker*, portrayed a little band of Park Avenue citizens movie-bound in dinner jackets and sables, inviting their neighbors through the open window, "Come along. We're going to the trans-lux to hiss Roosevelt."

Some were alarmed by the expanding scope of federal regulation besides and beyond the NRA. In 1933, for example, Congress in the emergency transportation act extended the range of jurisdiction over the financially embarrassed railroads by setting up a temporary coördinator of transportation and strengthening the Interstate Commerce Commission's authority in reorganization proceedings. Two years later another law gave the ICC control over motor transportation by common carrier and contract carrier in the interests of safety, quantity of service and just fares, and in 1938 the Civil Aeronautics Authority was created to regulate air traffic. The transportation act of 1940 established a national policy for all carriers by land and water, empowering the ICC to help farmers by reducing railway rates on agricultural exports and discountenancing "unfair or destructive competitive practices" and promising "fair and impartial regulation." The great differences in the economic operation of trains and trucks, busses and boats made this a dire need.

Because of the impotence or timorousness of private credit agencies—savings banks, insurance companies, trust companies—the New Deal assumed additional responsibility over the flow of credit by enlarging the scope and lending powers of the RFC far beyond its Hoover infancy, thus enabling it to serve a great variety of industries and individuals. Though this was welcomed by the business community, at the same time it fed the fear that the government was acquiring a mortgage upon the assets of private enterprise. Also under the New Deal the Federal Reserve system was converted into a more effective mechanism for the expansion or contraction of credit, and by fixing the margin requirements for security purchases it could affect the volume of credit flowing into brokers' loans. In still other fields the New Deal offered help to the debt-ridden farmer by creating the Federal Farm

Mortgage Corporation and aided the distressed householder by setting up the Home Owners' Loan Corporation. By creating the Export-Import Bank it also assisted the shipper, as well as the foreign government needing credit to buy his wares.

Other strands of federal control over interstate industry were spun year by year. The public-utility act of 1935, already mentioned, sought not only to protect the small investor from the evils of holding companies, but also to safeguard consumers and the public interest by demanding reasonable rates and the opening of financial accounts to inspection by the Federal Power Commission. Such power-producing enterprises as Boulder (Hoover) Dam in the Southwest, Fort Peck Dam in Montana, Bonneville and Grand Coulee in the Pacific Northwest and the Central Valley project in California converted the government into an actual operator. Under the Tennessee Valley Authority it took still further strides and attempted something beyond the reach of private enterprise: to improve vocational opportunities, security and health, in other words the standard of living and social values of an entire region.

Here, and in the relief and housing programs, one saw the essential difference between government and private enterprise in the economic sphere. Public welfare was the mainspring of the former, profit motive of the latter. What the citizen needed, rather than what he could afford to buy, became the determinant in the new social-service concept of government—a government which, having envisaged these needs, set out to meet them not on the basis of cash in hand or calculations of ultimate profit, but with assurance that the bill would be paid by apportioning it among the taxpayers. The rôle of the state as provider presupposed its function as financier and tax collector. Under the New Deal, government itself came to be incomparably the largest enterprise in the nation.

The first exclusively New Deal budget, for the fiscal year

1934, increased federal expenditures two billion dollars over 1933, approximately sixty per cent of all appropriations going for "recovery and relief." Before the close of 1936 the national debt, despite higher taxes, had reached thirty billion and by 1940 forty-three. Like most American phenomena, it too had become big. A roving reporter, sampling opinion through the country, found that persons on relief naturally approved, as did also most of the younger generation. Considerable authority, even among professional economists, maintained that the debt need not be feared since the people owed it to themselves. On the other hand, critics charged that money was being spent on "crazy experiments," that steep taxes sapped business confidence, that they really hid a socialist scheme to nationalize the means of production. They argued further that such taxation merely passed on the brunt to the consumer in higher prices, which caused lower consumption and in turn more unemployment in a vicious circle.

In this spirit the National Association of Manufacturers condemned legislation in 1935 boosting inheritance and gift taxes, increasing the surtax on incomes of over fifty thousand dollars and imposing a graduated corporation income tax, as an abuse of federal power "to penalize thrift and success." * Another turn of the screw of sadism—as these critics interpreted it—came with the revenue act of 1936, which set up an undistributed-profits tax. Without these reserves, groaned executives, plans for expansion were impossible, and their outcry caused a later, more sympathetic Congress to let this tax lapse in 1939. New Dealers justified these levies as based upon ability to pay, while the bolder ones frankly declared that taxation should be used not merely to obtain revenue but to redistribute wealth.

Many states and some cities quickly caught on to the ex-

* At the close of their bitter arraignment the N. A. M. added, "In opposing unsound economic and social measures it is unnecessary to propose alternatives." N. Y. Times, Dec. 6, 1935.

ample set by Washington and joined the parade of taxing and spending until the annual cost of government—federal, state and local—rose from eleven billion dollars in 1929 to seventeen by 1938. The incentive to match federal funds was well-nigh irresistible, for thereby such assets as new school-houses, hospitals, parks, playgrounds, sewer systems and roads were acquired and the millstone of local unemployment was lightened. In the case of the states "protective tariffs" on commodities from beyond their borders multiplied, while the income tax continued to gain ground until about two thirds of them had adopted this tax in some form by the end of the thirties. Though graduated much less steeply than the federal levy, it was sufficient to yield over a third of a billion dollars in 1939.

The most important innovation was the sales tax. Introduced by West Virginia in 1921, it found no imitators until the onset of hard times led to its adoption by twenty-one states between 1930 and 1935. A few municipalities also followed suit. New York City's sales tax, for example, at the close of the decade was producing nearly sixty million dollars annually. Such taxes bore more heavily upon the poor than the rich. A laborer with a thousand-dollar yearly income was estimated to spend nearly sixty-one per cent of it upon sales-taxed commodities, while a millionaire might spend as little as one per cent. Hence, while favored by chambers of commerce and bankers' associations as a federal policy, the scheme gained no support from the Roosevelt administration and little from Congress.

With the repeal of national prohibition the states incidentally recovered a lucrative source of revenue. Kansas, Oklahoma, North Dakota and five Southern states chose for the present to remain dry; fifteen commonwealths made the selling of liquor a state monopoly, though seven of them allowed private sale under stipulated conditions. Later years of the era saw a spreading web of local-option laws. High taxes imposed on alcoholic beverages—by federal and state author-

ities avid for funds—so raised the price of the legal article
that a considerable traffic in bootleg still persisted. Popular
opinion and state laws outlawed old rituals of bar and saloon
in favor of bottle sales by special shops, drug stores, or gro-
cery stores, while the public serving of liquor became the
rôle of cocktail lounges, beer gardens, night clubs and restaurants, where sitting rather than standing, eating as well as
imbibing, and the presence of both sexes wrought at least
overt changes in American drinking habits.

Thanks to this shift from federal prohibition to state
regulation, the consumption of alcohol became less frenetic
and hazardous to health, but certainly increased among the
working classes and among those who disliked stealth and
inconvenience. At any rate, the American people continued
to register satisfaction over the change. A *Fortune* poll late
in 1937 found only one man out of seven and one woman
in three favoring the return of national prohibition.

The states also made new advances in welfare legislation.
For example, workmen's accident compensation laws, which
had come into considerable favor among the states earlier in
the century, were vastly strengthened during the fourth decade under the stimulus of the New Deal and its philosophy.
In the year 1937 alone, thirty-eight legislatures revised and
broadened their laws by increasing accident and death benefits, reducing the waiting period, extending coverage, widening the definition of occupational diseases, liberalizing
hospital, nursing, dental, prosthetic and rehabilitation provisions. Pay-roll taxes were also invoked to finance state
social-security systems, as will be seen later.

Meanwhile the orbit of federal authority grew constantly
greater. Government now was expected to do things for its
citizens which government had never done before in the
United States. Obnoxious as this assumption of new powers
was to conservative extremists, it proved equally displeasing
to radical extremists. Until Stalin in 1935 decreed a "united
front" of communists with liberals throughout the world,

his followers in America conducted a virulent attack against the New Deal. Earl Browder, Warren Jay Vinton, Benjamin Stolberg and other Marxists assailed the Roosevelt régime no less rancorously for betraying the masses than did John W. Davis, Ogden Mills and Hamilton Fish for betraying the Hudson Valley gentry and the "American way of life." *

The president, steering "a little to the left of the center" and seeking to temper the winds of world socialism and domestic economic discontent, saw the necessity for adhering mainly to a middle course. In a fireside chat after substantial completion of the New Deal's legislative program he observed,

> Different from a great part of the world, we in America persist in our belief in individual enterprise and in the profit motive; but we realize we must continually seek improved practices to insure the continuance of reasonable profits, together with scientific progress, individual initiative, opportunities for the little fellow, fair prices, decent wages and continuing employment.

His task was a singularly delicate one, calling not only for the harmonizing of tradition with social progress, but the drafting of highly complicated plans under emergency pressure and the maintenance of a precarious balance between recovery and reform. Merely to prime the pump to make the economic waters flow once more through the channels of commerce and high finance—if this could be done—seemed as dubious as a total neglect of recovery in a frenzy of reformist zeal. In practice the New Deal, beyond the instant tasks of relief, mobilized its first great efforts toward recovery, with the Blue Eagle for industry and the original Triple A for the farmer. "Our first task is to get the economic system to function so that there will be a greater general security,"

---

* "There is nothing the New Deal has so far done that could not have been done better by an earthquake," wrote Stolberg and Vinton in the concluding paragraph of their *Economic Consequences of the New Deal* (N. Y., 1935).

Roosevelt told a committee of social planners in 1934. "Everything that we can do with intent to increase the security of the individual will, I am confident, be a stimulus to recovery." The two aims were therefore implicated in his own mind from the start, but at this stage recovery held priority.

The year 1935 proved to be the pivot upon which the New Deal swung sharply toward reform, as if Roosevelt believed recovery assured or thought it hopeless further to appease Big Business. The collapse of the NRA added to the president's vexation, and personal abuse from the Liberty League probably played some part, too. His enemies interpreted the change as a vote-getting policy angled toward 1936, in which the Democratic Congress also had a stake, or else as a ruse to distract attention from his poor showing in resuscitating the nation's economy. Whatever the reasons, 1935 saw the passage of more social legislation than any other year in the nation's history, including the national labor-relations act, the social-security law, the wealth-tax act, the public-utility act and the most liberal relief program ever undertaken by any government, the Works Progress Administration.

The Works Progress Administration (later, the Work Projects Administration) soon became for millions the personalized symbol of Uncle Sam as friend, provider and employer. "I'm proud of our United States," declared a North Carolina tenant farmer living with his family in a one-room filling station, "and every time I hear the 'Star-Spangled Banner' I feel a lump in my throat. There ain't no other nation in the world that would have sense enough to think of WPA and all the other A's." Working for the WPA carried its own modest dignity, for it meant neither handouts nor just raking leaves. Many a wife whose husband had been jobless soon came to say in effect, with a touch of pride, "We aren't on relief any more—my man is working for the government."

This agency, above all others, effected a noteworthy change in the low-income worker's relation to government and politics. Unlike the state-administered FERA, it established a rapport between him and his Washington employer, and he quickly learned to distinguish between local governments and the federal authority, which seemed relatively superior in fairness and efficiency. And, despite the program's shortcomings, its psychological results went far to justify the avowed aim of WPA officials "to help men keep their chins up and their hands in." Over the New York World's Fair building erected in 1939 by the WPA ran the inscription: "Work is America's answer to the need of idle millions." Increasingly one heard that the right to work had become one of the basic guarantees of American government.

The advent of the WPA in the summer of 1935 marked the divorce of work relief from direct relief, for the latter, as has been seen, was now handed back to the states and localities. By 1939-1940 about three fifths of direct-relief expenditures came from state funds alone. Many of the two million beneficiaries—families and single persons—were at that time faring less well than under the old FERA, the monthly allowances per family averaging twenty-five dollars and, in certain states like Arkansas and Mississippi, no more than three or five dollars.

The employables, for whom the WPA was designed, had in general bettered their lot, however. Monthly wages averaged between fifty and sixty dollars, with the work week rarely exceeding forty hours. Under Harry Hopkins as chief the WPA allotted the largest possible slice of its funds to wages, and looked to the local tax-supported public body collaborating upon a given project to furnish most of the materials and tools.* Eventually this latter contribution was

---

* In March, 1939, the president told Congress that out of every hundred dollars spent by the WPA $86 went for wages, $10.50 for materials, and $3.50 into administration. F. D. Roosevelt, *Public Papers and Addresses* (S. I. Rosenman, ed., N. Y., 1938-1941), VIII, 162. D. S. Howard, *The WPA and*

gauged at a quarter of the total cost. To the state, municipality or county the finished product belonged. A poor state like Mississippi, unable to match funds, did less well than better-circumstanced commonwealths, losing schools, swimming pools and playgrounds as well as jobs for the needy. Spending about ten billion from the Treasury up to January, 1941, the WPA during these years gave employment to nearly eight million individuals, one out of five of all the nation's workers, and in all supported between twenty-five and thirty million persons.

From the start the WPA endeavored to seek out those tasks which both free enterprise and civic initiative were passing over or postponing. Impressive was its list of accomplishments. They included New York City's forty-million-dollar North Beach airport and nearly six hundred other landing fields through the country, more than half a million miles of roads and streets and over a hundred thousand bridges and viaducts. The building or rebuilding of a hundred and ten thousand public libraries, schools, auditoriums, hospitals, courthouses and similar structures stood also to its credit. Half a million sewerage connections and over a million new privies aided public health no less vitally than did WPA mosquito control, drainage ditches and water purification. In the South a sharp reduction in typhoid deaths promptly followed WPA innovations. Disaster work in the wake of floods and hurricanes loomed large in 1937 and 1938.

Equally notable were the serving of nearly six hundred million school lunches up to January, 1941—at which time the WPA maintained fourteen hundred and sixty nursery schools—and the making of over three hundred million garments for needy children and adults. Sewing groups, which comprised the bulk of the WPA's female employees, mustered three or four hundred thousand at peak strength. Educa-

Federal Relief Policy (N. Y., 1943), 145-150, 608, 797, discusses the interaction of federal and state participation, finding the former much superior to the latter.

tional and cultural aspects of the agency will be discussed later, though one may note in passing the renovation of nearly eighty million books, chiefly in school and public libraries. Even the harshest critics admitted that the WPA greatly enhanced convenience, sanitation and neatness among American communities. In a less tangible way the WPA's ideal of equal employment opportunity regardless of race, color or creed—though occasionally violated in the South respecting the Negro—had also a salutary effect upon the spread of practical democracy.

The record of a single fortnight's activity, selected at random, offers a hasty map of the various zones in which government through the WPA touched the daily life, particularly of disadvantaged groups. During such a period in January, 1940, a million and a quarter attended naturalization, vocational-training, art, nursery and other classes; seventeen thousand completed immunization for smallpox, diphtheria or other diseases; a quarter of a million received medical and dental examinations and treatments; and more than a million attended twenty-five hundred free musical performances.

At first the average community hailed the WPA as a rich bargain in whose sunshine civic improvements might flower after a long winter of municipal deficits and the restraints of a group-poverty complex. To get new bridges, parks, assembly halls and public golf courses "at a little more than half of their cost to the local taxpayers," as a Middletown editorial phrased it, was blandishment indeed. Uncle Sam was regarded somewhat naïvely as a fount of beneficence quite unrelated to the citizen's pocketbook. As time wore on, however, the expectation of steady funds and eagerness for still greater sums battled in the citizen's mind with worries about bureaucracy, the coddling of loafers and the decline of states' rights.

For obvious reasons, chronic WPA workers were apt to be less efficient than the cream of man power skimmed repeatedly by private industry. Besides, the inevitable spongers exposed the whole program to criticism. During the recession of 1937-1938, for example, when the WPA bought fifteen million dollars' worth of clothing from the factories in order to prime industry and still more to outfit the jobless, some with no right to relief were reported to have received free overalls, shirts, bedding and other supplies. Jokes about "shovel-leaners," centering around the man who was injured when his shovel gave way, grew current in the latter thirties.

The WPA, like any government agency dispensing bounty to the masses possessing little save a vote, was often accused of buying good will, but beyond reasonable alertness to the logic whereby ballots tend to follow benefits, its high command seems to have kept a steady hand upon the purse strings and maintained a clean record. Local employees, however, were not always so scrupulous. Campaigning by the WPA staff in Pennsylvania, Kentucky and Tennessee in the 1938 elections led to much unfavorable notice and to the passage of the Hatch act of July, 1939, curbing "pernicious political activities" by federal appointees.

Private industry continued to lag under the pump-priming of both WPA and PWA.* While the federal outlay for construction rocketed from an annual average of $188,000,000 between 1925 and 1929 to that of $1,630,000,000 between 1933 and 1938, private construction during this latter period never attained half the predepression figure. A careful study under auspices of the National Resources Planning Board concluded that the tonic effect of federal public works upon national income and the sum of business activity was disappointingly small. Thus the economic results of pump-priming tended to bear out the critics of the New Deal at the

---

* The fluctuating and seasonal imbalance of private employment greatly complicated the problem. A survey of more than a thousand families in thirteen cities who left relief rolls for private industry in the summer of 1935 found that three fifths were driven back to seek relief within the next twelve months despite the nation's general advance toward recovery. J. C. Bevis and S. L. Payne, *Former Relief Cases in Private Employment* (WPA, Wash., 1939), 9.

same time that the gains in employees' morale gratified its
friends.

The public-works program was of course not perfect, nor
planned very logically. Like the people themselves, the administration was loath to admit that relief had become apparently a chronic problem. From this optimism stemmed
much of the program's makeshift character, its vacillating
theories concerning the federal obligation. Also, in retrospect
it seemed as if the WPA, with its free spending and quick
maneuverability to meet relief emergencies, should have come
prior to the cautious expenditure, the enmeshing of federal
with private enterprise, of the PWA. Yet in practice the cart
emerged before the horse.

The campaign of 1936 brought to the fore the whole New
Deal conception of government. Certainly the administration's activities seemed to offer targets vulnerable because of
their size and multiplicity. Here was Uncle Sam financing the
buying and vending of goods and the operation of ships and
railroads, managing currency and seeking to control prices,
generating and selling electric power, destroying and storing
agricultural commodities, teaching the farmer how to plow
and plant, supervising the diet of school children, draining
swamps, trafficking in real estate, sponsoring literature and
drama and art and folk dancing, and all the while describing ever widening circles of deficit financing. Opponents
turned their guns upon the New Deal's paternalism, its shapes
of concentrated power and monopoly, the alignment of class
against class, and a drift toward the "providential state" such
as one saw in advanced stages in Russia, Germany and Italy.
Under the régime of the state as regulator always lurked the
danger that what paraded as the "public interest" would
really become the interests of a group—if not of industrialists, bankers or war veterans, then of farmers, union labor
or the masses of the ne'er-do-well.

The editors of Middletown burnished up the old axiom
that "any man who is willing to work hard and to be thrifty

and improve his spare time can get to the top. That's the American way, and it's as true today as it ever was." Sniffing the springtime of recovery, many an elder American turned instinctively to the sarsaparilla of self-reliance. Such folk remarked that nobody ever got to the top "by working forty hours a week." Dale Carnegie's *How to Win Friends and Influence People,* published in 1936 and destined to be the nonfiction best seller to the tune of eventually three million copies, came like a breath of inspirational salesmanship wafted down the years from Timothy Shay Arthur and Orison Swett Marden. And in this year the National Association of Manufacturers sponsored a series of movie shorts, scoring "isms" and the rising cost of boondoggling, denying that machines destroy more jobs than they create and, above all, upholding the prestige of the Constitution.

The Republican leaders, assembling in Cleveland, discovered their bond of unity in the words of Senator Arthur H. Vandenberg: "I belong to but one bloc and it has but one slogan—stop Roosevelt." Their platform, however, betrayed significant concessions to the New Deal's concept of the service state. While looking to "the energy, self-reliance and character of our people" as the bulwark of economic security, the G. O. P. granted society's duty "to promote the security of the people by affording some measure of protection against involuntary unemployment and dependency in old age" and called upon the federal government to set standards for state systems and match funds for old-age pensions. Furthermore, "the necessities of life must be provided for the needy," though with sharper separation of public works from relief and of politics from relief, with the main responsibility for the latter falling upon nonpolitical local agencies. The farmer should be aided with benefit payments for soil conservation, abundant credit, the retirement of nonproductive land and federal encouragement of coöperative marketing. Labor was promised collective bargaining "without interference from any source," including bureaucrats. The platform also favored state measures to outlaw child labor and sweatshops and to protect women and children against economic exploitation notwithstanding that the Supreme Court, which most Republicans hailed as the palladium of liberty, had just invalidated a New York minimum-wage law for women as infringing "freedom of contract" between workers and employers and thus had seemingly shut the door upon all state regulation of working conditions. The candidate, Alfred M. Landon, mild, diffident and colorless in personality, took up the battle as best he could against overwhelming odds.

The Democrats, who offered the New Deal as their essential platform for 1936, renominated Roosevelt at Philadelphia with thunderous acclaim and sat back to hear an acceptance speech from which flew sparks and one fighting phrase, "economic royalists." His tutelary genius in the campaign seemed to be the ghost not of Jefferson but of Old Hickory, a more rugged champion of the people against the moneyed interests, and on election day, for luck, he wore Jackson's heavy gold watch chain. The most militant of his speeches was reserved for Madison Square Garden. Recalling "Nine crazy years at the ticker and three long years in the breadlines! Nine mad years of mirage and three long years of despair!" he continued, "Powerful influences strive today to restore that kind of government with its doctrine that the Government is best which is most indifferent." He exulted in their opposition:

> Never before in all our history have these forces been so united against one candidate as they stand today. They are unanimous in their hate for me—and I welcome their hatred.
> I should like to have it said of my first Administration that in it the forces of selfishness and of lust for power met their match. I should like to have it said of my second Administration that in it these forces met their master.

A postelection analysis of the campaign funds—nearly nine million dollars for the Republicans, five and a quarter for the Democrats—served as commentary on these words. Whereas in 1928 and again in 1932, bankers had been among the heaviest contributors to the Democratic purse, their revolt in 1936 was conspicuous. Heads of investment houses, magnates of steel and chemicals, chain-store and mail-order executives, individuals like Hearst the publisher and J. Howard Pew the oilman, poured funds prodigally into Republican coffers. On the other hand, motion-picture producers, theater owners, a fair representation from the liquor and tobacco interests and many members of the professions and organized labor swelled the Democratic fund. In the background stood millions of farmers, paid for not raising crops, and millions more on relief who could not give the president anything but love—and a vote.

Roosevelt achieved a reëlection victory such as no other president of modern times had won, capturing almost sixty-one per cent of the popular ballots in a contest which drew nearly six million more voters to the polls than the 1932 election, which had given him a mere fifty-seven per cent. Jubilant at their sweep of forty-six states, Democrats paraphrased an old saw, "As Maine goes, so goes Vermont." Hearst, among the most implacable of Roosevelt's enemies, grudgingly admitted a few days after the election that no man in American history save Jackson had enjoyed "an equally overwhelming popular appeal and popular victory." True to the Jacksonian touch, Roosevelt provided that the reviewing stand for the inaugural parade of January, 1937, should be a replica of the Hermitage.

In bullish mood the president was already planning to get the upper hand of his old adversary, the Supreme Court. Unmistakably from early in 1935 the tribunal had begun to do deadly execution among the tender brood of New Deal legislation: not only the NRA, the agricultural adjustment act, the Frazier-Lemke farm moratorium act, the Guffey-Snyder law seeking to stabilize labor conditions in the soft-coal fields, but even so innocent-seeming a measure as the railroad retirement act for pensioning employees, which was crushingly damned as irrelevant to interstate commerce and as denying due process of law "by taking the property of one and bestowing it upon another." Justices Harlan F. Stone, Louis D. Brandeis and Benjamin N. Cardozo usually constituted themselves a minority of liberal dissent, who upon occasion (such as the invalidation of New York's minimum-wage law for women) were joined by Chief Justice Charles E. Hughes. Five members of the bench, however, seemed invincibly conservative. A widely read book of the time, Professor E. S. Corwin's *The Twilight of the Supreme Court* (1934), argued that the judiciary had become the great stumblingblock of social progress.

So felt President Roosevelt when in February, 1937, he proposed to reorganize the entire federal bench, asserting that senility tended to hamper the pace of business. His scheme provided that for every justice who failed to retire at seventy an additional one be appointed up to a total membership of fifteen on the Supreme Court. Of the six septuagenarians then sitting, Brandeis alone was a convinced liberal.

This proposal to "pack" the Court caused a furor, swamping Congress with letters and telegrams and provoking protests from several legislatures, while a host of "Committees to Preserve Our Liberties" or "Associates for America" mushroomed over the nation. Opposition came naturally to the Roosevelt haters, who, however, were joined by many middle-of-the-road citizens sincerely fearing that the ideal of constitutional government was in danger from the inroads of personal domination. To many eyes Roosevelt's strategy looked both flippant and evasive, and to the collective symbol of the Nine Old Men group protectiveness rallied. In April, 1937, a Gallup poll asking, "Would you favor a constitutional amendment requiring Supreme Court Justices to retire at some age between 70 and 75?" reported an affirmative majority of sixty-four per cent, but in June, in response to the query, "Should Congress pass the President's Supreme Court plan?" the negative won by fifty-eight per cent, and a September poll registered sixty-eight per cent against his "fight to enlarge the Supreme Court."

In the spring of 1937 the tribunal itself cut the ground from beneath the advocates of change, at the same time appearing to vindicate the doubters of its Olympian detachment. Justice Owen J. Roberts now shifted his weight toward the liberal wing. The allegiance of Chief Justice Hughes seemed also to grow steadier. Accordingly, the Court upheld the railway labor act and the revised Frazier-Lemke farm-mortgage moratorium. Moreover, it sustained the minimum-wage law of the state of Washington, the Wagner labor-relations act and the unemployment-insurance tax provisions of the social-security act—all by a vote of five to four. The resignation of archconservative Justice Willis Van Devanter shortly permitted Roosevelt to name his first appointee to the bench, Senator Hugo L. Black, and assure a wider margin of victory for the New Deal.

Meanwhile in August, 1937, the Senate rejected the president's Supreme Court proposal. Though Roosevelt had failed to achieve his means, he attained his ends, and in the next year looked back upon the contest as "a lost battle which won a war." The new temper of the judiciary respecting the sphere of federal action may be sufficiently indicated by citing a decision in 1938 upholding the right of the PWA to finance municipal construction of distribution lines in competition with private facilities. Thus was cleared the most formidable road block in the path of the Roosevelt revolution, and the highest court in the land began to bestow its accolade upon many New Deal innovations.

CHAPTER VI

Unions on the March

IF the unfolding New Deal served to set one faction of the nation inflexibly against Roosevelt, it recruited corresponding support for him among the ranks of labor. Under his administration organized labor, which numbered a bare three million in 1931, strengthened its position as never before and discovered the leverage it could exert in politics. No development of the times loomed larger than this in the thinking and daily life of many Americans.

This new prestige had burst forth shortly after the clouds seemed darkest for organized labor. In 1929, following a postwar decade which saw management firmly in the saddle and union membership shrinking, labor leaders had small grounds for either complacency or hope. The once strong United Mine Workers, for example, suffered from internal strife and nonunion competition from the lower-cost bituminous fields; an attempt to organize Southern textile mills provoked the savage Gastonia riot but ended in failure; such major industries as steel and automobiles bore no trace of unionism. At this juncture came the onrush of mass unemployment, spelling further reduction in the ranks of dues-payers and in the power of collective bargaining.

Legally, however, labor won two important victories in the Hoover administration. After years of mounting wrath in labor circles against employer-sponsored company unions, the Supreme Court in the Texas & New Orleans Railway case in 1930 unanimously decided that an employer's attempt to force a company union upon his workers constituted interference with their rights. And in March, 1932, Hoover signed the Norris-La Guardia act outlawing "yellow-dog"

107

contracts, which had bound employees not to join unions, and forbidding federal courts to issue injunctions as weapons against organized labor. This law rested upon the premise that an individual worker was helpless save as he gained power through "association, self-organization, and designation of representatives of his own choosing, to negotiate the terms and conditions of his employment." Like other aspects of progressivism latent in Hoover days, it bore seed from which the New Deal sprouted in the fertile season of 1933.

Section 7A of the national industrial recovery act repeated phrases from the Norris-La Guardia act with more trenchant emphasis, promising employees "the right to organize and bargain collectively through representatives of their own choosing" under no restraint. Promptly capital and labor set to work to turn the guarantee to contrary purposes, the former striving to multiply company unions and use Section 7A as a prop for the open shop, while labor sought to destroy company unions and make its own unions the exclusive bargaining units. John L. Lewis, head of the United Mine Workers and most aggressive of organizers, sent forth evangels with the garbled gospel, "The President wants you to join the union"; as a result, membership in the UMW rose from one hundred and fifty thousand in 1932 to four hundred thousand by 1935. Less spectacularly, between midsummer, 1933, and midsummer, 1936, the rolls of the American Federation of Labor as a whole increased almost seventy-five per cent.

A floor under wages and a ceiling over hours were, as has been seen, mandatory for employers signing up under the NRA. Although some quibbling, evasion and violation occurred and though labor grumbled constantly at the lag between wages and rising prices, the requirement as to hours, later reiterated by the Wagner act, operated with depressed conditions to effect a much greater change in the work week than ever known in short order before. By 1936 the average laboring week was estimated at about nine hours less than in

1929, a five-day stint had become the rule rather than the exception, and the Saturday closings common in large cities provided longer week-ends. In smaller towns and in the South the resistance was greater, but no stratum of business or industry remained wholly unaffected.

To umpire the tug of war between management and re-surgent labor the president in August, 1933, created the National Labor Board of employer and union representatives with Senator Robert F. Wagner of New York as chairman. Its powers of enforcement were scant, however, and in June, 1934, Congress, taking back some of the authority which it had let slip into executive hands, substituted the National Labor Relations Board with quasijudicial functions. Composed of three labor-relations experts, the NLRB was supposed to be strictly impartial, but management began to complain when it almost invariably sided with the worker. If the New Deal in general and this Board in particular tended to favor labor oftener than management, their partisans pointed to the long ascendancy of the latter which now called for redress. Perhaps its most important decision, and the one most bitterly opposed by the National Association of Manufacturers in appeal to the courts, was that against the Houde Engineering Corporation, in which the Board held that under Section 7A an employer could not bargain with a minority, but must deal with a majority as the sole collective agent for all, although employees were under no compulsion to join this organization.

Upon labor the days of the Blue Eagle had effects important psychologically, as well as legally or judicially, by re-affirming the importance of collective bargaining and making unions more respectable in the popular eye. Following the collapse of the NRA and with it of the NLRB, labor was strong enough to press for congressional legislation to salvage its gains. After many years' submission to Samuel Gompers's policy of "voluntarism" for bettering industrial relations and of relying upon the unions' internal strength rather than the intercession of government, a large rebellious regiment of labor now demanded bolder tactics. In response, the Wagner labor-relations act of July 5, 1935, forbade interference with unionizing and collective bargaining and brooked no refusal to deal with employees' representatives, no promotion of company unions, no discrimination in the matter of employment.* To administer the law and hold employee elections, a new three-member National Labor Relations Board was established. Several states now passed "little Wagner acts" imposing similar restrictions upon intrastate enterprises.

A series of federal court decisions, following the lead of the Supreme Court, gave the NLRB virtually a free hand. Under the guise of preventing even "subtle coercion" the right of employers to talk was sharply limited, though critics urged that freedom of speech and debate was as desirable in labor disputes as immunity from unfair pressure and that the two were not mutually exclusive. Up to the end of January, 1941, the Board dealt with almost thirty-three thousand cases involving nearly seven million wage-earners; 3166 strike cases concerned 400,000 workers, and of these 2383 were settled, while almost a thousand involving 200,000 workers were averted. This did not mean the absence or quick settlement of all strikes, since no provision for compulsory arbitration, as practised for example in Australia, was even seriously debated save at the very close of the era in respect to defense industries.

Indeed, the middle years of the decade witnessed great industrial turmoil, the result both of labor's depression-dated bill of grievances and of its new self-assertion under encouragement of the administration. The summer of 1934 brought such a groundswell of strikes as had not been seen

* *U. S. Statutes at Large*, XLIX, 452-457. The LaFollette civil-liberties committee was formed largely to assure better enforcement of the Wagner act by investigating "the violations of the rights of free speech and assembly and undue interference with the right of labor to organize and bargain collectively." Quoted in Mary H. Vorse, *Labor's New Millions* (N. Y., 1938), 251.

for years. In late May the Communist Dunne brothers in Minneapolis organized a general truck drivers' strike, which led to bloodshed. In San Francisco a longshoremen's walkout, begun in May, involved sympathetic unions in a four-day general strike in July, the biggest of its kind since 1919. A poll by the men ended this effort, to the disappointment of its chief organizer, Australian-born Harry Bridges, whose alleged Communist ties and resistance to deportation resulted in a legal battle that raged through the late thirties. In September, 1934, a cut in production and hence in take-home pay, sanctioned by the textile code authority, caused three hundred and fifty thousand Southern cotton mill workers to drop their tools. A mediation board, appointed by the president and headed by New Hampshire's former Governor John G. Winant, found considerable justice on the strikers' side and recommended creation of the Textile Labor Relations Board.

To meet labor's growing power and in alarm at occasional signs of radical infiltration, management began to patronize more heavily the secret agents of Pinkerton and Burns and to engage company detectives, "stool pigeons" and incipient strike breakers under such euphemisms as Ford's "service division." Facing unionization in the automobile industry, General Motors from January, 1934, through July, 1936, spent close to a million dollars for private detectives.

This threat to management in motors arose from a new and militant force in American labor, the Committee for Industrial Organization. The more aggressive elements in the American Federation, notably the leaders of the United Mine Workers, chafed under stodgy methods and relatively slow expansion. The head of this bloc, burly, rhetorical John L. Lewis, argued that the traditional "horizontal" or craft structure of the A. F. of L. hampered its growth and bred disdain by the "aristocrats of labor" for low-wage mass-production workers. He wished to supplant it with industrial unionism, a type represented by his own organization, the International Ladies Garment Workers, the Amalgamated

Clothing Workers and the International Union of Oil Field, Gas Well and Refinery Workers.

Lewis and other leaders of "vertical" unions in November, 1935, formed the CIO inside the A. F. of L. to extend this principle of organization to other fields, a start having been made with the chartering of the United Automobile Workers in August, 1935, and the United Rubber Workers a month later. In January, 1936, the executive council of the parent body ordered the rebels to disband, and in August, when the dissident unions were "suspended," the total secession of Lewis's cohorts shortly followed. In 1938, with their four million members overtopping the Federation by nearly half a million, these unions rechristened themselves the Congress of Industrial Organizations. The American labor movement was thus rent from top to bottom. Industrial unionism aligned itself with bold fighting tactics and a legislative program to the left of the New Deal, leaving to craft unionism the conciliatory traditions which William Green as president had inherited from Samuel Gompers. Yet, even after the great schism, influence surviving within the A. F. of L. still urged it with partial success to "go industrial" and also to take livelier interest in the political scene.*

Spearheaded by the CIO, organized labor in the latter thirties developed into a force for political action never before seen in the United States, lining campaign chests, ringing doorbells, campaigning by stump and poster and radio, getting out the vote on an impressive scale. While the A. F. of L., in its tradition of standing by labor's friends and opposing its foes, gave only indirect support to the New Deal and

---

* Such a development within the A. F. of L. during the latter years of this era as the jurisdiction accorded the Machinists' Union over workers of all kinds in the aviation industry, virtually erased the vaunted division line between Federation and CIO. Far from weakening the A. F. of L., this fission seemed beneficial, shocking it into more vigorous leadership, yet leaving it with a conservatism in some employers' eyes which led them to bargain here rather than at the door of the CIO—so that by early 1941 the A. F. of L. boasted an all-time record of 4,500,000 dues-paying members to its rival's static 4,000,000.

made no effort to raise funds through its central organization, the CIO disavowed such timidity. Out of labor's donation of seven hundred and seventy thousand dollars to the Democratic cause in 1936 nearly half a million came from the CIO in gratitude and hope. Labor's Non-Partisan League, created by Lewis, Sidney Hillman and Major George Berry, rallied support for the president, its New York branch, called the American Labor party, polling nearly a third of a million votes. In the next presidential campaign, even though Lewis in personal pique deserted Roosevelt to return to his lifelong Republicanism, the rank and file remained loyal, the CIO members in particular giving the president so thumping a vote of confidence that Lewis had no choice but to fulfill his preëlection pledge and resign as its head, while retaining his leadership of the miners.

Whatever the vicissitudes of politics, it was a noteworthy trend of the era that labor had at last become an active participant in elections, eager to use the fulcrum of government for attainment of its ends. The New Deal in turn, aware of its heavy commitment to a prolabor policy and grateful for working-class support, manifested great reluctance to lay a restraining hand upon the unions, however irresponsible they might become. Earlier administrations had often behaved in just this way toward Big Business.

Closely linked with the emergence of the CIO was the technique of the sit-down strike, by which the worker downed tools and "sat on his job" inside the factory. For the workers this policy of passive resistance possessed many advantages. Not only did physical possession of the plant bar the entry of "scabs," but it was more comfortable for the men than picketing. It also heightened their sense of solidarity as they got to know each other under siege and ran the managerial blockade to bring food and hot coffee to the garrison. Not infrequently, however, they failed to observe the rules of their own game by infiltrating the plant with substitutes.

Successfully tried in 1933 by employees of the Hormel Packing Company in Minnesota and in 1935 by Goodyear workers in Akron, the sit-down first attracted national notice late in 1936 as the CIO's chief implement of assault upon the automotive industry. In 1934 forty-five per cent of the auto workers had been receiving less than a thousand dollars a year. In the big sit-downs of 1936-1937, however, the immediate issue at stake was not pay but union organization and recognition of the United Automobile Workers as sole bargaining agent. Beginning in November, 1936, at Flint, Michigan, with a strike against General Motors, the vortex of disturbance spread until it engulfed fourteen states and a hundred and thirty-five thousand men. Michigan's Governor Frank Murphy, declining to call out the militia, offered instead his services as negotiator, which in February, 1937, ended the affair with substantial success for the union. Other big motor companies succumbed to the same tactics.

The mere threat of a sit-down won a still greater victory against the United States Steel Corporation when in March the thunderstruck public learned that this giant and its compeers of "Big Steel" had without a blow hauled down their flag to unionization and a ten-per-cent boost. This triumph marked the zenith of Lewis's prestige. Meanwhile the technique of the sit-down spread to such diverse groups as bakers, shipbuilders, the chocolate makers of Hershey, Pennsylvania, wet nurses in Chicago and gravediggers in Kansas City—a contagion reminiscent of the dancing mania of the Middle Ages. Between September 1, 1936, and June 1, 1937, sit-downs involved a total of 484,711 workers.

This unprecedented spectacle of the wage-earner wielding the big stick alarmed public opinion, which by instinct favored a balance of power between capital and labor. In February, 1937, a Gallup poll reported fifty-six per cent of the people as siding with General Motors against the CIO. Another poll a month later found sixty-seven per cent hoping that sit-downs would be ruled illegal, as A. F. of L.'s Presi-

Americans in Flight.

"Arkies" at "home."

dent Green asserted they were despite sporadic instances within his own ranks. By midsummer of 1937 fifty-seven per cent agreed that "the militia should be called out whenever strike trouble threatens" and half admitted that their attitude toward labor unions had changed in the past six months. The Senate in 1937 and the Supreme Court in 1939 sharply rebuked the sit-down as infringing upon property rights, a violation of the law of trespass.

The tide of CIO success turned in the spring of 1937 when it challenged "Little Steel." On Memorial Day in South Chicago, pickets at Republic Steel clashed with police, bringing death to ten strikers. Under Tom M. Girdler, a leader as tough and tenacious as Lewis himself, "Little Steel" fought the unions to a bitter finish in July and bested them—even though the NLRB later condemned the methods as illegal and terroristic and ordered the companies to reinstate discharged strikers and enter upon collective bargaining.

Over this deadlock between "Little Steel" and the CIO, the president exclaimed, "A plague on both your houses," but in retrospect he considered the year 1937—with its record toll for the decade of 4720 strikes, of which 2728 had been waged over the right of organization—a season of "growing pains" for labor, essentially a healthy symptom. The more aggressive unionists, however, had grudgingly to recognize that the sit-down, for all its triumphs, quickly outlived its usefulness and strained the patience of both the public and the government.

Although the Wagner act specified that the term employer "shall not include the United States, or any State or political subdivision thereof," thus lending no aid to collective bargaining or strikes against the government, efforts, largely from the left wing, were nevertheless made to organize relief workers. A union of FERA employees flourished briefly, to be succeeded by the Project Workers' Union, which exerted fairly strong pressure against WPA wage cuts and layoffs despite the president's denial of their right to strike. Apparently the most vigorous organization enrolling relief clients and the unemployed was the Workers' Alliance, formed early in 1935 under Marxist auspices and boasting at its peak nearly a quarter of a million members. "Boring from within" in approved Communist fashion, it sought to honeycomb disadvantaged groups with its spirit of discontent, promoting hunger marches, protesting WPA discharges, picketing state legislatures in Wisconsin and Pennsylvania, demonstrating on Capitol Hill in 1937 and claiming credit for preventing deeper relief cuts. The total impact of these organizations, however, was small.

The decade brought certain changes in labor attitudes in the United States. An impetus, begun by the Depression and continued by the New Deal, made the workingman, particularly in the big industrial centers, class conscious as never before—to the gratification of leftists and a gloomy apprehension among conservatives that American traditions, individual ambition and fluid opportunity were being "Europeanized." The laborer as "proletarian" became also an object of absorbing interest to numerous writers and artists, as will be seen later. Even though their efforts were addressed chiefly to the highbrow, a residue did help to bolster the worker's importance and self-esteem. A new sense of solidarity appeared. Labor leaders sought increasingly to make the union the focus of community and recreational life, with clean, attractive quarters that contained rest rooms, game rooms, dance halls, restaurant, library and movies. In the larger cities social activity included dances, card parties, bingo, banquets, beer fests and, in more isolated regions, square dances, baseball games, picnics and hay rides. This development recalled the salad days of the Grange two generations earlier among the farmers.

But labor's new ascendancy also had its dark side. Symptoms of the same greed, arrogance and irresponsibility which "the interests" had shown when in the saddle now appeared among certain of its leaders and unions. Some seemed to want all the fruits of labor-saving methods and technology to be passed on to them in the form of higher wages and shorter hours rather than to share them with other segments of the population in the form of lower prices and greater consumption. Others sought to restrict the supply of labor in particular crafts and industries, acting on the theory that restraint of trade was a game at which two could play, while the consumer sat by unhappily. In 1939 and 1940 the department of justice strove to break the obstructiveness of several artisans' unions. Labor had waited long for its innings, and such behavior was natural, if ill-advised.

Rivals in the labor movement strove to top each other's gains in higher wages and shorter hours, with little heed for the common weal or the ultimate best interests of the unions themselves. Following the widespread disapproval of sit-downs, these aggressive elements came popularly to be epitomized by John L. Lewis, who with his fierce eyebrows, black cigar, limousine and cool assurance that government should knuckle to his will, might have doubled for a "robber baron" of the nineteenth century. In 1921 he had obeyed an unfair injunction with the words, "We cannot fight the government"; twenty years later he persisted in paralyzing the nation by a coal strike in a grave season of national defense.

More reprehensible than the labor boss, however, was the labor racketeer. A graduate frequently of the rum-running and dope-peddling underworld, he was schooled in extortion, violence and murder. In the early thirties "union czars" with a stranglehold upon workers in the building trades, motion-picture operators, bakers, furriers, poulterers and produce-market vendors—and often feuding among themselves for mastery—aggravated the industrial turmoil of cities like New York, Chicago and Detroit. In 1932 the president of the Chicago Crime Commission, Frank J. Loesch, reported that "fully two thirds of the unions in Chicago are controlled by or pay tribute directly to Al Capone's terroristic organizations." At this date Capone already lay under an eleven-year penitentiary sentence for income-tax evasion, and other gangsters soon began to tumble into the federal net.

But with the bigger membership and importance of organized labor under the New Deal, a host of new racketeers sprang up until in the latter thirties, as remarked by Mary Heaton Vorse, stanch friend of the labor cause, the A. F. of L. in Chicago was constantly working hand in glove with hoodlums and the most rotten elements in local politics. In the New York area young Thomas E. Dewey, as special prosecutor in 1935 and two years later as district attorney, built a national reputation by helping to break up some of the country's worst rings of labor racketeers. Nevertheless at the end of the era certain important unions continued to be veined with graft and extortion, including those in the movie industry.

The recession late in 1937 was widely blamed by the conservative press upon industrial turmoil and work stoppages. At all hazards the new tide of unemployment which it brought weakened, as always, the bargaining power of labor, so that 1938 saw only 2770 strikes, involving a third the number of the previous year, or less than 690,000 workers. In this latter year, however, despite a setback in the new puissance of the unions, unorganized workers won a legislative victory of the first importance. Paradoxically enough, the president and his aides in Congress carried the fair-labor-standards act through in face of apathy or downright skepticism from both CIO and A. F. of L. leaders, the latter tending to quote Gompers that the minimum wage often becomes the maximum. At heart perhaps they had little interest in the welfare of the workers outside the pale of their own memberships, or else begrudged gains won in any other fashion than by collective bargaining.

As embodied in the original Black-Connery bill, the proposal had been pressed upon Congress by the president in May, 1937, and urged again by him six months later with the recession in full swing. Opposed by some Southern congressmen as undermining their peculiar institution of regional differentials, and regarded by others as too prolix and complicated in phraseology, the measure was worsted in December —"the first time," as Secretary of Labor Perkins reflected, "that a major administration bill had been defeated on the floor of the House." In June, 1938, however, after the chastening of a winter's recession and further political strategy on behalf of a modified and simplified bill, Congress passed it. "Except perhaps for the Social Security Act," the president told the nation, "it is the most far-sighted program for the benefit of workers ever adopted in this or in any other country."

Its forebear was the Walsh-Healey public-contracts act, passed late in 1935, which had established the forty-hour week for all government contractors supplying more than ten thousand dollars' worth of goods and required them to pay minimum wages fixed by the secretary of labor upon the basis of "prevailing wages" for such work in the particular neighborhood. The doctrine of prevailing wages had also entered into the setting of WPA relief workers' pay. The fair-labor-standards act of 1938 extended to all work "affecting interstate commerce," exempting only agriculture, fishing and certain types of selling and service. It instituted a normal maximum work week of forty-four hours (to be reduced gradually to forty), with time-and-a-half pay for overtime except in certain seasonal occupations. The minimum wage was fixed for the first year at twenty-five cents an hour, with automatic raises looking toward an eventual floor of forty cents. Such gradualism was designed to ease the employers' period of readjustment. The act also abolished child labor in the making of goods for interstate commerce.

This federal regulation of wages and hours—more potent than state controls, which often resulted merely in transplanting industry into less progressive regions—had a far-reaching effect upon the American wage-earner. The chief beneficiaries were the nonunion, unprotected workers:

women, minors and the rank and file of the unskilled. The immediate effect was to raise the hourly pay of an estimated 300,000 employees to twenty-five cents and to shorten the work week for 1,300,000; the next year's wage increase to thirty cents benefited some 690,000, and the reduction to a forty-two-hour week about 2,382,000; while the innovation of the forty-hour week in 1940 affected roughly 2,000,000. Unanimous validation by the Supreme Court on February 3, 1941, signified that the act had become part of the durable fabric of industrial relations.

After 1939 defense and war needs tended to increase employment, absorbing at length that reserve pool of man power which so long had been left stagnant by the receding tides of private labor demand. In the brimming flood of prosperity every employable American, whether in factories or the armed forces, was in demand.* Thus came the ultimate pump-priming—which the dictators of Europe had discovered early as a palliative for depression and social unrest, but which Roosevelt had eschewed as perilous and unproductive until necessity forced his hand. By 1941 the real weekly earnings of factory workers stood at an all-time high.

Even in the deepening shadows of world crisis, labor disputes were not wholly at an end, but the time for strikes was swiftly running out. A measure of this new urgency was use of the army by presidential order to break the CIO-North American Aviation strike at Inglewood, California, in June, 1941. After the entry of Soviet Russia into the European war later that month, the more radical elements in American labor ceased to boycott the so-called "imperialist struggle," and a period of almost halcyon industrial peace and coöperation followed.

To both labor and management these years brought a quickened awareness of federal power, whether as indulgent

* In December, 1942, a year after the attack upon Pearl Harbor, the president ordered the administrator of federal works to close down all relief projects by February 1, 1943.

father or stern parent. And simultaneously the average citizen, whatever his economic and political interests or allegiances, felt the same regulatory hand upon his shoulder, whether he liked it or not. An inescapable sign of the new functions of government and the vastly expanded scope of the executive arm was the reorganization act of 1939, bringing under a single Federal Works Agency diverse welfare activities like the PWA, the WPA and the United States Housing Authority, and seeking in other ways to set in order the manifold improvisations of the New Deal.

In his annual message to Congress early in that year the president boldly said,

> We see things now that we could not see along the way. The tools of government which we had in 1933 are outmoded. We have had to forge new tools for a new role of government operating in a democracy—a role of new responsibility for new needs and increased responsibility for old needs, long neglected.

A few days later, at the Jackson Day dinner—in the spirit of his exemplar "who fought to the last for a united democratic nation"—the president surveyed the work of his hands and his administration which had wrought an even more arresting reorganization in American life, observing that the people

> have greatly changed their attitude toward government in this—our—generation. We of this modern day take our politics less seriously. And we take our government more seriously. . . . Today there is emerging a real and forceful belief on the part of the great mass of the people that honest, intelligent and courageous government can solve many problems which the average individual cannot face alone in a world where there are no longer one hundred and twenty acres of good free land for everybody.

And, with vision sweeping the ranges of social advancement
—as President Roosevelt and his friends conceived it to be—
he stoutly vowed that "by the Eternal, we shall never have
to strike our colors."

CHAPTER VII

TOWN AND COUNTRY IN A CHANGING WORLD

JUST as they had gazed upon separate facets of the Depression, so the urban dweller and the farmer looked upon the New Deal from different points of vantage. The city, first to feel the clutch of economic disaster, remained longer and more doggedly at grips with unemployment and the ogre of starvation than did either the small town or the rural community. In 1935, for example, the ten biggest cities alone accounted for one out of every five of the nation's employables on relief. The organization of municipal relief tended to be more efficient than in small towns, and the initial shame of accepting a hand-out considerably less in the vast metropolitan anonymity.

Furthermore, urban dwellers had fewer scruples about self-reliance and rugged individualism. In the twentieth century the city had become the seed plot of innovation and reform. Besides the quickened ferment of ideas, the strength of organized labor and the visible stratification into economic classes, another reason lay in the uprooted status of the typical urbanite. If he came from a small town, village or farm, that fact itself generally stamped him as a progressive, nonconformist or malcontent, and still more frequently its effect was to strip from his roots adhesions of the cake of custom. On the other hand, if he were foreign-born or the child of immigrants—as were nearly two of three of the inhabitants of cities with a million population and over—he was apt to feel no invincible prejudice against ideas which ruralites suspected as counter to the "American way." It was not surprising, therefore, that the New Deal's work-relief, social-security and housing programs found no warmer friends than in the great metropolitan centers, nor that Roosevelt so spectacularly swept the urban vote in successive reëlections—even in the forties when, as we shall see, many farmers began to fall out with the New Deal.

Relieving the burdens of impoverished householders and clearing slums for low-cost model dwellings were two activities which brought the federal power intimately into the lives of city folk. Government, chiefly municipal, had previously entered the sphere of housing with restrictive legislation, such as building codes and zoning ordinances, but in this decade, under federal leadership, it assumed a positive rôle, first offering home loans cheaply and then stimulating new construction in the low-rental field.

To achieve more direct succor of distressed homeowners than Hoover's Home Loan Banks had undertaken, the New Deal in June, 1933, set up the Home Owners Loan Corporation.* All loans were refinanced at five-per-cent interest, with fifteen years in which to repay; needed repairs were made under supervision, and those costs added to the loan. During its period of lending, which ended in June, 1936, the HOLC granted over a million loans, amounting to three billion dollars, and assumed about a sixth of the urban home-mortgage indebtedness in the United States. The number of foreclosures —which had quadrupled between 1926 and 1933—had by 1937 fallen to half the number in 1933, with hundreds of thousands of families saved from eviction.

This program, however, did not meet a large and more importunate area of need. The "one-third of a nation ill-housed, ill-clad, ill-nourished," to whom the president alluded in his second inaugural address, rarely had the property or prospects envisaged by the HOLC, nor were they catered to by the building and loan associations aided by

---

* The Federal Home Loan Bank Board henceforth supervised the lending activities of the HOLC as well as continued its program of assistance to building and loan associations begun under the previous administration.

Home Loan Banks.* This situation prompted further measures. Housing activities, like much of the New Deal, kept in view the twin objects of recovery—the hoped-for stimulus to private construction—and of reform, with increasing emphasis upon the latter. In June, 1933, the PWA set up an Emergency Housing Division to finance through private contracts the clearance of slum areas and erection of decent homes with light, air and space. The nation's first public slum-conversion project began in Atlanta, where eleven blocks, rated the city's worst district, became the site of Techwood Homes. Cleveland's notorious Whisky Island tenement-house area was expunged in favor of a PWA enterprise called Lakeview Terrace. In Chicago the Jane Addams Houses enhanced the neighborhood long served by the founder of Hull House. Largest of all was Brooklyn's project, Williamsburg Houses, supplanting twelve slum blocks with cheerful modern apartments accommodating nearly six thousand persons. On the other hand, two promising ventures in New Orleans were dropped by the PWA after the Huey Long-controlled legislature in 1935 smothered them under a blanket of local bossism.

Rentals averaged twenty-six dollars per month, and if the income of a resident family rose to five or six times this charge, it was required to leave. These rentals met the need of manual and white-collar workers rather than of the very poor; but even such rates were really a subsidy in disguise, for the prospect for self-liquidation was remote on construction costs running to seventeen hundred dollars per room—a result of the PWA's "mania for durability." Before its termination in November, 1937, this program sponsored about fifty developments, comprising nearly twenty-two thousand dwelling units.

* Roosevelt's famous allusion will be found in *Public Papers and Addresses* (S. I. Rosenman, ed., N. Y., 1938-1941), VI, 5. Prior to the New Deal it was stated that "at least half of America's 30,000,000 families are not even decently housed." *Housing America*, by the Editors of *Fortune* (N. Y., 1932), 115.

Meanwhile in June, 1934, the national housing act created the Federal Housing Authority, largely to help owners finance the repair, renovation and enlargement of already existing homes and to spur private building by federal mortgage insurance. The guarantee of loans at moderate interest rates, insistence upon certain standards of construction and the benefit of expert engineering and architectural advice were among the FHA's most salutary features. By the end of 1940 it had underwritten loans of a billion and a quarter dollars to modernize three million dwelling units, and nearly three billion dollars for the erection of six hundred thousand small homes and over three hundred rental projects.

In 1937 a renewed attack was made upon the problem of low-cost housing with the passage in August of the Wagner-Steagall act, which set up the United States Housing Authority. An enormous amount of unfinished business confronted this program. Under jurisdiction of the department of the interior the USHA was empowered to lend or, less commonly, to give $500,000,000 (later increased to $800,000,-000) to local housing agencies for slum clearance, repairs and new construction under federal planning and supervision. Localities were expected to assume certain responsibilities for operating costs, ordinarily in the form of exempting the property from their tax rolls. This agency absorbed earlier housing projects and directed its major effort toward providing decent shelter costing not more than a thousand dollars per room (increased to $1250 in cities with over half a million population). Rentals were pegged to annual incomes not exceeding $1150, and sometimes as low as $600 in the North and $300 in the South.

In this manner war was declared against the tenements ringing Chicago's Loop, New York's "Hell's Kitchen," the "corrals" for the Mexican poor of San Antonio, the Tin-Can Alleys and Poverty Courts all over the nation. Maximum window space, sun decks, terraces or strips of greenery and playgrounds were the new order of the day. One of the most conspicuous beneficiaries was the urban Negro, whether a denizen of the "arks" of Memphis and New Orleans or of Harlem's slums where more than two hundred and thirty people lived per acre and one stretch was known as "the lung block" because of the ravages of tuberculosis. Almost a third of the low-cost dwelling units federally financed in this era —some 47,500 in North and South—were for Negro use. Even though the number fell far short of the need, it was a brave beginning, leading Gunnar Myrdal, Swedish expert on American race problems, to declare that the USHA gave the Negroes "a better deal than has any other major federal public welfare agency."

"In 1939, for the first time in a hundred years, the slums of America ceased growing and began to shrink," exultantly wrote USHA administrator Nathan Straus, noting that the net cost to the federal government averaged about a hundred and twenty dollars yearly for each family housed. By January, 1941, nearly two hundred thousand family units had been provided, while penetration into lower economic strata proceeded year by year. Yet outside the orbit of USHA activities a measure of truth remained in earlier criticism that federal housing tended to benefit the lower middle class more than the truly underprivileged. In terms of the FHA's continuing loan activities, for example, less than thirty per cent of the new borrowers on one-family homes in 1940 had incomes below two thousand dollars, and only five per cent less than fifteen hundred. Private initiative unsupported by federal aid made only occasional forays into the medium low-cost field. In 1938 the Metropolitan Life Insurance Company embarked upon an attractive fifty-million-dollar project for New Yorkers with middling to small incomes, and later expanded this investment idea to other communities. Certain other corporations also launched model-housing projects for employees.

In 1939, for the first time since the start of the Depression, residential construction passed the billion-dollar mark, but deficiencies remained so acute that in the next year the nation was said to be still four million units short. In 1941, because of defense needs, purely private residential construction was virtually prohibited, while all the country's building resources were poured into the fabrication of emergency dwellings near aircraft, shipbuilding and munitions plants, and still more urgently into industrial construction until the latter attained a level nearly double the high-water mark of 1920. Upon the eve of American entry into the Second World War it was clear that defense scarcities, soldier marriages, population shifts leading to concentration in factory areas and, above all, deteriorations and arrears inherited from several decades, all conjoined to render America underhoused and badly housed.

The readiest answer was prefabricated houses. At Chicago's World's Fair in 1933 they had been hailed with enthusiasm, yet by 1936-1937 only about fifty companies were making them, their total annual output less than a thousand units. Among the chief brakes were restrictive building codes, opposition from trades threatened with displacement, real-estate and mortgage interests seeking to shield existing structures from obsolescence, failure of the budding industry to achieve satisfactory mass production at low cost and, perhaps as decisive as any, stereotypes of sentiment regarding what a home should look like. To many, however, prefabrication appeared the inevitable solution of the problem of sanitary and attractive living among poorer families.

Another important development involved the city-planning movement. A lively interest in city planning, flowering in the second and third decades of the century, withered on the vine under the blight of depression. By 1933 at least forty-five city, county and regional boards had been scrapped outright, and about a hundred and thirty were reported "inactive" or officially dismissed as "frills." But with the New Deal's public-works and housing programs and hearty encouragement from the National Planning Board and its successors, the movement sprang to life again. By 1940 the number of planning boards stood at eleven hundred, virtually double the peak figure of the twenties. Practically all the legislatures had provided for city-planning commissions, and well over half had approved county-planning agencies as well. Parks, playgrounds, zoning, pollution of air by "smog," transportation and utility networks were among their basic concerns.

Greatest of municipal headaches was the traffic problem, unrelieved even in the abyss of the Depression since, as has been remarked, Americans tend to cling almost wistfully to their automobiles through all vicissitudes. In the middle of the decade it was estimated that the handling of urban traffic cost the taxpayers more than two billion dollars annually. Multiplication of traffic lights, control towers, stop streets and boulevards and the staggering of office hours to reduce commuter congestion served as palliatives. Parking meters had their vogue, particularly in middle-sized towns, but could do no more than penalize overparking. Underground and roof-top parking lots, a costly solution, grew apace in the bigger cities. But in the face of opposition from merchants fearful of losing what once had been called the carriage trade, municipal authorities were loath to decree the spread of nonparking areas downtown.

Yet in certain ways the social force of the internal-combustion engine was quite contrary to that wrought by the age of steam, whose effect upon population had been powerfully centripetal. The era of the motor car, allied with that of electricity, wrought a diffusive influence, separating the spot where one worked from the place where he slept and played. The mounting volume of traffic, pouring into the canyons of the metropolis each morning and debouching upon the hills and dales of suburbia at dusk, bore witness to this change and also posed its own problems in speed and regulation. This commuter's web raying away from the city, when joined to the rising tide of cross-country haulage by truck and van, forecast an ultimate dilemma in planning—between the Highwayless Town, its residential districts barred to major travel, and the Townless Highway, with under and overpasses for arterial crossings. The latter thirties, with their works programs, saw a vast proliferation of freeways or parkways for motor traffic at high speeds. With scenic planting and occasional areas for picnicking or sight-seeing they enhanced the suburban landscape while making traffic at once faster and safer by systems of access and departure ramps and intersections of clover-leaf or other ingenious design.

Statistics likewise showed that decentralization was building supercommunities whose economic and cultural influence transcended the bounds of municipal government and taxation and whose power was "more realistic in many ways than the existing political states" of the Union. Already in the decade prior to 1930 the population within the core cities of ninety-six metropolitan districts had grown only a fifth, while their fringes increased almost two fifths. This trend continued through the thirties, the number of metropolitan districts advancing from a hundred and thirty-three in 1930 to a hundred and forty ten years later, at which time they comprised forty-two million people in the central areas and twenty million on the periphery. Thus, while Americans showed their incorrigible attraction to metropolitan civilization, they revealed an increasing desire to escape from its nuclear tyranny.

In the zone between city and country citizens hoped to have the best of both worlds. During the 1930's, while the nation's population was augmenting a little more than seven per cent, urban areas eight per cent, and that of the farm remaining almost stationary, the ranks of rural nonfarm or small-village folk leaped fourteen per cent. The commuter's train and bus as well as the private automobile, the lure of outdoor life for health and pleasure and the greater leisure decreed by the Depression and technological efficiency were important factors. Wives and children rather than breadwinners were the main beneficiaries; suburbia's social structure was largely a matriarchy.

Chiefly to aid needy city dwellers longing for a foothold in the soil, the Resettlement Administration soon after its creation in 1935 planned as demonstration units three "greenbelt towns." Under direction of Rexford G. Tugwell, undersecretary of agriculture, communities at modest rentals were laid out near Washington, Cincinnati and Milwaukee to accommodate some five to eight hundred families each. Examples of minuscule regional planning, they avoided main highways and utilized sunlight, playgrounds and parks, making these settlements almost ideal habitations for children. Each village—with post office, stores, school, community center, water supply and other facilities built largely by WPA labor—was girdled by farm and woodland, offering the productive resources of a garden home to city workers. For the first time in American history, the suburban middle ground had been discovered as a sphere for federal planning. To the anti-New Dealer these projects smacked of "collectivism," and an adverse court decision in 1936 caused a fourth project, near Bound Brook, New Jersey, to be abandoned, throwing the whole program momentarily into jeopardy.

The Resettlement Administration, which in 1937 was absorbed into the new Farm Security Administration, also trained its sights upon other types of need. An FERA study of rural problem areas found, for example, that from half to three fourths of all relief families in thirty Southern counties were existing in houses unfit for human habitation. Even many not on relief—sharecroppers, owners of gullied and eroded land from Illinois to Florida, tillers of parched or worn-out acres on the Great Plains—were faring hardly better. Homeless, farmless and jobless families, seeking cheap rent, low taxes and accessibility to relief rolls, migrated in increasing numbers to the agricultural village, whose settlers augmented during depression years at more than twice the rate from 1924 to 1930. In the Middle Atlantic states such places drew largely from the city's idle factories; in the South, from the farm tenant class; in the Middle West, from victims of the drought.

The prime object of resettlement was to give people the chance to move from bad land to good, exchanging discouragement and dependency for self-support. The "infiltration" type of project helped stranded and destitute rural families to purchase, with long-term federal loans, individual farms scattered here and there in the heart of good agricultural regions; the "community" type involved federal acquisition of relatively large tracts for subdivision among individuals, for lease or purchase, often with development of a whole network of new facilities like roads, schools and water supply. The land from which many such farmers were liberated, being poor and exhausted, was bought by the government and turned into forest, wild-life sanctuaries, pasturage, parks or Indian reserves. These projects provided new homes for about ten thousand families and a livelihood for some forty thousand persons.

Since the difficulties of the submerged farm population were multifarious—not only bankrupt soil but poor management, scant credit and crushing debts, ignorance, drought and flood and pests—no single prescription could minister to all. Among the unhappiest victims were the jobless farm laborers, unwanted by the city because of its own unemployed millions. Such workers were denied the benefits of federal and state laws regarding wages and hours and unemployment insurance as well as the New Deal's collective-bargaining guarantees. By the end of this era only four states had any kind of workmen's accident compensation applicable to agricultural laborers, although not infrequently their tasks were hazardous.

Under the buffetings of the Depression, the steady mechanization of the farm and Nature's oscillation from unwanted surpluses to equally desperate scarcities, it was not surprising that three and a half million rural households—

one out of four in the United States—succumbed to public or private relief in the 1930's. This was a new departure in American life, the capitulation of a group whose tight-lipped independence had long been proverbial.

Ironically enough, until this rural poverty was fully appreciated, the early depression years saw a reversal of the traditional flow of population from farm to city, which in the previous decade alone had netted an urban increase of six million persons. Between 1930 and 1933, for the first time in the annals of the United States, this current slackened abruptly and actually began to run the other way. Idle youth left the sidewalks of the metropolis to take refuge with rural relatives and friends; ill-fed families decided to try their hand at raising food; jobless miners of West Virginia, Tennessee and Kentucky returned to their old submarginal acres. During the year 1932 the farm showed a net addition of nearly three hundred thousand individuals, and by 1935 some two million were living on farms who had not been there five years before.

From the middle thirties onward, however, the old trend was resumed, though at such a retarded tempo that for the decade as a whole the city registered considerably less than half its gains of the twenties. This coincided with the slow climb toward recovery. Also it followed the revelation, upon the return of the native, that country folk had grown threadbare, too, and that recollections of bright lights, movies and plumbing could be even more nostalgic than memories of hay and apple blossoms. Furthermore, as relief and public works passed into federal hands, life on the farm revealed other disadvantages. Aid was usually harder to get, the family allotment smaller, and rural exile involved forfeiture of residence requirements. Hence many compromised by camping upon the outskirts of population centers. And, as always, the call of the city continued irresistibly to sound in the ears of ambitious youth.

Between the traditional high fertility of farm families and

the huge proportion of persons in their twenties found in urban areas, it was plain that a steady transfusion of vigorous blood still recruited the veins of the city. During the 1930's a net migration of about one and a half million young people occurred from farms and villages to larger communities. Regarding the selective factors no truly scientific study has been made, but the Wisconsin sociologist Edward A. Ross uttered a widespread opinion when he compared the depleted areas to "fished-out ponds populated chiefly by bullheads and suckers."

The greatest fertility and the most indurated defeat existed among the sharecroppers. They belonged to the bottom rung in a ladder of landlord-tenant relationships. Cash-renting, by which the tenant supplied the working capital, paid a fixed rent and kept all the profits, was the most self-respecting. Fairly common north of the Mason and Dixon Line—comprising in 1930 more than a quarter of all tenants—southward it remained virtually unknown. Crop-share renting, with the landlord meeting certain production expenses and the tenant furnishing labor, work animals, tools and seed, as well as paying rent in the form of a proportion of the marketable crops, was commonest of all in the North and Middle West. A similar sharing of assets and profits, called livestock-share leasing, flourished in the dairy and cattle-raising zones of the Midwestern states.

But in the cotton kingdom sharecropping prevailed, a system under which the tenant customarily contributed nothing but his own and his family's labor in return for half the cotton and a third of the grain he raised. The needy cropper borrowed from the landlord to purchase food and clothing, or else turned to a credit merchant whose charges might run up to fifty per cent. Too often these loans amounted to a perennial dole, chaining the hapless debtor to virtual peonage on soil as ruinously exploited as himself. Finding whites more recalcitrant, many landlords came to prefer blacks, whose sense of arithmetic was more naïve and docility greater.

White croppers were thus forced into the ranks of farm laborers or to drift from one season's stand to another. A third stayed no longer than a year in one place. Methods of cultivation and upkeep thus fostered slovenly waste, with little thought given to conserving soil, mending roof or fences, sending children to school or striking root in the community's social or church life. "What's the use? I don't get nothing but a living nohow," served as a stock reply to all criticism.

Farm tenancy in the South dated from Reconstruction days. Early in the twentieth century the system spread to the corn belt until by 1940 Illinois, Iowa, Kansas, Nebraska and South Dakota had more tenant farmers than Virginia, Kentucky and Florida. But in the Middle West the arrangement bred no pandemic misery. Indeed, some agriculturalists chose to invest their capital in equipment rather than acres, while others were steadily rising from hired labor to tenancy and thence to ownership. The impact of depression, however, drove hordes of small owners throughout the nation into the precarious status of enforced tenancy, with a loss between 1930 and 1935 of three quarters of a million farms by foreclosure and bankruptcy sales. From the Dakotas to Oklahoma desperate farmers rallied in 1932 and early 1933 to save their properties by vigilante methods, cowing agents of banks and insurance companies while making their own nominal bids for a cow or harvester. At Le Mars, Iowa, they dragged an intransigent district judge from his bench and hanged him by a rope until he fainted. Governors of Minnesota, North Dakota and Idaho issued proclamations against forced sales, and several legislatures hastily passed mortgage moratorium laws, anticipating the federal Frazier-Lemke act of June, 1934 (later annulled by the Supreme Court, but replaced by a more modest law of the same purport), which postponed the foreclosure of mortgages for six years if the farmers concerned meanwhile paid a rent fixed by a federal district judge.

Despite all these measures agrarian dispossession continued as a prime factor in the growth of tenancy. Early in 1937 the President's Committee on Farm Tenancy reported an accretion over the past decade at the rate of forty thousand recruits annually, until two out of every five farmers belonged to this class as against one out of four half a century earlier. In the wake of this comprehensive survey Roosevelt sent a message to Congress in February, 1937, invoking a program to improve the lot of tenants, croppers and farm laborers.

Behind this urgency also lay the popular interest quickened by Erskine Caldwell's novel *Tobacco Road* (1932), dramatized into the decade's greatest box-office attraction, and the same author's *Kneel to the Rising Sun* (1935), as well as the photographic documents which this Georgian and his wife, Margaret Bourke-White, were gathering throughout the nation. Still others learned about the sharecropper from the mordant novels of William Faulkner, movies like "Cabin in the Cotton" (1932), or the solid studies in rural sociology by Howard W. Odum, Arthur Raper, Rupert B. Vance and others of the Chapel Hill coterie.

In the background, too, lay the protest and agitation of the Southern Tenant Farmers' Union, organized in Arkansas in July, 1934, by a small band of white and black tenants. The implication of racial equality no less than its savor of radicalism alarmed the average cotton farmer. But in spite of floggings and night-rider opposition reminiscent of the Klan, the Union grew to about thirty-five thousand members in 1937, chiefly in Arkansas and Oklahoma, and at that juncture affiliated with the CIO. It maintained a lively lobby in Washington and helped to bring about the first legislation to redress the plight of the humblest farm workers.

The Bankhead-Jones act of July 22, 1937, set up the Farm Security Administration, with an initial appropriation of ten million dollars (raised to twenty-five in the next year, forty in the following) for making forty-year loans at three-per-cent interest to agricultural laborers, croppers and other needy tenants to buy their own places. From the start the number of applicants far exceeded the available funds. Repayment began with gratifying promptness, averaging over ninety-seven per cent. The FSA likewise granted small loans for debt adjustments with creditors; for tiding over periods of flood, drought and crop failure; and for the setting up of rural coöperatives to provide needed equipment and services, including group medical care for impoverished communities. As incidental but highly important services the FSA county supervisor taught the borrower lessons in thrifty management and encouraged the production of milk and vegetables for better dietary standards, while the home economist instructed the farmer's wife in the use of pressure cookers and scientific methods of canning. Still other FSA activities included the management of one hundred and sixty-one homestead projects for demonstration and experiment, some of which were run along coöperative lines by the residents.

In all, between efforts of the Resettlement Administration and its heir the FSA, about a million and a quarter were given some form of financial aid looking toward self-support between 1935 and 1939. And by the close of the decade, for the first time in history, a modest reversal from tenancy to ownership was apparent, particularly among whites in the South. The FSA naturally could not claim sole credit, but certainly its pull had been stoutly in that direction.*

These efforts of the New Deal on behalf of the landless

* Roosevelt, *Public Papers*, VI, 80-85; Administrator of the Farm Security Administration, *Report* (Wash., 1939), 1-18. The census of 1940 disclosed that the number of white owners and managers in the cotton states rose in ten years from 1,250,000 to 1,384,000, while white tenants declined by 150,000; Negro tenants decreased by 192,000, but the number of Negro owners also shrank from 183,000 to 174,000. U. S. Sixteenth Census (1940), *Agriculture*, III (*General Report*), 151. Problems of cotton production and marketing, discussed later, undoubtedly played a powerful rôle in these changes. Growth in size of the average Southern farm and disappearance of more than a million mules since 1930 pointed alike to greater mechanization and slow liquidation of the sharecrop system. For comment, see Jonathan Daniels, "A Native at Large," *Nation*, CLII, 474 (April 19, 1941).

and disadvantaged by no means tell the complete story of the federal government and agriculture. Among the thirty-two million people living on farms in 1940, the typical family had neither been on relief nor dwelt so close to the borderline of want as did the vast majority of tenants and seasonal laborers. The lot of the independent farmer, nevertheless, was not a happy one. Thanks to his chronic depression in the years after the First World War, his share of the national income dropped from fifteen per cent in 1920 to nine in 1929 and thence to seven in 1933. The causes were many: the teeming surplus of a world momentarily beating its swords into plowshares; the Hawley-Smoot tariff of 1930; the domestic encirclement of Big Business, forcing the farmer in the marts of trade always to receive a low price and pay a high one; lack of capital to mechanize his acres abreast of large producers; droughts and soil depletion. In addition, he had to face the bewildering problem of changing consumer tastes. The cotton farmer sadly pondered not only the cheaper production of new regions like Arizona and California, the Orient and South America, but also the rise of synthetic fabrics.* As for dietary habits, it was clear that cereals, potatoes and meat were slipping in popularity with a generation which eschewed the epic meals of its ancestors.

To be sure, certain agriculturalists fared better. Helped by the vitamin campaign, the per-capita consumption of citrus fruits nearly doubled from 1920 to 1940. Also by the later year, thanks to health education and the lighter diet of an increasingly urban civilization, the milk business attained the vast total of $1,355,000,000, outranking any branch of the meat industry and far exceeding any single farm crop. Similarly the truck gardener profited from the fact that the average family was using twice as many succulent vegetables as fifty years before. But, through vicissitudes of good seasons

---

* The output of rayon jumped from a mere 33 million pounds in 1920 to 458 in 1930, thence to 1948 in 1938. I. W. Duggan, "Cotton Land and People," *Journ. of Farm Econs.*, XXII (1940), 197.

and bad, the majority of farmers invariably grumbled t.
they, least of all producers in the national economy, coi
control the price of their product. This complaint both .
Hoover and Roosevelt administrations sought to meet.

The first important bill was Hoover's agricultural marketing act of June 15, 1929, creating the Federal Farm Board.
By setting up farmers' coöperatives and financing stabilization corporations to buy and control surpluses, the Board
hoped to steady farm prices and cut out the fat profits of
commission men, but it ran into two bad miscalculations.
First was the imminence of world depression. Secondly, its
slogan of reduced output ("grow less, get more") failed to
convert the average horny-handed individualist, who in hope
of profit speeded up production, ignored voluntary controls
and forced prices still lower. The Board's operations, chiefly
in wheat and cotton, cost three hundred and forty million
dollars, enriching speculators but failing appreciably to block
the avalanche.

When the year 1931 brought the South its third biggest
cotton crop on record, the Board desperately proposed that
every third row of growing cotton be "plowed under." But
the fecund land continued to be overwhelmed by surpluses,
and among later anti-New Deal critics of plowing-under few
recalled that the idea had been broached in a Republican administration. By midsummer of 1932 cotton was selling
below five cents, wheat under fifty cents and corn at thirty-
one. At last sensing the magnitude of the problem, the Board
called vainly for legislation to permit federal control of farm
output. In the end, after two harried years, the Board gave
up the effort and offered its surpluses as gifts to the Red
Cross. The lessons of its experience, however, were recol-
lected by the New Deal.

The typical husbandman, believing that hard work was
the best antidote to poverty, seemingly was spurred by the
Depression to work longer hours, with his wife and children
toiling beside him. Yet the economic results were ever more

disheartening. The year 1932, probably the blackest in history for American farmers, saw shapes of revolt arising on every hand. Late in the summer the National Farmers' Holiday Association, formed in 1927 in Iowa, declared a "holiday" until prices should recover. Led by fiery Milo Reno, the Association held Council Bluffs and Sioux City under virtual siege, with roads blocked to incoming wagons and milk cans emptied into ditches. Similar demonstrations took place in Nebraska, Minnesota, the Dakotas and scattered regions of the South and East. Prices showed no rise, however, and the revolt shortly subsided. In early May, 1933, with their plight unrelieved, these embattled farmers voted a nation-wide strike, but called it off at the last moment to give the New Deal's program a chance.

On March 27, 1933, the president consolidated all agricultural credit agencies—including the Federal Farm Board, Farm Loan Board and certain functions of the RFC—into a single Farm Credit Administration. Its chief purpose was to aid farmers bogged in debt by scaling down their mortgages and interest payments, with the result (buttressed by general recovery) that for the year ending March 15, 1936, mortgage foreclosures were only twenty per thousand as compared with thirty-nine in the spring of 1933.

On May 12, 1933, the agricultural adjustment act, popularly called the "Triple A," began a new era in farm economy. To raise prices it provided for "adjusted production" of seven basic commodities—wheat, corn, cotton, hogs, rice, tobacco and dairy products—to which nine others were later added under some political pressure. The producer who entered voluntarily into partnership with the government to reduce surpluses, and hence boost the market value of the remainder, would get "benefit payments" on his restricted allotments. Large growers with greater alacrity than small ones, the knowledgeable more promptly than the illiterate, fell into line behind this program. Agents of the department of agriculture went among millions of farmers in the early summer of 1933, preaching the gospel of crop control until the nonconformist began to feel ill at ease in the surge of converts. At last collective action had reached the farm community, under a widespread recognition that problems of marketing were currently more vital than production methods.

As if to test their new faith to a heroic degree, the AAA asked several million producers to do a thing that violated their deepest instincts: destroy the fruits of their labor. Southern cotton growers were preparing in the summer of 1933 to harvest a bumper crop from forty million acres, which meant that at least sixteen million bales would thus be added to the huge carry-over of recent seasons. Though it was too late to check planting, the AAA sent forth twenty-two thousand agents, chiefly volunteers, to persuade farmers to plow up about a fourth of their acreage in return for cash payments ranging from six to twenty dollars an acre. They returned with agreements to take more than ten million acres out of tillage.

The press reported that the Southern mule, trained to walk between rows, stubbornly refused to trample growing cotton as he pulled the plow of destruction. His master, who seemed at first more tractable, proved so reluctant early next season to sign up for crop limitation—hoping to reap the benefit of rising prices—that Congress passed the Bankhead cotton-control act in 1934. By laying a heavy tax on all fiber brought to the gin in excess of a grower's assigned quota, it introduced a measure of compulsion into the AAA; and its running mate, the Kerr-Smith tobacco-control act, imposed similar taxes upon overproduction in another Southern staple, where plowing-under had also been practised in 1933.

Prospects for a short wheat crop in 1933 exempted that commodity from destruction; but in the corn-hog belt the ruinous prospect of two-dollar hogs, plus the corn-crop reduction planned for the following spring, doomed to death six million pigs and breeding sows. "It was a foregone conclusion that the public would not like the idea of slaughtering baby pigs," wrote Secretary of Agriculture Henry A. Wallace, the Iowa farm-journal editor converted from Republicanism to the New Deal. While regarding the destruction of farm products as "a shocking commentary on our civilization," and vowing that it should never happen again, he felt that desperate conditions warranted desperate remedies. New Dealers argued that it was more defensible than industry's policy of plowing out millions of surplus workers in 1930-1932.

A hundred million pounds of dry salt pork from this slaughter were processed at government expense and given to jobless families by the Federal Surplus Relief Corporation. The same autumn it purchased sixteen million bushels of wheat, to be parceled out as flour, and in 1934 over seven million head of cattle in twenty-four drought-ridden states. Although plowed-under cotton was, of course, unreclaimable, federal stocks of cotton were distributed among the jobless in the form of mattresses and garments. By the end of 1935 this agency had spent nearly three hundred million dollars for such purposes.

Starting in Rochester, New York, in May, 1939, and spreading to over a hundred cities by the close of 1940, a new scheme called the Food Stamp Plan was devised for dispensing surpluses of fruit, vegetables, pork, butter and eggs to needy consumers. For every dollar's worth of orange stamps bought by a relief recipient he got fifty cents' worth of blue stamps free, and the latter, eventually redeemed by the government, were accepted by grocers in exchange for foods currently designated as "surplus commodities." A similar Cotton Stamp Plan, begun in Memphis in May, 1940, remained only regional. These varied uses of farm surpluses tended to be forgotten by foes of the AAA in their criticism of its subsidies and regimentation and its swath of destructiveness in 1933.

Time and the Supreme Court's adverse judgment early in 1936 wrought changes upon the AAA. Some farm folk, among them a sprinkling of backwoods preachers, had felt in their bones that crop control was as immoral as birth control and had seen in the drought of 1934 God's punishment for plowing under cotton; but most scoffed at the Court's "states' rights" argument, asking whether markets, winds and flood erosion respected state lines. The judicial nullification was taken "calmly" in only one out of ninety-six rural communities sampled by two sociologists. In response to agrarian sentiment Congress in February enacted the soil-conservation-and-domestic-allotment act, dropping the processing tax, to which the Court had objected, and shifting the basis of operation from crop reduction to conservation. Farmers were now to be paid for curtailing their acreage planted to soil-depleting crops like cotton, corn, wheat, rice and tobacco, and devoting it instead to legumes, grasses and green-manure crops. They were also expected to follow scientific methods of terracing, plowing and fertilizing.

The new plan was only a legislative makeshift, and its oblique approach to the problem of surpluses proved inadequate when 1937 brought further bumper crops and price recessions. The majority of agriculturalists were looking to the president to outmaneuver the judiciary. In the early autumn of 1937, on the heels of his defeat over "packing the Court," Roosevelt took a swing around the circle, chatting to audiences in the corn belt and Far West about crop-reduction benefits, irrigation, conservation, hydroelectric rates. Among the throngs in Stetsons and sunbonnets, go-to-meeting clothes and levis, an observer heard him called "our President" and "the greatest since Lincoln." A conservative newspaper editor growled: "That 'our President' stuff is something new in politics. Some of the farmers and other people I know must think Mr. Roosevelt belongs exclusively to them—and maybe they're right."

As to the affinity between benefits and ballots, the situation here was not unlike that among the unemployed. Was it possible to distinguish between concern for the farmer and concern for his vote? The agricultural economist Joseph S. Davis voiced the doubts of the skeptical when he wrote,

> Regardless of the purity of motives of the Administration, a subtle form of political corruption is involved; for farmers' votes are effectually influenced when their income seems to depend increasingly on political measures, and less and less on the economic value that society sets on their products and services.

In February, 1938, the president and his advisers pulled forth the long-awaited rabbit from the legislative hat. The new agricultural adjustment act returned to the old problem of regulating production at the same time that it continued conservation payments to the faithful. National acreage allotments for wheat, corn, cotton, tobacco and rice were set at levels sufficient for domestic use, export and reserves. Conformity was voluntary but shrewdly encouraged, since those planting beyond their individual allotments were ineligible to receive "parity payments" or to get commodity loans (on the basis of surpluses stored under government seal) at such favored rates as coöperators enjoyed. In order to withhold surpluses of these five commodities from the market until prices rose to or above "parity"—that is, the purchasing power which any such commodity had had during the supposedly normal period of 1909-1914—marketing quotas could be imposed upon all farmers, under penalty, after such quotas were approved by a two thirds' vote of the producers involved. Equally significant, the surpluses from good years were not to be dumped recklessly on the market, destroyed or given lavishly for relief, but stored against a day of shortage. Thus was realized Secretary Wallace's dream of the "ever-normal granary," a reservoir to stabilize supply and demand, equate good seasons with poor ones. By 1940 some six million farmers were coöperating in the program. Henceforth, in meeting the needs of a war-ravaged world, these reserves grew increasingly important.

The ultimate effects of the AAA upon the economy and habits of the average farmer are not easy to gauge. As an emergency measure the original plan did raise prices and reduce cutthroat competition. The cotton grower's income showed spectacular improvement, a total gain of seven hundred and eighty million dollars (including four hundred and fifty-two million dollars in benefit payments) during the first three years of this program, while the tobacco planter's more than doubled in two seasons. Cash earnings of the American farmer in 1933 increased nearly a quarter over the previous year; the two following years saw successive rises of fifteen and sixteen per cent respectively. Of course, AAA payments always made up a substantial part of this income, drawn from taxes passed on to the consumer as higher prices—prices which to some degree canceled the urban worker's benefit from improving wages. Including government payments, the national farm income in 1939 was reported to be eight and a half billion dollars, nearly double that of 1932, though only a little more than half that in 1919.

This prosperity was not always evenly spread. Producers outside the magic circle, notably poultry raisers and truck gardeners, complained that Uncle Sam had forgotten them. Still more gravely, particularly in the cotton kingdom, AAA largess tended to find its way into the pockets of landlords and independent farmers, while the tenant, too ignorant or timorous to complain, found himself poorer than before. The New Deal assumed almost all the risks of production for the landowner, but it set up no effective safeguards to prevent his passing on to the tenant the brunt of reduced acreage and seasonal fluctuation. In 1937, for instance, the average operator of a plantation grossed a cash income of $8328, of which $833 came from AAA payments, while a tenant family made $385, of which only $27 came from the government. Proportionately at least, the principle—or application—of the AAA seemed to be: to him that hath it shall be given. Indeed, the only form of risk insurance for the tenant was relief. "The government wouldn't let us plant, so we had to go on relief," was a typical hard-luck tale. Another angle was presented by an Oklahoma landlord, whose not uncommon experience he recounted in 1938: "In '34 I had I reckon four renters and I didn't make anything. I bought tractors on the money the government give me and got shet o' my renters."

The plight of families "tractored off the land" was only indirectly related to the AAA and certainly unforeseen by its original advocates. Yet the logic was simple. Upon beginning to recover from a long slump in agriculture, the landowner found himself with cash in hand, and inside his head a new psychology of businesslike methods, notions of crop restriction to augment profits and of economic planning and foresight fostered from Washington. The era of hit-or-miss had ended; innovation was in the air. The cold shock of the Depression followed by the warm interest of the New Deal quickened the farmer's sense of calculation as nothing else could have done.

One of his first thoughts was to overcome the lag of mechanization. Between 1930 and 1940, while the number of automobiles owned by farmers showed practically no gain, trucks increased sixteen per cent and tractors seventy per cent until almost two million of the latter were bearing the heavy work of the nation's agriculture and altering production methods, ways of life and of thinking. More of a potential threat than a reality, the vibrations of the mechanical picker, humming swiftly along a few cotton rows, were already beginning to shake the whole base of Southern rural economy —in a section already apprehensive over the threat of cheaper Brazilian cotton, which had rushed into the world market to fill the vacuum created by restrictions under the Triple A.*

* The Rust brothers, John and Mack, who built the first mechanical picker in 1930, displayed rare social conscience in seeking to temper the winds of technological change, setting up the Rust Foundation in 1938 to rehabilitate displaced croppers and laborers and to subsidize research on Southern poverty. See S. M. and Laura Rosen, *Technology and Society* (N. Y., 1941), 456, and

Meanwhile, regions of farmed-out cotton land like the "black prairie belt" of central and northern Alabama were being turned into grassland to make way for beef and a dairying industry utilizing all the resources of the electrical age for production and processing. This also meant dispossession of many tenant families, in effect like the old English enclosure movement, with added prosperity for those who survived.

In the Middle West mechanical corn pickers, especially the two-row type that came into use between 1928 and 1933, were estimated before the end of the decade to have displaced from a third to a half of the itinerant labor which Iowa's crop formerly employed. In one of Ohio's best corn-growing counties sixty per cent of all maize harvested off the stalk was so picked. In the wheat belt the harvester-combine enjoyed a similar popularity, with the "baby" model of 1935 and the "midget" of 1939 catering to the small farmer. By reason of nearly universal adoption of these machines, seasonal labor in the wheat fields had by 1939 become almost a thing of the past. For every one hundred farm-labor jobs offered, two hundred and thirty-six unemployed agricultural laborers were available.

Many tillers of the soil were beginning to grasp the fact, set forth in 1937 by the National Resources Committee, that income tended to vary with the degree of mechanization. Thus Alabama, with the lowest gross income per agriculturalist in the whole country—$492 per annum—showed only 1.5 horse power available and $142 invested in machinery; while Montana, with 22.5 horse power and $953 worth of machinery, enjoyed a gross income of $1798. This demonstration, naturally enough, proved more potent to the

P. S. Taylor, *Power Farming and Labor Displacement in the Cotton Belt* (U. S. Bur. of Labor Statistics, serial no. R 737, 1937). A report of the National Resources Committee, *Technological Trends and National Policy* (Wash., 1937), 143, remarked that, whether for good or evil, this machine hit at the greatest single source of employment in America for women and children. For the international outlook in cotton, see P. F. Drucker, "Exit King Cotton," *Harper's Mag.*, CXCII (1946), 473-480.

average husbandman than did the wraith of technological unemployment in the background.

The modernizing of the farm was greatly speeded by the Rural Electrification Administration, set up in May, 1935. Refusal of commercial distributors to build lines to the farm had denied central-station light and power to about nine out of ten agriculturalists. The REA offered low-interest loans to states, municipalities and coöperatives, along with WPA labor, for the purpose of extending power cables to rural homes—for lighting, refrigeration, milking and separation, heating incubators, mixing feed, pumping water and manifold uses. By the autumn of 1938 more than three hundred projects so financed had been launched, five sixths of them by coöperatives. Such activities, though resented by most privately owned utilities, wrung from them better and more extensive service at lower rates. Thanks greatly to acceleration by the REA, the 225,000 farm homes which in 1925 were connected with central power plants—less than four per cent of the total—had risen by 1940 to 1,700,000, a quarter of the total.

These developments pointed up the great paradox of farm life in the thirties—that, while efficiency was steadily encouraged, it was accompanied by unemployment and overproduction, the latter reflecting the insufficiency of efforts to stimulate foreign trade and raise domestic standards of consumption. As a secondary paradox, the AAA in communities of scant, poor and backward acres tended to subsidize inefficient farming, but in regions of larger holdings and progressive instincts it fostered market utilization of the best land only. Many small and depressed cotton growers in the Deep South kept straggling on solely by grace of the AAA, while producers in the corn states often found themselves in quite another situation. Thus the AAA acreage reduction decreed in 1937-1938 trimmed the maize-growing area by eight per cent; yet production rose by about seventeen per cent.

Besides the selection of choice land and the superior methods of tillage promoted by this agency, the widespread adoption of hybrid corn—the decade's most important agricultural innovation—helped to compound the increase.* Husbandry in these regions had become less a way of life and more a high-pressure business, alert to profits and often run by absentee management. A typical phenomenon was the "suitcase farmer," generally a small business man from the city who bought one or two farms, mechanically planted and harvested his acreage each year, but had no thought of living on the soil. Another product of scientific agriculture and the machine—single-crop farming on the mammoth scale, as practised from the Texas Panhandle to the Dakotas with fleets of tractors and gang plows—also promoted impersonal efficiency.

Hence another paradox could be deduced. One set of forces, represented by the Resettlement Administration, Farm Security Administration, Rural Electrification Commission and home economists of the department of agriculture, worked toward an ideal of subsistence farming and diversified methods, invoking rural coöperatives and a live-at-home program. Another, embodied in certain operations of the Triple A and the extensive lending activities of the Farm Credit Administration, conspired with technology and the new science of farm management to make agriculture into Big Business.

Whatever the contradictions and crosscurrents of the times, in the wake of recovery community life began to feel its morale reviving. Coöperation, rehabilitation, modernization, were new words of magic. This development was en-

* Hybrid corn had first become available in 1929. In 1933 about 40,000 acres were planted to it; but 1939 saw its increase to 24,000,000 or about a fourth of the national acreage, resulting in an augmented yield (from 15 to 20 per cent) of some hundred million bushels. Its resistance to certain blights and great "standability"—promoting use of the mechanical picker—became universally recognized. Bureau of Agricultural Economics, *Technology on the Farm* (Wash., 1940), 20-21. Also spectacular was the rise of soybean production, under pressure of new industrial uses, from less than thirty million bushels in 1936 to eighty three years later (24).

hanced by the growing cultural uniformity of rural America. Older immigrant groups, including the Scandinavian and German, had largely been assimilated or gathered to their fathers; a steadily dwindling number of foreign-born now tilled the soil. Motor cars, movies, consolidated schools and the radio all helped to erase lines of provincial nonconformity between town and country. The stimuli which bombarded rural life emanated more and more from the city. Whether in fashions, reading matter, entertainment or ways of thinking, urban taste tended to call the tune.*

As in the nation at large, the lodges and secret orders popular a generation before now appeared to be in retreat before organizations less interested in ritual than in community welfare: coöperatives, parent-teacher associations, county planning boards, athletic and other recreational groups, along with those fomenting some political or economic crusade like the Townsend and Social Justice clubs, which struck firm root in certain rural sections. The 4-H clubs, sponsored by the department of agriculture, whose young adherents were ardent missionaries for rural innovation and progress, had grown in twenty years to one and a third million members by 1940. The Future Farmers of America, sired in 1928 by the Office of Education to foster vocational education and the intelligent choice of careers in agriculture among high-school students, had by the end of this era recruited almost a quarter of a million, while for Negro youth the New Farmers of America promised well.

In many rural regions, especially the South, the New Deal took on the aspect of a popular movement, rejuvenating old

* "Hands should be soft enough to flatter the most delicate of the new fabrics. They must be carefully manicured, with none of the hot, brilliant shades of nail polish. The lighter and more delicate tones are in keeping with the spirit of freshness. Keep the tint of your fingertips friendly to the red of your lips, and check both your powder and your rouge to see that they best suit the tone of your skin in the bold light of summer." So read the beauty column of the *Idaho Farmer*, April, 1935, cited in Dept. of Agr., *Yearbook for 1940*, 162. See also A. M. Schlesinger, *Learning How to Behave* (N. Y., 1946), 65-66, 70.

efforts for community betterment and starting fresh ones. Outside "interference" was often resented at first, but, given time, local pride commonly conquered local apathy. Attempts to think through neighborhood, national and world problems, to draw blueprints for a better future, to enhance adult education and culture—such matters came to engross many earnest, frequently baffled minds in rural America. "In a period where bread itself became a primary necessity for millions," wrote two rural sociologists, "the conviction deepened that man lives not by bread alone."

More was done for the farmer under the New Deal than ever attempted before by federal action. In reply to queries as to how long these heavy expenditures should continue, Secretary Wallace in December, 1939, gave answer: "As long as agriculture is at a serious disadvantage in bargaining power with other groups, and as long as low farm income makes it impossible for farm families to conserve our basic land and human resources for the future." Talk of human resources normally envisaged such social values as the healthfulness and physical vigor of rural life, its satisfying creativeness, its simplicity and its high birth rate ("the most important agricultural surplus consists of young persons," wrote the economic historian of the Social Security Board). These virtues were judged vital enough to warrant subsidy of a larger number of farm families than were really required to raise the nation's food—and a time-honored American instinct, smacking of Jeffersonian logic, seemed to indorse this point of view.

Nevertheless, before the end of the era, large areas of American agriculture showed growing signs of disenchantment with the New Deal. Many farmers of substance who heartily approved the AAA began to share the urban business man's misgivings toward other types of federal spending, particularly when the recession of 1937-1938 brought a renewal of large relief expenditures, mounting debts and tacit assumptions that mass unemployment was here to stay. Being

taxed to support the alleged wastrels of the city—where joblessness was regarded as laziness in disguise—vexed many an
independent husbandman, who years since had begun to
identify himself with the employer interests. The so-called
coddling of union labor, its automatic greed and penchant
for striking also stuck in his craw. In the Middle West the
reciprocal trade agreements promoted by Secretary of State
Cordell Hull—unconditional most-favored-nation pacts
which enabled Canada, the South American republics and
other nations to ship beef and certain agricultural products
to the United States in return for advantages reciprocally
granted—proved on the whole unpopular. And finally, having recovered much of his prosperity under the New Deal,
the midland farmer who had voted for Roosevelt in 1932
when frightened, and again in 1936 when gratefully convalescent, now, feeling the ground secure beneath his feet,
turned comfortably back to his traditional conservatism.

Hopefully watching these developments, the Republican
party in 1940 nominated Senator Charles L. McNary, co-
author of the McNary-Haugen bill of nostalgic memory, for
the vice-presidency, with Wendell Willkie as head of the
ticket, and in its platform pledged continuation of soil-con-
servation payments while calling for the elimination of crop
control. Whatever the grievances and the blandishments, the
results of that election, though favorable to the administration, showed that the farmer-labor coalition which had long
sustained the New Deal was beginning to crack. True, the
South continued "solid" politically, being also the region of
impoverished agriculturalists, and the conservation-minded
and progressive West Coast still loved Roosevelt; but elsewhere the flag of rebellion flew high. Roosevelt swept every
city in the nation of four hundred thousand population and
upwards save Cincinnati, while New York City carried the
day against revolt upstate, and Chicago counterbalanced that
downstate. On the other hand, nine of the ten states he lost—
Indiana, Iowa, Kansas, Nebraska, Colorado, North and

South Dakota, along with invincible Maine and Vermont—
had a larger-than-average proportion of rural folk. The
home state of the father of the agricultural New Deal, Henry
Wallace, now candidate for vice-president, sharply turned
against him, though not by so wide a margin as in its rejection of another native son for president in 1932. Was
this the ingratitude of agrarian commonwealths? An ardent
New Dealer might well have thought so.

CHAPTER VIII

OLD SECTIONS AND NEW REGIONS

THE budding of city, county and state planning boards in the heyday of the New Deal and the growing stress upon foresight in agriculture occurred within a wider frame of reference that might be called the rise of the region. A region could be defined in diverse ways, as the "constellation of communities" envisaged by Carl Dawson and Warner Gettys, Stuart Chase's "area where nature acts in a roughly uniform manner" or Isaiah Bowman's *"ensemble de rapports* between man and the natural milieu." Its borders were not conceived like those of states and other political subdivisions, which, for example, favored the river as a boundary line though its effect was really to unite the communities on both sides.

In essence, as planners of the 1930's liked to say, regionalism recognized no boundaries, only centers. A citizen might think of himself as belonging to one region for a given purpose and to an adjacent one for another. Within the region a harmony should be kept among the various interests— agriculture and manufactures, production and distribution, town and country, private enterprise and public welfare— yet this ideal of a partly self-sustaining life ought to foster neither "autarchy" nor isolation. Indeed the interrelation of regions and the fabric of the nation as a whole, argued the planners, would be strengthened by such developments. By the same token, haphazard, sporadic, politically inspired measures, such as the traditional river-and-harbors legislation, would give way to long-term programs weighing all the needs of a locality as well as the needs of other localities, with a federal umpire in the background.

Regional ways of thinking were, of course, no novelty.

Concepts like New England or the Mississippi Valley over-stepped state lines, whereas others like Virginia of the tide-water or the piedmont were contained within them. Cities had taken occasional strides toward local regional adaptation. Greater Boston's program of park, water and sewer planning inaugurated at the close of the nineteenth century was ampli-fied a generation later in a vast blueprint for the metropolitan New York area, addressing problems of harbor and water-way improvement, transit and transportation, parkways and the reclamation of marshland in twenty-two counties in three states. For all its achievements in these and other places, how-ever, metropolitanism was not identical with true regional-ism, since the city, insatiable as an octopus, tended to draw all nutriment to itself and dominate the scene.

The states had also essayed minor approaches to regional-ism. Interstate compacts as provided for by the Constitution had long been invoked regarding such matters as crime con-trol and regulation of interstate utilities, but their use in the sharing and conserving of natural resources came compara-tively late. The Port of New York Authority, set up by New York and New Jersey in 1920 as a virtually autonomous public corporation, had soon proved its worth. Two years later the Colorado River Compact, ratified by six states, sought to apportion the waters of that vital stream, but, hamstrung by jealousies and friction, the results fell short of expectation. Yet the nation's resources seemed to possess a definite regional pattern, whether one surveyed great water-power areas like Niagara Falls and the Columbia River, the iron and lumber of the Great Lakes or the petroleum fields of the Southwest. And in one project much bruited about in the thirties, the St. Lawrence seaway, regionalism promised to overleap international lines.

If the great city with its magnetic pull and the state with its rigid bounds and obstructive pride seemed ill-adapted to regional planning, the federal government enjoyed superiori-ties over both, its avowed concern being for the good of the whole. Having found it cumbersome to treat simultaneously with forty-eight states of assorted sizes, Washington had long since redivided the country into bigger units for various administrative purposes—for example, the Federal Reserve Board's twelve districts, the war department's nine corps areas, the Interstate Commerce Commission's seven zones and similar schemes adopted by more than seventy federal agencies. Some of these divisions ignored state lines altogether, particularly those addressing economic interests like banking, railroads, cotton, wheat, timber and water. The New Deal, assuming bigger interstate responsibilities and authority, created certain bodies—such as the AAA's production-planning section, the FERA's rural-research unit, the WPA's division of sectional economic research and the petroleum administrative board—which powerfully advanced the notion of regional administration.* In July, 1933, the National Planning Board was set up to coördinate planning, urban and rural, physiographic and sociological, while gleaning data about the nation's human and economic geography upon a scale never before attempted.† In fostering regional thinking its influence was great.

While an occasional theorist in the thirties plumped for a "United Regions of America," critics hostile to regionalism foretold the "Balkanization" of the Republic. Both, however, missed the point. The regional approach, in the minds

---

* William B. Munro, expert on government, suggested at the threshold of this era the possibilities of regional government: "As entities of government we accept the nation and the states, both artificial creations, and obtrusively decline to make full use of the natural divisions which the primal architect of the universe thrust in between." *The Invisible Government* (N. Y., 1928), 151. In 1935 he renewed his argument for regional governments—in a day of multiplying bureaucracy and resurgence of the spoils system—as buffers against that federal centralization which tends to "apoplexy at the center and paralysis at the extremities." "The New Deal and a New Constitution," *Atlantic Mo.*, CLVI (1935), 617-624.

† In 1934 it became the National Resources Board, in 1935 the National Resources Committee and in 1939, with functions steadily broadening, the National Resources Planning Board. Under criticism from New Deal foes Congress in 1943 finally ended its life by withholding further appropriations.

of most of its exponents, involved not the erection of super-states, but rather the acceptance of a new concept of administration and the coördination of existing local machinery of government for that purpose. Nor was the new regionalism to be confused with the old sectionalism despite the efforts of a handful of agrarian traditionalists to color it with the faded hues of the Bonny Blue Flag.

In this spirit a symposium by twelve sentimental Southerners called *I'll Take My Stand* (1930) proposed "to support a Southern way of life against what may be called the American or prevailing way" and, after renouncing urban industrialism with all its evils, espoused the theory that "the culture of the soil is the best and most sensitive of vocations." During this decade Allen Tate, John Crowe Ransom and (somewhat less brashly) Donald Davidson wrote persuasively about regionalism so conceived in terms faintly nostalgic of Calhoun and Robert Toombs. A more creative interpretation of regionalism stemmed from the North Carolina school of sociology and Howard W. Odum in particular, inspired in part by the later writings of the historian Frederick Jackson Turner, who saw sectionalism as aggressive and egocentric, regionalism as rational and reciprocating. In a series of books and articles through the decade Odum and his colleagues expounded this view and documented it with the most painstaking analysis.

It was no coincidence that so much of the debate over regionalism was pivoted upon the South. That part of the Union, by reason of economic geography, climate, people, history and traditions, had inherited the most unyielding, least assimilated, of all types of sectionalism and was quickest to resent outside interference or criticism. Some of her sons regarded this fact with complacence or melancholy pride—Davidson, for example, remarking that "the differences go so deep as to seem practically ineradicable, and they beget loyalties that cannot be overridden without damage to the human spirit"—while others like Odum saw in this attitude "a sort of arrested frontier pattern of life," dooming the South to "ingrowing patriotism, cultural inbreeding, civic immaturity, and social inadequacy." As if to add the final irony to this set of circumstances, one of the South's most backward regions, the Valley of the Tennessee River, became the only example of carry-through in regional planning ever attempted in the United States. Here in precipitation, side by side, were the two elements almost in their pure state.

Popular interest in the South—or Souths—was stimulated by a flood of books both fictional and scholarly. Literature ran the whole gamut from honeysuckle to hookworm. The former was the essence of Caroline Miller's novel *Lamb in His Bosom* (1933), Stark Young's *So Red the Rose* (1934) and Margaret Mitchell's *Gone with the Wind* (1936), which was also turned into a highly successful technicolor movie.* The Florida backwoods received idyllic treatment in Marjorie Kinnan Rawlings's *The Yearling* (1938), while the charm of Negro lore inspired such stage productions as Marc Connelly's "The Green Pastures," adapted in 1930 from the book by Roark Bradford, and DuBose Heyward and George Gershwin's "Porgy and Bess" (1935), first musical production of the Theatre Guild.

Of sharper realism was Thomas S. Stribling's trilogy, *The Forge* (1931), *The Store* (1932) and *Unfinished Cathedral* (1934), portraying both the tarnished gentry and the miserably exploited Negro croppers and white tenants in Alabama. Ellen Glasgow's novels *The Sheltered Life* (1932) and *Vein of Iron* (1935) showed the scions of Virginia pioneers and planters seeking to adjust themselves to modern civilization —to parvenus and noisome factories. William Faulkner's *Sanctuary* (1931) presented the South of pure melodrama, but his less popular books—like *As I Lay Dying* (1930), about the trek of a poor-white family, and *Light in August*

---

* Miss Mitchell's book, the century's best seller with nearly 4,000,000 copies, was reported by a Gallup poll in 1938 to be running neck and neck with the Bible in popularity.

(1932), concerning miscegenation—held deeper sociological values. In like spirit Paul Green's novel *This Body the Earth* (1935) depicted the chain gangs of North Carolina's penal system and the cropper families whose hapless and sodden lives Erskine Caldwell also took as his theme. Josephine Johnson's *Now in November* (1934), winner of a Pulitzer prize, recorded a ten-year struggle with the land, culminating in ordeal by drought, fire, mortgage foreclosure and the eviction of sharecroppers.

Books of solid social fact, like Rupert B. Vance's *Human Geography of the South* (1932), Arthur F. Raper's *Preface to Peasantry* (1936), Odum's *Southern Regions of the United States* (1936) and John Dollard's *Caste and Class in a Southern Town* (1937), seemed likely to remain definitive. These sociologists, together with the novelists of realism, educators like Frank P. Graham and Homer P. Rainey and a handful of such newspaper editors as Jonathan Daniels, Virginius Dabney and Mark Ethridge, strove manfully for the self-understanding of the South and its emancipation from the fetters of sectionalism.

Their labors were not without effect. For example, a Citizens' Fact-Finding Movement arose in Georgia in 1937 after an affliction of four years under Governor Eugene Talmadge, hillbilly champion of "white supremacy." Its reports called attention to the fact that, while the state ranked among the highest in church attendance, in education it stood near the bottom, annually spending less per pupil ($30.96) than any save Arkansas, failing to enroll a seventh of its school-age youth and condemning nearly three quarters of its Negro children to one-room schools and wretched equipment. Furthermore, three out of five tenant farmers moved every year, and within a decade some four hundred thousand young Georgians had left the state for opportunities elsewhere.

The major impulse to improvement, however, came from President Roosevelt. As a humanitarian, leader of the Democratic party and frequent sojourner at Warm Springs, Georgia,

he showed a lively concern for the South's welfare. Addressing a conference of Southerners in 1938, he described their
homeland as "the Nation's No. 1 economic problem," adding
(in words that disclosed the regional drift of his own thinking) that this was "the nation's problem, not merely the
South's. For we have an economic unbalance in the nation as
a whole, due to this very condition of the South." A few
weeks later at the University of Georgia he drew from these
words the sting to sectional pride by observing that "in these
past six years, the South has made greater economic and social progress than at any other period in her long history."
Once the forgotten section, it had become under his administration the proving ground for some of the most thorough-
going New Deal innovations—in crop control, rural resettlement, soil conservation, electrification, public health and
other measures, including the one striking epitome of physical and social engineering in the Tennessee Valley. Only the
more cynical Democratic politicians asked privately whether
such federal outlays were not wasted upon the "Solid
South."

The need for swift and effective action was imperative.
While the South shared only nine per cent of the national income, it possessed twenty-one per cent of the population and
the highest birth rate.* Wasteful methods of agriculture and
deforestation had for generations been corroding her natural
assets, which included the most diversified soil in the Republic
and two fifths of its woodland. With the largest number of
farms of any section she averaged the smallest acreage per
farm. At the same time much of her mineral wealth
and great hydroelectric potential remained untouched.
Though her most abysmal poverty was rural, even in industry the common laborer in 1937 got sixteen cents an hour

* The South's Place in the Nation (Public Affairs Pamphlet, no. 6, 1936),
8, 14. The thriving Southwest, customarily excluded from the Southern picture—Texas, Oklahoma, New Mexico, Arizona—with only six per cent of
the nation's population, received six per cent of the collective income.

less than elsewhere, while an annual average wage of $865 contrasted with $1291 for the rest of the United States.

Under the circumstances half the people, rural and urban, were ill-housed; sickness and death rates ran unusually high, with from sixty to eighty-eight per cent of the poorer urban families ill-fed and more persons dying without medical attendance than anywhere else in the country. To meet her problem of educating a third of the nation's children the South commanded only a sixth of the total school revenues. These states reaped proportionately in taxes about half as much as the country as a whole, with the brunt of their levies —such as the sales tax, which in the later thirties every Southern commonwealth save one used to raise sixty per cent of the revenues—falling upon those least able to pay. Absentee ownership of the bulk of Southern industry failed to contribute its fair share of taxes in support of local schools and other institutions.

The smaller outlay for education meant overcrowded and dismal schoolhouses and the nation's highest illiteracy rate (about nine per cent in 1930). Among the bleak schools of the Georgia highlands the teachers' salaries in 1930 averaged $436 as compared with $816 for the state as a whole and $1420 for the nation. Poverty affected other aspects of cultural life as well. Virginia alone approached the national average in books per capita in public libraries, and the whole South trailed the rest of the Union in the circulation of forty-seven national magazines. As a consequence of such conditions the brightest and best youths tended to leave home, enriching other areas with their productivity and leadership. From the turn of the century to 1936 the South showed a net loss by migration of over three million four hundred thousand people, including a large proportion of educators, scientists and technicians. Homekeeping youth was frequently second pick.*

* H. W. Odum, *Southern Regions of the United States* (Chapel Hill, 1936), 51, who adds, "The measure of the region's leadership in national management

At the heart of the South's unyielding sectionalism—her pride and defensiveness as well as her distinctive socioeconomic pattern—lay her biracialism. Nearly a third of the people were of Negro stock; in Mississippi and parts of other states around a half. To label this phenomenon any longer the "Negro problem" seemed both smug and old-fashioned; with the passing years it was seen just as truly to be the white-man problem. As the Institute of Southern Regional Development observed, "One of the most obvious reasons for the social and economic retardation of the South is the unwillingness of the white man to face the fact that his own fate and that of the region as a whole are inseparable from the fate of the Negro."

To add to his chronic poverty, the Negro shouldered more than his rightful burden of unemployment, both in North and South. In 1933 no less than two million were on relief —twice as many as should have been in terms of the national population. A saying recurrent in hard times described the Negro as "the first man fired and the last man hired." In the South the Depression virtually erased the category known as "Negro jobs," such as heavy toil in the building trades, unskilled industrial labor, street cleaning, garbage collecting and, for women, employment as domestic servants. As whites began to compete, blacks were dismissed.

In the early stages of the relief program in the South the race faced discrimination on this front as well. In Mississippi in 1933, where they formed a slight majority and admittedly stood in more grievous need, only nine per cent received relief as against nearly fourteen per cent of whites; but such administration later grew more equitable. The proposal of the NRA to pay equal wages to the two races also choked in

is generally considered less than five per cent as compared with its approximately 21 per cent of population, 17 per cent of area, and 12 per cent of wealth. In the great majority of the dominant national groups the southern representation on the executive or controlling boards is negligible. The same is true in most of the New Deal units of administration in contrast to the large representation in Congress."

the gorge of white supremacy, although its sponsorship by a Democratic administration somewhat sweetened the pill. The acreage reduction of the original AAA left the typical Negro husbandman worse off than before, but the later AAA almost imperceptibly crossed an old sectional taboo in setting up annual elections to permit cotton farmers, including tenants and sharecroppers, to ballot on marketing quotas. No indignant voice arose, and if the fact was void of political meaning, it did accustom both races to the spectacle of going jointly to vote.

The Southern Negro had not yet graduated beyond a "second-class citizenship," but his dissatisfaction with it was growing. By the end of the decade only three Southern states —North Carolina, Louisiana and Florida—had repealed the poll tax, a measure still effectually disfranchising not only the black but the poor white. County boards of education tended to allot to white institutions a disproportionate share of public-school funds, leaving Negro schools with meager support from taxes and hence poorly trained teachers, short terms and primitive equipment. Significantly enough, the margin of inferiority was least where white schools were best and white community standards high. In December, 1938, the United States Supreme Court ruled in the Gaines case that Missouri should provide equal accommodations "within the state" for law students irrespective of race. This was apparently an entering wedge for better professional education of the Southern Negro.

Diffusion of the race outside the South continued to convert a sectional into a national issue, with not infrequent complaints by migrants that the North was "going southern." Though the net migration between 1930 and 1940, estimated at three hundred and seventeen thousand, fell far short of the seven hundred and sixteen thousand in the previous decade's industrial boom, it swelled the colored population of several large Northern cities by as much as a quarter. The pinch of poverty and grosser forms of discrimination sent many from the Southern seaboard to New York's Harlem, from the central South to Chicago and Detroit and from Texas to St. Louis and Chicago. Rarely indeed did they seek farm work, and as they gained a measure of prosperity in the cities, they often collided with Jim Crow in the guise of zoning ordinances and restrictions. Moreover, many A. F. of L. unions barred them, and individual workers resented their incursion.

Whether in the North or South, even after economic recovery began, the black man's chances for employment remained slim. In May, 1935, for example, about three million Negroes in the nation—approximately one in four—were being supported by public funds. To discourage migrants, many Northern states established residence requirements up to five years, but still they came, hoping for odd jobs or charity from friends until relief eligibility was established. In Detroit from 1936 onward a vigilante band of whites called the Black Legion sought to revive the terrorism of the Klan, a threat which in the South—along with the kindred iniquity of lynching—appeared, at least temporarily, to be on the wane.*

In general, the New Deal won the Negro's friendship and strikingly modified his age-old allegiance to the party of Lincoln. The disservice done the race was inadvertent—by reducing crop acreage and the number of sweatshop jobs—or unforeseen, like the indirect effect of social-security legisla-

---

* The annual lynching toll for the decade averaged about ten. Gunnar Myrdal, *An American Dilemma* (N. Y., 1944), I, 561. Some incidents, however, failed to be tabulated because unattended by publicity: the victim "disappeared" at the hands of a clandestine group (II, 1350). Salutary work was done by the Commission on Interracial Coöperation and by the Association of Southern Women for the Prevention of Lynching, the latter denying that mob law offered their sex any protection. The longest sustained friction of the decade was generated by the Scottsboro case, following arrest in 1931 of nine Negro youths charged with the rape of two white women of promiscuous habits. Their trial was a field day both for Southern bigots and Communist agitators, but at least mob action was kept at bay. The case inspired a 1934 Theatre Guild production, "They Shall Not Die."

tion in leading some employers under compulsion of new responsibilities to oust black workers for white. On the credit
side the New Deal did more for the Negro than any other
administration since the Civil War. Relief funds, housing
projects in the wake of slum clearance, rural resettlement,
land-utilization schemes providing parks and picnic grounds
and beaches for colored folk, greater federal attention to their
education and health—these things were scarcely more important to group morale, after the poverty and pessimism of
the early thirties, than the personal friendliness of the President and Mrs. Roosevelt. Hopefulness was again astir.

As spokesmen for the Negro's rights were certain Southern
political figures generally identified with the New Deal, such
as Maury Maverick of Texas, Claude Pepper of Florida,
Hugo L. Black and Lister Hill, both from Alabama. Together with progressive journalists and educators they spoke
out more boldly than their fathers without meeting quite
the reflex of resentment that always followed a stranger's
criticisms, particularly if he came from the North, bore a
Jewish name and was suspected of radicalism. For the first
time in history, moreover, the scattered liberals, over twelve
hundred of them, met as the Southern Conference on Human
Welfare in 1938 at Birmingham and two years later at Chat-
tanooga, with leaders of the Negro race playing an important
part.

Voices of bigotry were still articulate in Southern politics,
like Theodore G. Bilbo and John E. Rankin of Mississippi,
"Cotton Ed" Smith of South Carolina and "Gene" Talmadge of Georgia, and as the decade progressed, they came to
speak more and more for economic reaction as well. But,
outside the calculated hysteria of politics, gross prejudices
were rarely vented in books and articles, however much they
still figured in private talk. As a whole, the South had been
coaxed into taking a few more steps away from antique prejudices by enlightened leadership at home, party ties, widespread admiration for the president and the need of federal

funds. Mob violence and peonage had declined, the quality of the police and law courts slowly improved, and appeals to the sense of fair play seemed to be growing.* "In the South, in particular," wrote the distinguished colored educator Charles S. Johnson at the end of this era, "there has been manifest over the past decade a disposition, stemming from economic and regional necessity, to conceive the Negro population, in the total planning of the region, as something more than a temporary and burdensome adjunct to the white population . . . ."

For white and black alike, the key to the South's economic welfare lay in using her natural resources with keener social intelligence. True, conservation was no novelty even in this prodigal, easy-going land. After the Civil War some South Carolinians had built up a modest but thriving industry in preparing phosphates for soil enrichment, and in 1918 the South's only president since that conflict, Woodrow Wilson, had caused the construction of a dam and two nitrate plants at Muscle Shoals on the Tennessee River in northern Alabama to make explosives and fertilizers for war and peace. Henry Ford and other industrialists long cast covetous eyes upon this development, and for years it remained a bone of political contention. Meanwhile the Tennessee basin, draining portions of seven Southern states with a population of four and a half million, continued like the rest of the South to denude its topsoil, deny it replenishment and squander other resources like timber, minerals and water power.

For this region of income and living standards not only well below the national average, but even under the Southern median, a new destiny began in May, 1933. Thanks to a

---

* "The Southerner's attitude toward the Negro is incredibly more humane than it was in the South I knew as a child," wrote the South Carolina educator John A. Rice, *I Came Out of the Eighteenth Century* (N. Y., 1942), 195. The Swedish sociologist Myrdal, after an exhaustive four-year study sponsored by the Carnegie Corporation, reached a similar conclusion. *American Dilemma*, II, 998-999. Yet antilynching bills in Congress continued to meet with fanatic opposition from the traditional Southern bloc.

twelve-year battle waged by Senator George W. Norris and other conservationists and to Roosevelt's conviction that power resources belong to the people, the Tennessee Valley Authority was created to promote flood control, navigation, electric-power production, proper use of land and forest and "the economic and social well-being of the people." The new agency was to deal with all natural resources as a single big problem and make decisions without constant reference to Washington. Interstate in character, it worked coöperatively with seven state governments and scores of local ones. At last regional planning on a large scale had been given the signal to go ahead.

Though the TVA could invoke the power of eminent domain in matters like flood control, the essence of its program affecting the people's daily life was voluntary. Under a planning council six divisions—representing agriculture, forestry, industry, engineering and geology, land use, social and economic aspects—maintained "demonstration units," which became the chief means of individual persuasion. While still engaged in building locks and dams and power plants, it began the retirement of submarginal lands, soil conservation, afforestation, the introduction of better farm machinery and the fostering of local manufactures, public health and education.

The hill dweller of Tennessee, Alabama and North Carolina inclined to stubbornness, conservatism, suspicion—the traits of ingrained sectionalism. In the lowlands a few oldsters at first avowed that, rather than move, they would just sit in their rocking chairs till the water came up to drown them. New-fangled methods of plowing and household gadgets also left them dour. But as the program progressed— with vast works of concrete and steel rising skyward and transmission wires spanning the valleys, brown water turning deep blue, ragged hillsides changing into rich green— inertia yielded to curiosity and then appreciation, with youth and the better educated taking the lead. Sharecroppers, white and black, found jobs with the TVA which gradually converted them into skilled craftsmen or mechanics; many were glad to exchange ramshackle cabins for the prefabricated workers' dwellings whose example began to raise housing standards in the Valley. Malaria control and the curbing of stream pollution enhanced regional health at the same time that the TVA health and safety department was supervising the medical needs of workers and setting a remarkable record of freedom from industrial accidents.

Library service for these thousands of workers in an area of few books and periodicals, operating through state and local library boards, equipped "bookmobiles" which came to be the nucleus of permanent regional library systems in Tennessee, Alabama and North Carolina, tax-supported and open to nonemployees. A lively adult-education movement likewise spread from workers to the larger community, while under stimulus of a few TVA demonstration parks, state and county authorities awoke to new interest in public recreation and Tennessee created its first conservation department.

In spreading the gospel of the TVA among hill farmers the chief missionaries were the twenty thousand husbandmen who agreed to show what could be done with scientific methods like terracing and contour plowing and, specifically, the use of concentrated mineral phosphate produced in electric furnaces from the fossilized bones of animals that lived around that prehistoric sea once covering middle Tennessee. These farmers quickly demonstrated their superiority, holding down corn acreage to avoid overproduction but so augmenting the yield of hay that they doubled or tripled their number of beef and dairy cattle and their consumption and sale of meat and dairy products. Community life grew not only more prosperous but exciting. Even conservative elders began to praise the TVA "because it keeps the young folks at home," while among its partisans the sense of achievement waxed almost lyrical. Homes were repaired, schools painted or rebuilt. A communal pride burgeoned.

Instead of the capricious, destructive river and its tributaries of the old days, a chain of lakes presently stretched across the Valley, stocked with fish and offering nine thousand miles of shore line for recreation. A private organization called the Tennessee Valley Waterway Conference devised, with aid from TVA technical experts, a series of public-use terminals linking the railroads and truck highways with a navigable channel six hundred and fifty miles long. In January, 1937, when an Ohio River flood drowned some nine hundred victims and left half a million temporarily homeless, the TVA received its most dramatic vindication, demonstrating that even under torrential rains the Tennessee River was a giant safely chained in the service of man. Three years later, as the war crisis deepened, the energies of the TVA were mobilized to the end foreseen by President Wilson: the Muscle Shoals ammonium nitrate plant went into big-scale munitions production and the white clay of the Valley was poured into aluminum.

Meanwhile the once backward region had become the second largest producer of power in the United States, with municipalities and coöperatives in partnership with the TVA supplying electricity to consumers at three cents a kilowatt hour instead of ten. Responsibility for the distribution of this current fell largely to local boards made up of public-minded citizens. While home consumption of electricity for the nation increased sixty-three per cent between 1934 and 1942, that in the Tennessee Valley (beginning at seventeen per cent below the national average) almost doubled. Freezing lockers, electric pumps, hay driers, motors to grind feed and cut wood—these were the sinews of new might, instruments for promoting agricultural efficiency and enhancing standards of living.

Although some branches of private industry, eager to sell more electric ranges and other appliances, rejoiced at these developments, the private purveyors of electric power abominated the new agency. Roosevelt's contention that TVA rates constituted "yardsticks so that the people of this country will know whether they are paying the proper price for electricity of all kinds" provoked hot debate. Cost factors of the TVA could be figured variously—in terms, for example, of allocation between electric power, navigation and flood control, or of estimates for depreciation and amortization and the interest to be charged theoretically to the investment (since the TVA, financed largely by congressional appropriations, paid virtually no interest). Its bookkeeping was further complicated because it paid nothing for benefits provided by other federal services, such as materials and labor furnished by the WPA and Civilian Conservation Corps, workmen's compensation under the United States Employees' Compensation Commission, the franking privilege and low freight rates on land-grant railroads.

While its foes argued therefore that its rates did not cover true costs but flourished a yardstick as pliable as the "rubber dollar," its friends replied that TVA wholesale charges were actually high enough to cover all these disputed items, plus its payments to states and counties in lieu of property taxes of 12.5 per cent of gross revenues, roughly equivalent to taxes borne by private utilities. This issue, a matter of exhaustive congressional inquiry, was extremely complex. If, however, TVA rates failed to furnish an exact yardstick, they did serve to deflate excessive profits in the private-utility field, not only in the Tennessee Valley but through the nation. Thanks to this and other causes, the average residential rate for the whole country declined from 5.52 cents in 1933 to 3.67 in 1942.*

For several years the TVA and local subsidiaries of Commonwealth and Southern, the chief utility corporation in this

* In the seven years prior to the TVA's creation this national rate fell only 2 per cent; in the next seven years, 23 per cent. 76 Cong., 1 sess., *Senate Doc.,* no. 56, pt. 3; David Lilienthal, *TVA: Democracy on the March* (N. Y., 1944), chap. iii. The TVA's percentage payment to local bodies in lieu of taxes (since states may not tax federal property) was fixed by the amended TVA act of June, 1940.

region, worked together in a precarious harness of enforced coöperation. But upon expiration in 1936 of the TVA's contracts to use private transmission lines, open war broke out, with the corporation's president Wendell Willkie leading the squadrons of private enterprise. A limited victory for the TVA, gained from a Supreme Court decision in 1936 holding that construction of the Wilson Dam was constitutional, was enormously reënforced three years later when the tribunal ruled that private companies had no legal right to protection from TVA competition. Seeing that the game was up, Willkie sold the facilities of the Tennessee Electric Power Company to the TVA, and other utilities in Tennessee, Alabama and Mississippi followed suit.

Through its power of appropriation Congress alone held a whip hand over this half-a-billion-dollar property, which would require several more years of construction beyond the end of this decade to complete its twenty-one dams and at least thirty years of operation before it became a "paid-out" investment. With a few notable exceptions, such as Tennessee's pork-barrel devotee Senator Kenneth D. McKellar, the majority of the lawmakers acquiesced in the view of TVA Chairman David Lilienthal that "a river has no politics." Its personnel were chosen and promoted on the merit system under the TVA's exclusive responsibility, the sole instance of this method in the whole system of permanent federal agencies. Not only did the staff appear to be well insulated from political tampering but, in accord with the philosophy of regionalism, they represented a wide geographical selection, and were frequently loaned to junior projects, like the Northwest's Bonneville Dam or South Carolina's Santee-Cooper development.

Though the TVA offered the only completely integrated project in regional planning—a "demonstration unit" not merely for the nation but the world, as its steady stream of visitors bore witness—kindred developments were in the bud. The president and his National Resources Committee tended to stress the river valley as the unit of regional planning. On June 3, 1937, he recommended that Congress create six more projects, conceived at this stage, perhaps out of deference to congressional caution, less as "little TVA's" possessing executive authority than as planning boards. They were designated for the Atlantic Seaboard, the Great Lakes and Ohio Valley, the Missouri and Red rivers, the Southwest drainage systems (from the Arkansas Valley to the Rio Grande), the Colorado River and adjacent Pacific Coast, and the Columbia River basin. This last was alone given a jurisdiction approaching that of the TVA.

With the storm of world war gathering and an undertow of conservatism beginning to flow, the years after 1937 marked a legislative and political retreat from regional planning. The very turn of the tide was symbolized by the president's exuberant speeches in September and early October, 1937—at Bonneville, Oregon, where a great dam and hydroelectric plant had just begun operation; at Grand Coulee, Washington, with its dam, still four years short of completion, "the largest structure . . . that has ever been undertaken by man in one place," designed to add a million and a quarter acres to the nation's arable land; and at Fort Peck, Montana, where a dam "four times bigger than any other earth-filled dam in the whole world" would supply irrigation and power —this last address being followed in Chicago two days later by Roosevelt's famous "quarantine" declaration against aggressor nations.

In other respects as well, the conservation of the nation's natural resources under the second Roosevelt had gone forward even more swiftly than under the first. The Soil Erosion Service (later the Soil Conservation Service), set up in October, 1933, began to dot the map with model projects undertaken in partnership between the farmer and his government. By 1940 five hundred and thirty-four of these ventures were in operation, each averaging twenty-five thousand acres and serviced in large part by CCC camps in the vicinity.

With a similar purpose in view the Taylor grazing act of 1934 authorized withdrawal of eighty million acres of the public domain from the overgrazing abuse which had so aggravated drought and wind damage, thus halting further homesteading on the range. In the same year an executive order allocated fifteen million dollars for planting a "shelter belt" of trees, a hundred miles in width, from Canada to the Texas Panhandle to act as a windbreak and conserver of moisture. Despite the political ridicule which ultimately curbed this program, many agriculturalists were converted to its wisdom.

The urgent reason for these steps was best seen in the instance of the "Dust Bowl," containing over a hundred counties in Kansas, Oklahoma, Colorado, New Mexico and Texas, an area broken by the plow during and after the First World War at a time when submarginal agriculture promised profits and rainfall averaged better than usual. The settlers literally reaped the whirlwind in a series of droughts and storms beginning late in 1933. That winter and the next year wind stripped the farm lands from the Dakotas to Oklahoma, blackening the sky at noon, burying fences and machinery and desolating thousands of families; and the erosion of human resources followed the flight of the topsoil.* Though less spectacular than some other holocausts, these gales spelled grief for a much greater number.† A common sight along the highways of the Southwest came to be that of hungry and bewildered men and women trundling handcarts and baby carriages piled high with shabby household goods, their children trudging behind. Others set forth in ramshackle

---

* For the Resettlement Administration the young producer Pare Lorentz made a powerful documentary film, "The Plow That Broke the Plains" (1936), dramatizing conditions like those which cost the nation three hundred million tons of soil blown away in the "black blizzard" of May 11, 1934. His sequel, "The River" (1938), dealt with the erosion by water, entailing an estimated three billion tons of solid material annually washed out of the country's fields and pastures.

† The principal other natural disasters of the era were southern California's earthquake in 1933, the Ohio floods of 1937 and the New England hurricane of 1938, the last destroying seven hundred lives and two billion trees.

flivvers, with bedding, water jugs and skillets strapped on for easy access. Certainly such attitudes of defeat and drift were a sad departure from America's rural tradition. Speaking for these wayfarers, the poet Archibald MacLeish wrote:

> We wonder whether the dream of American liberty
> Wasn't the standing by the fence to tell them:
>
> And we're not standing by the homestead fence
> And telling any man where he can head for:
>
> Not in these parts: not with this wind blowing:
> Not with this wind blowing and no rain. . . .
>
> Men don't talk much with the road to stand on.

An estimated million persons took to the road during the worst depression years, whether as refugees from the Dust Bowl, uprooted tenant farmers or laborers rejected by agriculture and industry. The FERA's transient relief program aided about two hundred thousand families, the highest monthly registration (341,428 individuals) coming in April, 1935. It offered food, clothing, shelter or camping ground, ambulatory medical care and wages for doing local odd jobs. The vast majority of the recipients were native-born whites, stable and self-supporting prior to 1929; only about a fifth were chronic wanderers. The Farm Security Administration, which began by making small subsistence grants to several hundred thousand stricken families in the Dust Bowl and the South to dissuade them from joining the exodus, took over from the FERA most of its activities in the later thirties, providing in addition some educational opportunity. Various critics of these programs charged them with promoting vagrancy and shiftlessness at federal expense, but proposed no positive substitutes.

While foot-loose individuals came generally from cities—New York, Chicago, Pittsburgh—transient families tended to stem from the farming regions, with Oklahoma, Texas and

Missouri leading a tally made in 1935. This human erosion was one of the prime reasons why between 1930 and 1940 the number of white farmers in Oklahoma and Texas fell six or seven per cent and why, still more strikingly, the rural Negro population of those states shrank twenty-seven and thirteen per cent respectively. The Sooners of 1890 and their children, the nation's last big bloc of homesteading pioneers, now gave up the struggle in disheartening numbers. From about 1935 onward these "Okies" and their neighbors, the sharecropping "Arkies," became the most famous migrants of modern America. Westward they took their way, the jalopy doubling for the pioneer's Conestoga wagon and a wistful sense of hope for the boldness of the argonaut. Their straggling march over U. S. Highway 66 into the orchards, truck gardens and vineyards of southern California found its Anabasis in John Steinbeck's novel *The Grapes of Wrath* (1939).

During the four years beginning in midsummer of 1935 about three hundred and fifty thousand Dust Bowl farmers crossed the Arizona border into the Golden State. Their frightful poverty stirred such alarm that southern California's All-Year Club began to advertise: "Warning! Come to California for a glorious vacation. Advise anyone not to come seeking employment." Many of the newcomers, however, found precarious seasonal work under the prevalent system of corporate farming. Out of California's one hundred and fifty thousand farm proprietors in 1939, fewer than three thousand large-scale operators, belonging chiefly to an organization called the Associated Farmers, employed at starvation pay most of the two hundred thousand migrants then in the state. This body strongly resented the unionization of agricultural labor which the CIO undertook in 1937, and tension mounted until the exigencies of war industry raised wages and enforced a truce.

Meanwhile the Dust Bowl began to contract, thanks to the shelter belt of trees, the department of agriculture's lessons in dry-land farming, the development of small irrigation works and building of reservoirs, the enlargement of farms and restoration of ranching in some areas, resettlement and rehabilitation under the FSA, and other measures worked out jointly by federal and state agencies. From more than six million acres under severe erosion in 1935-1936 the area declined to less than a million, mainly on the fringes, by 1939. Increased rainfall also helped, but its maximum benefit would have been lost without such foresight.

What were the lessons afforded by the New Deal's sally into regionalism? In the first place, it was clear that coöperative effort—essentially the self-education of the people under the guidance of experts federal and local—could accomplish wonders impossible either to the people or the government alone. In the second place, workable segments of the Union, each with its peculiar conditions and cohesion of interests, seemed able to plan in a way which weakened neither the national economy nor loyalty (as considerations of sectionalism were apt to do), but rather strengthened them. "Unity through diversity" was the ideal, the ultimate application of the principle of interstate commerce to embrace not only mercantile traffic but social and cultural intercourse as well.

As for the administrative side of regionalism, admittedly there were potential risks. "Federalists" of some newer deal, fanatic do-gooders, conceivably might weaken local initiative, diversity and administrative democracy, laying upon citizens' shoulders the heavy hand of bureaucratic paternalism and technological determinism. In the ardor of conserving land, water, timber and minerals and the exhilaration of huge engineering schemes the individual might be forgotten as the real beneficiary. Fortunately, in policy makers like David Lilienthal and Harcourt Morgan, the TVA early found leaders who understood the danger. "In the last analysis," as Lilienthal himself observed, "in democratic planning it is human beings we are concerned with."

Furthermore, the TVA's insistence upon independence

from Washington in the making of practically all decisions meant not only that grass-roots responsibility was substituted for bureaucratic "buck-passing," but that technicians and officers had to live and work among the people whom they served. Absentee management was abolished. Collaboration with local groups—whether governments, farmers' associations or citizens' power boards, which occasionally vetoed TVA schemes—remained an astringent against federal consolidation, even the kind (as the phrase ran) which applied Hamiltonian means to gain Jeffersonian ends. The TVA, as its chairman fully appreciated, had a contribution to make to the philosophy of government at a time when, in order to curb the growing centralization of industrial and financial power, government itself had taken rapid strides toward centralization and might in turn develop the pathology of power.

CHAPTER IX

YOUTH IN SEARCH OF A CHANCE

THE talisman of "planning," which the economic shocks and innovations of the thirties invested with new magic, might cast its spell over the breadth of a region or else contract to the microcosm of a family, foreseeing the future of child and oldster. The urge for personal planning lay behind the social-security act, the consumer and coöperative movements, group medicine and a variety of other developments. Youth had the longest road to chart, hence the greatest number of hazards to encounter and the largest claim upon society to see that he did not begin this journey as a handicap race.

For many years the growth of cities, higher living standards, the emancipation of women, reduced immigration of the more fecund peoples, late marriages and contraception among the upper and middle classes had been whittling down the size of the American family. Population continued to increase, but at a much slower pace than formerly. The Depression's impact by pointing up the expense of rearing many children accelerated the trend. Between 1930 and 1940 the size of the average family shrank more rapidly than in any previous decade.

This reduction was largely deliberate—the result of "planned parenthood," as the "race suicide" of the first Roosevelt, the "birth control" of the twenties, had become, by a signal triumph of semantics. At the start of the era there were only twenty-eight contraceptive clinics in the nation; Charles G. Norris's novel *Seed* (1930), an honest, if labored, attempt to present both sides of the issue, was hailed by reviewers for accosting "a subject that is much discussed but rarely gets into print." The so-called Comstock law, enacted by Congress in 1873 and imitated by all the states save North Carolina and New Mexico, still hedged the matter with archaic legalisms.

Chief defenders of the old order were the rural South and, more actively, the Catholic hierarchy. In the South, where child labor remained a substitute for mechanization, many fathers still regarded big families as an economic blessing. In June, 1931, the Southern Presbyterian General Assembly withdrew from the Federal Council of Churches after the latter indorsed birth control. Official Catholic opposition persisted despite a marked decline in Catholic birth rate since 1920. But in 1931 Pope Pius XI in his encyclical "Christian Marriage" approved the so-called natural method or "safe-period" theory. The American market was promptly flooded with books about the Ogino-Knaus ("O. K.") cycle. This technique, though deemed none too reliable by the Birth Control Clinical Research Bureau, helped at least to bring Catholic theory into closer harmony with what seemed to be Catholic practice.

Other elements of public opinion moved more decisively in the same direction. A poll among *Farm & Fireside* readers early in the Depression showed two to one for giving medical advice on planned parenthood, and during the thirties the Sears, Roebuck catalogue began to list contraceptive wares. A straw vote of subscribers by the Protestant *Churchman* in January, 1935, revealed almost unanimous approval for birth control, while in the next year, among all sorts and conditions, a Gallup poll agreed with a *Fortune* survey in finding two out of three favorable. This majority, moreover, rose steadily in later years, with women outranking men in the warmth of their indorsement.

Results speedily appeared. In 1936 an important decision by the United States Court of Appeals liberalized interpretations of the federal law which had hampered physicians in advising patients on contraception; and in June, 1937, the American Medical Association tardily recognized the subject as a province of legitimate professional practice, with a host of state medical societies following suit. By 1940 the giving of professional advice on pregnancy-spacing for reasons of health had been legalized in every state save Massachusetts and Connecticut, where Catholic opinion in the latter thirties joined forces with unreconstructed Protestantism to padlock birth-control clinics. The close of another year found seven hundred and forty-six such centers in the country, all medically directed and nearly a third supported by public funds.

North Carolina in 1938 set up the first state-sponsored clinics, which within three years were giving medical counsel to four out of every hundred underprivileged wives in seventy-five counties. South Carolina promptly emulated her neighbor's example, and Alabama followed early in 1941. In 1939 the Birth Control Federation (shortly rechristened the Planned Parenthood Federation) reported that its rural health program had made contact with 23,500 mothers, 1500 of them in migratory camps, in thirteen states. Despite relatively small numbers and limited coverage this campaign remained one of the most significant developments of the era for the alleviation of poverty.

For the nation as a whole, fertility in the poorest areas was seventy-seven per cent in excess of the need for replacement, while among zones with the highest living standards the birth rate fell seventeen per cent below such requirements. The fecundity of many families on relief provoked widespread irritation against "dole babies," along with regrets that the stock best able to care for and educate offspring showed the greatest reluctance to bear them. Though medicine, public health and living habits increased the average life expectancy at birth from fifty-six years in 1920 to sixty-four in 1940, the proportion of children in the nation steadily diminished. Thus in 1938 there were some 1,600,000 fewer children under ten years of age in the United States than five years before—a situation already mirrored in the decline of pupils in elementary schoolrooms.

The Great Depression bore with special harshness on growing youth. As the crisis deepened, hunger and want overtook several million children, some from homes once prosperous and others in substandard families ranging from the slums of Brooklyn to the pine barrens of Georgia. The relief census of October, 1933, listed forty-two per cent of all recipients as under sixteen years old, yet they comprised only thirty-one per cent of the population. A year later the Committee on Economic Security reported eight million children on relief.

Beyond the huge sums spent on immediate help and work relief for the family's breadwinners, the New Deal addressed certain special programs directly to needy youngsters. The FERA hired unemployed nurses to look after small children and embarked upon its free school-lunch program. More durably, the social-security act of 1935 authorized $24,750,000 annually to aid dependent children, $3,800,000 for maternal and child health, $1,500,000 for homeless and neglected children and $2,850,000 for crippled children. This program, resting upon state collaboration, elicited in most regions hearty indorsement, and in 1939 Congress increased its appropriation. What Henry Wallace termed the "genetic basis of democracy" found impressive recognition. Largely as a result of the better care provided for mothers, maternal mortality rates for the nation fell a fourth between 1934 and 1938.

As for wage-earning children, forty per cent of the boys between the ages of fourteen and nineteen were so engaged and twenty-three per cent of the girls in 1930, a marked reduction from earlier times. In the next decade child labor continued to retreat, thanks partly to legal restraints and partly to the requirement of more schooling, until by 1940 these percentages had lowered to thirty-five and nineteen.

In the summer of 1933, when hearings on the NRA cotton code began, the textile manufacturers at a dramatic moment offered an amendment abolishing mill labor for persons under sixteen. Considering the new minimum-wage levels this was a relatively cheap concession, but the action roused cheers in the committee chamber, applause through the nation. It resulted in the discharge of one and a half million youngsters. Yet when President Roosevelt told Congress on January 3, 1934, that "child labor is abolished," he apparently overlooked a large area of neglect. Agriculture, outside NRA supervision, remained a heavy employer, keeping in the fields about half a million between the ages of ten and fifteen. The children of Southern croppers, toiling for the landlord from the age of six or seven, were among the worst sufferers.

After the NRA's invalidation in 1935 child labor increased somewhat; hence the Walsh-Healey act of 1936 required employers holding substantial government contracts to bar such toilers, and in the next year a law restrained child employment by sugar-beet farmers enjoying federal benefits. In 1938 the fair-labor-standards act went further, banning industrial work by youths under sixteen and forbidding employment under eighteen in hazardous and injurious occupations. It offered no protection, however, for the nonfactory worker and the laborer in purely intrastate concerns.

Meanwhile, under the fulcrum of an adult labor surplus and firmer intrenchment of minimum wages, twenty-three more legislatures between 1931 and 1941 approved the child-labor amendment to the Constitution, first submitted in 1924. Only eight states short of the necessary thirty-six remained to ratify. A Gallup poll in 1937 reported a favorable majority in every state and an over-all indorsement by more than three fourths. As might be supposed, managerial interests in commonwealths employing heavy child labor lobbied against the reform, while sentiment in other states was wedded to local regulation. Thus in 1938 two industrial commonwealths favoring their own systems, New York and Massachusetts, and one major agricultural employer, Mississippi, rejected the proposal. Claims that after so long a time the amendment had become a dead letter were ended by the Supreme Court in June, 1939.

Youth encountered the obverse side of the employment situation when, upon the threshold of maturity, it set forth in quest of a job, expecting not the pittance paid children but a living wage. The gap between leaving school and the first job, always a no man's land of uncertainties, widened under the Depression. In the middle 1930's more than a quarter of the youths in their late 'teens and early twenties had never had regular work; for the entire group the waiting period averaged about two years after quitting school. Four out of five were still living with parents, including nearly half of those married. The American Youth Commission in 1935 estimated the number of job-seeking youth at 4,200,000—a third of the nation's idle man power—while many of the 4,000,000 still attending school or college were so doing largely as an alternative to "just hanging around." Commentators upon the census of 1940 soberly concluded that "youth have suffered more unemployment than any other element of the labor force."

At an early stage of the Depression youngsters often took to the road in search of work and adventure, reasoning that at home there would be one less mouth to feed. Upon the Missouri Pacific, for example, the number of bums and freight-car migrants (including repeaters) increased from thirteen thousand in 1929 to nearly two hundred thousand in 1931. In Los Angeles alone, free flophouses and midnight missions gave asylum in 1932 to more than two hundred thousand. In the summer of 1932 most railroads gave up trying to block this traffic, and trains began to carry one or more box cars with open doors to forestall the temptation of breaking into sealed cars.

Railroad men, social workers and police agreed that the great majority of these nomads were neither criminals nor vagrants, and but for the Depression would have been in school or at work. Among five thousand boy transients studied on the West Coast, three fifths possessed at least a ninth-grade education and most had participated in school or church activities. Nearly two thirds stated that they had left home for economic reasons, a fifth blamed family quarrels or broken homes, a seventh admitted wanderlust, and one out of thirty some personal maladjustment, such as escape from compulsory schooling or petty crime.

Surprisingly enough, the Depression's effect upon crime, especially in the case of homeless and pliant youth, was not striking. In Massachusetts, for example, a perceptible drop occurred in the state's juvenile-delinquency rate between the latter twenties and the early thirties, though adult crimes against property mounted. Only sporadically did increased delinquency appear, taking such forms as stealing, willful trespass and running away from home. Youthful crimes against property generally rose when relief measures slackened; and offenders under twenty-one made up a third of all arrests for major crimes in New York City in 1939. Including both young and old, the prison population of the United States numbered a hundred and eighty thousand in 1939, an increase of nearly two fifths during the decade.

The most spectacular crime wave, which reached its crest between 1932 and 1934, had nothing to do with juvenile delinquency and bore only an oblique relation to the Depression. It was the work of racketeers turning from rumrunning and other activities of waning profit to the kidnapping of children and adults. An aroused Congress passed severe laws against interstate abductions in 1932 and 1934, with penalties involving death if the victim were harmed.*

* N. Y. *Times*, June 23, 1932, and May 16, 1934. See also E. D. Sullivan, *The Snatch Racket* (N. Y., 1932). The decade's most famous abduction, that of Charles Augustus Lindbergh, jr., first-born of the aviator, on March 1, 1932, was, however, perpetrated by an amateur. The frantic search, appeals to the underworld, discovery of the child's body, arrest of the murderer in 1934 through tracing of the gold certificates extorted, his trial and electrocution in 1936, evoked mass emotions of an intensity scarcely seen before—morbidness, vulgar curiosity, national anxiety, neighborly grief and sympathy. S. B. Whipple, *The Trial of Bruno Richard Hauptmann* (N. Y., 1937).

One effect was to glorify the Federal Bureau of Investigation, its chief J. Edgar Hoover and his special agents, the "G-Men" (underworld cant for government men), into hero-hood for the romantic public and the young. By 1936 movies, juvenile literature, radio serials and budding organizations of "Junior G-Men" were attesting to the fact that law enforcement had at last grown more glamorous than lawbreaking.

Greater concern for the predelinquent child—school truancy, health problems, emotional make-up, educational needs—inspired special-service adjuncts of the public schools and more progressive police departments, as well as child-welfare projects staffed by the WPA. The movies gave casual publicity to the "Dead-End Kids" as types of urban delinquency, and to Father Edward J. Flanagan's "Boys' Town" in Nebraska offering healthier surroundings to the under-privileged.

The Depression's full toll upon susceptible youth was hard to assess because in large measure it resembled a payment deferred. That its sum was not greater was due appreciably to the Civilian Conservation Corps, created in April, 1933, to keep idle youngsters from "riding the rods," living off soup kitchens and sleeping in hobo "jungles." Incidental to the task of saving youth was that of saving natural resources. The idea, worked out by Secretary of Labor Frances Perkins and Senator Robert F. Wagner, owed something to the work camps of pre-Hitler Germany, something also to the philosopher William James, who a generation earlier had called for "a conscription of the whole youthful population to form for a certain number of years a part of a great army enlisted against *Nature*."

The CCC was voluntary, but its discipline and spirit were mildly military, though drilling, saluting and marching were taboo. The war department directed the building of camps and also supervised the boys' health, morale and welfare. The administration of the corps, however, became wholly civilian before the close of 1939. Each youth received a monthly wage of thirty dollars, part of it as a family allotment. A spruce-green uniform was worn in winter, and in summer the olive drab which many soon would don again with a more military cut.* When the CCC's peak enrollment of nearly half a million was reached in the autumn of 1935, Negroes comprised about a tenth, and those aboriginal woodsmen, the Indians, a smaller fraction.† At first, needy lads were accepted from both relief and nonrelief families, but in 1935 the latter were eliminated and the age span set at from seventeen to twenty-eight. In practice, among the 2,750,000 recruits who served up to the end of 1941, the great majority were in their 'teens.

The turnover was rapid, thanks to the beckoning reality or mirage of a regular job, restlessness, hankering for old haunts or rebellion against discipline. All in all, about half left before finishing their term of from six months to two years. The bulk of those who stayed, however, benefited from the experience. It gave them better food and more regular habits than they had known at home, taught lessons of hygiene, physical agility and manual "know-how," often engrafted ambition and self-confidence. Per capita the CCC proved the most expensive form of relief, costing about eleven hundred and seventy-five dollars annually to maintain each lad; but to offset this cost, in addition to gains in health and self-respect, roads and trails were built, forest fires

* Between July, 1940, and June, 1941, no less than 300,000 enrollees completed training and left CCC camps for military service and jobs in defense industry. Kenneth Holland and F. E. Hill, *Youth in the CCC* (Wash., 1942), 124.

† Fostering a New Deal for the Indian, the Wheeler-Howard act of 1934 sought to conserve the tribal domain, provide a larger measure of self-government and safeguards for civil rights, resettle landless persons and prevent spoliation of natural resources. Under Commissioner of Indian Affairs John Collier livestock coöperatives, arts and crafts and other tribal enterprises took a new lease on life. For good writing and photography on this subject, see Oliver La Farge and Helen M. Post, *As Long as the Grass Shall Grow* (N. Y., 1940).

checked or prevented, gullies stopped from erosion, wild life preserved and some two billion trees planted.

The CCC enjoyed more consistent popularity than any other New Deal agency. A Gallup poll, which in 1936 reported three out of five citizens, for example, against the AAA, recorded in the same year more than four out of five supporting the CCC. Youth busy in the great outdoors appealed to the public's imagination. Moreover, its heavily patronized voluntary educational program and library facilities added to the value of the experience. Employers looked favorably on "graduates" of the CCC, feeling that its practical lessons—learning to do a full day's work, carry out orders, take pride in results, often acquire special skills—approached more closely those taught in private industry than did the lax disciplines of other work-relief programs or school-administered projects.

The National Youth Administration, begun in June, 1935, was a "sort of junior WPA," designed for lads between sixteen and twenty-five years of age unwilling or physically unsuited to go off to a CCC camp, for those eager to finish school, and for girls, in whose case the camp idea, tried modestly in the mid-thirties on a coöperative plan, had not worked well. From the standpoint of cost it was the cheapest work relief, combining part-time employment with little equipment and overhead at a yearly average of two hundred and twenty-five dollars apiece.

At its peak month (April, 1937) the NYA numbered six hundred and thirty thousand in its two major programs— of whom no fewer than seven eighths were receiving student aid and the remainder employed on out-of-school projects. The latter group, mainly from relief families, lived at home and by working about forty-four hours a month averaged earnings of fifteen dollars. Making and lettering street signs, repairing discarded toys for poor children, building school furniture, constructing footbridges for rural school paths, soil-erosion control and sewing were typical activities. Vocational-guidance programs sent many boys into manual work-shops and girls into domestic-science classes, and in under-privileged zones of cities NYA community youth centers sprang up.

The much larger group of beneficiaries, nearly two million in all, were high-school and college students who needed financial help to continue their education. Faced with a sharp drop in undergraduate enrollments since 1932, the FERA in February, 1934, had launched a program of student aid averaging about fifteen dollars a month for seventy-five thousand boys and girls. The NYA took over and greatly expanded this plan. Soon the young people were engaged at such tasks as mending and cataloguing library books, typing, compiling statistics and bibliographies and assisting in campus maintenance and repair. In scholastic standing they stood above average in a majority of colleges surveyed.*

The NYA, however, never captured such public favor as did the "tree army." The wisdom or folly of its program hinged almost entirely upon local management. Quite often young state and city administrators were appointed who lacked both tact and experience in dealing with senior community leaders. NYA funds, moreover, were always too scanty for grappling with big problems. For this or other reasons projects frequently turned into boondoggling. Yet, by holding back the torrent of unemployment, the prolonging of education through any means equipped youth better for the economic struggle ahead. Under widespread joblessness, the number of high-school pupils grew from about four and a half million in 1929 to six in 1935—an increase of a third —and the trend continued. Many boys and girls, who in piping times would have dropped out after grammar school or brief experience with high school, thus profited from ad-

* Betty and E. K. Lindley, *A New Deal for Youth: the Story of the NYA* (N. Y., 1938), 169, citing a study made in 1935-1936 of 270 colleges, which showed superior grades by NYA students in 168, no essential difference in 71, and inferior standing in 31.

versity. The rising enrollment, coupled with the falling birth rate, wrought a significant shift between 1934 and 1936 in the structure of American education. Though the number of public high schools rose by nine hundred, elementary schools shrank by about four thousand. Some fifty public and two hundred private institutions of higher learning also came into existence.

The plight of public schools early in the Depression was often desperate. A municipal-economy drive, backed by citizens' committees and chambers of commerce, had picked education as its initial victim. In Chicago in 1932-1933, where tax delinquency and bad government had long afflicted the community, the teachers, unpaid for a year and victimized still longer by the issue of scrip and tax warrants, in April, 1933, staged a demonstration which drew nation-wide attention. In New York City eleven thousand teachers were idle in 1932 and 1933, while at one stage five out of six of Alabama's schools were closed. Throughout the country twenty-six hundred schools, largely rural, had ceased by the beginning of 1934; shut doors and shortened terms affected nearly ten million children. Only gradually did these conditions improve with the nation's economic upturn.

"Progressive" education, particularly in urban schools, continued in the saddle, but the Depression stripped away some of its faddism. Cross-fertilization between private and public schools served the advantage of both, helping to save the former from eccentricity and snobbery, the latter from mechanical routine and notions of mass production. In elementary education the "child-centered" instruction of the twenties yielded to the "community-centered" school, fostering more projects built about social and economic themes. In the high schools, as at the college level, much talk was heard about the unification of knowledge for the benefit of daily living and the practical welfare of mankind. "Integration," "orientation" and "frames of reference" became the pet jargon of educators in revolt against mere memorizing, fact gathering or learning *in vacuo*.

Noteworthy also was the spread of adult education. Many communities in 1930-1932 set up rather haphazard education programs for the jobless, but most of them bowed out before the Federal Emergency Adult Education Program instituted in the fall of 1933 by Harry L. Hopkins, which utilized unemployed teachers to instruct other groups of the unemployed. By April, 1935, the scheme had engaged 43,722 persons to teach 1,190,131 enrollees, of whom the vast majority were able-bodied literate adults. With federal encouragement "depression colleges" and junior colleges were also set up in various places to attract members of this new leisure group. With the end of the FERA these activities were continued vigorously by the WPA.

The universities also underwent change. The 1920's had resembled a gold rush, with huge numerical increases paced by bigger and better endowments, and horizons of collegiate spires broken by an occasional skyscraper. Funds provided by the oil millionaire Edward S. Harkness on the eve of the economic crash enabled Harvard and Yale to launch great building programs which carried them triumphantly through the darkest depression years. Harvard unrolled her "House" plan along the banks of the Charles in the colonial Georgian style but of a magnificence never dreamed of by the Puritan worthies, Dunster and Winthrop, while under New Haven's elms Yale built her "Colleges" in the Gothic taste which Edwards and Trumbull might have found popish. At both places this reorganization meant an enhancement of personal faculty-student relations, which in the East had begun to win general favor before the end of the twenties, invoking tutors, faculty advisers, vocational counselors, campus psychologists and personnel bureaus.

In most cases, however, the Depression robbed campuses of present hope for multiplying either buildings or faculty. Holding the line was enough. As gifts fell off, interest from investments shriveled and tax support declined, capital expenditures dropped about eighty-six per cent between 1929-1930 and 1933-1934. Appropriations for libraries and laboratories had to be reduced, salaries pared, and though the number of professors remained virtually unchanged, instructors' ranks were thinned. Numerous young M.A.'s and Ph.D.'s, along with the fledgling doctors, lawyers, chemists, engineers and architects hatched by alma mater in expectancy of limitless demand, now joined the unemployed, which by 1933 included some two hundred thousand certified teachers. Unwanted elsewhere, they had to pocket pride and professional training and try their luck selling insurance and vacuum cleaners, perhaps with stretches of labor in the fields or orchards and not infrequently a spell on relief.

Despite this rebuff to the hardy old belief that higher education pays off in cash, young people retained their faith in its ultimate and perhaps nonmaterial values. Though the first jolt of depression reduced enrollment between 1930-1931 and 1933-1934 by some eighty thousand—eight per cent of the total—the year 1934-1935 reversed the tide, notably among institutions with modest or no tuition fees. Thanks to readjustment to a more austere living scale, attended by small economic gains and support from the FERA and later the NYA, registration in forty-four state universities and land-grant colleges rose within the year eight and a third per cent, and henceforth the increases continued. By 1940 one in every six or seven college-age youth was enrolled on some campus—their total nearly one and a half million—thus setting an all-time national and world record.

For both teacher and student the shock of hard times loosed ancient educational moorings. Recalling that Horace Mann had achieved his great work for free schools following the Panic of 1837 and that the high-school movement flowered mightily after the Panic of 1893, some observers surmised that catastrophe served a useful purpose in smashing decayed wood and encouraging educators to experiment. Far more than in the 1920's, stereotypes like entrance units, required courses, examinations, college credits, even grades and degrees, were challenged. Fresh attention was drawn to unconventional colleges founded in the mid-twenties like Bennington and Sarah Lawrence, now joined in 1934 by newly revamped Bard College, under the wing of Columbia University, and coöperative Black Mountain College, opened about the same time in North Carolina. In 1934 that progressive Quaker institution, Swarthmore College, abandoned the credit-hour system, declaring for thoroughness in fewer subjects rather than the traditional smattering in many. Here and elsewhere "honors courses," cast in the Oxford pattern and designed to free individual curiosity from the shackles of routine, enjoyed mounting favor.

The storm center of innovation, however, was the University of Chicago under the régime of Robert M. Hutchins, who took over in 1929 at the age of thirty. He sought to end the "old traditional time-serving course-credit requirements" by permitting the bright student to travel as fast as he pleased toward a bachelor's or graduate degree. Students lacking high-school diplomas were admitted, and those who did not want a bachelor's degree might take an inferior award, Associate in Arts, while the true scholar would persevere to one of the four higher divisions: humanities, biological sciences, physical sciences and social sciences.

With less success in his own institution, Hutchins espoused certain ideas about the medieval "quadrivium" of grammar, rhetoric, logic and mathematics, over which metaphysics should preside as queen of the disciplines, unifying all knowledge. Hutchins's colleague, Mortimer J. Adler, explained in his best seller *How to Read a Book* (1940) some aspects of a reading program for adults centered largely in the "world's hundred best books," while in another region educators friendly to such ideas remolded the curriculum of Maryland's old St. John's College about this core. Hutchins and his followers did not go unchallenged. Harry D. Gideonse, for example, who after leaving Chicago became president of Brooklyn College, agreed with the attack upon sloppy and diffuse learning, but questioned Hutchins's so-called basic principles, which upon scrutiny looked suspiciously like that unity-by-mandate dear to totalitarians abroad.

The issue of free inquiry versus authority assumed fresh urgency in a world over whose face the waters of political dictatorship were rising fast. It formed a dominant theme at Harvard University's Tercentenary in September, 1936, attended by savants, scientists and men of letters from all parts of the earth. This occasion pointed up, as did no other event of the decade, the recent cumulative losses of Europe to America in research enterprise, intellectual leadership and the pursuit of disinterested learning. In place of the Old, the New World now held primacy in the advancement of knowledge.

What did young people in and out of college think about this troubled civilization which willy-nilly would be their inheritance? Youth began the decade with considerable apathy toward politics, prone to repeat time-worn sayings about pull, machine politics and graft; but the Depression and the New Deal gradually overcame this indifference. Questions of economics and history, sociology and social justice proved vastly engrossing to those with intellectual curiosity. A poll of Maryland young folk found that the great majority believed the federal government ought to participate more intimately in the lives of citizens, regulating wages and hours, assuring living standards of "health and decency," maintaining agencies like the NRA and WPA. In summary, the analyst concluded that these youths seemed to subscribe to the doctrine that "the best government is that which governs most." Others confirmed his findings. In this era, unlike the twenties, youth (it appeared) neither flamed nor strove. Conservative oldsters disappointedly pronounced it a generation of hitchhikers, seeking to thumb a ride from Uncle Sam, and put the blame on the New Deal. Liberals argued that youth did no more than insist upon its birthright: free education and a job. "Today's young people want to *live*—not simply to accumulate," wrote a university observer in the mid-thirties.

Decent food, clothing and shelter and, still less, the chance to begin a career and marry—such things had ceased to be automatic guarantees of American youth. A system promising their return through social planning was bound to appeal. "If someone came along with a line of stuff in which I could really believe," said a lad in the depths of 1932, "I'd follow him pretty nearly anywhere." Even Republicans might rejoice that the man who came along was not a homespun version of Hitler or Stalin but Franklin Roosevelt, whom polls repeatedly showed standing higher in favor with youth than with their elders. As for the alleged dependence and physical softness of this generation, obviously its true potentialities could only be plumbed by a global crisis such as still lay over the rim of the world.

New to American life were the nation-wide gatherings and student unions which tended to rally opinion slightly or far to the left of center. An amalgamation of over a thousand local and national organizations in 1934 comprised the American Youth Congress. Its second Congress, in 1935, drafted an "American Youth Act," espousing public-works jobs for youth at trade-union or prevailing wages, a federal apprenticeship program at guaranteed pay and hours, federal scholarships in high school and college free from barriers of sex, race, creed or politics. By 1937 Youth Congress objectives shifted heavily to the international scene, with resolutions demanding economic sanctions against treaty breakers, abolition of trade barriers and federal ownership of the munitions industry. For mutual support it joined hands with the World Youth Congress.

Beyond doubt, a variety of self-styled youth organizations lent themselves to manipulation by pressure groups and adult agitators with axes to grind. In this company were the Student League for Industrial Democracy and the National Student League, soon fused into a single leftist-pacifist body called the American Student Union in 1935. It clamored for the united front "against war and fascism" lately decreed from Moscow. Though its paid-up membership probably never exceeded nine thousand, its devotees proved highly articulate in student mass meetings and campus newspapers. Application of the strike technique to academic life helped enlist support, as the Student Union first demonstrated in April, 1936, when half a million collegians walked out of lecture halls at a given day and hour to protest against future wars—or as a pretext for cutting classes. Faced with the dilemma of resisting domestic fascism by disarmament or blocking foreign fascism by preparedness, the Union soon found itself a house divided. Upon domestic issues, however —Negro rights, collective bargaining and socialization of the means of production— it displayed greater accord. Throughout it was swayed by a communist-socialist bloc.

Such testaments of youth, spontaneous or imitative, alarmed conservative elders, whose fears were further fed by alleged exposures of the congressional committee "to investigate un-American activities," headed by publicity-loving Martin Dies. Evidence of economic heresy among the young —its spread often greatly exaggerated since the majority tended to despise the average campus radical as a "drip"— led the older generation to inferences like those the solid citizens of Athens once drew concerning the disciples of Socrates: the teacher must be to blame.

A rash of accusations broke out, from New York to California and from Illinois to Georgia, against "leftists" in the public schools and universities. Discussion in social-science classes of topics like communism and race relations, use of textbooks by Harold Rugg and Rexford G. Tugwell, reading of liberal weeklies like the *Nation* and *New Republic*, might serve as immediate causes; but in the background lay the challenge of the New Deal to the sacredness of property and *laissez faire*, with answering voices from the Hearst and Bernarr Macfadden publications, the American Liberty League and spokesmen for such organizations as the American Legion and Daughters of the American Revolution. Teachers'-oath laws, which Rhode Island had pioneered in 1917 under war hysteria, spread from California, Montana, North Dakota and Washington in 1931 to New York in 1934, and thence to Arizona, Georgia, Massachusetts, Michigan, New Jersey, Vermont and Texas in 1935.

But the year 1936 marked a slackening in this campaign, due to the usual recoil that follows such alarums. Already in 1935 seven legislatures had rejected similar bills, while the governors of Maryland and Delaware vetoed others. A Gallup poll in May, 1936, asking, "Should schools teach the facts about Socialism, Communism, and Fascism?" mustered an affirmative vote of nearly two out of three, with almost as many agreeing that college teachers should "be free to express their views on all subjects, including politics and religion." Such findings indicated that the value of honest inquiry was being more generally recognized, along with distinctions between a teacher's private views and his utterance in class, between objective discussion and propagandizing outside the field of his authority.

What of the mores of youth? In its attitude toward sex, free love and marriage this generation parted company with the jazz age. Of course, conventional wooing and honest wiving had formed the habit of a majority of young people even in the heyday of Scott Fitzgerald, but the coterie which got itself talked about had flouted "middle-class" morality, and its most daring focus, the Greenwich Village set, had degenerated from bathtub gin and fornication in the early twenties to the "wild party" and experiments with drugs and homosexuality later in the decade. The onset of the Great Depression meant that an old age was out, and time to begin a new: among those in whose blood the fires of rebellion burned, economic rather than sexual heterodoxy came to be flaunted as the red badge of courage. If idleness served to whet sexual craving, the cost of courtship—movies, refreshments, transportation, party clothes—acted as a deterrent. "You can't have dates without money," said the lad, while the girl was apt to explain ruefully, "I don't have the clothes to go out in," or "You can't get married on what the boys make."

On the other hand, sex freedom, though no longer vaunted, was often taken calmly as a biological need or the individual's right to happiness.* A questionnaire answered by nearly fourteen hundred college students from coast to coast in 1937 indicated that half the men and a quarter of the girls in the junior and senior years had had premarital intercourse, while two thirds of all the young women avowed themselves willing to do so for true love. Youth both in and out of college condemned promiscuity as "cheap, vulgar, immoral." This generation believed that marriage, if possible financially, was "the best of human institutions." A *Fortune* poll in 1936 reported that three out of five college girls and half the men wanted to wed soon after graduation and about half of each sex hoped for children. As a jobless youth in an upstate New York industrial town wrote in his diary,

> Always a lover, never a husband. God, ain't it awful? . . .
> To hell with that. It may fit the twenties but it sure don't fit the thirties. They gotta take me as I am, with everything I ain't got, or nothing stirring, sister. I ain't looking for a girl-friend but a wife.

During the early depression Eddie Cantor popularized over the radio a song called "Now's the Time to Fall in Love," with the blandishment that since prices were falling

---

* "American civilization and the Catholic church are in open conflict on practically every phase of sex," wrote the Reverend F. X. Talbot, editor of the Jesuit weekly *America*, rebuking the continued laxity of the mores. "The Catholic view holds sex and its manifestations as sacred: the American view regards it as somewhat more serious than a sneeze." Harold Stearns, ed., *America Now* (N. Y., 1938), 538-540.

"two can live as cheap as one on what you're makin'." But converts at first were few. The marriage rate of 1929—over ten per thousand of population—dropped by 1932 to the lowest recorded point in American history, less than eight, or three fourths of the annual average for the previous decade. Divorce was also less frequently resorted to in these years. Desertion, "the poor man's divorce," increased as job-hunting husbands left unhappy homes, but legal divorce was an expensive business. Not unexpectedly, therefore, the rate fell from 1.66 per thousand of population in 1929 to a low (unmatched since the year of the Armistice) of 1.28 in 1932 and 1.31 the next year.

A discouragement to divorce and argument for marriage, potent during the decade's middle years, was that both employment opportunity and federal relief were granted more readily to a married man, better still if he had children or a pregnant wife. Reviving prosperity brought a gradual climb of the divorce rate, however, to an all-time record of two per thousand people in 1940. As for the resurgence of marriage, biology was proverbially impatient, nor prone to be satisfied with makeshifts like those suggested by the rise of both illegitimacy and prostitution between 1929 and 1933. Readjustments of attitude occurred: millions learned they could get along on less money, brides waived expensive weddings and often a home of their own, the spread of contraceptive knowledge promised deferment of offspring and, of course, the economic revival greatly helped. After 1933 the trend soon outran the pace of recovery. The year 1934 brought a return to the 1929 level, while 1937 boosted the number to more than eleven per thousand of population, the highest since the bumper crop of postwar weddings in 1920.

The outbreak of the second German war and the passage of the peace-time selective-service act accelerated the marriage rate as young men hastened to wed the girls they might have to leave behind them. The year 1941 recorded nearly thirteen marriages per thousand. Soon young wives with infants, living on servicemen's pay and cheerfully following the camps, could be seen crowding railway waiting rooms and drab hotels all over the land. Nevertheless a lag remained. In 1938 it was estimated that, despite the attempts to make up for time lost, about one and a half million young people who would normally have married had been forced to postpone the event, often still living under the parental roof. For a minority a further deterrent arose from the fact that during these years twenty-six states passed laws demanding pre-marital blood tests, while the number requiring advance notice of intention to wed increased from seventeen to twenty-six.

Neither the stress of prolonged economic crisis nor the even greater tensions of imminent war could long keep youth from mating. The liturgy's ancient pledge—for better for worse, for richer for poorer—overshadowed the Victorian injunction concerning maintenance of the bride in her accustomed style. The thing which according to observers this generation most wanted—security—remained so teasing a mirage that youth came to doubt its reality. Hence in the quest for personal contentment they seemed more ready than their parents to throw material prudence to the winds. When each had found his own, the pair believed that they were justified in salvaging whatever happiness they could from the world's dark uncertainties.

CHAPTER X

AGE IN QUEST OF SECURITY

AT the time of the Civil War only one American out of forty was sixty-five or older. By 1940, when the United States Public Health Service established its first unit on gerontology to study senescence and its socioeconomic problems, one out of fifteen had reached this age, and for 1980 the ratio was forecast as one in six. While causes already explored were slowing down the birth rate, better diet, closer medical supervision and scientific advances in the prolongation of life were stretching out the span. "The American nation," wrote two statisticians in 1939, "is now well on the way to becoming the most aged aggregation of people on the face of the earth."

This condition, unluckily, went along with certain factors tending to make the elderly less solvent and self-sufficient. In 1890, when they comprised only three per cent of the population, a mere quarter of them were not gainfully employed, but by 1930, when they made up five and a half per cent, more than two fifths had quit their jobs. Ironically, those likeliest to continue working—bankers, lawyers, farmers, business executives—generally had much less economic reason for doing so than did machinists, miners and factory laborers, who were often fired at forty-five or fifty. The phrase "old at forty" met its gesture of rebuttal in the title of a best seller in 1932, Walter B. Pitkin's *Life Begins at Forty*, which thereafter became a wishful byword. Aggravating the problem was the shrinking size of families, which meant that the burden of supporting dependent parents now fell upon one or two children instead of perhaps half a dozen.

While the majority of European nations, members of the

British Empire and several South American republics adopted systems of compulsory old-age insurance during the first quarter of this century, the United States seemed laggard in presenting a humane alternative to "sending the old folks over the hill to the poorhouse" or county farm. Hardly more than one out of twenty in 1928 drew a pension from private industry, while masses of state and municipal employees knew no such security as that furnished to federal workers. On the eve of the crash eight commonwealths had acts permitting counties to pay old-age pensions if they chose, but most of this legislation was too loosely drawn to have much practical value, with only Wisconsin and Minnesota offering aid to such counties as assumed these responsibilities. Moreover, the backlog of life savings among the low-income group was the least adequate of any in affording a shield against disaster.

The impact of depression converted a mild chronic problem into one of importunate misery. Along with other aspects of relief, this charge first fell upon private charity, then the municipalities and states and, finally, the federal government. By 1934 the FERA was providing temporary aid to nearly three quarters of a million persons over sixty-five, and by 1936 the number dependent upon public relief was at least a million, with about half the remainder—three and a quarter million—receiving some assistance from children, other relatives or friends. The back-breaking load and personal bitterness which this need sometimes laid upon the younger generation's shoulders were displayed in Josephine Lawrence's novel *Years Are So Long* (1934), a homely American version of Lear and his daughters. Agitation for workable state pension systems reached such pressure that by the middle of 1934 no fewer than twenty-eight states, together with the territories of Alaska and Hawaii, had passed old-age acts, of which twenty-three were now mandatory.

For most of the elderly, reëmployment offered scant practical remedy, and their plight grew no better through the middle 1930's. Among three classes strikingly in need of direct relief—children, the blind and the aged—by far the heaviest expenditure in 1932 went for dependent children, but by 1936 assistance to age had come overwhelmingly to hold first place in both city and rural areas, representing eighty-five per cent of the total outlay for such purposes. That politicians and charlatans as well as idealists should hearken to the old folks' cry was inevitable. Unlike children, these senior citizens could vote, agitate, give pennies and dollars to the cause.

California, with its lure of climate for the enfeebled Iowa farmer and Kansas storekeeper—contributing to a state-wide ratio of nearly eight oldsters out of a hundred inhabitants— proved to be the happy hunting ground for social-security schemers. Practical-minded newcomers, caught in the grip of reduced income from modest investments or the collapse of banks and building and loan associations, joined self-help organizations, coöperatives and barter groups in unprecedented numbers; but more articulate politically were organizations such as the short-lived Utopian Society, founded in Los Angeles in 1933, which within a year attracted half a million followers through its promise of a wonderland where machines should perform all the drudgery and everybody retire at forty-five.

Against a background mainly of grass-roots or small-town conservatism transplanted in later life to a land of ease, then cruelly overtaken by penury, sprang up also in 1933 the crusade of the novelist Upton Sinclair. Having run unsuccessfully for governor as a Socialist back in 1926, he turned now to the more reassuring Democratic label, offering his candidacy because, as he said, "I saw old people dying of slow starvation, and children by the tens of thousands growing up stunted by the diseases of malnutrition." These conditions he described in a book *I, Governor of California and How I Ended Poverty* (1933), which sold nearly a million copies and helped to finance his race. Sinclair advocated stiffer income and inheritance taxes, a tax on idle land, a fifty-dollar monthly pension to needy persons over sixty, and a huge network of coöperatives to stimulate production, consumption and employment. His slogan was "End Poverty in California," happily shortened to EPIC. When he led the field in the primary election, his campaign could no longer be dismissed as a joke, and only by the most strenuous efforts of the press, movie industry and conservative citizens was he nosed out in November, 1934, by his Republican opponent Frank Merriam. The movement quickly collapsed, leaving in its wake the mute evidence of EPIC cafes, New Economy barbershops and Plenty-for-All stores, which long survived in backwater communities.

In January, 1934, while EPIC was still soaring, a simpler panacea for prosperity, compounded exclusively for the aged, issued from the same region with Dr. Francis E. Townsend's incorporation of Old Age Revolving Pensions, Limited. The founder, a gaunt physician who had struggled long years homesteading in Kansas and doctoring folk in the Black Hills, had finally migrated to Long Beach, California, as assistant health officer. Under the watchword "Youth for work and age for leisure," he proposed that the proceeds from a universal two-per-cent transactions tax should pay two hundred dollars monthly to every unemployed person of good character over sixty years of age, this stipend to be wholly spent before the next pay day. The notion of rapidly circulating money —"the myth of velocity," skeptical economists called it—strongly appealed to the naïve, despite statisticians' figures that nearly half the national income would be required to meet Townsend's demands on behalf of eight or ten million persons. Moreover, like all sales taxes, this levy would fall most heavily upon wage-earners.*

* Townsend claimed that his crusade was inspired by the sight of three elderly women rummaging in garbage cans; but probably he was imitating a proposal current in Seattle to give the old a pension for compulsory spending. R. L. Neuberger and K. Loe, "The Old People's Crusade," *Harper's Mag.*, CLXXII (1936), 427; Carey McWilliams, *Southern California Country* (N.

The Townsend crusade gained recruits from the defeated EPIC forces, spreading over the nation and raising almost a million dollars in two years by donations, card parties, dances, quilting bees, raffles and box suppers, as well as by subscriptions to the *Townsend Weekly,* where homey inspiration was interlarded with advertisements for trusses and artificial teeth. This agitation undoubtedly speeded passage of the social-security act in 1935. The next year the founder claimed five million members. Some politicians in both parties hopefully plumped for it, but the 1936 presidential election demonstrated that the Union party, formed by Townsendites and other irregulars with Congressman William Lemke as their nominee, could command no better than nine hundred thousand votes. The fact that Roosevelt and most New Dealers opposed the scheme had disheartened followers of little faith. A congressional investigation of Dr. Townsend and his conviction early in 1937 of contempt of the House helped also to discredit the movement, suggesting that a pathetic crusade had fallen prey to demagogy and the profit motive.

Its decay provided the humus from which sprang another California mushroom of hope and heresy. The promoters were more worldly than Dr. Townsend and essentially cynical: a technocrat named Roy Owens, the brothers Lawrence and Willis Allen (who gained apparently the lion's share of the proceeds) and one Robert Noble (who later went to prison for fascist agitation in the Second World War). This was the so-called "Thirty Dollars Every Thursday" plan, which promised "Ham and Eggs" to all the faithful. Specifically, it would give to every unemployed Californian over fifty a pension, to be financed from the circulation of one-dollar warrants on which each holder must affix a two-cent stamp every week prior to spending it. Narrowly defeated in

Y., 1946), 299. For the plan and its fallacies, see H. S. Pritchett, "The Old Age Pension as Related to American Life," Carnegie Foundation for the Advancement of Teaching. *13th Ann. Rep.* (1935), 15-26.

the state elections of 1938, "Ham and Eggs" won a million signatures for a special referendum the next year only to fail more decisively. Henceforth the movement rapidly ebbed. In comparison, a scheme rejected by the Ohio voters in November, 1939, seemed almost pedestrian. Devised by the Reverend Herbert S. Bigelow, ex-congressman of Cincinnati, it promised all the unemployed over sixty fifty dollars a month, the sum to be raised by heavier state income taxes and a two-per-cent land tax on real estate valued at more than twenty thousand dollars an acre.

Among stump speakers and radio orators dangling utopian bait in the waters of discontent, none attracted more notice than Senator Huey Long and the Reverend Charles E. Coughlin. Long, scion of a Louisiana family of poor whites, had worked up from peddling patent medicines and lard substitutes to become one of the shrewdest lawyers in the South, publicizing his early battles with Standard Oil, and as governor seeking particularly to benefit the small independent farmers with better roads and bridges, free school-books and reduced power and telephone rates. In the course of doing so, however, the "Kingfish"—a title he borrowed from the radio comedians "Amos 'n' Andy"—built up a ruthless political machine which destroyed democratic processes in Louisiana.

Long confidently expected to be president, and the title of his autobiography, *Every Man a King* (1933), which he claimed to have lifted from William Jennings Bryan, was matched in significance by its sequel, published after his assassination in his new state capitol in September, 1935, *My First Days in the White House.** His bid for that office took

* According to Long, "William Jennings Bryan said: 'Behold a Republic! where every man is a King, but no man wears a crown.' " *Every Man a King* (New Orleans, 1933), 297. Carleton Beals's biography of Long in 1935 and H. T. Kane's in 1941 ascribe this quotation to the Cross of Gold speech, but actually the nearest resemblance seems to occur in Bryan's speech "Imperialism" in the 1900 campaign, where he spoke of "a republic in which every citizen

the form of the "Share-Our-Wealth" campaign, a vague scheme for redistributing enormous fortunes so that every "deserving family" in the nation might have sufficient income to own a car, a home and a radio over which presumably it should hearken to the master's voice. A *Fortune* survey in July, 1935, indicated the deep root which this proposal had struck, particularly in the Middle West and still more on the Pacific Coast; and a nation-wide poll by the Democratic national committee shortly before his death suggested he might gain three or four million votes on a third-party ticket.* Beyond much question Huey Long's pyrotechnics helped passage of the wealth-tax act in August, 1935. Indeed, stealing the thunder of demagogues and scaling down their promises to workable size became the strategy of the New Deal in its middle years.

A comparable messiah in the North was Father Coughlin, Catholic priest of Royal Oak, Michigan, who gradually revealed himself a Jew baiter and Nazi apologist. From radio sermons Coughlin passed in early depression years to politics, extolling the New Deal with cries of "Roosevelt or Ruin!" In 1934 he organized the National Union for Social Justice, advocating the nationalization of banks and credit, utilities and natural resources. In January, 1935, he began flaying the administration for turning "its precious attention to foreign affairs while we are still surrounded with domestic turmoil" and directed the Union's boasted nine million members to swamp Congress with protests against joining the World Court—with results that probably played some part in the Senate's negative action. Coughlin openly became a scoffer at democracy ("the magic of numbers"), and in 1938 formed an anti-Semitic organization called the Christian

is a sovereign, but in which no one cares or dares to wear a crown." W. J. and Mary B. Bryan, *Memoirs of William Jennings Bryan* (Phila., 1925), 501.

* J. A. Farley, *Behind the Ballots* (N. Y., 1938), 249-250. A minor anti-Semite and frank admirer of Hitler's Reich was the Reverend Gerald L. K. Smith, sometime Shreveport pastor, chief organizer under Long of "Share-Our-Wealth" and his would-be heir.

Front, which spread to many cities and, when war came, took a stand of benevolent neutrality toward the Axis. With his New York counterpart, Father Edward L. Curran of the *Brooklyn Tablet*, Coughlin represented the fascist wing of Catholicism, but as the true nature of his opinions grew clearer, his popular influence waned.

Whatever evil they did, these salesmen of panaceas, even the most cold-blooded and cynical of them helped in their fashion to hasten the adoption of social security. Other influences were at work, however: European example; the social conscience sensitized by depression; the proof that many individuals would not save systematically unless compelled; the belief that unemployment was just another type of industrial hazard, whose whole cost the victim should not have to bear alone; and a spreading conviction that industry ought not to exploit labor for huge profits during flush times, then throw upon society the whole burden of unemployment and threadbare old age. In June, 1934, the president appointed a committee to draft a program, and fruition came with the signing of the social-security law on August 14, 1935.

For the aged it provided two types of assistance. An annuity system, the only feature of the act directly administered from Washington, offered benefits upon retirement at the age of sixty-five, based upon earnings under the law. Employer and employee matched funds; and participation was compulsory save for public servants, domestics, casual laborers, merchant seamen and employees in charitable, religious and educational institutions. By 1940 fifty-two million citizens had each his "social-security number" under this plan.* Income from savings and investments did not prevent the drawing of benefits, but any employment paying over fifteen dollars a month did, which meant that, since all annuity pay-

---

* A provision to raise the rate of contribution from one per cent of wages to an ultimate three per cent in 1949 was not carried out, the contribution being "frozen" at the minimum figure.

ments were modest, this provision sometimes proved irksome.

The second kind of assistance consisted of grants for persons already past their earning power or outside the pale of the annuity system. The federal government offered to collaborate with the states for the relief of indigent old age, up to a combined total originally set at thirty dollars monthly and later raised to forty. By the close of the decade nearly two million elderly poor were enrolled under state systems. Payments, however, averaged only twenty dollars over the nation, with six Southern commonwealths granting mere pittances and California at the other extreme offering close to the maximum. Pensioners in this category, augmented by fifty thousand blind, and nine hundred thousand crippled, neglected and dependent children entitled to similar benefits, occasioned the chief expense of the social-security act to the national government.

Still another provision of the act set in motion unemployment insurance. To create the necessary reserve a three-percent federal pay-roll tax was levied upon employers (with the exceptions named above, and those having less than eight employees). Against ninety per cent of this tax the employer might credit contributions paid into an approved state unemployment compensation system—thus in effect forcing state compliance—while the federal government made the major rules and paid the administrative costs. Benefit payments varied according to previous earnings and length of employment, ranging between about five and fifteen dollars weekly and limited in most cases to a fourteen or sixteen-week period. Quitting work voluntarily, discharge for misconduct and, in many states, striking disqualified the employee; also, if a suitable new job were rejected, the benefit ceased.

The act bore assault from various quarters. Many critics looked askance at the huge reserves anticipated from these levies, with billions in purchasing power withdrawn from the volume of circulating money. Others attacked the federal bookkeeping which used these funds for paying current government expenses, leaving I.O.U.'s in the reserve account. A company of liberals who had battled long for social security assailed the act as invoking a hodgepodge of forty-eight state systems, and some doubted whether unemployment funds accumulated in the heavily industrialized states, whose economy always stood in precarious equilibrium, would be adequate to meet a real test.*

A minor crisis was weathered successfully in late 1937 and early 1938. In August began a business recession which anti-New Dealers promptly dubbed the "Roosevelt depression." It came about partly because of sharp retrenchment, at their insistence, in the WPA and other agencies of federal spending. Additional factors were stock speculation, overproduction and big inventories that outpaced purchasing power, contraction of credit under more stringent bank-reserve requirements, labor troubles and business's continued distrust of the New Deal. The president's census in the autumn disclosed nearly six million totally unemployed, two million jobless save for relief work and three and a quarter million partially employed. This was better than the fifteen or sixteen million of March, 1933, though not spectacularly so. That the hardest problem of all, unemployment, had not been mastered by the New Deal, was plain.

The general economic structure of the country, however, proved distinctly firmer than five years before, as Roosevelt noted in observing that "banking and business and farming are not falling apart like the one-hoss shay as they did in the

---

* Eleanor L. Dulles, "Financing Old-Age Insurance," Am. Acad. of Polit. and Social Sci., *Annals*, CCII, 176-183, reviews a considerable body of this criticism but thinks it unwarranted. An attack by a social-security pioneer is Abraham Epstein's "Our Social Insecurity Act," *Harper's Mag.*, CLXXII (1935), 55-66. A more temperate critic is P. H. Douglas, *Social Security in the United States* (rev. edn., N. Y., 1939), chap. ix.

terrible winter of 1932-1933." The president and Congress shifted the whole spending program back into high gear early in 1938, increasing outlays by about five billion for the WPA, PWA and lending activities of the RFC, and the edge of individual misery was further blunted by the social-security act. Thirty states in 1938 paid approximately four hundred million dollars to their unemployed. Presently recovery began once more to flow and, save for a milder setback early in 1939, carried the nation's economy steadily forward into the full employment of the war years.*

Meanwhile, modifications of the social-security act occurred. Amendments at the close of the decade added benefits for survivors and dependents of annuity policyholders, and by attaching the United States Employment Service to the Social Security Board enmeshed job insurance with job placement. The Federal Security Agency, formed in 1939 to embrace also the Office of Education, Public Health Service, the NYA and CCC, henceforth became the chief instrument for federal welfare activities.

Whatever economic ups and downs the future might bring, the thirties had firmly planted in American life the principle of social security. A few reactionaries, like the radio commentator Upton Close, might lament the passing of the glorious spirit of risk which had inspired the frontiersmen, but most citizens felt otherwise. A Gallup poll in 1938 found that no less than nine out of ten persons approved old-age pensions. However critical of ways and means, even the party of the opposition in its national platforms acknowledged that social security had come to stay. It was no coincidence that the number of social workers almost doubled between 1930 and 1940, most notably in the huge industrial

* With rapid growth in the number covered by unemployment insurance, the volume of benefit payments of all kinds rose until the end of 1940, then rapidly ebbed in the year 1941 when better wages and opportunities for defense jobs bred increasing reluctance to retire at sixty-five. *International Year Book for 1941*, 596.

Fontana Dam, one of the largest in the world.

A demonstration farm on the left, an old eroded one on the right.

Transforming the Tennessee Valley.

Scholars, gathered at the Harvard Tercentenary from all over the world, attested the value of free inquiry for civilization.

states of New York, California, Pennsylvania, Illinois and Ohio.*

A Martian observer might have concluded that social welfare was the new American religion. With eyes upon the mounting ascendency of the social—or socialistic—gospel over formal theology, Paul Hutchinson, managing editor of the *Christian Century*, in 1937 cried emotionally, "It is either on to Moscow, or back to sin!" This development was less the cutting of a new channel than the deepening of an established one. An exhaustive study of the church and society, carried on from 1920 to 1934 by the Institute of Social and Religious Research, repeatedly stressed the trend of Protestantism toward social interpretations of the faith and the ministry of human welfare. Similarly, American Catholics put forth new efforts in response to the principles of social justice expounded by Pope Pius XI in his encyclical *"Quadrigesimo Anno"* (1931). while the Central Conference of American Rabbis in the next year drafted its "Program of Social Justice" and the Federal Council of Churches reaffirmed its stand on collective bargaining and social security.

Clerics seeking a message for the age were apt to take their cue from John A. Ryan, John Haynes Holmes, Ernest F. Tittle, Ralph W. Sockman or Harry Emerson Fosdick. A poll of nearly twenty thousand ministers in 1934 disclosed that nearly three out of five favored a "drastically reformed capitalism" and almost a third socialism. Social and economic themes waxed in popularity as sermon topics, and prayer meetings often turned into discussion groups for canvassing "problems in human relationships."

In early depression days the churches turned actively to feeding and clothing the poor, but as public agencies shouldered the burden, they tended to slacken their efforts. As a

---

* By contrast, the number of nurses gained by little more than a fifth, while teachers lost one per cent and the ranks of clergymen shrank by ten per cent. *Social Work Year Book for 1945*, 448.

result, a certain disenchantment arose among the destitute with churches and semireligious bodies like the Y. M. C. A. The Catholics kept more successfully in touch with their unemployed than did most Protestant denominations, but the Mormons in Utah achieved a conspicuous record. Proudly refusing federal aid and not a little wary of New Deal financing, they made each "ward" of Latter Day Saints responsible for its needy, and higher units came to the rescue when local capacity was overtaxed. The chief aim was to make the family self-sustaining through such means as coöperatives, colonization schemes, home canning and handicrafts and the vigilance of church employment agencies.

Financially the Depression put the majority of Protestant churches "in the most desperate plight in their history." Part of it was due to indebtedness contracted in the flush 1920's to build million-dollar edifices and some multimillion-dollar apartment-hotel-churches, with swimming pools, recreation halls and other resources which might better have been communal than sectarian. Now collections sharply declined, falling almost half between 1930 and 1934. Urban ministers' salaries were pared to the bone, while in rural areas and villages many flocks dispensed with a "regular" preacher.

Toward the fact of the national economic disaster religious attitudes varied. Fundamentalists of the Moody Bible Institute and their affiliates—millenarianists who had hailed the First World War as the beginning of the end—now saw the catastrophe of world-wide unemployment as a similar portent. Catholic teaching ran less to the apocalyptic than the purgatorial, stressing the theme of present suffering to be rewarded in the life to come. Sterner preceptors of Rome saw depression as a healthy astringent to the lush pagan materialism of American life. In general, however, acceptance of the Depression as a punishment for sins, national and personal, arose from the Protestant pulpit. Hosts of preachers, editors of evangelical periodicals and pious business men like

Roger Babson avowed that depressions came because men forsook Christ to follow selfish ends.

It was freely predicted that hardship would lead Americans back to the faith of their fathers, but in fact no wave of revivalism, wholesale conversion or even increased church attendance occurred outside the pale of certain new and eccentric cults. Lack of decent clothes to wear and of money to drop into the collection plate—though many churches discontinued "free-will offerings"—discouraged even normal habits of churchgoing. And upon those in whom such habits were weak, the growing secularization of the Sabbath exercised its pull toward the new municipal swimming pool, golf links or tennis courts laid out by WPA labor. Women's interest in church work was reported in 1931-1932 to have reached a new low, doubtless under pressure from vocational and other worldly pursuits, while periodical literature also mirrored the declining prestige of organized Christianity. Even in the village and small town, where lay the core of evangelical strength, institutional religion seemed on the wane, with falling attendance and donations and among the leaders a planless bewilderment in the vortex of social forces.

Between 1930 and 1940 the nation's churches lost twenty-seven members per thousand of population, a total deficit of almost three million. According to a Gallup poll in 1939, half the people attended worship less often than their parents and less than a fifth exceeded their parents. Asserting that earlier crises had evoked a contrary reaction, the editor of a popular Protestant journal found the difference lay in a relatively new conviction that so-called economic laws, unlike the laws of Nature, are man-made and therefore can be cured by human initiative rather than by prayer or penitence.

Youth, little schooled in the old-time gospel, was probably the least devout group. While a majority still clung to nominal church membership, scarcely more than a third were actively interested or considered religion a helpful or vital part of their lives. A survey in 1934 reported lower classmen in college more prone to belief than juniors and seniors, and that of the faculty the less eminent scientists numbered more believers than their colleagues—although physicists and like specialists, presumably knowing least about society and the mind of man, took more stock in religion than did biologists, social scientists and psychologists. Inconclusive though such data were, they served as straws in the wind indicating a continued drift away from institutional creeds.

Religion as an inner experience—fruition of America's long tutelage to the Protestant spirit—was probably much less impaired. Upon the highest intellectual level it still flourished, for example, in the writings of the theologian Reinhold Niebuhr, whose Gifford lectures at Edinburgh appeared in 1941 as the first volume of *The Nature and Destiny of Man*. Here he expressed a rather somber view of man caught between the upper and nether millstones of his supernaturalism and his naturalism, the latter often deluding him into erecting "idols" like rigid systems of philosophy or social schemes for perfecting the race, though Niebuhr himself paradoxically supported liberal ideas. Basically he taught—in the tradition of Denmark's Kierkegaard, rediscovered by intellectuals in this generation through the writings of Karl Barth—that religious faith has no connection with and requires no verification by reason; God exists, and man's contact with Him is life's most certain and significant fact, even though man cannot conceive God as He truly is. Under long depressions and times of frustration, religious philosophy tends to magnify man's helplessness, looking to God for all strength and wisdom.

Upon the popular level religion found expression in the best-selling inspirational novels of the clergyman Lloyd Douglas, like *The Magnificent Obsession* (1929) and *The Green Light* (1935), and in such works as Henry C. Link's *The Return to Religion* (1936), which sought to endow men with a spiritual purpose against selfish immersion in the tide of circumstance. A cherished American tradition was thus streamlined to an age of depression and incertitude. Henry Wallace, brash oracle on many subjects, contributed *Statesmanship and Religion* (1934), while many of Franklin D. Roosevelt's public utterances rang the changes upon themes of human dignity, neighborliness and democracy as practical Christianity.* The president, an Episcopalian, stirred sectarian rivalry upon a single notable occasion. The announcement on December 24, 1939, of the precedent-shattering appointment of Myron C. Taylor, steel magnate and Episcopal layman, as the president's personal envoy to the Vatican under the crisis of war, provoked a storm in some Protestant circles.†

In general, partisan rivalry appeared on the decline. In 1929 the Congregationalists combined with their friends of the Christian Church. Ten years later the old *ante-bellum* rift between Northern and Southern branches of the Methodist Episcopal Church was healed by the union of these two with the Methodist Protestant wing. In 1940 the Reformed Church in the United States fused with the Evangelical Synod of North America. Late in the thirties a merger of the Episcopal with the Presbyterian Church was proposed, but opposition from High Churchmen in the one camp and rock-ribbed Calvinists in the other postponed accomplishment.

Short of the ultimate gesture of union, coöperation between faiths increased. In 1931 the National Catholic Welfare Conference, Federal Council of Churches and General Conference of Rabbis formed a Conference on the Permanent

---

* From the opening words of his first inaugural address concerning the "day of consecration," to such later allusions as in the annual message to Congress in 1939: "Religion, by teaching man his relationship to God, gives the individual a sense of his own dignity and teaches him to respect himself by respecting his neighbors." F. D. Roosevelt, *Public Papers and Addresses* (S. I. Rosenman, ed., N. Y., 1938-1941), VIII, 1.

† Thirty denominations or conferences vainly rebuked this alleged overture to Rome or asked Taylor's recall. *American Year Book for 1940,* 663.

Preventives of Unemployment, and three years later Catholics, Protestants and Jews organized a nation-wide Committee on Religion and Welfare Activity to support more effectually all religious agencies for social betterment. Despite occasional signs of ancient prejudice and friction among irreconcilable members of these doctrinal camps, brave efforts went forward toward common understanding, largely under the banners of religious liberty and minority rights, which elsewhere in the world were being trampled underfoot.

An array of minor religious cults attracted notice. The so-called Oxford Group movement, sired by Dr. Frank N. Buchman and cradled in the jazz age, undertook on the eve of the Second World War a great publicity campaign for "Moral Rearmament," preaching (in the words of the founder) that "if men will be good, there will be no more wars." But the pacifism of "MRA" was soon overwhelmed by the world upheaval, and the Groups—which once boasted contact with such dissimilar figures as Neville Chamberlain and Heinrich Himmler—entered an eclipse.

A more hardy and primitive opposition to the coming struggle arose from Jehovah's Witnesses, who declined either to salute the flag or serve in the armed forces. They became a storm center in communities ranging from Maine to Texas and often the victims of mob violence. Started earlier in the century by "Judge" Joseph F. Rutherford, a Missourian, the Witnesses developed into a folk sect not unlike that of the Millerites and first-generation Mormons of a hundred years before. Appealing to the poor and frustrated, they "made hate into a religion," attacking Catholicism with singular ferocity, courting martyrdom by defying civil authority and preaching the imminent Last Judgment. From door to door they played gramophone records of sermons, and on street corners hawked or gave away tracts. In the year 1939 their forty thousand field workers distributed over fifteen million documents and six million copies of the *Watchtower* and similar periodicals. The gathering storms of war failed to shake their conscientious objections, stirring fresh outbreaks against them and presenting the Supreme Court with a long series of civil-liberty suits.

Perhaps the gaudiest cult was that of the Negro evangelist Father Divine (born George Baker of Georgia) who, after years of obscurity on Long Island, entered Harlem in triumph at the depth of the Depression in 1932 to establish his reign under the credo that "the real God is the God who feeds us," and the incantation, "Peace, it's wonderful!" Before long his "Heavens" spread from Manhattan to the colored population of other cities, offering devotees the benefits of a common purse and shrewd business management and providing ample food and the shelter of country estates and resort hotels.*

Equally delirious was the Great I Am movement, fathered by a self-styled mystic named Guy W. Ballard shortly after he settled at Los Angeles in 1932. Offering to unlock the wonder-working secrets of the medieval necromancer Saint Germain and other "ascended Grand Masters," he promised his followers healing, wealth and power. At its peak the movement claimed a third of a million converts in a dozen major cities, but the trial of its leaders in the early forties upon charges of using the mails to defraud brought exposure, ridicule and decline.† A kindred enthusiasm called Mankind United, devised in 1934 by another California seer named Arthur Bell, blended spiritual magic with pseudoscience. Its proposal to usher in a fabulous age of freedom from want and luxury for all by tapping sources of primal energy at the earth's center attracted in its heyday about fourteen thousand believers. This group, too, ran afoul of the law, for shortly after the Japanese attack on Pearl Harbor the leaders were convicted of violating the sedition statutes.

* R. A. Parker, *Incredible Messiah* (Boston, 1937).

† The Supreme Court ruled in 1944 that the defendants' lack of good faith in their own claims might be challenged, though the truth or falsity of miraculous healing and alleged communication with the spirit world was irrelevant to the case. United States *v.* Ballard, 322 U. S., 78.

The growing secularization of American life for millions made security here and now seem more real than those rewards which the Communists derisively termed pie in the sky. But for many the two sorts of hunger were inevitably mingled. And so these will-o'-the-wisps of cultism in the thirties are perhaps as revelatory of the popular mind as were more practical and material achievements in the domain of social security.

CHAPTER XI

THE NEW LEISURE CLASS

ON no aspect of American life did the Depression have a more striking effect than the use of leisure. Net sales of amusement and sporting goods dropped from half a billion dollars in 1929 to little over a quarter of a billion in 1933. Federal taxes paid by recreational groups—city athletic clubs, country clubs, golf and tennis clubs—declined more than half between 1930 and 1934. Golf clubs alone lost about a million members, and under acute financial stress many private links were sold and converted to the daily-fee system of operation. Social clubs and fraternal organizations appeared to share the same eclipse.

On the other hand, simple home games—jigsaw puzzles, "monopoly," checkers, chess, dominoes, backgammon, pitching quoits and horseshoes—became immensely popular whether as time killers or diversions from anxiety. Roosevelt's best-known diversion, stamp collecting—not unrelated to the fecundity of his administration in issuing about a hundred new varieties during its first five years—publicized a pastime which recruited the number of philatelists from an estimated two million to nine. Bridge, for low stakes or none, gained under the fillip of novelty lent by the variant called contract. Ely Culbertson, author of best sellers on this pastime, estimated that despite the hard times the nation spent ten million dollars on bridge lessons alone in 1931 and, including purchase of playing cards, nearly a hundred million in all. In suburbia, staying at home promoted a renascence of badminton, ping-pong and *al fresco* suppers and stimulated hobbies like amateur carpentry, mechanics, pigeon

219

racing and others reported on a popular radio program called
"Hobby Lobby."

The lunatic fringes of sport dear to the twenties, such as
marathon dancing and flagpole sitting, persisted but with
diminishing vitality. A brief vogue for being buried alive
in 1934-1935 and a passing collegiate ardor for swallowing
goldfish, begun by a Harvard freshman in 1939 and carried
to strenuous heights by a Chicago student who devoured
three phonograph records, seemed afterthoughts from a
vanished day. Equally ephemeral was the passion for miniature golf which in the summer of 1930 mushroomed into a
hundred-million-dollar business, but quickly ebbed, leaving
the face of the nation pitted with greens made of dyed cot-
tonseed. The mid-thirties witnessed fashions for slightly de-
mented parlor games: a sign language called "handies"
favored in 1935, a routine of outrageous puns in 1936
prefaced by the words "Knock, knock—who's there?" and
a modified version of the charade called "The Game" eman-
ating from Hollywood two years later.

Of collegiate sports football in particular displayed a new
sobriety. In 1931, for the first time in years, the receipts of
the "Big Ten" fell below two million dollars; soon it was
remarked that "students in general seem less excited than
formerly over the outcome of games." With easy money no
longer lining the pockets of alumni, deliriously alcoholic
week-ends declined no less visibly than did the "buying" of
promising athletes, while the stadiums built in the twenties
by huge bond issues now hardly met the interest on their
indebtedness. Some excellent teams were turned out, though,
and one of the most famous pigskin heroes, Byron ("Whiz-
zer") White of the University of Colorado, combined his
all-American rank with a Phi Beta Kappa key and election
to a Rhodes Scholarship. With an audacity unthinkable to
most, the University of Chicago in 1940 capped its heresies
by abolishing intercollegiate contests. From the decade's
middle years, however, professional football with a spirit

frankly uncollegiate won favor in many cities as a spectator
sport.

Professional baseball remained a hardy perennial, followed
over the radio by millions, its stars like "Pepper" Martin,
Lou Gehrig and Joe DiMaggio shining on every sports page
in the land. In the year 1939, observed as the centenary of
the National Game, the New York Yankees set an all-time
record by winning their fourth straight World Series only
to lose in the next year to the Cincinnati Reds. In 1940 and
again in 1941 the Brooklyn Dodgers after twenty years'
obscurity emerged as challengers for national recognition,
and with their colorful style and cocky self-assertion excited
popular imagination as no other team had ever done.

Heavyweight boxing, moribund since Gene Tunney's retirement in 1928, woke to new life with the advent of Joe
Louis, a powerful Negro youth who came up from Alabama
by way of the automobile factories of Detroit to garner an
almost unbroken string of victories. His knockout of Max
Baer in New York's Yankee Stadium in 1935 drew the first
million-dollar gate since 1927. Bested by Max Schmeling
in 1936, the "Brown Bomber" so mauled his adversary in
the first round of a return engagement two years later that
Nazi Germany's premier athlete had to be hospitalized. After
flooring "Jim" Braddock in 1937 Louis possessed the world's
championship in a grasp so firm that public interest and the
gate receipts once more began to flag. Meanwhile juvenile
talent in the ring was fostered by the Golden Gloves tourna-
ment, which spread from national to international competition, and furnished the milieu for one of Clifford Odets's
successful plays, "Golden Boy" (1937).

In two other sports the retirement from amateur competition of old masters let down the bars to a host of younger
aspirants. After setting an all-time record in 1930 by winning the American and British amateur and open golf
championships, Robert T. ("Bobby") Jones left the field
to such contenders as Johnny Goodman, Olin Dutra, Lawson

Little and Byron Nelson. In tennis William T. Tilden by turning professional in 1931 relinquished the spotlight to youths like Ellsworth Vines, Donald Budge and Frank Parker, while in the women's ranks Alice Marble succeeded to the crown of Helen Wills Moody. After long holding the Davis Cup, probably the most famous international trophy, the United States lost it to Australia in 1939, just as the curtain of war fell upon competitive tennis.

The Depression and New Deal not only deflated costly sports and athletic spectacles but also fostered mass participation. In seeking to redress past neglect the conscience of the thirties considered the needs of low-income groups, particularly the growing generation. With municipal budgets badly slashed, however, the authorities could hardly rise to the occasion. The supervision of many playgrounds would have broken down completely in 1932-1933 save for the volunteering of some citizens as recreation leaders aided by a skeleton staff of paid workers. From 1933 onward, however, the start of huge public-works programs gave the cause of mass recreation a propulsion never before known.

The initial emphasis fell upon parks and forest reserves, whose growth, according to a National Park Service official in 1935, was advanced a normal half-century by the first two years of CCC labor. Lakes were created, cabins built, trails carved to mountain peaks. In July, 1933, federal funds made possible the purchase of a vast area in the Great Smoky Mountains as one of the most attractive national parks. The next spring the Biological Survey, headed by an intransigent Republican but ardent conservationist, the cartoonist J. N. Darling ("Ding"), persuaded Congress to set up fish and game sanctuaries in the national forests.

Under such pace-setting and the availability of CCC labor to enhance state and community parks, local governments awoke to the opportunity. Virginia, West Virginia, South Carolina, Mississippi, New Mexico, Nevada and Montana all acquired their first state parks during the initial two years of the New Deal. California created seven new ones in 1933 alone, and Texas set aside nearly a quarter of a million acres in the Big Bend of the Rio Grande River. In brief, more than six hundred thousand acres were added to state preserves between 1933 and 1936, while the annual federal purchase of forest land, mainly for parks and wild-life refuges, rose from a pre-Roosevelt average of about half a million acres to two million in 1935.

The public was not slow to accord approval. In 1934, the first year national parks kept travel statistics, six million visitors were reported; by 1938 the total surpassed sixteen million. Facilities like camp sites and picnic grounds and the spread of the youth-hostel movement fostered hiking as a pastime. By 1937 in New England alone seventy-six hostels at fifteen-mile intervals stretched along a thousand-mile chain of trails. The rise of the American Camping Association was another significant development, as was the formation of the Cub Scouts, an adjunct to the Boy Scouts designed to promote outdoor life and manliness among lads aged seven to ten.

For both youth and adults winter sports increased in favor. In 1930 a New England railroad scheduled the first snow train. Two years later the winter Olympics at Lake Placid kindled widespread interest, and this fact, coupled with the park facilities and ski runs and jumps built by the CCC on the public domain and with commercial ventures like the Union Pacific's well-advertised Sun Valley in Idaho, resulted in such trains carrying tens of thousands out of Boston, New York, Pittsburgh, Chicago, Salt Lake City, Portland, San Francisco and Los Angeles.

Nor did urban recreation fail to benefit. Between 1930 and 1940 the number of cities reporting parks grew from nine hundred to almost fifteen hundred, their acreage from three hundred thousand to nearly half a million. During the last five years of the decade attendance at playgrounds doubled, at swimming centers almost doubled and at picnic centers increased tenfold. Here, too, the New Deal contributed funds and labor. The PWA spent over forty million dollars building athletic facilities under local supervision; and the NYA with a much smaller budget in 1937 reported that sixteen thousand of its employees were improving parks, while fifteen thousand served as leaders in crafts, dancing, drama, music and the like.

The greatest benefactor, the WPA, constructed tens of thousands of swimming pools and tennis courts, laid out or improved hundreds of municipal parks, golf courses and playing fields and, in collaboration with schools and extension services, supervised innumerable sports programs, employing more than forty thousand persons as of June, 1939, in the rôle of recreation leaders. About half this recreation program dealt with physical exercise, including softball, archery and shuffleboard. The rest lent great encouragement to the depression-sired revival of square dances, folk dances, singing games and amateur drama.

New Deal expenditures, involving at least one and a half billion dollars for permanent recreation facilities, were by no means solely responsible for increasing the nation's play life. Many municipalities took a vigorous stand. For example, when Fiorello LaGuardia early in 1934 became mayor of New York, he and his indefatigable park commissioner, Robert Moses, launched a program, supported by local and federal funds and the sinews of seventy thousand relief workers, which started by destroying fashionable Central Park Casino and building on its site a children's playground. Moses drained the swamps of Flushing Meadow to make a World's Fair ground, and cleansed sewage-polluted waters and outfitted Jones Beach on Long Island for the accommodation of more than a hundred thousand people for swimming and sun bathing.

The greatest good of the greatest number was the new keynote of recreation. In most cities the formal landscape park, prized by the later nineteenth and early twentieth centuries, sacrificed some of its scenic perfection to make way for pools, playgrounds, bridle paths and the like: the sign "Keep Off the Grass" grew rarer. Similar democratization filtered into organized games. The national lawn-tennis and golf associations began sponsoring public-parks championships, the winners playing in the national finals. In 1939 the tennis champion was Seymour Greenberg, a Jewish lad from Chicago, who thus obtained a place on the Junior Davis Cup squad, while the victor in golf was Andy Swedzko, a Pittsburgh steelworker.

Minor fashions came and went, such as the cycling revival of 1933-1935, which temporarily boosted the annual output of bicycles above the half-million mark for the first time since 1899 and, incidentally, helped introduce women's slacks. The firm grip of the automobile, however, was not to be dislodged. In 1935 no fewer than thirty-five million vacationers were still thronging the highways. The tourist camp, catering to purses from those of "Okies" up to wayfarers desiring promenade terraces and dancing pavilions, continued to flourish until the advent of gasoline restrictions late in 1941. A Kentucky commercial traveler named Duncan Hines sold hundreds of thousands of his guides to good restaurants and lodgings along the highway. Despite the appeal of new models with draft ventilators, sloping radiators, free wheeling, "airflow" design, hydraulic brakes and hydromatic gears, numberless Americans clung to old cars longer than ever before. In all, over thirty million cars and trucks were in use by the close of the era.*

For a time the innovation of the trailer looked portentous. In 1929 a bacteriologist named Arthur G. Sherman built a house on wheels to be towed behind his car, made several for his neighbors and exhibited one at the 1930 Detroit Auto-

---

* The production in 1929 of over five and a half million cars and trucks fell to below one and a half million in 1932, then commenced a slow climb to regain predepression figures by 1937. World Almanac for 1941, 587, which reported the world total of automobiles at only forty-five million.

mobile Show. Competitors quickly entered the field, and by
1936 fifty thousand a year were rolling off production lines,
costing six or seven hundred dollars apiece and containing
cooking as well as sleeping units. Many homemade ones also
joined the highway procession. To the restless and uprooted,
seeking adventure or a job and wary of taxes and rent, this
self-sufficient vehicle held the lure of house boat or tramp
steamer. By the summer of 1938, however, the novelty had
worn thin, and sales slumped badly.

The eclipse of the trailer, with its cumbrous sway on
curves and blocking of visibility, undoubtedly served the
interests of safety. That consideration needed every aid in an
era of increasing congestion and high speeds which exacted
an annual toll of forty thousand deaths and a million and a
quarter injuries, two thirds of them manifestly preventable.
A gory description of highway mortality, "—And Sudden
Death," written by J. C. Furnas for the *Reader's Digest* in
1935 and distributed also in four million reprints, had little
visible effect, for nearly two thousand more fatalities occurred in 1936 than the year before. After the attainment
of a record high in 1937 the accident rate fell somewhat for
the rest of the era, thanks probably to stiffer penalties for
lawbreakers, safe-driving pledges and local newspaper campaigns against "mixing alcohol and gasoline."

For many persons bus travel offered substantial savings
over rail fares, if at some sacrifice in comfort. A popular
movie, "It Happened One Night" (1934), presented such
overland journeys in romantic guise. The number of passengers, including children in school busses, rose from fewer
than one and three-quarter billion fares in 1933 to more
than four and three-quarter billion in 1941.

Passenger bus and freight van had made considerable inroads upon railway traffic even before the Depression struck.
With their overcapitalization the lines were caught short,
and between 1929 and 1933 both passenger and freight
revenues declined fifty per cent. In consequence almost a

third of the nation's total mileage tottered into receivership
or bankruptcy despite early and prolonged resuscitative efforts by the RFC. To stimulate patronage the Western companies shrewdly slashed passenger fares from 3.2 to 2 cents a
mile, with a fifty-per-cent gain in business. When Eastern
railroads seemed reluctant to follow suit, their hand was
forced in June, 1936, by the Interstate Commerce Commission, and the whole national picture brightened. Meanwhile,
public-works projects in many localities undertook to eliminate grade crossings for faster and also safer operation.

Seeking to make rail travel more alluring, the roads began
to adopt air conditioning. "Manufactured weather"—
promptly taken up by many shops and movie houses for the
comfort of patrons and by industrialists for the efficiency of
workers—developed into a seventeen-million-dollar annual
industry by 1935. Air-conditioned Pullmans and coaches
became standard equipment on all crack trains, vastly promoting seasonal travel in the South and arid Southwest and
on some roads increasing summer traffic by as much as a
fourth. Another improvement was the use of Diesel engines.
In 1934 the Union Pacific pioneered a complete Diesel-
powered train constructed of duralumin, and its competitor
on the Chicago-Denver run, the Burlington, quickly followed with the first of its flashing stainless-steel "Zephyrs."
These trains running at speeds up to ninety miles per hour
brought the Rocky Mountains within overnight range of
Chicago. Thereupon most of the big railroads went in
heavily for "streamlining," pervasively influencing automobile design as well.

Aviation underwent a far greater transformation. At the
start of this era the age of barnstorming, flying circuses and
sight-seeing tours from local airports was only just past its
prime; among the three and a half million Americans who
flew in 1929 the great majority went up for the thrill. Six
thousand planes were being manufactured a year, with sales
totaling eighty-seven million dollars. Depression brought a

temporary decrease, but by 1937 the business had rallied to reach an annual hundred and twenty-four million. The outbreak of the Second World War in Europe found the industry with a capacity of fifteen thousand planes a year, giving employment to fifty thousand workers. WPA and other expenditures on the construction of airports and landing strips then amounted to about a hundred and seventy-two million, which jumped another hundred million in 1941 alone.

In April, 1930, the Lindberghs set a dawn-to-dusk transcontinental record of fourteen and three quarters hours, and in 1931 Wiley Post and Harold Gatty rounded the globe in eight days and fifteen hours—records which by the close of the decade seemed primitive indeed, with flyers spanning the continent in seven hours and girdling the earth in less than four days. Not only the records but the heroes of yesteryear were gone, with Post, accompanied by the beloved humorist Will Rogers, a crash fatality of 1935 in Alaska, and Charles A. Lindbergh laboring under a cloud of isolationism and mystic racism.

These years saw other developments as well. A clash in 1934 between the Roosevelt administration and the nation's seventeen commercial air lines over mail contracts resulted in the army's disastrous attempt to fly the mail and then in the passage of an improved air-mail act in 1935. The next year the "China Clipper" made its initial flight to Manila and in 1939 passenger service was begun to Europe. Coast-to-coast travel in giant air cruisers at two hundred miles an hour, with overnight sleepers and navigation steadily improved by radio beacons, helped to make aviation no longer an adventure or amusement but the channel for a huge traffic, carrying by 1940 about three million passengers over a hundred and twenty million miles, along with fourteen million pounds of freight. Besides public carriers some sixteen thousand private planes were ranging the skies on the eve of the Second World War. Thanks in large part to the Civilian Pilot Training Program instituted in 1939 to teach college-age youths to fly, the number of certified civilian pilots, which stood at less than sixteen thousand in 1937, had by the end of 1941 attained a hundred thousand. The air-mindedness of young America, among students in manual-arts and engineering schools and amateur mechanics who a generation earlier would have tinkered with flivvers, forecast development of the world's largest aircraft plants and the servicing of the mightiest aërial fleet mobilized for that struggle.

Of the sedentary diversions of these years none surpassed that of listening to the radio. In 1929, when the cost still averaged over a hundred dollars, twelve million families owned receiving sets. The Depression not only brought lower prices but also great audiences with time to kill: four million families purchased radios during the abysmal years 1930-1932. By the beginning of 1940 twenty-eight million homes, or eighty-six per cent of the population, owned a total of forty-four million sets, with saturation nowhere in sight. By this means an increasing proportion of the people absorbed a varied fare of news, politics, advertising, information and entertainment. The Office of Radio Research, set up in 1937 by Rockefeller funds to study the impact of broadcasting upon American life, hopefully suggested that radio aided more than it impaired the reading habits of listeners. It was doubtful, however, that the place of reading in the home remotely rivaled the four-and-a-half hours during which the average household radio was in daily use.

According to the radio act of 1927 and the communications act of 1934 the air waves belonged to the public domain for use "in the public convenience, interest, and necessity." Stations were simply lessees of part of that dominion, whose limits were thought to be staked out irrevocably by the eighty-nine wave lengths possible for broadcasting without interference. But the number of practicable frequencies suddenly bade fair to multiply after the disclosure in 1935 by Professor Edwin H. Armstrong of Columbia of frequency modulation (FM), by which static could be eliminated as well as greater tonal fidelity achieved. In 1940 the Federal Communications Commission, a regulatory body set up by Congress in 1934, authorized commercial operation of FM stations.

The public's thirst for news analysis and clarification lent a new popularity to commentators—Raymond Gram Swing, H. V. Kaltenborn, Lowell Thomas, Gabriel Heatter and others—to whose opinions about the Munich crisis, the Sino-Japanese conflict, the invasion of Poland and the fall of France millions intently listened. Moreover, between 1932 and 1939 the volume of news carried by radio almost doubled. In the summer of 1939 a *Fortune* poll asking, "Which of the two—radio or newspaper—gives you news freer from prejudice?" reported fifty per cent for radio, seventeen for the press and almost a third undecided or disposed to give them parity.

Yet, in face of the world crisis, radio's policy often mirrored the timidity of owners and advertisers. Alexander Woollcott the "Town Crier" was taken off the air in 1935 by an uneasy sponsor after rude remarks about Hitler and Mussolini; Du Pont's excellent dramatizations of history, "The Cavalcade of America," officially eschewed all such issues as war and peace, the class struggle and religion; and a canvass by the FCC of all broadcasts during the first six months of 1941 revealed the curiously lackadaisical rôle played by local stations in educating the public against the day of military decision.

The New Deal's best radio propagandist was President Roosevelt himself, whose warm democratic salutation "My friends" had been adopted as early as his vain campaign for the vice-presidency in 1920. His direct, intimate appeal to the people built a personal leadership unprecedented in its influence; not infrequently fifty thousand letters a day followed a "fireside chat." Recordings of these speeches through the years show changes in Roosevelt's technique, from the old-fashioned sonorous style with oratorical pauses learned in preradio days, to a lower pitch and softer, relaxed, more engaging address better suited to the unseen audience.

That the radio had become an immense political force was being demonstrated in another way by the Axis dictators as well as by home-grown demagogues like Father Coughlin and Huey Long. Not only did it carry nuances and subtle emotion denied to print, but it tended to arrest in the listener those critical impulses that often led a reader to turn back to the dubious or imperfectly understood. Startling evidence of its hypnotic effect on the mass imagination was afforded by a broadcast of the young actor Orson Welles on the evening of October 30, 1938, a month after the Munich crisis. Based upon H. G. Wells's *War of the Worlds* and punctuated by announcements that should have carried reassurance, the sketch purported to describe a rocket-borne invasion of Martians, equipped with flame throwers and heat rays, who proceeded to ravage the New Jersey countryside until slain by the disease bacteria of this planet. Not pausing for that dénouement, at least a million auditors became upset or terror-stricken, many forsaking their homes afoot or by car in panic.

The potency of the air waves was not overlooked by the advertiser. While newspaper advertising never regained its 1929 peak of eight hundred million dollars, radio salesmanship mounted year by year until in 1941 it was doing a two-hundred-million-dollar business—over a third of that vouchsafed its competitor—with magazines occupying third place. Growing constantly more blatant, radio advertising featured the singing commercial, the middle commercial flanked by those incidental opening and closing plugs called by the trade "cowcatchers" and "hitchhikers," and the "give-away" to reward a listener's correct answer to a telephone call from the studio. The ratio of commercial to noncommercial or "sustaining" programs appeared steadily on the wane, advertisers' demands relegating some of the best public-service features to unpopular listening hours.

Helpless to throttle the radio as an advertising medium,

the newspaper press for a time tried to prevent its access to a regular flow of the world's news. In 1934, however, the feud was composed by the so-called press-radio agreement and formation of the Transradio Press Service, which outlasted that pact. At the same time newspapers rapidly increased their ownership of stations, sometimes monopolizing all the news outlets in a given community. Within the single year 1935 the number of stations so owned doubled, and by 1940 no less than a third of the nation's eight hundred licensed stations were tied in one way or another to newspapers. Concentration also characterized the national networks, whose slickly professional programs, originating chiefly in New York and Hollywood, were piped to local stations all over the land. Three big chains commanded the field: the National Broadcasting Company, whose Red and Blue networks in 1938 controlled a hundred and forty-eight stations by ownership or affiliation, the Columbia Broadcasting System with a hundred and fifteen, and Mutual (a newcomer dating from 1934) eighty-three.

Though educational programs were the exception rather than the rule, certain of them attained a nation-wide following, notably "The University of Chicago Round Table," "Invitation to Learning," "Science on the March" and "Art for Your Sake," which presented knowledge stripped of the husks of pedantry typical of old-fashioned lecture methods. In 1935 began the "Town Meeting of the Air," staging a brisk debate over current issues which sought to recapture the atmosphere of New England's historic institution. The perplexities of wealth and poverty, war and peace, stimulated the public forum not only on the ether but in other surroundings, including the "Town Hall" idea which spread in the thirties to cities in Ohio, Michigan, Illinois, Iowa, Texas and elsewhere. By 1936 the United States commissioner of education stated that, out of three hundred and fifty public forums regularly attracting half a million persons, more than two thirds had been started since the onset of the Great Depression.

Fashions in entertainment came and went. After the success in 1936 of "Professor Quiz," question-and-answer programs like "Information Please" and "The Quiz Kids" burgeoned mightily. Such unrehearsed contests reflected a vogue similar to that featuring sidewalk interviews, guessing games and amateur hours, with a large element of audience participation. The radio serial proved to be a universal favorite, illustrated early in the era by the vast popularity of "Amos 'n' Andy," blackface comedians whose voices could be heard of a summer evening echoing block after block as one walked the streets of any suburb, or the plenitude of "soap operas" which later in the decade came to rule the daytime hours, dedicated to the praise of soap flakes and washing powders between interstices of tears and laughter in their plots of homely romance.* For juveniles the decade's hero was the "Lone Ranger," who made his début in 1933—a stalwart without fear or vices, whose cry "Hi-Yo, Silver!" heralded his arrival upon that trusty steed to redress wrong and succor the weak. By the close of the era radio's best-known personality had come to be an impudent puppet named Charlie McCarthy, creation of the ventriloquist Edgar Bergen.

Music occupied over half of radio's daily log, and more of it than ever before was of high quality. In 1930 Columbia began its Sunday broadcasting of New York Philharmonic concerts; the following year the National Broadcasting Company launched its Saturday-afternoon series of grand operas from the Metropolitan; and in 1937 it persuaded the world-

---

* According to a Manhattan columnist, "Toni Jo Henry, a 26-year-old murdress, . . . told this interviewer about the thoughts of a condemned person. 'I'm worried a little about "Abie's Irish Rose," a radio serial,' she stated. 'Every day I used to listen to it. But they discontinued the serial till September. I won't be here in September.' The producers . . . are forwarding to Miss Henry a short synopsis of the story which will be broadcast in installments from September until June." "What Do We Know about Daytime Serial Listeners?" in P. F. Lazarsfeld and F. N. Stanton, eds., *Radio Research 1942-1943* (N. Y., 1944), 3-33.

famous conductor, Arturo Toscanini, to undertake a memorable series with its own symphony orchestra. Over ten million families, according to a 1939 estimate, listened to such music; a poll in this year indicated that, save on the farm and at the bottom of the economic scale, those who enjoyed "classical" music outnumbered those desiring exclusively "popular." When in 1940 the Metropolitan Opera Company in severe financial straits appealed to its invisible audience, they contributed a third of a million dollars to "save the Met."

Music appreciation in the home saw the performer's rôle steadily supplanted, however, by the auditor's. While the radio was outstripping even the phonograph in popularity, father's fiddle gathered dust, and in affluent homes the piano remained oftentimes as a piece of prestige furniture. In 1939 only sixteen million copies of sheet music were sold as compared with forty-five million records of popular melodies. The invasion of music by radio, whether "live" or "canned," was greater still though harder to measure, while the life expectancy of a popular song, under furious exploitation by the "Lucky Strike Hit Parade" and similar programs, grew vastly shorter.*

Both radio and phonograph fostered the continued popularity of dancing, which had swept the twenties under the heady inspiration of jazz, that powerful if almost indefinable rhythmic style. About 1931, when a popular song was urging the depressed to "wrap your troubles in dreams, and dream your troubles away," the plangent bravado of jazz temporarily faded from fashion before the soothing hypnotic strains of "sweet" bands like those of Guy Lombardo, Wayne King and Eddy Duchin. An advance-guardist of new

---

* Music publishers computed the lifetime of a preradio favorite at nearly two years as against four months or less under the constant titillation and quick satiety wrought by radio. Novelties like "The Music Goes Round and Round" (1935) and "Flat-Foot Floogie" (1938) wore out in from six to eight weeks, but ballads like "The Last Round-Up" (1933) enjoyed better than average durability.

modes in jazz who died in that year—the trumpeter Leon ("Bix") Beiderbecke—would later be recalled nostalgically by Dorothy Baker's fine novel of the artist as jazzman, *Young Man with a Horn* (1938).

Early in 1934, perhaps as a harbinger of recovery, the spirit of jazz was reborn, largely by the superb clarinet recordings and dance-band broadcasts of Benny Goodman, exponent of what European connoisseurs called *le jazz hot*. It soon gained a new name, swing. A more dynamic form of syncopation and superimposed rhythm, an intense yet easy floating that "gets there on time"—and in expert hands capable of rich improvisation—swing retained the essence of its parent, jazz. " 'Swing' is to jazz what the poetic spirit is to poetry," wrote one lyric journalist in the winter of 1935-1936 when "jam sessions" and Hot Clubs were springing up over the nation. An incidental term in high favor was "boogie-woogie," signifying piano music in which an insistent rolling left-hand pattern mingled with the fancy-free inventions of the right.

Millions of youthful feet indorsed the new style. Fervent connoisseurs called themselves hep-cats, and the actively devout jitterbugs. When they "got in the groove" and "went to town," the results were apt to be more kinetic than graceful. Late in 1937 a dance called the Big Apple conquered the country, bearing some likeness to the old square dance in which a "caller" at the center of the floor summoned one couple after another to "rise and shine." Among the more popular turns were the Suzy-Q, truckin' or shagging, while in 1938 the Lambeth Walk, cockney importation for group dancing, vied in favor with a local routine called the Lindy Hop. The dancing mania of youth, with its accompanying argot and the "drape-shape" or "zoot-suit" clothes affected by certain zealots near the end of this era, puzzled elders often to the point of alarm. In the main, however, the cult of swing was more athletic than erotic, and the sartorial extremes sometimes associated with it were the compensatory mechanisms (to borrow another sort of jargon) devised by certain submerged juvenile groups, notably Negro and Mexican, in the big cities. The jitterbug age was youth's last fling before the bugles sounded war.

Motion pictures—the nation's fourth largest industry in the previous decade—remained the topmost commercial amusement. The initial thrill of the "all-talking, all-singing" picture, particularly the delight of hearing the voices of stars long adored in silent films, helped to tide the industry over depression's first shallows, although about a third of all regularly operated movie houses had closed by midsummer, 1933, shortly before the current of recovery began to flow. By 1939 box-office receipts at the country's fifteen thousand motion-picture theaters had risen to nearly seven hundred million dollars, a yearly average of twenty-five dollars per family. "Five years ago million-dollar films were so rare that the trade papers gave editorial ravings to their announcement," observed the *New York Times* on October 24, 1937. "Today they get no more than a few lines on an inside page."

Technicolor, essayed in several mediocre scenarios in 1929-1930 while the processes were still crude, proved at first a disappointment; but in 1932 a new three-color method was launched successfully by Walt Disney in his animated cartoon "Flowers and Trees," first of his "Silly Symphonies" in color, and triumphantly in "The Three Little Pigs" (1933), its theme, "Who's Afraid of the Big Bad Wolf?" just suited to the nation's rally in morale. Disney had arrived in Hollywood in 1926 from the Middle West and two years later created Mickey Mouse, a failure in silent films before the talking picture "Steamboat Willie" (1928) started the all-resourceful rodent on his way to world herohood. As the thirties waned Mickey was reported to be losing ground before a later Disney creation, Donald Duck. Was it possible that Donald's strident panic was closer to the new *Zeitgeist* than Mickey's brassy individualism? The author of these "fairy tales of the machine age" also exhibited his versatility in "Snow White and the Seven Dwarfs" (1938), his first full-length picture, photographed from nearly half-a-million paintings in sequence, and "Fantasia" (1940), a bold attempt to blend classical music with pictorial and often abstract art.

The content of most motion pictures still was designed for escape, the majority reflecting the tastes of tired or jaded adults seeking a never-never land of luxury and melodrama, sex and sentiment—far less wholesome fare for young movie addicts than Disney's world and fruitful of dubious social effects. Irony also lay in the fact that this Hollywood product increasingly went to markets all over the globe, where it passed for something it had been designed specifically not to represent, namely, average American life. Its milieu appeared not merely one of passion, licit or illicit, interlarded with gunplay, but also dedicated to glamourizing urban above small-town or rural civilization, wealth instead of moderate means, heroes from the leisure classes, Big Business or the professions rather than from the ranks of agriculture or labor. Such presentations of life, though no more gravely out of perspective than those of the theater, were seen daily by many millions, and to an era of social responsibility these facts seemed more disturbing than to the mind of the 1920's.

Not surprising, therefore, was the rise in the thirties of two movements concerned with the cinema's public obligations, one looking to morality, the other to economic and social education. Early depression days found Hollywood apparently oblivious of the crisis but pursuing sex themes, started in the jazz age, into the new medium of sophisticated repartee and innuendo made possible by the talkies and adorned by such talents as those of curvaceous Mae West and sultry Jean Harlow. This preoccupation with sex was generally blamed, not upon the public who seemed to like it, but upon the movie makers, in the main Jewish Americans. The paradox of the home-loving Jew with his strong family solidarity and loyalty, transgressing the public moral codes of a Gentile civilization with the highest divorce rate in the world, was not without its piquancy. "The Christian wishes to protect society at large, even if he should himself violate some of its rules of morality," wrote a thoughtful Jewish observer. "The Jew wishes to exploit society, while he himself exercises restraint."

Under leadership from a group of Catholic bishops the Legion of Decency was formed in April, 1934, to ride herd on these film executives. Moral suasion went hand in glove with the threat of boycott by the faithful and support from many devout Protestants. Will Hays, Hollywood's official conscience as chief of the Motion Picture Producers and Distributors, promptly dusted off a production code drafted in 1930 to curb screen portrayal of license and crime and appointed an Irish Catholic, Joseph I. Breen, as its policeman. The results were almost sensational. Hollywood, wavering between the two biggest successes of the past year—Mae West in "She Done Him Wrong" and Katharine Hepburn in "Little Women"—now plumped heartily for pigtails and gingerbread, summoning to the studio "Mrs. Wiggs of the Cabbage Patch," "Anne of Green Gables" and "The Girl of the Limberlost." Even Miss West's next vehicle, anticipatively billed as "It Ain't No Sin," demurely emerged as "The Belle of the Nineties." Henceforth the quota of pictures blacklisted by the Legion of Decency shrank to a small fraction, largely foreign films and bootleg productions on the "sex circuit." The most effective censorship bloc in Hollywood's history admittedly had scored its point.

Less localized, the second movement arose from the pervasive conviction in some circles within and outside the industry that movies should be something more than an escape hatch. An instrument for rousing mass emotions and implanting ideas, the cinema in times of crisis held a responsibility so huge that timid producers seemed averse to essay themes drawn from unemployment and the Great Depression, or of class and race conflict, farm peonage, delinquency and penology, freedom and totalitarianism.

Oftener perhaps than the big studios, independent producers felt the urge to experiment, as illustrated in the pictures made by the veteran actor Charlie Chaplin. His first with music and sound effects, "City Lights" (1931), briefly touched upon the ironies of unemployment and showed Charlie, the starving tramp, dissuading a broker from suicide by slapping his own puny chest and exhorting the titan to buck up. More explicit was "Modern Times" (1936), a view of regimentation in the machine age, with class riots, jails, Hoovervilles, the speed-up and other forms of exploitation, until finally the little man went mad and fled the hive of mass production. Banned from Italy and Germany, this film was succeeded by "The Great Dictator" (1940), assailing even worse kinds of regimentation. Although Chaplin's ability to mimic Hitler no longer seemed very funny to audiences at that late hour, the actor made amends by an impassioned closing plea for personal liberty, racial and religious tolerance.

Among major producers the Warner Brothers pioneered in controversial themes. Their box-office success "I Am a Fugitive from a Chain Gang" (1932) induced competitors to follow. In 1934 "Our Daily Bread" dealt with subsistence farming, while "Imitation of Life" shyly approached racism. The next year "Black Fury" attempted an impartial portrayal of coal strikes, and 1936 brought "Fury," a stark vision of lynch law that conceded a sentimental end, and "Millions of Us," an anonymous Hollywood product on the subject of joblessness and unionization. The following year marked the apogee of Hollywood's social consciousness, with such pictures as "They Won't Forget," treating mass hatred and mobs; "Black Legion," about race terrorism in the Middle West; "White Bondage," the sharecropper's struggle for life; "Make Way for Tomorrow," the tragedy of old age lacking social security; "Dead End," the slums as breeding grounds for crime, a topic soon better handled in "Boys of the Street"; and "The Life of Emile Zola," penman of social justice. Not infrequently the stock plot of the mid-thirties—in pictures like "One More Spring," "Little Man, What Now?" "My Man Godfrey" and "Mr. Deeds Goes to Town"—showed poverty and unemployment miraculously solved by luck, chiefly in the person of an eccentric philanthropist.

Political themes of international import were not lacking, though Hollywood shelved Sinclair Lewis's antifascist novel *It Can't Happen Here* as too hot to handle in its foreign market. A picture of 1934 called "The President Vanishes" disclosed a plot by bankers and munitions makers (currently under scrutiny by the Nye committee) to start a second world conflict and their frustration by the chief executive. The same year saw release of the grim newsreel shots which Laurence Stallings pieced together under the significant title "The First World War." In 1939, however, Hollywood began to prepare for the next war, with "Confessions of a Nazi Spy" and "Espionage Agent" and a series of patriotic shorts like "Sons of Liberty," "Remember the Alamo" and "Teddy Roosevelt." Henceforth war pictures and subjects drawn from American history swelled to a flood, while a streamlined newsreel series called "The March of Time" (started in 1935 by editors of *Time*) produced in "The Ramparts We Watch" (1940) a stirring recollection of the First World War.

Some pictures primarily for entertainment reached higher levels of technical finish and maturity of content than the best of the twenties. The hallmark of quality appeared in films as diverse as the dancing comedies of Fred Astaire and Ginger Rogers; "The Informer" (1935), its titular rôle played by Victor McLaglen, a tragedy of the Irish revolution; "Dodsworth" (1936), with Walter Huston in the lead; "The Good Earth" (1937), Luise Rainer's portrayal of Chinese motherhood; "Ninotchka" (1939), a witty satire upon the Soviets; Philip Barry's social comedy "The Philadelphia Story" (1940); and "Citizen Kane" (1941), the tale of a newspaper tycoon destroyed by his own corrosive ego, written, acted and directed by Orson Welles.

Distributors intent upon making movie attendance seem both a bargain and a chance to get something for nothing resorted to various devices. First came the double feature. Except in thrifty New England this innovation was unknown until 1931 when Hollywood applied pressure to theater chains and local managers to accept block booking—that is, a certain quota of second-rate films along with the good, and a bigger yearly total than actually needed. Exhibitors acquiesced, hoping that more entertainment, or at least more time-killing, would attract depression customers, as apparently it did, and within a year double billing had been adopted by one out of five of the "better" accounts and hordes of the less prosperous. The general effect of block booking and double features was to imperil quality, leading youthful habitués to prefer two movies to a single picture however good. A Gallup poll in 1940 found nearly three out of five persons disliking double features, but strong affirmative majorities from youth and poorer patrons. This poll also revealed that weekly attendance at the films averaged fifty-four million— far below what the industry had long claimed for itself. In this same year a federal suit in equity brought by independent exhibitors and their allies against the eight major film companies, charging that block booking was a combination in restraint of trade, reached compromise with help from the department of justice. In a modest antitrust victory, sales were limited to blocks of five pictures instead of the fifty common before.

A second development designed to coddle mediocre movies was Bank Night, sometimes styled Prosperity Night or Movie Sweepstakes. Begun in 1933 in the small Colorado town of Delta, it spread within five years to at least half the nation's picture theaters. With luck one might win a car or a several-hundred-dollar jackpot for the price of only two tickets, the first to obtain a lottery number and the second for admission on the night of the drawing. Among other similar schemes movie houses would offer substantial give-aways at "banko" or "screeno," their version of a simple gambling game which millions played from 1935 onward under names like "bingo," "beano" or "keno." Each player received a board filled with squares numbered in haphazard order; as numbers were drawn and called out, beans or other markers were laid upon the corresponding number until the first player to fill out a straight line shouted "Bingo!" and claimed the stakes.

When the game was employed as a fund-raising device for churches, lodges and local charity, the "house" reaped a profit from each player's entry fee. The Catholic hierarchy— which frowned upon gambling only if the odds were patently unfair or if it tempted the player to hazard what he did not own—gave bingo its august blessing as a parochial money-maker. Protestant ministers, keepers of the Puritan conscience which taught the sinfulness of invoking God's will in matters of trivial chance, often took a sterner view and continued to stake their faith upon the collection plate.

The spirit of the times, however, favored gambling. Reacting perhaps against the long drought of the Depression, many a person grabbed for the cup of fortune and hurriedly gulped or spilled it. With the repeal of national prohibition thousands of newly opened taverns and roadhouses installed slot machines, pinball games and punchboards, while amusement arcades, clubs and lodges did likewise. After a few drinks the bored patrons would challenge the "one-armed-bandit" slot machine and proceed to play one device or another all evening, taking little account of losses because each venture was so small. Nickels were the standard diet of these machines. From time to time a player would hit the jackpot and the machine disgorge a cascade of coins, although chances always heavily favored the "bank." The annual take of such

"The Will o' the Wisp."

Three would-be messiahs: Gerald L. K. Smith, Father Coughlin and Dr. Townsend.

Social Panaceas.

Popular Diversions.

devices was computed in the latter thirties as between half and three quarters of a billion dollars.

Pari-mutuel betting, legal in only six states at the close of the twenties, had spread to twenty-one by the latter thirties, the exigencies of raising revenue having mastered moral scruple. Harlem's besetting vice was the "numbers" game, operated as a daily lottery based upon any regularly published set of figures in the newspaper: clearing-house statistics, produce sales and (most favored of all) pari-mutuel totals. Honeycombed with racketeering, occasionally tinged with thuggery and murder, this game drained off cash from hundreds of thousands of poor families, involving nearly a third of a billion dollars annually in wagers.

Not years of spectacular plunging and gambling, the thirties produced no "Diamond Jim" Brady, Jay Gould or "Dick" Canfield, but they were extraordinarily fertile in small rackets, mild and often sugar-coated gaming, whose results looked impressive only in the mass. A Gallup poll in November, 1938, reported that outside the stock market more than half the nation's adults admitted indulgence in some form of gambling during the past year. Nearly one out of three had patronized church lotteries, one in four punchboards and a similar number the slot machines, one in five played cards for money, while a slightly smaller fraction fell for the "numbers."

One imaginative journalist ventured to suggest that relief, the social-security act and the Securities and Exchange Commission had so cushioned American life against mishap that petty plunges at bingo and pinball were about the only outlet left to man's risk-taking nature. It might be conceded at any rate that gambling, like other recreations indoor and out in this decade, tended to lower the cost of individual participation and broaden the base of its following. In sport and amusement, as in other aspects of life in America, the hallmark of caste and the stamp of prerogative had grown perceptibly dimmer.

CHAPTER XII

READING, WRITING AND REVOLUTION

ON the verge of the Depression about nineteen in twenty
adults were newspaper readers, three out of four read magazines and one in two read books. The economic crisis
wrought only minor damage to the patronage of news stands
and magazine racks—where a single outlay was always small
—but upon the book world it cast a severe blight while
simultaneously booming public-library circulation at a time
when such institutions found themselves strapped for funds.

Idle millions discovered the public library as the poor
man's club, a warm quiet place to browse or drowse. The
American Library Association estimated in 1933 that between three and four million new borrowers had been added
since 1929, while the total circulation of books had increased
nearly forty per cent. "If it hadn't been for the library, I'd
have gone crazy or killed myself," patrons occasionally told
librarians. Fiction was the great gainer at first, but as time
passed, a good many readers of Wild West novels and light
magazines graduated to books on technical and intellectual
subjects. Unhappily, however, at this moment of greatest opportunity, library authorities groaned under a burden of poverty. In sixty large cities book-buying funds dwindled from
an annual two and a third million dollars in 1931 to less
than a million by 1933. The Chicago library, in the exposition year when that city strove to put its best foot forward,
faced its third consecutive season with no book funds what-
soever. Inability to replace worn-out volumes, poor service
and shortened hours were common handicaps until the nation's reviving economy in the middle years began to restore

the standards which had long made American public libraries the world's best.

Newspapers in small cities, towns and rural communities suffered some impairment of circulation between 1931 and 1935; but the prosperity of the great metropolitan journals was never gravely affected and, in general, peoples' reading habits continued that trend which from 1920 to 1940 swelled the daily output of news presses from twenty-seven to forty-one million copies. Prolonging another major drift of the century, mergers as well as financial casualties steadily shrank the number of journals while fortifying the surviving fittest. By the forties only about a hundred and twenty cities possessed more than a single newspaper management, the net rate of mortality between 1930 and 1941 amounting to no less than forty-eight per cent. The weekly, traditional stand-by of small towns and farming communities, also declined until by 1941 the total had fallen to 10,800 from 12,-600 in 1930.

Meanwhile the ramification of newspaper chains, remaining during the decade at about sixty and controlling over three hundred papers, remorselessly continued to consolidate power, enjoying a substantial monopoly of wire services, feature syndicates, Sunday magazine supplements and the best newsprint supply. The launching of the *Chicago Sun* in 1941 by the liberal millionaire Marshall Field III provoked an acrimonious struggle between this independent journal and the tyrant of press services in that region, Colonel Robert R. McCormick's *Tribune*. Some argued that concentrated management promoted a better product; others saw danger in giants overlording the fields of publicity and communication.

The tabloid paper, adapted to the commuter's elbow-room and the psychology of "subway minds" at a price suited to the depression budget, rose in number from twelve in 1930 to thirty-five dailies and one Sunday specimen within six years. A survey of New York City youth in 1935 disclosed that two in three read the tabloids while nearly a fifth perused no other kind of newspaper. Effortless absorption and eye appeal—in terms of garish captions, big type and comics—characterized the tabloid, plus unblushing exploitation of news involving lust and violence and sexy photographs. The principal exception was Manhattan's *PM*, started in June, 1940, a liberal tabloid eschewing advertisements in its early years and using sensational methods to stir interest in political and social reforms.

Explicit proof of the visual-mindedness and (according to some) the immaturity of the mass mind lay in the doubling between 1930 and 1940 of the newspaper space given to comics and pictures. The former now seemed a misnomer, for among the one and a half billion copies of cartoon strips circulated weekly at the decade's end, a very large proportion made no claim to humor but spun endless adventure yarns like "Tarzan," "Terry and the Pirates," "Superman" and "Little Orphan Annie." So vast was the demand that, apart from serialization in the press, some eighteen million comic books were sold monthly in the early forties upon news stands, an estimated half of them to adults.

The growing stress upon photography led to technical improvements, notably for transmitting pictures by wire and radio, with color facsimile added in 1937. Upon the eve of the Second World War these developments had spread to vast areas of the great globe itself. A still more vital advance, affecting not only the press and radio but also brokerage offices, air lines needing constant weather reports, and other enterprises, was the teletypewriter or writing telephone, bought by American Telephone and Telegraph interests in 1930 and henceforth widely adopted.

The syndicated public-affairs columnist, little known a generation before, filled an average of two and a half columns in the metropolitan press by 1940, to be joined upon the brink of the Second World War by the military expert. These autocrats of the breakfast table sought to clarify the thickening complexity of the news and pierce the dark shadows of the future. Walter Lippmann, carried by nearly two hundred papers with perhaps ten million readers, wielded vastly greater power over the daily thinking of Americans than any Horace Greeley or Henry Watterson of an earlier day. Others, catering to all shades of opinion, competed for the public's attention—among them Dorothy Thompson, strenuous-minded feminist waging a personal war against Hitler; Eleanor Roosevelt, chatty observer and friend of the underdog; politically disillusioned Frank Kent; progressive Raymond Clapper; pinkish Heywood Broun; sedately old-fashioned Mark Sullivan; and the perpetually angry Westbrook Pegler. That their imponderable sway was always used wisely few would argue, but from the standpoint of the public at least some safety resided in numbers.

The views of Americans *en masse* about issues of the day were themselves caught in the mirror of collective-opinion polls and beamed back to the public in the form of syndicated reports published by hosts of newspapers and several magazines. Improving upon the old random technique of straw votes and *Literary Digest* polls, a young Iowan named George Gallup and an experienced marketing consultant, Elmo Roper, learned in the mid-1930's by representative sampling to forecast election results with fair accuracy and also to gauge popular opinion on current issues, to which politicians began to hearken with growing respect. Gratifying to believers in democratic government was the image which emerged from this welter of evidence, of a balanced, sensible and even foresighted mass mind.

To supplement their daily paper and perhaps in silent criticism of inadequate reporting, more and more people turned to weekly news digests, notably *Time,* fast becoming a giant after its infancy in the twenties, and *Newsweek* and *Today,* each dating from 1933 and merged four years later under the former's name. All promised to tell the news behind the news, and their crisp manner and studied pertness exercised considerable effect upon modes of expression of other periodicals. Henry Luce, emboldened by his success with *Time*, turned the trick twice more by founding *Fortune* in 1930 and *Life* in 1936, both committed in the main (like their elder brother) to articles of nameless and generally composite authorship—a touch of collectivism which apparently did not worry their conservative owner. *Fortune*, intended "to give business a literature" and angled toward a wealthy clientele with a ten-dollar subscription price, seemingly could not have been cradled under more inauspicious stars, yet from the early thirties it steadily prospered. *Life*, with a name purchased from the great humor magazine of an earlier day, hit the mass jackpot as a pioneer pictorial weekly, inspiring *Look* and a dozen other imitators during its first two years, with a total combined circulation said to be sixteen million.

Such periodicals appealed not only to the growing visual-mindedness of readers, but still more specifically to the candid-camera craze of the thirties. The importation, chiefly from Germany, of Leicas and other small cameras and their parts increased fivefold during the lean years between 1928 and 1936, while the domestic business more than doubled from 1935 to 1937 and the yearbook *U. S. Camera* crashed best-seller ranks. A candid-camera shot of Princeton undergraduates at compulsory chapel, revealing postures of boredom, sleep, newspaper reading and so on, prodded the trustees into abolishing that ordeal. The vogue served more impressive ends at the hands of Margaret Bourke-White, Dorothea Lange, Walker Evans and other artists in photography who documented the sharecropping South, the migrating Dust Bowl, the casuals of flophouse and bread line with indisputable fidelity and overtones of irony. Indirectly such techniques probably exerted a strong influence upon books of "social reportage" like Edmund Wilson's *The American Jitters* (1932), James Rorty's *Where Life Is Better* (1936), Nathan Asch's *The Road* (1936), James Agee's text in *Let Us Now Praise Famous Men* (1941) and the still more brilliant evocation of "the camera eye" in John Dos Passos's novels.

Magazines generally remained firm under the Depression's assault, gaining somewhat in circulation, with weeklies holding an edge over monthlies. Shrinking book sales combined with the new leisure to the magazine's profit. True-story and love magazines, opiates of escape, boasted in 1935 a total circulation almost a third greater than in 1921; but another supposed solace, the humorous weekly, failed conspicuously to rally, standing by 1935 at little better than half its predepression popularity. Aside from *Ballyhoo's* temporary success, "laughing off" this crisis fell short of the need. Religious journals continued to wane, but popular science and mechanics held their own. Liberal and radical periodicals reached a record high in 1931, lost nearly half their circulation in the year ensuing, hit bottom in 1934, but climbed a little from 1935 onward.

Women's periodicals, their twelve million subscribers not greatly reduced by hard times, continued to purvey romance and sentiment with only small concessions to the rising tide of economic and political debate. The first magazine exclusively for men, *Esquire*, was begun in 1933. A later newcomer called *Scribner's Commentator* presently assumed the tinge of official Nazi propaganda, while a once reputable veteran, the *Living Age*, fell into the clutches of Japanese agents. On the other side of the totalitarian barricade the *New Masses* (suspended awhile in 1933) continued to take its cue from Moscow.

Among the *avant-garde* in arts and letters, *transition*, best known of the "little magazines," survived till 1938 as the darling of American exiles in Paris, and the *Partisan Review*, set up in New York in the winter of 1933-1934, deserted its rigid Stalinism three years later to reappear as the favorite forum of such advanced aesthetes as William Carlos Williams, E. E. Cummings, Kenneth Patchen and Karl J. Shapiro. A strange fruit of Huey Long's régime in Louisiana was the endowment of the *Southern Review*, a highly intellectual quarterly of criticism published at the State University from 1935 to 1942.

The *Reader's Digest*, a pocket-sized monthly with a quarter-million subscribers at the start of this era, was approaching seven or eight million copies by its close, including foreign-language and Braille editions. This was the largest magazine circulation ever known. Its success arose partly from the Depression—when families unable to subscribe to several magazines adopted this all-purpose one—and partly from its practice of skimming the cream, or at least condensing the milk, of other publications. Its fare ranged from articles in quest of the silver lining or the larger hope, to gay life stories by the halt and blind, mingled with yarns about intelligent dogs and chipmunks and sedately off-color jokes such as one might hear after the breaking-up of a ministerial association. In the latter thirties the editors began increasingly to publish original pieces and to "plant" others elsewhere for the purpose of culling them; it started likewise to compress full-length novels and nonfiction works in the manner which *Omnibook* also popularized.

The book trade, severest sufferer in the publishing field, saw its total production of new titles fall from nearly a quarter-billion copies in 1929 to slightly more than a hundred million in 1933 before the flow gradually resumed. Dollar reprints of best sellers, begun a quarter-century before, gathered momentum in the *Star* and *Blue Ribbon* series, with drug and cigar-store sales almost matching those through bookshops. Tapping a still greater potential market, Robert F. de Graff, former publisher of *Blue Ribbon Books*, launched in 1939 *Pocket Books*, furnishing full texts of classics and quondam best sellers in convenient miniature size at twenty-five cents. Sold at news stands, drug stores and aboard trains and ferries, casually bought, read, swapped or abandoned, they neatly fitted the mobility of hotel-room and army camp life in the early forties, selling about ten million copies in 1941 and doubling that figure in the following year.

The trend toward fewer titles but wider circulation, begun in the previous decade, persisted through the thirties with the continuing growth of book clubs. Book-of-the-Month-Club selections mingled potential best sellers with an occasional *succès d'estime* which its judges had the experimental courage to back. Its chief competitor, the Literary Guild, tended increasingly toward the sure-fire historical romance. In the late 1930's each organization was approaching a million subscribers. In their wake sprang up special book clubs for children, science and mystery fans, Marxists and Catholics, and early in the forties Sears, Roebuck & Company sponsored a Peoples' Book Club which submitted likely new books to a jury of housewives, farmers, white-collar workers and other average citizens.

Americans wanted apparently to have their reading chosen for them whether by digest magazines or book clubs. The reason may have been busy lives, distrust of their own judgment or merely the desire to read at a given time what everybody else was reading. If this habit discriminated against many unusual and worthy books, it unquestionably quickened the circulation of some good ones and greatly widened the orbit of buyers.

What of the books themselves? The thirties proved to be thin years for poetry, drama, philosophy and religion; irregular ones for the novel, whether romantic or hard-boiled; lively for criticism; excellent for history and autobiography, science and medicine; and, from the base line of past records, best of all for economics and sociology, whose titles virtually doubled between 1929 and 1939. These shifts mirrored certain changing attitudes among both readers and writers.

The bank crashes and devaluation of the dollar in the early thirties brought back to America, physically and spiritually, a host of expatriates who found themselves not a little like Rip Van Winkle. Main Street was being repaved by the

WPA, which was also laying out a municipal golf course and
building a better high school; Babbitt, his real-estate business
shot to hell, no longer orated at lunch; Elmer Gantry found
the revival racket stale and unprofitable; Dodsworth banished thoughts of castles on the Rhine, and his womenfolk
their urge to get presented at Court; the man who "knew
Coolidge" had almost forgotten that quaint fact. Ann Vick-
ers, the driving social worker, now took Sinclair Lewis's
spotlight, while in the background loomed the shape of a
demagogue rehearsing for a fascism that might "happen
here." The Bible Belt seemed less absurd as a haven of funda-
mentalism, more challenging as a plague spot of race prejudice, poor schools and hospitals, sharecropping and wasted
resources. Not even Boston's Watch and Ward Society or
Manhattan's Society for the Suppression of Vice looked quite
so formidable after Judge John M. Woolsey in December,
1933, struck the shackles of censorship off James Joyce's
Ulysses and made way for greater candor in the printed word.
All in all, literary folk discovered closer affinity with the
Muckrakers of the century's early years than with the de-
bunkers of the 1920's whose behavioristic psychology had
tended to return man to his animal origins and laugh at his
consequent discomfiture.

Some young writers, who had once copied H. L. Mencken's disdain for the masses, now turned in the penitential
mood of a Maundy Thursday to laving their feet and poul-
ticing the bruises of oppression.* What Robert Frost termed
"the tenderer than thou" school convened. A number of superficial, rather patronizing books addressed the lives of the

---

* Mencken, whom P. W. Slosson, *The Great Crusade and After* (*A History
of American Life*, XII), 421, rightly called the "dominant figure in American
criticism" in the preceding period, was left stranded by the changing *Zeitgeist.*
From the editorial tower of the *Baltimore Sun* he took pot shots at "Dr." Roosevelt and the New Deal, thus proving faithful to his essential toryism, which had
once passed almost for radicalism when he was assailing the *bourgeoisie*. More
benignly, he continued to overhaul his monumental *The American Language*
(4th revision, N. Y., 1936) and write mellow remembrances of things past in
Happy Days (N. Y., 1940) and *Newspaper Days* (N. Y., 1941).

"little people"—the down-and-outers, waifs and strays always present, whom the jazz age loftily had ignored.* Others, moved by authentic knowledge and an awkward earnestness, ignored the principles of literary craftsmanship; their very lack of schooling became a publisher's blurb. Today the novels of Albert Halper, Meyer Levin, Michael Gold, Grace Lumpkin and Albert Maltz are almost unreadable. Doctrinaire communism, in particular, seemed curiously at odds with good writing, as if Marx's own ineptitude were inherited by his cult.

Better examples of proletarian fare were Robert Cantwell's *Land of Plenty* (1934), Leane Zugsmith's *A Time to Remember* (1936) and Thomas Bell's tender story of love in the Bronx, *All Brides Are Beautiful* (1936). Erskine Caldwell wrote vivid and often ribald chronicles of the Southern poor white, while Richard Wright, understandably a left-winger like so many other able young Negroes, presented a powerful, violent story of race tension in *Native Son* (1940). The most impressive work in this general vein was James T. Farrell's trilogy of South Chicago, *Young Lonigan* (1932), *The Young Manhood of Studs Lonigan* (1934) and *Judgment Day* (1935), a cycle of youth's degeneration under brutal surroundings and the joblessness of the Great Depression. Somber and pedestrian in his realism, Farrell missed the verbal brilliance and technical skill of John Dos Passos's trilogy about the coming-of-age of Big Business, the postwar boom and the bubble blown to bursting, in *The 42nd Parallel* (1930), *Nineteen Nineteen* (1932) and *The Big Money* (1936), presently assembled under the title *U. S. A.* (1937). A Marxist in these middle years, Dos Passos gave indication in *The Ground We Stand On* (1940),

* A different spirit is displayed in Joseph Mitchell's preface to his Bowery sketches written near the close of this era, *McSorley's Wonderful Saloon* (N. Y., 1943): "The people in a number of the stories are of the kind that many writers have recently got into the habit of referring to as 'the little people.' I regard this phrase as patronizing and repulsive. There are no little people in this book. They are as big as you are, whoever you are."

under the approach of war, of his growing reliance upon the moorings of Jeffersonian liberalism.

Organized radicalism in the early depression days clustered around the John Reed clubs (named for the hero of American communists) which sprouted in many large cities, sustaining a half-dozen local magazines and attracting impoverished, discouraged young writers. Dissolved on orders from Moscow in 1935 as too partisan, these clubs delivered their membership almost intact to the League of American Writers, which added a fair quota of professionals and liberal "fellow-travelers." This group held four Writers' Congresses in New York City during the latter thirties, penned excited resolutions and manifestoes, waxed strong in working for the Spanish Loyalists, then crumbled after the Nazi-Soviet pact of 1939 disillusioned many a devout Marxist, like Granville Hicks, literary editor of the *New Masses*, who had trusted in the sincerity of Soviet ideology.

In the entire field of fiction the premier novelist was Ernest Hemingway, who began this era with *A Farewell to Arms* (1929), a poignant story of love in the shadow of war and death, and closed it with *For Whom the Bell Tolls* (1940), kindred in theme but enacted against the backdrop of a newer struggle, the Spanish Civil War and free-lance American participation in it. Hemingway's spare writing, staccato dialogue and devotion to man as an extrovert strongly influenced this generation, his disciples of the hard-boiled urban school being tougher than the master. Notable products were John O'Hara's sardonic and sensual novel of the country-club set, *Appointment in Samarra* (1934), James M. Cain's brutal novelette of adultery, crime and punishment, *The Postman Always Rings Twice* (1934), and Jerome Weidman's tale of a "wise guy" in the garment trades, *I Can Get It for You Wholesale* (1937). By contrast John E. Steinbeck, from the open spaces of California's Salinas Valley, looked simple, romantic, almost sentimental, even in melodrama like *Of Mice and Men* (1937), built about two ranch hands snared in the trap of fate, or in his handling with neither rancor nor doctrinalism such proletarian themes as those of his strike novel *In Dubious Battle* (1936) and his tale of the Okies' hegira, *The Grapes of Wrath*, three years later. While Cain and O'Hara offered a catharsis of terror without pity, the latter was Steinbeck's best ingredient.

Still farther removed from Marxian bias were Thomas Wolfe's unforgettable pictures of the Great Depression: the poor of Manhattan huddled for warmth in the City Hall latrines, the denizens of cheap boarding houses, the shabby, lonely men who haunted the subways and all-night coffee stalls. Whether in the heart of the metropolis or the North Carolina highlands or in Central Europe trembling upon the abyss of going Nazi, Wolfe, with a gusto for experience richly exhibited in novels like *Of Time and the River* (1935) and *You Can't Go Home Again* (published two years after his untimely death in 1938), symbolized the American lost in the bewilderment, glory, frustration and death-premonition of life itself.

Wolfe owed his early recognition to the praise of Sinclair Lewis in the latter's speech in 1930 accepting the first Nobel Prize to be won by an American man of letters. This decade brought two other Nobel awards to native writers—in 1936 to the dramatist Eugene O'Neill, who save for a New England tragedy on the Greek model, "Mourning Becomes Electra" (1931), and a carefree comedy of youth, "Ah! Wilderness" (1933), lapsed into a sterile phase; and in 1938 to Pearl Buck, whose novel *The Good Earth* (1931) related the struggles of a Chinese family with flood, drought and economic exploitation in a manner arresting to the age of the Great Depression.

Of considerable passing acclaim was Hervey Allen's novel *Anthony Adverse* (1933), a long swashbuckling tale of more glitter than gold, while Margaret Mitchell's even longer *Gone with the Wind* reflected the same depression-born passion for cubic bargains in books. Shaped by the adroit hands of Walter D. Edmonds and Kenneth Roberts, the American historical romance marched on to further popularity with the former's *Drums along the Mohawk* (1936) and *Chad Hanna* (1940) and the latter's *Northwest Passage* (1937) and *Oliver Wiswell* (1940).

Poetry, more than ever before, forsook her ivory tower for the pageant of national history, the forum and even the soapbox. In 1929, for the first time since Longfellow, a long narrative in verse thrust its way among the best sellers with Stephen Vincent Benét's exciting Civil War epic, *John Brown's Body;* seven years later, in "Litany for Dictatorships," this poet voiced his countrymen's revulsion against the sadists engaged in torturing the free spirit and snuffing out the divine spark in peoples. Edna St. Vincent Millay, once the laureate of flaming youth, turned from the pure poetic contemplation of *Fatal Interview* (1931) to earnest talk of social and political issues in *Conversation at Midnight* (1937). Archibald MacLeish, no longer musing that "it is a strange thing to be an American," began to write verse plays and radio dramas like *Panic* (1935), about the Wall Street crash and a march of the jobless, and *The Fall of the City* (1937), showing how some dictator schooled in the strategy of terror might seize a metropolis without firing a shot. Carl Sandburg, into whose paean for the nation's virility a note of uncertainty had crept in *Good Morning, America* (1928), responded to New Deal idealism with *The People, Yes* (1936), avowing that while "the tycoons, big shots and dictators" loom momentarily against the sky, the people, though often baffled and cheated, remain always the earth's builders and the final source of wisdom. And from Iowa's cornlands young Paul Engle added his testimony in *American Song* (1934).*

---

* To be sure, a few dissenters continued in evidence, notably Robinson Jeffers, self-styled recorder of social decay and mordant skeptic of all economic planning; T. S. Eliot, English expatriate of long standing, who continued to find solace in Anglo-Catholic mysticism; and Ezra Pound, another in-

History, criticism and biography all mirrored the cultural rediscovery of America. A wide audience followed James Truslow Adams in his *Epic of America* (1931), Charles A. and Mary R. Beard in their *America in Midpassage* (1939) and Frederick L. Allen and Mark Sullivan who also recalled and savored the nation's recent past. Helping to round out the picture were such professional studies as Frank Luther Mott's *A History of American Magazines* in three volumes (1930-1938), Charles M. Andrews's *The Colonial Period of American History* in four volumes (1934-1938), Ralph H. Gabriel's *The Course of American Democratic Thought* (1940) and Marcus Lee Hansen's *The Atlantic Migration* (1940). Margaret Leech's lively picture of the nation's capital in its greatest ordeal, *Reveille in Washington* (1941), caught the popular fancy, while Paul H. Buck's *The Road to Reunion* (1937) in more scholarly vein told the aftermath of that struggle. In 1934 Congress created the National Archives to preserve federal records deserving permanent care. Housed in a handsome building completed by 1937, it henceforth became an indispensable workshop for many aspects of American studies.

Van Wyck Brooks in deft poetic vignettes described the literary past in *The Flowering of New England* (1936) and *New England: Indian Summer* (1940), a region whose charm, even with gently satiric overtones, multiplied the readers of George Santayana's novel *The Last Puritan* (1936) and J. P. Marquand's *The Late George Apley* (1937). Brooks, once the analyst of damaged souls crushed by the philistinism of American life, now extolled its new-found beauty and significance, and in *Opinions of Oliver Allston* (1941) lashed the coterie of despair. With subtler criticism F. O. Matthiessen in *American Renaissance* (1941) examined the creative spirit of the 1850's, while such vigorous and salty books as Constance Rourke's *American*

curable exile, whose brooding over usury, Western capitalism and social credit led him to espouse the fascism of his adopted Italy.

Humor (1931) and Bernard De Voto's *Mark Twain's America* (1932) testified to a new spirit that no longer condescended to the frontier.

Civil War biography and Lincoln in particular attracted a people aware of a modern house divided over war and peace, and craving a rebirth in patriotism. Besides a spate of Lincoln movies and radio plays, Robert E. Sherwood produced his moving drama "Abe Lincoln in Illinois" (1938) and Sandburg wrote his four-volume *Abraham Lincoln: the War Years* (1939), while Southerners could rejoice in Douglas S. Freeman's four-volume *R. E. Lee* (1934). Lytton Strachey's vogue had ended, and renouncing flippant wit biographers chose subjects whom they admired rather than despised. Such instances were Henry James's *Charles W. Eliot* (1931), Allan Nevins's *Grover Cleveland* (1932), Marquis James's *Andrew Jackson* (1933-1937), Tyler Dennett's *John Hay* (1934), Claude Bowers's *Jefferson in Power* (1936) and Carl Van Doren's *Benjamin Franklin* (1938). Ray Stannard Baker added the last six volumes to his massive *Woodrow Wilson*, and Ralph Barton Perry in *The Thought and Character of William James* (1935) wrote perhaps the decade's best intellectual biography.

Autobiography set a varied table, its fare running from Lincoln Steffens's memoirs in 1931—a crusader and Muckraker who in old age had argued himself into cynicism upon almost every subject save Russia—to *The Autobiography of Alice B. Toklas* (1933), a gay and lucid self-portrait by Gertrude Stein, high priestess of the "cult of unintelligibility." In the latter 1930's doctors' reminiscences proved uncommonly popular, led by Harvey Cushing's *From a Surgeon's Journal* (1936), Victor Heiser's *American Doctor's Odyssey* (1936) and Arthur Hertzler's *Horse and Buggy Doctor* (1938).*

---

* By the light of future events a somewhat sinister book from a doctor's pen reached the best-seller lists in 1935, *Man the Unknown*, by Alexis Carrel, a surgeon of French birth long domiciled in America. In view of his col-

Ideas, social, political and economic, aroused keener interest and debate than in the twenties. John Chamberlain's *Farewell to Reform* (1932) uttered a premature funeral oration over the old progressivism, Lewis Corey preached doctrinaire communism in *The Decline of American Capitalism* (1934), and Max Lerner demanded a faster pace toward the goal of democratic collectivism in *It Is Later Than You Think* (1938). Edmund Wilson's *To the Finland Station* (1940) surveyed with equanimity the grand forces fomenting revolution in the modern world, while Walter Lippmann in *The Good Society* (1937) urged the safer path of controlled capitalism to attain more efficient production, rising standards of living, freedom and voluntary order. A Yale law professor and New Dealer, Thurman W. Arnold, in *The Symbols of Government* (1935) and *The Folklore of Capitalism* (1937), argued (sometimes with tongue in cheek) that "justice" and "injustice" were purely relative terms like "up" and "down," that successful government had to sell itself over and over to the public as if it were a dentifrice, and that "from a humanitarian point of view the best government is that which we find in an insane asylum" whose aim is "to make the inmates as comfortable as possible."

In the field of scholarship the *Journal of Social Philosophy* was launched in 1935, the *Journal of the History of Ideas* in 1940, while between 1930 and 1935 were published the fifteen volumes of the *Encyclopaedia of the Social Sciences,* edited by Edwin R. A. Seligman and Alvin Johnson. In 1938 appeared the first of a four-volume *Dictionary of American English,* a University of Chicago project, and in 1939 the *Linguistic Atlas of New England,* edited by Hans Kurath, broke ground for a projected monumental *Linguistic Atlas of the United States and Canada.*

---

laboration with the Nazis a later reader might ponder his proposals for a high council of the intellectual élite to rule the world for its own good, setting right the heresies of democracy and denying to stupid people all legal rights whatever.

The rapport between writers and scholars seemed closer than in the twenties. While the University of Iowa pioneered in accepting poems and novels in lieu of research dissertations and taught painters by strictly empiric methods, a growing number of colleges and universities sponsored summer writers' conferences, maintained experimental theaters and provided fellowships for authors. Indeed the salaried writer—whether supported by universities, magazines, movie studios, radio stations or the federal government—was increasingly a phenomenon of the later years. A refugee from the Great Depression, the average author tended as never before to welcome the assurance of steady income.

Most striking of the new departures was the WPA's Federal Writers' Project lasting from 1935 to 1939. At its peak it supported over six thousand journalists, free-lance writers, novelists, poets, Ph.D.'s and other jobless persons experienced in putting words on paper. Hacks, bohemians and local eccentrics jostled elbows with highly trained specialists and creative artists of such past or future distinction as Conrad Aiken, Maxwell Bodenheim, Vardis Fisher, John Steinbeck and Richard Wright. In all, the members of the project completed three hundred and seventy-eight books and pamphlets published through commercial channels with the royalties going to pay other than labor costs or else into the federal Treasury. The major emphasis was placed upon collective tasks, chiefly the preparation of guidebooks to states, cities, highways and waterways.* Several volumes of folklore were

* According to a letter of January 17, 1945, to the author from Dean Harlan Hatcher of the Ohio State University, former state director of the FWP, "The dilemma with which I was constantly confronted was that of preparing and publishing a guide with the help of relief personnel, and at the same time I was duty bound to help these people whom I had trained, to find jobs in private employment. One of my best people who worked on the 'Essays' got a fine job in the midst of our labors and went up to a prosperous career. This also happened to one of the key men on the 'Tours' who went into college teaching, and with our supervisor whom Archibald MacLeish was kind enough to employ at the Congressional Library at a responsible position."

garnered, ranging from ex-slave narratives to tall tales of South Dakota and special studies like those of Swedes and Finns in New Jersey and Armenians in Massachusetts, with photographs embellishing each volume. The *Guides* proffered a rich documentation of the American map, mile by mile, unearthing legends and bypaths that might otherwise have perished, or silhouetting local economic situations with sudden clarity.

The WPA's Historical Records Survey, instituted in 1936, sent forth relief workers to take inventories of local public records stored in city-hall cellars, courthouse garrets and library lofts, to index old newspaper files, to make abstracts of court cases wherein nuggets of local history were embedded, to examine business archives and church records and even to scrutinize moldering tombstones for vital statistics. The allied survey of federal archives combed the land for national administrative and historical documents. Luckily, the recent perfecting of microfilm rendered possible the photographic preservation of millions of pages crumbling into decay. A special division (eventually absorbed into the National Park Service) measured some twenty-three hundred historic buildings, making thousands of diagrams, sketches and photographs for posterity. In this way the negligence of many communities in preserving their past was to an important degree redressed.

Under brunt of the economic storm the theater creaked distressfully. Two thirds of Manhattan's playhouses were shut in 1931, the Shuberts plunged into receivership, eight out of ten offerings in the 1932-1933 season failed, and thousands of actors faced penury. In 1932, in desperate hope of a job with the "talkies," no less than twenty-two thousand registered with Hollywood casting bureaus. Vaudeville troupers, chorus performers, extras, stagehands, stage mechanics and musicians were also hard hit. Little wonder that in such circles the leftist gospel exerted a strong appeal, expressing itself through "agit-prop" troupes playing to metropolitan workers and intellectuals, and in propagandist drama presented at New York's Theater Union between 1933 and 1937. The better-known Group Theater discovered the outstanding young Marxian dramatist in Clifford Odets, who followed his "Waiting for Lefty" (1935), a crudely powerful moment in a taxi drivers' strike, almost immediately with "Awake and Sing," describing the struggle against poverty of a Jewish clan in the Bronx. Elmer Rice shifted from the realistic reporting of "Street Scene" (1929) to social and political themes in "We, the People" (1933), "Judgment Day" (1934) and "Between Two Worlds" (1934), while Lillian Hellman ran up her anticapitalist flag in "The Little Foxes" (1939).*

Thanks largely to this professional slump, amateur theaters enjoyed a season of rapid growth. The heretofore popular label "little theater" tended to yield to "community theater," following the example set by pioneers like Pasadena's Community Playhouse as well as the social bent of the times. State colleges and state universities, community recreation agencies and even the Extension Service of the department of agriculture helped to spread rural theaters and local drama festivals until by 1940 nearly a thousand amateur and semiamateur groups were producing plays for audiences reckoned at fifteen million people annually.

As in the case of unemployed writers, the federal authorities moved early to ameliorate the actors' plight. First under auspices of the CWA and then the FERA, plays to benefit jobless performers were staged in New York, Boston, San Francisco and Los Angeles. In August, 1935, soon after the WPA's establishment, Hallie Flanagan, head of the Vassar experimental theater, undertook to direct the Federal Theater Project. With an annual budget of seven million dollars it

* Quite innocent of Marxism but full of the overtones of the Great Depression were the plays of William Saroyan, California-born Armenian and self-taught writer, who treated engagingly the hopefulness born of comradeship in adversity in improvisations like "The Time of Your Life" (1939).

was soon supporting about twelve thousand five hundred actors through the nation at an average "security wage" of eighty-three dollars monthly, better and steadier pay than most had ever received before. Enthusiastic Mrs. Flanagan relished the aesthetically venturesome more than routine presentations, however lucrative the latter might be. Experiments in dramatic art, not infrequently touched with boondoggling, thus tended to get the upper hand over considerations of economy, although at its peak the project grossed about a million dollars yearly in box-office returns. At first there was no admission price, stress being put upon performances before CCC camps, schools, hospitals, veterans' homes and prisons, but later small fees were charged the general public, comprising an estimated twenty to twenty-five million people, of whom a majority had never seen a play before. By means of portable stages on trucks for open-air performances, marionette shows for children, a traveling circus and road companies penetrating the Dakota prairies and rural South, all parts of the country and all classes were reached.

The Theater's chief technical innovation was the "Living Newspaper," a blend of radio-play methods and movie newsreel, which sought to turn current events into the stuff of drama and had the advantage of using masses of relatively mediocre actors. The initial offering, in New York in 1936, "Triple-A Plowed Under," depicted the farmer's plight under a recent Supreme Court decision; then came "Power," showing Everyman's search for cheap utilities and his discovery of the promised land of the TVA; and "One-Third of a Nation," high-lighting the slum problem. A nation-wide hit, "It Can't Happen Here," dramatizing Sinclair Lewis's antifascist novel, opened simultaneously in eighteen cities and drew over a quarter-million spectators in its first few weeks. Another big success was "Macbeth," adapted to a Haitian setting by Orson Welles, star of the Manhattan outfit, who soon left to found his own experimental Mercury Theater. "The Hot Mikado," also employing Negro performers, proved still more popular. Another paraphrase of Gilbert and Sullivan, "The Swing Mikado," originating in Chicago, became such potent "box-office" that private interests offered to employ the cast in a Broadway production. Brooks Atkinson, drama editor of the *New York Times*, called the Federal Theater Project "the best friend the theater as an institution has ever had in this country."

Given the attendant circumstances, the Federal Theater inevitably exhibited spots of political pink and sometimes undisguised Marxism.* The sensibilities of conservative congressmen were frayed even by New Deal propaganda praising the AAA and TVA and union labor. Following a Dies committee report in January, 1939, that "a rather large number of the employees on the Federal Theater Project are either members of the Communist Party or are sympathetic with the Communist Party," the sound of sharpening axes could be heard off stage. Resolved to "put Uncle Sam out of the show business," Congress cut off all appropriations as of June 30, 1939, and the project closed.

On the commercial stage the lacquered, sophisticated comedy of manners never wholly expired—witness the continued successes of Philip Barry—but it no longer held ascendancy. Robert E. Sherwood turned from the gay romance of "Reunion in Vienna" (1931) to lament the "impotence of the intellectuals" in a bruisers' world in "The Petrified Forest" (1935), thence to "Idiot's Delight" (1936), portraying the folly of war, darling of capitalists and nationalists, and finally to "There Shall Be No Night" (1940), showing the valor of war, physical and spiritual, against totalitarian aggression. Maxwell Anderson moved from high Elizabethan tragedy to an analysis in "Both Your Houses"

* Atkinson himself thus epitomized one of its plays for children in 1937 called "The Revolt of the Beavers": "Beavers of the world, unite! By uniting and shooting down the chief's company police with revolvers and machine guns concealed in their lunch boxes, the hungry beavers joyfully overthrew their industrial oppressors." *N. Y. Times*, May 21, 1937.

(1933) of the collision between idealism and hard-boiled politics behind the scenes of the New Deal, discovered a historical theme in "Valley Forge" (1934), and wrote in "Winterset" (1935) an eloquent commentary upon the Sacco-Vanzetti case. Similarly, Thornton Wilder, forsaking his earlier romances of escape, wrote a simple, moving play of New England village life in "Our Town" (1938).

Satiric comment on the American scene found an ideal vehicle in the musical play. In the Hoover régime George and Ira Gershwin had lightened the encircling gloom with "Of Thee I Sing" (1931), a rollicking travesty on politics and life in the White House, while in 1937 George M. Cohan in George S. Kaufman and Moss Hart's lively farce "I'd Rather Be Right" portrayed Roosevelt in his most jovial mood as a harum-scarum president. The same year a youthful composer named Harold Rome demonstrated in "Pins and Needles" that tuneful romance could be pressed into proletarian service. Produced with some assistance from the Federal Theater by the International Ladies Garment Workers Union, this production on a shoestring soon found itself in the big money and on national tour. The social temper of the time did not, of course, preclude a crop of melodious revues in the conventional style, such as Cole Porter's "Gay Divorce" (1932), introducing the perennial torch song "Night and Day," his "Red Hot and Blue" (1936) and Jerome Kern's "Roberta" (1933).

On the more serious side of musical art, Deems Taylor ventured his grand opera "Peter Ibbetson" at the Metropolitan in 1931, while the rediscovery of American subjects was reflected in Howard Hanson's "Merry Mount" (1934) and the "folk opera" of Douglas S. Moore and Stephen V. Benét, "The Devil and Daniel Webster" (1939). Roy Harris, from an Oklahoma farm, showed rare skill in the elaboration of folk tunes in his "Song for Occupations" (1934) and "Farewell to Pioneers" (1935) as well as in portions of the four "Symphonies" he wrote during this decade. Increasingly,

Hollywood employed the talents of the better composers. Moore, for example, provided the music for such documentary films as "Youth Gets a Break" and "Power and the Land," and Aaron Copland, writer of symphonic odes and chamber-music pieces, served similarly for "The City," "Of Mice and Men" and "Our Town." Younger composers included Paul Creston, whose "First Symphony," played by the NYA Symphony Orchestra of New York, won the Music Critics' Circle award for 1941, and Earl Robinson, whose "Ballad for Americans" in the WPA production "Sing for Your Supper" (1939) stirred audiences at a time of increasing national peril. Its wider popularity owed much to the magnificent bass of Paul Robeson, who shared the primacy among Negro artists with the great contralto Marian Anderson.

The hard times, combined with inroads of the talkies and radio, had thrown perhaps fifty thousand musical performers out of work on the threshold of this era. Rallying to their need, the WPA in July, 1935, set up a Federal Music Project which presently was supporting about fifteen thousand persons. They gave a total of some hundred and fifty thousand programs, heard by more than a hundred million people, while their free music classes drew monthly over half a million pupils, of whom a majority could never have afforded private lessons. Although devised essentially to help performers rather than composers, the project consistently stressed American music—names like Copland, Harris and Virgil Thomson now growing familiar to unaccustomed ears—while its Composers' Forum-Laboratory brought such artists into direct contact with their audiences. "It is safe to say," wrote Deems Taylor in 1938, "that during the past two years the WPA orchestras alone have probably performed more American music than our other symphony orchestras, combined, during the past ten." Furthermore, thanks to the FMP, some two thousand primitive and vernacular songs—from folk melodies of the Kentucky hills and Creole bayou chants to Negro spirituals and cowboy ballads—were collected on phonograph records.

Painters and sculptors received comparable aid from the government. Beginning late in 1933, the Public Works of Art Project, sponsored by the Treasury with CWA funds, hired nearly four thousand needy artists who before the project closed in the next summer turned out about seven hundred murals and over fifteen thousand other art works, featuring American history and the native scene. Public schools, libraries, courthouses, hospitals, orphanages, of which the vast majority had never possessed a picture before, profited from the talents of rising young artists like Frank Mechau, Peter Blume and Henry Mattson.

The Treasury then launched a somewhat different venture, creating a Painting and Sculpture Section looking less to relief than to the decoration of federal buildings, particularly post offices, by the most competent artists available. Under this sponsorship Thomas Hart Benton, Boardman Robinson, Rockwell Kent, Maurice Sterne, George Biddle and others covered huge wall spaces, fostering an unprecedented flowering of mural art which, responsive to the new social consciousness, sought not only to portray American life but to criticize it. Favorite themes were strikes and strike breakers, bread lines, mobs, sharecroppers, Dust Bowl and flood erosion. Speeding this trend was the inspiration of José Clemente Orozco and Diego Rivera, who in 1932-1933 had brought a mural art to the United States spicing the primitivism and warm colors of their native Mexico with a gusto for Marxian satire. Notable examples were the former's "Quetzalcoatl" series for Dartmouth College, and the latter's designs for the Detroit Institute of Arts as well as the ones politically unacceptable to the owners of Rockefeller Center.

With the relief need uppermost, the WPA in 1935 established the Federal Art Project, enrolling at its peak over five thousand persons. Before it came to a close in 1939 the members of the project painted additional murals for public

buildings, designed stage sets for the Federal Theater, conducted free art classes averaging sixty thousand students
monthly, and maintained sixty-six community art centers
which attracted a total of six million visitors. The emphasis
upon grass-roots themes and culture was most notably served
by a program called the Index of American Design which
under the direction of Constance Rourke gave employment
to about a thousand artists. They ransacked antique shops
and museums, historical societies, New England farmhouses,
Shaker barns, California missions, for specimens of early arts
and crafts, which occasionally they photographed but usually
painted with minute fidelity to color and texture.

This aspect of the Art Project, comparable to the WPA's
endeavors in preserving other rich layers of local culture,
possessed probably greater significance than most of its original productions, which contained their full complement
of arty daubs and doctrinaire canvases. But the undertaking
also helped to sustain worthy artists in the lack of other patronage, it diminished the awe and snobbery which enshrined
Old Masters to the neglect of living moderns, narrowed the
gap between the artist and his public, and fostered appreciative curiosity about art as a creative process. Yet, even in
the higher brackets of the FAP itself it was recognized that
indefinite federal patronage would likely foster a pensioners'
roll of mediocrities, and that competition among reputable
artists for government contracts at self-respecting wages in
the longer view was fruitful of better results.

The elder realists of the American scene—through whose
eyes so many of the younger generation trained themselves
to look—included Charles Burchfield with his sepulchral
farmhouses and crossroads stores under dark and snowy
skies; Edward Hopper, bringing an equally sharp fidelity to
lonely tenements and deserted streets as well as tō lighthouses
and silos; Charles Sheeler with his absorption in the homespun folk art and crafts of Shaker Pennsylvania; and John
Sloan with his vivid multitudinous depiction of the side-

walks of New York. Georgia O'Keeffe, preferring delicate and often abstract perceptions of form and color inspired by the Southwestern plateau country, found fewer imitators. The smoothness of Grant Wood's landscapes and the angularity of his farmers, the savor of romantic drama in John Steuart Curry, the sardonic comment upon village life in Thomas Hart Benton along with his sympathy for sharecropper and Negro, all reached a nation-wide public through color reproduction in the magazines. Distinctly leftward was the caustic limning of George Grosz's New York and the masterly restraint with which William Gropper conjured up mob violence and the terrors of war. This camp also embraced such painters of the depression mood as Joseph Hirsch, Mitchell Siporin, Philip Evergood, Jack Levine and Ben Shahn.

The Federal Art Project, moreover, supported many needy young sculptors, while both government and private patronage subsidized those already known to fame and the establishment of new art museums increased popular appreciation of both sculpture and painting. It was under federal sponsorship, for example, that Gutzon Borglum completed after more than a decade the colossal Mount Rushmore Memorial begun in 1927 in South Dakota's Black Hills, glorifying Washington, Jefferson, Lincoln and Theodore Roosevelt. The most important of the new museums was the National Gallery of Art in 1941 at Washington. Announcement had been made four years earlier of Andrew W. Mellon's gift to the American people of his superb collection of European paintings and statuary reputedly valued at thirty-five million dollars, and supplemented by fifteen million more for a building and endowment. In 1939 Samuel H. Kress enriched this collection by nearly four hundred Italian paintings.

The decoration of Rockefeller Center evoked sculpture in the modern manner, as in Lee Lawrie's "Atlas" in the forecourt and the carved panels by William Zorach and Gaston

Lachaise for the RCA building. Several famous craftsmen, like Carl Milles and Alexander Archipenko, were newcomers from the Old World. The ranks of native sons included Jo Davidson, whose "Will Rogers" in the national capitol drew great popular approbation; John Flannagan, less famed but of higher critical esteem, with his expressive sculpture wrought from field stones; and Alexander Calder, whose specimens of movable sculpture ("mobiles") seemed the final application to art of Yankee gadgeteering. The decade's most ambitious commission, executed between 1930 and 1936 by Malvina Hoffman, was the modeling of a hundred heads and figures representing basic types among the races of mankind for the "Hall of Man" in Chicago's Field Museum.

The national capital enjoyed the greatest concentration of new buildings, including the huge but undistinguished pile of the department of commerce, the marble majesty of the Supreme Court, the handsome marble annex of the Library of Congress, the miniature jewel of the Folger Shakespeare Library next door and the Palladian grace of the Thomas Jefferson Memorial. Dedicated by President Roosevelt in 1943, the Jefferson Memorial, with a statue of heroic size by Rudolph Evans, rounded out the cruciform design traced by an axis running from the Capitol to the Lincoln Memorial and intersected at the Washington obelisk by another line drawn from the White House to the bank of the tidal basin. Its completion on this site—like the beginnings of the Jefferson National Expansion Memorial on eighty acres of the St. Louis water front—attested the growing herohood of democracy's founder on the anniversary of his two-hundredth birthday.

Thanks to the sumptuous restoration of Colonial Williamsburg through Rockefeller munificence between 1927 and 1936, the scene of Jefferson's college days was also recaptured, while throughout the land the classic taste he had done so much to domesticate continued to find favor as the "official" style—from handsome new post offices such as those in Philadelphia and Minneapolis to the Doric simplicity of San Francisco's Opera House, destined a decade later to be the first meeting place of the United Nations. The Gothic mode waned steadily save for a few churches and college buildings, but at the other pole the so-called "international" style advanced in favor, thanks to the world leadership of Frank Lloyd Wright, with practitioners like George Howe and William Lescaze (architects of the Philadelphia Savings Fund Society Building) and European newcomers like Walter Gropius at Harvard, Laszlo Moholy-Nagy of Chicago's "New Bauhaus" and Richard Neutra in California.

Simplicity, clean lines, space, sunshine, sanitation and common sense—virtues which in a measure the modern hospital had taught to architecture—seemed to be increasingly prized in metropolitan communities. For its homes the public tended to accept glass bricks and molded corners with appreciation, but still looked askance at glass walls, planes of reënforced concrete and sun decks jutting like fungi from the parent trunk, and it regarded with little more than amusement the mast-suspended "dymaxion" house of Buckminster Fuller. More decisively, modernism made headway in factory designs for maximum lighting, the radical provision for space utilization in the Bronx's Hillside Housing Project, the TVA's buildings with their pure functionalism, San Francisco's Golden Gate Bridge, and a host of structures such as broadcasting studios or airport buildings and hangars respecting whose appearance no stereotypes had yet had time to harden.

CHAPTER XIII

The Consumer and Science

IN 1935-1936, on the basis of field work done by the WPA, the National Resources Committee endeavored to answer the question: how does the consumer spend his dollar? The population, it reported, comprised thirty-nine million consumer units—families or lone individuals—whose annual income averaged $1500. As a matter of fact, more than two thirds got less than this amount, two fifths less than $1000 and a third of the nation less than $780. Since this lowest third spent $1207 million more than it earned, it was hardly surprising that one in three among this group fell back upon some type of relief during the year. Upward toward the economic apex, about one consumer unit in eight enjoyed an income over $2500, one in thirty $5000 or better, and one in a hundred $10,000 or higher. Thus surveyed at the first thaw ending the Depression's long winter, disparities still existed comparable to those before the fateful October of 1929, and in the lower brackets showed even greater aggravation.

More novel was the emergent pattern of a whole nation's consumer habits, revealing that, with fifty billion dollars available annually for current expenses, Americans spent seventeen billion on food, nine and a half on housing, five and a quarter on clothing, five and a third on household operation and nearly one and a half for household furnishings and equipment. Besides these primary needs, personal care absorbed a billion; the nation's automobiles, $3.8 billion (but all other kinds of transportation only $884 million); recreation, $1.6 billion; and tobacco, $966 million. Reading matter, on the other hand, took but $551 million, and private expenditure for education, $506 million. In the latter case, however, government and endowed institutions swelled this outlay to a grand total of nearly $2.4 billion.

While education was thus recognized as a public concern, medical care emphatically was not. The $2205 million spent by private individuals far outstripped the mere $516 million contributed by government. Moreover, the poor were the worst neglected, households with incomes under $500 averaging but $22 yearly, while those with $20,000 and upward paid out $837 each. Similar discrepancies had been reported by President Hoover's Committee on the Costs of Medical Care, which stated in 1932 that, while medical care cost $30 a year per capita in the United States—$23 of it coming from private pockets and the rest from government and philanthropy—individuals with incomes between $1200 and $2000 spent only $13, those below $1000 a bare $9. Yet these two groups, even in the piping times of the latter twenties, composed about half the population. Added to absolute poverty was the burden of uneven costs, the difference between a year of good health and one entailing a major operation or a few weeks' hospitalization frequently meaning the margin between solvency and a long train of debt, misery and worry which itself retarded convalescence. Moreover, hospital accommodations fell far short of the need. Almost half the nation's counties, generally sparsely settled but comprising seventeen million people, contained no registered general hospital, while the majority of rural areas possessed no child-health centers or clinics.

A striking paradox lay in the contrast between the acute health-consciousness of the American people—mirrored in advertising, syndicated medical-advice columns, radio talks on hygiene, the huge drug-counter traffic and myriad symptoms of faddism—and the government's traditional timidity or parsimony in approaching public health. Thus the Hoover committee's majority recommendation that the costs of medical care "be placed on a group payment basis" through insurance or taxation got no further because of the bitter hostility of the American Medical Association. A minor advance, however, occurred in 1930 when the Hygienic Laboratory, dating from 1901, was reconstituted as the National Institute of Health, and under direction of the United States surgeon-general inaugurated a research program into human diseases.

The deepening of the Depression worsened conditions. In 1932-1933, for example, investigations showed that the highest sickness rate occurred among wage-earning families which had suffered abrupt losses in income and living standards, while in general it stood about forty per cent higher among the jobless than among the full-time employed. Childhood and youth naturally remained the principal victims, and in these years undoubtedly were sown many of the causes that led to the rejection in 1940-1941 by army medical examiners of almost half the first two million registrants examined under selective service.* To add to the difficulties, tax-supported municipal health centers in places like Detroit, Dayton and Los Angeles had to shut their doors for lack of funds. Even in 1929 half the nation's physicians had earned net incomes below three thousand dollars, and by 1932 the average doctor found himself idle between a third and half of his working time. Their own earnings dwindling, physicians grumbled at devoting their skill to charity practice and sometimes refused. In 1933 local units of the FERA undertook to pay private doctors to furnish free medical aid to patients on relief, but so pressing proved the need that this program was virtually swamped in the twenty-six states attempting it.

The New Deal envisioned but did not achieve a comprehensive program solving the basic problem of medical

---

* American Youth Commission, *Youth and the Future* (Wash., 1942), 189. This high rate of unfitness, like that disclosed in 1917 when a third of those examined for the draft were rejected on medical grounds, momentarily shocked public opinion. Under the urgencies of the Second World War these initial high standards were later modified.

A Scene from Robert E. Sherwood's "The Petrified Forest."

William Gropper's "For the Record."

Charles Burchfield's "End of the Day."

As the Artists Saw It.

costs. As part-way steps the social-security act provided funds for crippled children and maternal care, while specific diseases were attacked both from the standpoint of research— as by the establishment of the National Cancer Institute in 1937—and of prevention, inspection and treatment, as in the venereal-disease-control act of 1938. Moreover, considerable success attended federal efforts to foster coöperative self-help. Thus the Resettlement Administration early in 1937 took the lead in setting up medical, surgical, dental, hospital and nursing services on a group basis among drought-stricken and depressed farm families in the Dakota backcountry; and by January, 1940, over a third of a million persons were covered by county health associations and similar schemes worked out in thirty states by the Farm Security Administration in collaboration with local physicians. In 1940 the various federal public-health activities found new quarters at Bethesda, Maryland, in an imposing National Institute of Health, while about the same time federal reorganization shifted the Public Health Service from the Treasury to the Federal Security Agency.

In February, 1938, Senator Robert F. Wagner introduced a national health bill, proposing grants-in-aid to states to foster either tax-supported systems of general medical care or combinations of public medicine with universal health insurance. Meeting inflexible opposition from the American Medical Association, it failed of passage, even though a Gallup poll found a majority of doctors favorable to schemes of voluntary health insurance and Surgeon-General Thomas Parran in July, 1938, publicly observed that "at the present time people in general are beginning to take it for granted that an equal opportunity for health is a basic American right."

Short of compulsion the putting of medical and hospital costs on an insurance basis was indeed the innovation which the thirties brought to several million families, chiefly with modest incomes. Just as medical centers and private group clinics were a prime development of the previous period, so that of the new decade was the group health association and the hospitalization plan. Unlike the obligatory insurance systems of several European nations, this plan operated within the frame of private enterprise, costing the subscriber a fixed sum (averaging about twelve dollars a year for hospital care alone and from two to three times that sum for complete health coverage) which assured him free service whenever the need arose and similar care for his dependents at cost. At the threshold of this era not more than half a dozen hospitals in the country offered group insurance schemes, but after the American Hospital Association indorsed the principle in February, 1933, a new day began. By 1938 the plan had spread to about sixty cities, enrolling some three million subscribers.

Hospitalization schemes like the popular Blue Cross usually met less professional hostility than did the activities of group medicine. Of the latter type were the thriving and efficient Ross-Loos clinic in metropolitan Los Angeles, started in 1929 by request of some municipal employees, and the Group Health Association in Washington, established in 1937 on a still more coöperative plan at the urging of Federal Home Loan Bank employees, whose foes in the American Medical Association were declared by Assistant Attorney-General Thurman Arnold to be violators of the Sherman act by their attempted restraint of a wholly lawful "trade." On the edge of the Oklahoma Dust Bowl a flourishing coöperative hospital found its stoutest defender in the Farmers' Union. In 1936 the Coöperative League, headed by the surgeon James P. Warbasse, set up a Bureau of Coöperative Medicine in Manhattan to advise health coöperatives all over the nation. Before the end of this era it reported over a hundred organizations at work.

Whether for medical care or daily bread, the coöperative idea advanced rapidly in this decade after some slowing down in the twenties. Thrift, planning and communal endeavor were in the air. In the disastrous years between 1929 and 1934 the volume of farm supplies bought through coöperative societies doubled, reaching a quarter of a billion dollars. Gasoline and oil coöperatives flourished in many rural areas, the Tennessee Valley Associated Coöperatives bloomed under the sun of federal encouragement, while the Credit Union National Association, organized in 1934 at Madison, Wisconsin, applied the idea to banking, particularly for loans and installment buying. On the other hand, the number of farmers' associations for marketing grain and livestock declined with the advent of the New Deal, apparently because the AAA took over much that farmers had been trying to do for themselves, but coöps for purveying other agricultural commodities and for supplying farm needs grew with unprecedented vigor. By 1935 ten thousand farmers' buying and selling associations embraced over three and a quarter million members. Although the coöperative idea also made inroads upon the city, its taproot remained the farm, especially the old zones of German, Scandinavian and Finnish settlement.

The twenties had brought extraordinary blatancy and meretriciousness to advertising, and one of the Depression's early effects upon many manufacturers was to promote the substitution of smaller containers, looser packing, subnormal weight, misbranding and inferior materials. With the consumer impelled as never before to spend his dollar advantageously, a profusion of books like Arthur Kallet and Frederick J. Schlink's *100,000,000 Guinea Pigs* (1933), James Rorty's *Our Master's Voice: Advertising* (1934), Schlink's *Eat, Drink and Be Wary* (1935) and Ruth Lamb's *American Chamber of Horrors* (1936) appeared to warn him of pitfalls. American Medical Association committees spearheaded reform in the drug market, while its committee on foods, created in 1929, awarded grudgingly its seal of approval, rejecting two out of every three products submitted and insisting upon revised labels and deflated advertising claims for most of the remainder. This was a more rigorous procedure than that of the "Institute" run by *Good House-keeping,* which, though purporting to represent consumers, indulgently showered stars upon its best advertisers. More reliable were the standards and tests devised by groups like the American Home Economics Association and the American Standards Association, the latter a federation of trade associations, technical societies and federal bureaus.

Plainly enough, the shift from a producer's to a consumer's economy, from scarcity to abundance, had fundamentally changed the strategy of buying. The problem was no longer how to get goods at all, as in Adam Smith's day, but how to get the best at a fair price. By the decade's end some twenty-five thousand secondary schools were giving consumer education to over six million future housewives, whose credo henceforth would be distrust and comparison. University chemistry courses now often set students to analyze drugs, soaps and gasoline, while those in agriculture stressed meat buying and the grading of farm commodities. In 1938 Missouri's Stephens College set up an Institute for Consumer Education, endowed by the Alfred P. Sloan Foundation. Throughout the country women's clubs were spark plugs of the consumer movement, with strong leads taken by both the National League of Women Voters and the American Association of University Women.

Older and more sedate organizations devoted to the assaying of merchandise—like the National Consumers' League, its original concern being with the products of unsanitary and sweated industry—were elbowed to a back seat by livelier ones. Such were Consumers' Research, started in 1929 to foster the habit of buying by grade and specification rather than advertisers' claims, and Consumers Union, dating from 1936, which championed not only the consumer but also the union worker, gaining by its criticism of competitive capitalism a somewhat leftish repute. The findings of their laboratories, sent to subscribers under "confidential" seal as protection against libel suits, probably reached many more through loan and word of mouth than the hundred and fifty thousand families on their combined mailing lists.

The New Deal also took a hand in the matter. Besides short-lived efforts under the NRA, it set up the AAA's Consumers' Counsel, which in partnership with the Bureau of Agricultural Economics, Bureau of Home Economics and Bureau of Labor Statistics, inaugurated a biweekly bulletin called the *Consumers' Guide*. In addition, the Federal Trade Commission from 1934 onward obliged many advertisers to correct errors and temper the exuberance of their claims, and the Wheeler-Lea act in 1938 considerably strengthened such controls. Meanwhile demands increased for a sweeping modernization of the pure-food and drug act of 1906, notably after the death of over seventy users of an "Elixir Sulfanilamide" purveyed by a drug company. Despite apathy by the press and open hostility from many commercial concerns, but under urgent pressure from women's organizations, the food, drug and cosmetic act of June 24, 1938, scrapped obsolete legislation and widened the domain of federal authority, requiring adequate testing of new drugs before their introduction to the market, sharply defining adulteration and misbranding and prohibiting deceptions effected by containers and labels.

If the consumer had the cash or credit, he could buy more commodities—for health, efficiency, convenience and luxury —than any earlier American had been able to command. Multiplying the marvels of synthetic chemistry, industrial research poured forth a stream of new and attractive wares at low cost. Between 1920 and 1940 the number of industrial research laboratories grew from three hundred to more than two thousand, the scientists and technical experts they employed from six thousand to sixty, with General Electric, Du Pont, Radio Corporation of America and Westinghouse setting the pace. The miracles of applied chemistry shielded several big concerns from the worst consequences of the Depression, notably the Du Ponts, who embarked upon a sales campaign for the nonporous envelope called cellophane. The results were so successful that the public began to buy its prunes and caramels and cigarettes thus encased. The same concern pioneered a synthetic rubber under the name "duprene," utilizing a process devised by Dr. J. A. Nieuwland, announced in 1931. Its importance became evident ten years later when Japan sought to retaliate upon American oil and metal embargoes by choking off the flow of natural rubber across the Pacific.

In the novel field of chemurgy, which early caught the eye of Henry Ford as well as the Du Ponts, farm products ranging from soybeans to skim milk were converted into plastics, and in 1939 Congress subsidized regional laboratories for further research. From such materials as camphor, carbon, alcohol, urea, asbestos and formaldehyde still other synthetics were achieved. Nylon, a polyamide fiber made from coal, air and water, was introduced to an appreciative feminine public in 1939-1940, while coarser fibers of the same product went into toothbrushes. Plywood, fibers made from cellulose, and new steels containing molybdenum, vanadium, nickel, chromium and tungsten proved of immediate industrial and future military importance. Pyralin, fabrikoid, plexiglas, plastecele, lucite and vinylite were other innovations. Within a short space it dawned upon the average person that wonderful new substances now composed the fountain pen with which he wrote, the radio cabinet at his bedside, the sponge in his bathroom, the wheel by which he steered his car, his wife's dresses, and the motion-picture film which they saw projected on the screen. And, thanks to imaginative designers like Norman Bel Geddes, many such products tended to greater functionalism, beauty and clarity of color.

In the mid-thirties the process of cracking heavy oils, after extraction of gas and gasoline, added millions of barrels of fuel for consumers' use as well as raw materials for industrial alcohol, lacquers, plastics and synthetic rubber. As still another aspect of laboratory conservation, polymerization, a technique causing combustible gases to combine into gasoline molecules, promised eventually to add nine billion more gallons of gasoline to the nation's annual output.

Machines serving to replace man's senses, including the ability to gauge form and size and weight and to test pressure and temperature, were joined in 1930 by the first commercially practicable photoelectric cell. This "Aladdin's lamp of modern science" could see better and farther than the human eye, without error, fatigue or color blindness. It proved itself an incomparable servant for sorting articles, matching hues, counting passing objects, regulating light, automatically leveling elevators at floor stops, opening doors and guarding gates and prison walls. Television, hailed with great enthusiasm at the start of this era, hung fire disappointingly because of excessive costs and mechanical imperfections. Upon a limited scale, however, it was displayed at the New York World's Fair in 1939 and the next year the Columbia Broadcasting Company demonstrated the feasibility of color television. A less spectacular advance in the field of optics was the sodium lamp perfected in 1932 by General Electric. If its yellow color was generally unacceptable for use indoors, it was the most efficient of all long-life lamps and ideal for illuminating highways; while polaroid lamps and glasses, invented by Edwin Land of Boston, effectually prevented glare.

In practical acoustics the radio telephone attained its majority, its use on planes and ships presaging the "walkie-talkie" of approaching war days. In 1937 the coaxial cable entered commercial use: a single wire by means of the crystal wave filter and the vacuum tube could now carry two hundred and forty simultaneous conversations. Meanwhile the introduction in the mid-thirties of the electric organ—without pipes, reeds or other vibrating parts, yet capable of approximating pipe-organ standards—proved a boon to music lovers in small homes and apartments as well as to schools, churches and broadcasting studios. It did much to revive the popularity of organ music.

New processes also affected eating habits. The commercial adoption in 1930 of solid carbon dioxide ("dry ice") made possible vastly longer shipments of fresh edibles by land and sea, for its gradual release of carbon-dioxide gas killed or checked bacterial growth. The extremely rapid freezing of foods, preserving them with their natural flavors, had been devised in 1925 by Clarence Birdseye, and the method, bought by General Foods, was introduced to the retail trade in 1930. Four years later ten million pounds of such frozen foods as peas, corn, berries, oysters and other perishables were being sold. By the end of the decade the costs of refrigeration had been reduced by over three fourths, and though prices still remained higher than for fresh foodstuffs, the volume had grown to two hundred million pounds.

Even more sweeping developments in the American dietary came from physiological and medical research concerning vitamins. These investigations had begun before the First World War, but the modest total of forty-seven papers published on that topic in 1911 had grown to fifteen hundred annually by 1930. Knowledge advanced swiftly in regard to vitamin complexes, relations of vitamins to each other and to hormones, and their general effect upon metabolism, health, susceptibility to disease and longevity. The nature of vitamin A remained largely a mystery until the important work done in 1929 by Yale's M. D. Tyson and Arthur H. Smith; in the next year its plant source was identified with the pigment carotin. Vitamins A and B_1 were synthesized in 1936 and, largely through the researches of the Texan Tom D. Spies, nicotinic acid within the B_2 complex was discovered to be the cure for the Southern poor whites' scourge, pellagra. In 1937 Edward A. Doisy of St. Louis isolated vitamin K from alfalfa, and shortly afterward showed its potency in checking haemorrhage. On the other hand, these years brought into use the drug heparin, having precisely the opposite effect, and in the latter thirties this anticoagulant began to be employed with marked success in preventing thrombosis and in treating bacterial heart disease.

With vitamin potencies standardized by a League of Nations committee, manufacturers for the world market and particularly in the United States were soon selling huge quantities of concentrates in the form of tablets, capsules and elixirs. Thanks to publicity regarding malnutrition which the Depression evoked—with the American Medical Association's president, for example, declaring in 1935 that twenty million persons lived near or below the level of nutritive safety—many citizens, including the well-fed, began to ingest quantities of vitamin concentrates. A veritable mania of self-dosage occurred, harmless perhaps but not infrequently a needless expense. In the winter of 1938-1939 a trade journal reported vitamins as second in demand only to laxatives among all products sold over the drug counter, while manufacturers declared they were seven million pellets a day behind orders in a business grossing half a billion dollars annually. Food industries advertised the vitamin content of their wares, and commodities like condensed and fresh milk, bread, cereals, yeast, even chewing gum and lipstick, were sold with guarantees of extra vitamin enrichment.

Rather more sensibly, the publicity about vitamins helped to modify certain culinary practices. Housewives learned not to keep fresh foods too long before consumption as well as not to boil vegetables excessively and then throw out the water; increasing use of the pressure cooker was thought to preserve vitamins; and more vegetables were served raw than ever before. Brown and whole-grain bread gained in favor over white—reviving the dietary change effected during the First World War as a conservation measure—while citrus-fruit juices were drunk as a charm against colds, milk became still more of a national beverage for all ages, and liver won new esteem because of its advertised efficacy against anemia.

Physiology and medicine also recorded other important

advances. Greatest was the discovery of sulfa drugs, particularly sulfanilamide, sulfapyridine and sulfathiazole. Pioneered in Germany, they were perfected and applied to new uses in the United States, notably by Dr. Perrin H. Long and other Johns Hopkins clinicians, from the winter of 1936-1937 onward. In dreaded infections like pneumonia, meningitis, trachoma and erysipelas the sulfas often worked miracles, but their ill success with diseases such as virus pneumonia, typhoid and tuberculosis left other worlds still unconquered, and the damaging effects sometimes wrought upon the kidneys and blood-forming organs set up danger signals as well.

In 1931 Dr. Rolla E. Dyer identified the flea as the carrier of typhus. Nine years later Dr. Hans Zinsser, author of the 1935 best seller on this subject, *Rats, Lice and History,* announced shortly before his death the development of large-scale vaccine production methods invaluable in the Second World War. Researches begun in 1939 by Dr. R. J. Dubos of the Rockefeller Institute led to the discovery of gramicidin, an antibiotic product of a soil-inhabiting bacterium having great potency against pneumococci, streptococci and staphylococci. The widespread use by hospitals of dessicated blood plasma, perfected about 1940, held immense significance for the future. Rapid gains occurred in the thoracic field. In 1930, for example, the "artificial lung" was invented, enabling those with paralyzed chest muscles to survive, and new surgical techniques rendered it possible to remove an entire lung to check cancerous growth.

Along the borders of physiology and psychiatry occurred certain fruitful developments, such as the adoption in 1937 of the insulin shock treatment for schizophrenia. Beginning in 1934 F. A. Gibbs, Alfred L. Loomis, H. H. Jasper and other doctors studied the electric potentials of the human brain as recorded by electroencephalograms, thus shedding new light upon the diagnosis of epilepsy and the location of brain tumors. In psychology workers continued to refine and elaborate inquiries previously begun under such influences as Freudianism, behaviorism and the *Gestalt* school. Much work was also done in highly practical fields such as the psychology of traffic accidents, juvenile delinquency and adult crime, vocational psychology and testing.

Meanwhile exploration of the globe's little-known portions interested men of inquiring mind, whether the ventures of Admiral Richard E. Byrd into Antarctica in 1928-1930, 1933-1935 and again in 1939, or the continued investigations of the marine life and geology of the bathysphere by Dr. William Beebe of the New York Zoölogical Society, as recorded in his book *Half Mile Down* (1934). In one of the decade's most ingenious achievements Professor A. E. Douglass of the University of Arizona plotted an absolute weather chronology for the Southwestern United States, dating back to 91 A.D., by means of tree rings found in the beams of Indian pueblos and varying uniformly under cycles of drought and wet seasons.

Old problems of heredity and environment still exercised their fascination and slowly yielded more secrets. A host of timely queries—from the environmental issues posed by social workers and planners to those of heredity perverted into racial myths by Nazi apologists—turned to biology for evidence. In the United States, where freedom of research and speech continued unimpaired, allegations respecting absolute race purity or superiority were exploded anew by anthropologists like Franz Boas, Otto Klineberg, Margaret Mead and Ruth Benedict.* In genetics over two decades of experiments on the vinegar fly by Thomas Hunt Morgan of the California Institute of Technology conclusively proved the creative rôle played by mutation in evolution. Morgan's work, for which he received a Nobel Prize in 1933, disclosed

* The last two belonged to a growing band of distinguished American women in science. Others making significant contributions included Maud Slye in mouse-cancer research, Florence R. Sabin in diseases of the blood and bone marrow and Florence Seibert in tuberculosis research.

the geneticist's new world of chromosomes and their component genes, introducing subtleties unknown to the simpler scheme of Mendelian inheritance.

Meanwhile Hermann J. Muller showed that the bombardment of fruit flies with X-rays speeded mutations a hundred-and-fifty-fold, causing their progeny after a very few generations to exhibit radically new traits. Later, in 1933, Muller left his University of Texas laboratory to accept a position under Soviet patronage in Moscow's Institute of Genetics, with results ultimately unhappy when he found his research snared in an orthodoxy as fanatical as Hitler's and as hostile to free inquiry. On the threshold of this decade Professor Edward A. Doisy of St. Louis University announced his isolation of the pure hormone of the ovary (theelin) ; and when two years later the pure male hormone was isolated in European laboratories, these joint achievements advanced knowledge toward the old enigma surrounding the mechanism of sex determination, although its core still defied solution.

Though private industry, even in the Depression's darkest season, continued to pour rich subsidies into industrial chemistry and other investigations in applied science and engineering, the support given pure science by the great research foundations dwindled as their incomes melted away. Between 1930 and 1934 foundations for the advancement of science and learning—possessing capital funds of seven hundred million dollars—were forced to cut their annual grants by nearly three quarters. Research supported by state and federal funds also ran upon the shoals of poverty, only to get afloat again just before the opening gun of the Second World War in 1939. Among the few bright gleams in the darkness was the birth of the Institute for Advanced Study at Princeton, New Jersey, in 1930, with an endowment from the Newark merchant Louis Bamberger and his sister Mrs. Felix Fuld. A research institution free from degree-giving routines, it quickly attracted an eminent group of mathematicians, economists, political scientists and humanists. Yet by a triumphant paradox the thirties produced brilliant achievements in branches seemingly the remotest from immediate practical application, notably astronomy, cosmic radiation and nuclear physics. As a result, the United States came to stand at the forefront in fields as diverse as astronomy, atomic physics, radiation, biochemistry and physiological chemistry, affording further proof that the world capital of knowledge had moved westward across the Atlantic.

In 1930 the Lowell Observatory in Arizona reported the discovery of an eighth major planet, Pluto, out beyond those observed heretofore. Six years later Robert McMath and his University of Michigan colleagues adapted the spectroheliograph to take motion pictures of the sun, vividly showing in action the gaseous phenomena of its atmosphere. At the Mount Wilson Observatory Edwin P. Hubble, seeing that the apparent velocity of recession of nebulae as shown by the red shift of their spectral lines increased with the distance of the nebulae from the earth, conjectured that he held a new yardstick for cosmic measurement. In 1934 his colleague, Milton Humason, discovered the greatest velocity ever known, in a nebula of a cluster in Boötes that appeared to be rushing away at the rate of some twenty-four thousand miles a second.* Further discoveries awaited the use of a telescope with a two-hundred-inch reflector, whose cost had been provided from Rockefeller funds just before the Depression began. Cast at the Corning glassworks in 1934 and carried for grinding to Pasadena, this huge mirror was nearing completion in 1941 when the outbreak of war caused the suspension of many years' labor. When at last it should be installed

* The precise significance of the red shifts depended upon their origin. They might be due either to actual outward motions of the nebulae in an expanding universe, or to some hitherto unknown property of light reaching this globe from vast distances in a stationary universe. As yet the observational data did not suffice for the proper interpretation.

atop Mount Palomar, near San Diego, it would afford the penetration into space of more than a billion light years.*

Time, space, matter, ether, electricity and other concepts of classical physics continued to be reinterpreted in the wake of relativity, supplanting the orderly mechanistic causality of the old school with new ideas of space-time and a philosophy of science far less snug and deterministic. There were conflicting hypotheses regarding the nature of cosmic rays, now known to be bombarding the earth with more than a thousand times the energy per shot than man had ever before found to exist in any sort of atomic process, though the shots were so infrequent as to bring to earth only about the amount of energy involved in starlight. Robert A. Millikan and H. Victor Neher in 1932-1934 conducted elaborate world surveys of the variation of the cosmic-ray intensities with latitude and longitude, as did also Arthur H. Compton of the University of Chicago and his collaborators. Such inquiries yielded unmistakable evidence that these powerful rays assaulting the globe from all directions consist, largely at least, of electrically charged particles (presumably electrons) mixed in unknown proportions with photons—ether waves of the same nature as light. Experiments in 1936-1940 made by Millikan and Neher with instruments borne in pilot balloons nearly to the top of the atmosphere proved that this photon component cannot carry more than about a third of the total incoming energy, probably much less.

Meanwhile, in 1931, Harold C. Urey of Columbia found by spectroscopic means deuterium, the heavy isotope of hydrogen, whose nucleus consists, not like the ordinary hydro-

---

* At the other end of the scale the electron microscope, developed by two engineers of the Radio Corporation of America, Vladimir K. Zworykin and James Hillier, achieved a magnification of one hundred thousand times (as compared with the two thousand of an ordinary high-powered microscope) and revealed for the first time the structure of viruses and protein molecules. Dr. Zworykin also invented the iconoscope or "image scanner," which converted light into electrical signals and thus laid the basis for improved television methods.

gen atom, of a single proton, but of a close combination of a neutron and a proton. It weighs twice as much as the usual atom of hydrogen, and when replacing it in molecules of water, makes "heavy water." Through these and other discoveries the man in the street began to sense that sources of incredible power, undreamt of by Newton and Franklin, had now flashed across the horizons of human observation. One way to measure the stupendous particle energies was used in 1932 in the California Institute's laboratories by young Carl D. Anderson, who photographed the effect of such rays in a cloud chamber, finding that this invisible force struck from the atom a lightweight positive particle which he called the positron. For discovering this twin of the negative electron he was awarded a Nobel Prize.

The race for the artificial production of bombarding particles of even greater power than that with which the alpha particles are shot out from radium began in 1928 at the California Institute of Technology with Charles C. Lauritsen's million-volt X-ray tube, the pioneer of all atom smashers. The key to its operation consisted in shooting the charged atom through a succession of electrical fields in each of which it received added energy. Robert J. Van de Graaff at the Massachusetts Institute of Technology then constructed a machine which by increasing the number of such "kicks" drove the potency of atom-smashing particles up to several million electron volts. In 1932 another youthful candidate for science's highest honors, the University of California's Ernest O. Lawrence (Nobel Prize, 1939), built his first practical cyclotron, an eleven-inch magnetic resonance accelerator with metal walls. The work of Urey and Lawrence was to some extent complementary, for deuterium particles, when speeded by oscillating electrical fields of high frequency, become projectiles of greater energy than do similarly treated protons. The cyclotron ejected them in a bombarding stream with an energy of some twenty million electron volts against the nucleus of the atom to be smashed.

The public read curiously, if with vague comprehension, of these atom-smashing experiments. They had little prevision of their practical import. A new stage, however, began in 1939 with the disclosure from Germany that the uranium nucleus had been split by the assault of neutrons. Experts in half a dozen laboratories now began to strive for a "chain reaction" in the fission of uranium. In that autumn, after advice from Albert Einstein, a refugee in America, and others on the possible military value of atomic research, President Roosevelt appointed an advisory committee on uranium. A new radioactive element, plutonium (number 94), was presently obtained from uranium 238, and it also grew clear that one of its components is largely responsible for most of the fission observed when neutrons assault unseparated uranium. After the fall of France in the summer of 1940 a thick curtain of censorship was drawn over further progress in nuclear fission. It was the most secret of all the activities of the newly organized Office of Scientific Research and Development, the most unexpected result of that regionalism which had developed the vast hydroelectric potentials of the Tennessee and Columbia River valleys, and the eventual outcome became known to the world only with the explosion of the atomic bomb over Hiroshima on August 5, 1945.

Though scientists under patriotic need contributed in this and other ways to the destructiveness of impending war, a new departure showed in the fact that in the 1930's they displayed a social conscience more sensitive and articulate than in any previous era. "Our object," said Professor Urey, winner of a Nobel Prize in 1934, "is not to make jobs and dividends. We wish to abolish drudgery, discomfort and want from the lives of men, and bring them pleasure, leisure and beauty." However inadvertently, the achievements of scientists and engineers had contributed to the phenomenon of technological unemployment, and in recognition of this fact several sections of the American Association for the Advancement of Science as early as 1932 held an earnest symposium to discuss cyclical unemployment in the machine age. In 1937 the parent body resolved to take as one of its objectives "an examination of the profound effects of science upon society," inviting its colleagues through the world to coöperate "in promoting peace among nations and in intellectual freedom, in order that science may continue to advance and spread more abundantly its benefits to all mankind." The following year a group led by Karl and Arthur Compton, Urey, Anton J. Carlson and Franz Boas formed the American Association of Scientific Workers, an affiliate of the AAAS dedicated to the application of science to human welfare and the safeguarding of professional freedom. Both the social consciousness of the age of the Great Depression and the contrasting spectacle of Nazi brutality and suppression speeded this development.

Popular interest in the efficacy of applied science was evidenced in the winter of 1932-1933 in the short-lived vogue of Technocracy, a pseudoscientific scheme devised by a Greenwich Village prophet, Howard Scott, for converting the nation into an engineers' and technicians' paradise: money, banks, private enterprise and economic maladjustments should all bow before a planned economy where no one worked over four hours daily, everybody enjoyed the same income and prices reflected the energy units required to produce any given article. More significant was the surge of books dealing with the social responsibilities of technology. Stuart Chase's *Men and Machines* (1929), Ralph Flanders's *Taming Our Machines* (1931) and Arthur Dahlberg's *Jobs, Machines, and Capitalism* (1932) were followed in the Roosevelt régime by Harold Rugg's *The Great Technology* (1933), William F. Ogburn's *Living with Machines* (1933) and Lewis Mumford's *Technics and Civilization* (1934).

A year later a national survey, conducted by sixty technicians with some federal subsidy, reported that, if the nation's potential capacity for "the production of honest goods and services for the consumer" were utilized, the total output would in predepression dollars average about forty-four hundred dollars per family, or two and a half times actuality. Such innovations as air-conditioning equipment, plastics, prefabricated houses, the photoelectric cell, cellulose, synthetic rubber, television, gasoline from coal, the mechanical cotton picker and tray agriculture made it plain that, during the time when millions vainly sought work and hosts of factories rusted in idleness, technology had marched sturdily forward. In 1937 twenty per cent more goods and services could be produced than in 1929 with no additions to the labor force, and one engineer reckoned that something less than a twenty-four-hour work week could be made to serve all American productive needs. A Gallup poll in June, 1939, asking those on relief, "What do you blame for the present unemployment in this country?" reported that the largest percentage said, "machines taking the place of men"—a reason both dispassionate and intelligent.

An ingenious analysis and forecast appeared in a book widely read at the close of this era. James Burnham's *The Managerial Revolution* (1941) predicted that neither capitalists nor communists would inherit the earth, but the managers, for vital as was the continuing rôle of applied scientists and engineers, the keys to power in an industrial order were held by the coördinators: production managers, plant superintendents, finance executives. He also interpreted the New Deal as a managerial revolution in government, since federal superintendents had taken over huge fields of private enterprise, could operate at a loss and thus held a substantial advantage over agents of the profit system.

Less controversial and more tangible were the marvels of technology displayed by the three great fairs of these years. Chicago's "Century of Progress" drew about ten million admissions in its first season in 1933. Unlike her glorification of Old World culture in the exposition of forty years earlier, this occasion featured native achievements in invention and engineering, and its Hall of Science drew the largest number of visitors. The summer of 1939, febrile last season before the catastrophe of the Second World War, saw parallel exhibitions on opposite shores of the continent, with railways taking advantage of the circumstance by offering excursion rates to "See Two World's Fairs." San Francisco's Golden Gate Exposition, true to its architectural *motif* drawn from pre-Columbian and Spanish America, tended somewhat to play down modernism and technology save for the most ambitious floodlighting in color ever attempted and a lavish aeronautical display.

Bigger and more catholic was New York's "World of Tomorrow," its emblem of trylon and perisphere (a spire rising from the globe) symbolizing "the theme of social reconstruction." Its twenty-nine million admissions in 1939, including the king and queen of England on an unprecedented good-will tour, saw the début of fluorescent lighting on a large scale, radio broadcasting of facsimile newspapers and a ten-million-volt lightning bolt discharged at intervals "to show how man has chained the forces of nature." The "Town of Tomorrow," bristling with innovations in housing, and the "Electrified Farm," revealing the wonders of hydroponics (the soilless cultivation of plants), attracted millions. Foreign nations occupied twenty-two variegated pavilions flanking the Court of Peace, with Nazi Germany conspicuously missing. Czechoslovakia, her independence lately destroyed, attempted nevertheless to carry on; Italy featured a gigantic waterfall and Japan a Shinto shrine enclosing a replica of the Liberty Bell made of eleven thousand cultured pearls and four hundred diamonds; while over the Soviet building the colossal figure of a worker towered into the sky holding aloft the Red Star. It was indeed the World of Tomorrow in parables and ironies. But, whatever political allegories might have been fancied beneath the show, the triumph of technology stood clearly forth, with some forecast of its still unwritten and perhaps incalculable effect upon the fate of modern man.

CHAPTER XIV

RENDEZVOUS WITH DESTINY

UPON the threshold of the forties the mind of the nation manifested a complex of ideals, motives and emotions. The complacency of the twenties, scattered like last year's leaves by the chill winds of depression, had been followed by the springtide of the New Deal, hopeful, vigorous, luxuriant, reaching full flower in the overwhelming reëlection of Roosevelt in 1936; then, almost imperceptibly, sere and yellow hues began to show.

In the alleviation of want the New Deal's achievements had been solid and extensive. In effect, it took from the idle rich to support the idle poor and, when still more was needed, embarked upon deficit financing. Extreme New Dealers argued that redistribution of wealth *per se* was a prime function of modern government; extreme conservatives, noting that some of the relief recipients spent the little they had foolishly, asked sternly whether the taxpayer should be penalized for such irresponsibility. As a whole, the nation overwhelmingly favored even made-work to the corroding dole, but in certain moods took alarm at the mounting public debt and not infrequently felt that the government coddled the dawdler and ran unduly to boondoggling undertakings. In June, 1939, a Gallup poll asking the public to name the "greatest accomplishment" and also the "worst thing" done by the New Deal found that "relief and the WPA" led both counts by a considerable margin—surely the epitome of a divided mind.*

* As the New Deal's finest achievement 28 per cent designated the relief program and the WPA, 21 banking reforms, 11 the CCC, 7 social security, 5 the farm program, 4 labor policy, 3 prohibition repeal and 2 foreign policy.

The New Deal did not, and apparently could not, solve the basic recovery problem. Some of its works, notably the NRA, seem actually to have retarded revival, but others like the pump-priming PWA and WPA helped to accelerate domestically that improvement in economic conditions which from early 1933 set in through the world. Yet between six and ten million men remained a stagnant pool of unemployment throughout much of this era, while agriculture was kept afloat by lavish federal subsidies. By contrast, the third of the New Deal's "three R's" proved comparatively easy in the malleable mood of the mid-thirties. Beginning in the Hundred Days, reform, as has been remarked, took the spotlight from recovery after about 1935. The accomplishments were impressive and apparently of enduring import. Congressmen and local politicians climbed aboard the progressive band wagon; and art, literature, music and the movies resounded with strains of social significance. It now grew as customary to interpret history with a liberal Jeffersonian slant as in the nineteenth century a tinge of Hamiltonian Federalism had set the fashion, even up to the academic writings of Woodrow Wilson.

The lifelong idealist, emerging from his long hibernation in the torpid 1920's, drew a deep breath and joined actively once more in the quest for social justice. Others, hitherto insensitive or smug, were shocked, often deeply concerned, to learn from the president's speeches as well as from articles, novels and plays that one third of the nation was ill-housed,

For the worst, 23 per cent named the relief program and the WPA, 16 lavish spending, 12 the farm program, 6 labor policy, 6 foreign policy, 5 "interference" with business, 5 the Supreme Court plan, 4 the NRA, 3 prohibition repeal and 2 the raising of taxes. Citizens in the upper-income brackets credited Roosevelt with stemming the banking crisis, but severely disapproved his spending policy and handling of relief; those in the lowest brackets (including relief clients) applauded relief but deprecated plowing under cotton and the destruction of livestock as their chief grievance. Among farmers, 23 per cent lauded banking reforms as best, while 19 chose the agricultural program; as the New Deal's worst feature, 29 per cent specified relief and the WPA while 11 selected the AAA.

ill-clad, ill-nourished. Women's clubs, for example, devoted their programs increasingly to these matters rather than "mere literature" or flower gardens. The acute suffering of the Great Depression and its aftermath thus fostered a tenderer social conscience, calling attention to a stratum of chronic misery—among slum dwellers, sweated labor, underprivileged children, submarginal farmers, sharecroppers and other classes —that long antedated the current emergency. In response came a variety of reforms and palliatives like slum clearance and model housing, new legislation against child labor, wage-and-hour laws, rural resettlement, loans to struggling farmers and the furtherance of soil conservation.

Above all, the idea of social security took root in American life, seeking to protect the individual against hazards beyond his power to control, whether out-of-school youth in quest of his birthright, or maturity facing the risks of illness, industrial accidents and technological unemployment, or old age confronting the ultimate joblessness. Recalling James Bryce's analysis of this generation's fathers and grandfathers, the sociologists who in 1935 took another look at Middletown observed, "The most striking difference lies in the emphasis Americans placed, according to Lord Bryce, on the adventurous and the new in contrast to the emphasis Middletown now places on the tried and the safe." Many people in the 1930's staked their faith upon the New Deal's promise of security, while others pined for the old order "which had made America great," cherishing individual enterprise and free competition in their apprehension of radicalism and revolution. But from either side the basic urge remained curiously the same.

Roosevelt himself and the majority of his adherents saw nothing radical or revolutionary—in the pejorative sense— about the New Deal, arguing indeed that it promoted individual enterprise and free competition precisely because it favored small business over big business, the average citizen against monopoly, collective bargaining against concentrated managerial power. To them it was a new deal but with the same old cards, which as played in the labor mart, for example, tended to supplant the rules of auction with those of contract. Beyond any question, governmental intervention strengthened labor's hand in an age not only of rising demand for workingmen's security and fuller sharing in the profits of industry, but also one reflecting an even deeper discontent stemming from the dull impersonal grind, the deadly mechanical repetitions that robbed the worker of interests and creative satisfactions gone with the handicrafts and small factories of an earlier day. This pervasive unrest lay in the background of the unions' demands for greater collective prestige in politics as well as in the purely economic sphere.

Conservatives were prone chiefly to note the new arrogance of labor "czars," whose business was aggrandizement, or the lawbreaking tactics of labor racketeers. Moreover, the quasi-judicial National Labor Relations Board appeared from time to time to overstep its professed impartiality in assuring unions an opportunity to redress old grievances by swinging to the other extreme. Even in the shadow of the war emergency, leaders like John L. Lewis created the general impression that labor's exclusive goal was a larger share in the national income, not a due share in a larger national income. Many persons friendly to the labor movement in the early phases of the New Deal turned sour at the time of the sit-down strikes of 1937 and thenceforth tended to criticize the federal pampering of unions, just as they had disapproved the contrary tendency under Coolidge and Hoover.

Public opinion displayed less sympathy toward another stock charge of conservatives, namely, that the Washington government was meddling too much with personal freedom. A *Fortune* poll in the early autumn of 1940 found nearly two persons out of three sure that no undue interference existed, only one in four believing that it did and one in ten expressing no opinion; even among the prosperous, denials of such interference led by a very narrow margin. This and other surveys indicated that the majority of people took comparatively little exception to the New Deal's regulatory aspects, which as a whole bore most heavily upon the stock exchange, corporations, high individual incomes and inheritances. In so far as the New Deal touched the average citizen, he considered it beneficent, although, as a variety of polls showed, he might object to some phase not infrequently lying outside his own sphere, such as the farmer's qualms about the WPA and the urban relief recipient's regarding slaughtered pigs. In general, whether for good or ill, the Roosevelt administration fostered the habit of local dependence not only upon the bounty but the powers of decision in Washington, and also the growth of personal government.

The whole program of the New Deal—for relief, recovery, reform—was essentially experimental, with both the virtues and defects of fluidity in method, however steady its ultimate goal of well-distributed prosperity and social justice. Sometimes its improvisations seemed capricious, as in the monetary manipulations of 1933-1934, but never unfaithful to Roosevelt's early pledge of action, incessant action, whatever the sum of trial and error. A scion of William James's Harvard, he took pragmatism for his political tool, and the mind of America in this era of bewilderment, flux and transition gave its hearty indorsement.

That the New Deal had to attempt so much so hastily—achieving brilliant successes and a few patent failures—arose in no small measure from the need for rekindling that lamp of progressivism which had shone bright in the day of the first Roosevelt, Taft and Wilson, but had gone out in the excitement of the Great Crusade and never been relit in the stagnant air of the twenties. But with all the New Deal's mistakes and shortcomings, its level of public trust remained singularly high and its leadership sincere, so that posterity might well be puzzled to read of the almost pathological hatred which Roosevelt's name inspired in a considerable minority of people lacking neither intelligence nor civic responsibility. Among its multitudinous works the New Deal built much of its program into the structure of society and government. Even the Republicans in 1936 and 1940 promised somewhat vaguely to do many of the same things—only better and more cheaply. Other segments of the New Deal mosaic were tried, legally nullified, willingly scrapped or drastically modified. At some points of stress the onset of a new age of "normalcy" doubtless would cause further buckling. But that American life would never be the same again, both friends and foes agreed.

Toward the end of the thirties reform legislation slowed almost to a stop, holding its gains but attempting little more. Republican and Southern conservative advances in the 1938 election apparently marked a turning of the tide, for thereafter New Deal enthusiasms and innovations seemed to interest the public less and less. With increasing distance from the great national débâcle of 1929 and a considerable measure of recovery plus new preoccupations, reform in this generation had reached its fulfillment. As if calling for the confluence of the two streams which had parted in 1935, the president told Congress on January 4, 1939, "Our full energies may now be released to invigorate the processes of recovery in order to preserve our reforms." Seeing things now "that we could not see along the way," he observed that the reforms of the New Deal had been in the broadest sense a defense measure, not only salvation from internal economic disintegration but also the building of sounder bulwarks against foreign enmity. Undoubtedly Roosevelt also perceived the need for closer unity within his party and the country under the threat of impending world conflict. He required the Southern conservative vote and interventionist Republican support for rearmament at a time when certain congressmen who had supported his domestic program were forsaking him to sulk in the isolationist tent. This annual message closed with the solemn reminder that "dangers within are less to be feared than dangers from without. . . . Once I prophesied that this generation of Americans had a rendezvous with destiny. That prophecy comes true. To us much is given; more is expected."

On March 5, 1933, the front page of the *New York Times* had reported, in a column adjacent to an account of Roosevelt's inauguration, the latest news from Germany under the caption "Victory for Hitler Is Expected Today." Bonfires blazed on every hilltop along the Reich's borders "to signalize the Nazi ideal of an awakening nation," and henceforth the flame crept rapidly along the powder train leading to the Second World War. At first the rise of totalitarianism seemed to Middletown chiefly something to read about in the newspapers, hardly a matter of American concern. But columnists, radio commentators, roving journalists in their books and articles, educators and a few returned tourists began to take the measure of the peril. Steadily it advanced from Hitler's reintroduction of compulsory military service in 1935 and fortification of the Rhine in 1936 and Mussolini's concurrent subjection of Ethiopia to the collaboration of the Axis dictators in destroying the popular-front government in Spain in 1936-1938, thence to Hitler's subjection of Austria in the spring of 1938 and of Czechoslovakia in the autumn and following spring.

The refugee, whether the Gentile who hated Hitler on principle or the Jew whom Hitler hated on psychopathic grounds, was a harbinger of doomsday more commonly seen in cities and university communities than in Middletown. Between 1933 and 1939 some sixty thousand quota immigrants arrived from Germany alone, and even this number fell far short of including all who applied to American consuls for permission to migrate. The influx coincided with an abrupt decline in general immigration. In fact, with the promise of American life no longer beckoning so alluringly, many aliens already in the United States began to reverse their flow, returning to the Old World where lower living costs and family shelter awaited. In 1931, for the first time in history, the number departing exceeded the number arriving, a trend which persisted until 1936, when a slight gain at last reappeared and, augmented by the refugee traffic, grew steadily until after the outbreak of the Second World War. The decade as a whole offered a startling contrast to past ones. Whereas in 1921-1930 the sum total of immigrants reached 4,107,209, in 1931-1940 it sank to 528,431, the smallest decennial crop since 1820-1830.

Despite the talk long fashionable in intellectual European circles about the blemishes of American civilization—race riots, gangsters, corrupt politics, bloated capitalists and pandemic vulgarity—the United States reënacted its proverbial rôle as the haven of the liberal exile. These refugees, unlike the earlier waves of German and Italian farmers, mechanics and laborers, included a remarkably high percentage of physicians, scientists, scholars, musicians, artists and authors eager to contribute their best to the land of their adoption. Among them were the physicist Albert Einstein, the novelist Thomas Mann, conductors Arturo Toscanini and Otto Klemperer, composers Arnold Schoenberg, Paul Hindemith and Kurt Weill, the architect Walter Gropius, the painter George Grosz, the geneticist Richard Goldschmidt, the bacteriologist Carl Lange, the cultural historian Giuseppe A. Borgese and a former chancellor of Germany, Heinrich Bruening, domiciled as professor of public administration at Harvard. Most of the refugees found ready employment. The Emergency Committee in Aid of Displaced German Scholars helped to subsidize savants while they worked on campuses or with research foundations until their adaptability and value could be gauged properly, while Manhattan's New School for Social Research in 1933 set up a "University in Exile" which gave employment to a hundred and seventy-eight European professors.*

* Between September, 1939, and May, 1941—and in throngs just after Hitler's break-through in the West—nearly seven thousand European children

The prominence of Jews among the new arrivals added fuel to the flame of anti-Semitism—a relatively new phenomenon in the United States. Among certain groups it seemed as if the bacterial warfare of hatred, so zealously manufactured in the political laboratories of the Third Reich and imitatively in Spain and Italy, was now spreading its infection across the Atlantic. Or perhaps every man, like every section and nation, carried within himself the dormant virus of racial and religious prejudice and mob cruelty, and only a healthy state of mind and decency's innate power of resistance could keep such germs from multiplying. Organizations like Coughlin's Christian Front, George Deatherage's Knights of the White Camellia and Fritz Kuhn's German-American Bund, with support from periodicals like Gerald Winrod's *Defender* in Kansas, stirred the caldron of intolerance. Apparently the most fanatical, William Dudley Pelley's Silver Shirts, which started in North Carolina in 1933, inherited so completely the white-supremacy program and tactics of the moribund Ku Klux Klan that an observer was led to comment upon "the great shift from sheets to shirts." An estimate in 1936 placed the total membership of Jew-baiting organizations at fifteen thousand; certainly they never achieved much numerical strength.

Nevertheless, in 1938, an observant liberal like Alvin Johnson could report "a marked increase in anti-Semitism in America. Everybody knows that it is true." A *Fortune* poll in April, 1939, asking, "Do you believe that in this country hostility toward the Jewish people is growing or not?" found that nearly forty-six per cent said no, thirty-three per cent said yes, and twenty-one offered no opinion. While folk of the town, village and farm, where the Jew was rare, denied an increase of prejudice, city dwellers, white-

of sixteen and under, excluding those coming to join parents, found sanctuary in the United States by efforts of the U. S. Children's Bureau in collaboration with private groups and philanthropic individuals. Katharine F. Lenroot, "The U. S. Program for the Care of Refugee Children," National Conference of Social Work, *Proceeds. for 1941*, 198-207.

collar workers and inhabitants of the Northeast seaboard reached a different conclusion. Furthermore, about a quarter of those interviewed revealed anti-Semitic attitudes themselves. More serious than the professional agitator was the unthinking or disgruntled individual who expressed casually, irresponsibly and often flippantly a bias compounded of several things, chiefly the belief that Jews belonged to an unassimilable minority group and monopolized certain businesses and professions, together with such carefully planted absurdities as that they were all Communists (sometimes merely New Dealers), yet "international bankers." Few Americans felt anything but disgust at Hitler's overt persecution of the Jews, but a not inconsiderable minority thoughtlessly parroted Nazi talk.

Despite the growth of anti-Semitism, gullibility to foreign propaganda attracted more notice than ever before, stemming largely from the lurid tales about mutilated Belgian children and crucified Canadian soldiers spread during the First World War by Britain, France and America's own Creel committee. Writings of "revisionist" historians like Harry Elmer Barnes and, at a higher level of scholarship, Sidney B. Fay, buttressed by best sellers like Walter Millis's *Road to War* (1935), sought (with enthusiastic aid from Prussian Admiral Arno Spindler and Count Max Montgelas) to explode the "myth" of German war guilt in 1914 and often stressed the rôle played by British propaganda in persuading the United States to "pull Britain's chestnuts out of the fire." Such publications fed the rising isolationist sentiment of the 1930's.*

In the autumn of 1937 was set up in New York City a

* The economic interpretation of history played into the hands of pro-German apologists in the latter twenties and the thirties by creating a "merchants-of-death" bogey about Allied munitions makers and also by kindling sympathy for Germany as a "have-not" nation, forgetting that she was a "have" in 1914. Before the menace of Hitler became irrefutable, many liberals in the United States and other countries thus tended to admire "misunderstood" Germany and disparage "greedy" France.

nonprofit Institute for Propaganda Analysis under an advisory board including the historians Charles A. Beard and James T. Shotwell, the economist Paul Douglas and the sociologist Robert S. Lynd, its chief activity being the publication of *Propaganda Analysis: a Monthly Letter to Help the Intelligent Citizen Detect and Analyze Propaganda,* whether foreign or domestic. It classified the seven basic techniques as the name-calling device, glittering generalities, transfer in terms of approved symbols and sanctions, the testimonial, the plain-folks device, card stacking through falsification and build-up and, finally, the band wagon ("everybody's doing it").* While such students undoubtedly had much truth on their side and so helped to educate the nation beyond the effervescent innocence of the Great Crusade, they served to build a propaganda against propaganda which, particularly among the young, turned into skepticism, then hardened into cynicism respecting all national ideals, nourishing an isolationist apathy in the face of the totalitarian threat. Nor did such folk distinguish between the propaganda of dictatorships that tolerated only one kind, whether fascist or communist, and democracies which believed in the freedom, variety and decentralization of public opinion.

An obbligato of pacifism also ran through this era, in its early years attuned to economy as an argument for armaments reduction. "Sentimental peace impulses," wrote Willard M. Kiplinger's breezy *News Letter* of July 29, 1929, are "tied up with the domestic pocket-book, serving to emphasize that one of the qualities of war is expensiveness." Blaming rearmament for much of the Depression, Hoover in the spring of 1930 applauded the efforts of the naval-arms

---

* An unconscious example of the last technique, illustrating propaganda analysts' own inability to disengage themselves from propaganda, is found in Harold Lavine and James Wechsler's statement, regarding Hoover's Belgian relief activities, that "most Americans tend to agree that the enterprise was part of a build-up for American intervention in World War I." *Propaganda Analysis,* April 30, 1940, 2.

conference in London. The congressionally appointed War
Policies Commission, meeting a year later, heard much testimony about "taking the profits out of war," with dark hints
of a bankers' conspiracy, headed by J. P. Morgan, as a prime
cause of American intervention in 1917. Henceforth the
theme of war's cost to the taxpayer yielded to that of war's
profit to the capitalist. The year 1934 brought forth books
like H. C. Engelbrecht and F. C. Hanighen's *Merchants of
Death* and George Seldes's *Iron, Blood, and Profits* as well
as a widely read *Fortune* article called "Arms and the Men";
and a special Senate committee, headed by North Dakota's
isolationist Gerald P. Nye, sought to pry the lid off profit-
eering in the First World War. The reaping of excessive
gains was conclusively established, but the thesis which Nye
strove hardest to prove—that pressure from Big Business
had swayed Wilson in deciding upon war—found no con-
firmation among the tons of evidence so diligently collected.*

Moved by revulsion against "foreign entanglements,"
Congress in 1934 passed the Johnson act forbidding nations
with defaulted debts to the United States to borrow again
and, with South America's Chaco war immediately in view,
authorized the president to ban sales of arms to foreign belligerents. In 1935 the Senate again rejected membership in
the World Court, and Congress embarked on the first of a
series of neutrality acts. In effect, this legislation retreated
from traditional American claims to freedom of the seas,
prohibited the arming of merchant vessels, barred loans or

* The Special Committee Investigating the Munitions Industry, pursuant to
S. Res. 206, 73 Congress, published between 1934 and 1937 its findings in
thirty-nine parts. Part 5, for example, concerned E. I. du Pont de Nemours &
Company, Part 21 the lobbying activities of shipbuilders, and Parts 25-29
J. P. Morgan & Company. A student keenly in sympathy with the Nye committee's point of view, Charles C. Tansill, *America Goes to War* (Boston,
1938), 657, admits it found "not the slightest evidence" of Wilson's suasion
by industrialists. War sentiment in Congress and in the press was, of course, a
more complex matter. This campaign to "take the profits out of war" bore later
fruit in the excess-profits-tax law of October, 1940. See F. D. Roosevelt, *Public
Papers and Addresses* (S. I. Rosenman, ed., N. Y., 1938-1941), IX, 276.

credits to belligerents and imposed an embargo upon arms shipments with no discrimination between aggressor and victim.

Among the people pacifism took many shapes—from the Girl Scouts' change of uniform at the close of the twenties from "militaristic" khaki to gray-green (for them, no doubt, innocent of association with the German *feldgrau*) to the thunderous applause with which the National Education Association in 1935 greeted Senator Nye and then by almost unanimous vote condemned military training in tax-supported schools. Ladies' clubs campaigned against toy soldiers, and some proposed to abolish Memorial Day with its custom of decorating military graves. In New York a peace parade bore the picture of a one-armed veteran on crutches under the familiar recruiting caption, "The Army Makes Men." * For a time the peace movement bade fair to be snatched out of middle-class, idealistic and largely feminine hands by left-wing labor and radical groups, which saw in fascism capitalism's last stand and in war the ultimate convulsions of a dying order. One such organization, the Congress against War, formed in 1933 by Theodore Dreiser, Upton Sinclair and others, shortly blossomed into the Communist-supported League against War and Fascism.

The clergy, ruefully recalling how they had "presented arms" in 1917, now resolved in large numbers never to bless another crusade. A nation-wide poll in 1931 among nineteen thousand Protestant ministers found that twelve thousand believed the churches should register disapproval of any future war, while over ten thousand gave their personal pledge not to sanction or actively take part in one. A slightly larger poll in 1934 reported that three out of four wanted their denominations to oppose all armed conflicts, but, some-

* Cited with warm approval by H. C. Engelbrecht, *Revolt against War* (N. Y., 1937), 40, an emotional book mirroring the common pacifist assumption that America would never be attacked, but would seek war only to protect overseas investments under the guise of quixotic ideals.

View of Chicago's "Century of Progress."

Symbols of New York's "World of Tomorrow."

Two World Expositions.

Refugee Children Arriving in New York from Nazi-Menaced Britain.

what illogically, only a little more than half condemned defensive war.

Though the brunt of battle inevitably would be borne by youth, this group, while tending to regard all war as futile, evidenced less inflexible pacifism than a desire to avoid and discourage war. A *Literary Digest* survey of college undergraduates in January, 1935, indicated that twenty-one in twenty-five would fight if the nation were attacked, but that hardly more than four in twenty-five would join in invading another country. A poll of thirteen thousand young people throughout the population two years later disclosed that a third of the males would volunteer if war should be declared, another third go quietly when drafted, a twelfth would serve only if invasion threatened, while another twelfth would refuse under any circumstances. Girls, announcing their intention to dissuade brothers, sweethearts or husbands from serving, proved twice as numerous as male objectors.

In October, 1937, when the president launched as a trial balloon his Chicago speech proposing the "quarantine" of aggressors against world peace, a Gallup poll discovered that almost three Americans in four favored the Ludlow amendment which sought to prohibit Congress, save in times of invasion, from declaring war without a national referendum. Thanks, however, to the president's strong opposition and his moral support from international-minded Republicans like Henry L. Stimson, the House shelved the proposal early in 1938 by a narrow margin.

Meanwhile two bitter wars had broken out on opposite sides of the globe. In 1936 a fascist rebellion, abetted by Hitler and Mussolini, began under Francisco Franco to subdue the legal Spanish government, the latter gaining from Soviet Russia too little help to turn the tide but enough to alienate the Catholic hierarchy in America and thus assure powerful support in Washington for the imposing of an arms embargo, which in practice hurt the Loyalist régime. Some young American idealists and leftists enlisted under the Spanish liberal banner as the Abraham Lincoln Brigade; the showing of the Loyalist movie, "Spain in Flames," stirred excitement and recrimination; and citizens in general now learned of the "fifth column," agents of the Franco forces who bored from within.

The struggle destined more directly to affect the United States flared up in the Orient. In 1931 Japan invaded Manchuria; and though Hoover's Secretary of State Stimson protested, he evoked neither hearty response from the British nor keen popular concern at home. Having plumbed the abyss of indifference, Japan in July, 1937, launched a full-scale offensive against China. This time the Roosevelt administration protested, and many college girls forswore silk stockings and chain stores boycotted Japanese manufactures; but these gestures seemed impotent beside the accelerated sale of oil and scrap iron by American and British business firms to feed the emperor's war machine. Later in 1937, however, demands for Japanese apology and indemnification after the sinking of the American gunboat *Panay* got prompt results, although the National Council for the Prevention of War sought to bar the showing of films of this incident because of dialogue "directed against the Japanese and having an unquestioned effect of arousing the American temper." While requests for an embargo hung fire at the White House, a Gallup poll in 1938 registered an affirmative mandate from the people.

The grim logic of events rather than ardor steadily drew the nation closer to war. Thus while a Gallup poll in October, 1938, found a majority approving Prime Minister Neville Chamberlain's settlement at Munich despite still greater agreement that Hitler's claims were unjust, another sampling in January, 1939, reported barely more than two out of five still hopeful that the United States could stay out of another world conflict. In April the president sent messages to Hitler and Mussolini asking on behalf of neighbor states a ten-year nonaggression covenant, but met with tacit scorn. In late August the unexpected Nazi-Soviet pact at Poland's expense—a demonstration of appeasement still more cynical than Munich—executed a swerve so abrupt that its centrifugal force sent hurtling all fellow-travelers save those with an iron grip on the Communist line.* A week later Hitler invaded Poland, and Britain and France, though impotent to give more than moral aid, declared war upon Germany.

"This nation will remain a neutral nation," Roosevelt told the people in a fireside chat, "but I cannot ask that every American remain neutral in thought as well. Even a neutral has a right to take account of facts. Even a neutral cannot be asked to close his mind or his conscience." The next year saw the gradual mobilization of public sentiment—from benevolent neutrality implemented by "cash-and-carry" armaments (made possible by a revision of the neutrality act in November, 1939) to a surge of sympathy and of relief funds for Finland wantonly attacked by Russia, thence to "all aid for the Allies short of war" and "aid even at the risk of war," as Gallup polls reported to be the majority desire before the end of 1940. The president marched usually in the vanguard of mass opinion—both being some steps ahead of Congress—and sharpened its expression. Even the past seemed clearer by the light of the new conflagration, Gallup polls showing, in an unprecedented reversal of a popular verdict upon history, that citizens who believed America had mistakenly entered the First World War had fallen from sixty-four per cent in the spring of 1937 to a minority of thirty-nine in December, 1940. In the meantime, by October, 1940, Gallup reported nine out of ten favoring an embargo on all supplies to Japan.

* The reaction of a young American radical who had just foreseen this about-face, and spent the ensuing months trying to rebuild his philosophy of life and politics around a new core—his homeland instead of the "magnetic mountain" of Russia—is depicted in the diary of Walter Morris, *American in Search of a Way* (N. Y., 1942), 141 ff.

While isolationists like Senator Burton K. Wheeler and Congressman Hamilton Fish and their friends, banding together as "America First," continued to vociferate, at the other extreme the adherents of Clarence Streit, journalist and author of *Union Now* (1939), advocated merging the sovereignty of fifteen North Atlantic and Scandinavian democracies into a league for self-defense. Others looked less to the keystone of English-speaking peoples than to Pan-American solidarity in a world of chaos, rejoicing that Roosevelt's "Good Neighbor" policy had built a seemingly durable bridge of amity over the tottering old piers of "Yankee imperialism." * In view of these changed relations Secretary Hull could rightly say in July, 1940, that the essence of the Monroe Doctrine was a stake in the common safety, with no implied hegemony over the Americas.

His summary of the situation helped no less to buttress inter-American understanding than did the establishment in the next month of a joint Board of Defense between Canada and the United States.† In September American responsibility in the North Atlantic took still more concrete form under an executive deal whereby the nation acquired eight British bases on ninety-nine-year lease, stretching from Newfoundland to British Guiana, in exchange for fifty overage destroyers. William Allen White's Committee to Defend America by Aiding the Allies, formed in May, 1940, when Hitler overran Holland and Belgium, put into its name the

* The retreat from imperialism was actually begun by Hoover's withdrawal of the marines from Nicaragua in January, 1933. It was paralleled in the same month by the Hawes-Cutting bill looking toward independence for the Philippines, a plan further advanced by the Tydings-McGuffie act of March, 1934. For the "Good Neighbor" policy, see S. F. Bemis, *The Latin American Policy of the United States* (N. Y., 1943), 221-342.

† While Roosevelt's cherished scheme of the St. Lawrence seaway failed to pass the Senate, sweeping reciprocal trade agreements between the two countries served to hammer new links. At Kingston, Ontario, on August 18, 1938, the president said, "I give you assurance that the people of the United States will not stand idly by if domination of Canadian soil is threatened by any other Empire." *Public Papers.* VII, 493.

logic to which a growing number now subscribed. After another month only one major ally remained to fight the Axis, France having succumbed to the Nazi *Blitzkrieg*.

Production of armaments for the defense of Britain and the preparedness of the United States rose together in steady crescendo. With the retooling of aircraft factories, the conversion of tractor assembly lines into processions of tanks and gun carriages, the ceaseless hum of shipyards and precision-instrument workshops, America's own war potential was being modernized and expanded. This Anglo-American collaboration attained an important milestone in the lend-lease act of March 11, 1941, which undertook to supply materials to foes of the Axis according to their need rather than ability to pay. Tentative gestures to aid China by loans and, at last, the stoppage of Japan's imports of high-test gasoline and scrap metal in 1940, though popularly approved, attracted much less notice than did transatlantic events.

In response to the thickening war dangers the WPA turned increasingly to projects like housing for aircraft and munitions workers, camps for the National Guard, armories and rifle ranges until by October, 1941, one in three WPA workers was engaged in such tasks. Inevitably defense needs pyramided the national debt to new heights, but as an off-setting factor federal relief grew less and less necessary. By early autumn, 1940, the Federal Reserve Board's index of industrial production had risen nearly seven points and almost two million more persons had found private employment during this first twelvemonth of war in Europe. A different demand for man power arose from the nation's first peace-time selective-service act, signed on September 16, 1940. Within a few months clothiers' advertisements began to remark that "olive drab is what the well-dressed young man is wearing."

Adding to these portents was the excitement of another presidential election year. To the chagrin of organization

Republicans the party's national convention, bowing to popular demand, nominated Wendell Willkie, a vigorous, earnest Hoosier practising law in Wall Street and managing a big utilities concern, who had been a Democrat prior to quarreling with the New Deal's methods rather than its ideals. As a sincere internationalist, he had still less grounds for differing with the administration and hence refused to wage the sort of contest that might have split open the country in a demoralizing way. When, however, the Democrats "drafted" Roosevelt for a third term, Willkie sought to make a campaign issue of that break with precedent. The most challenging of all Roosevelt's opponents, Willkie impressed millions with his simple, forthright idealism and his quick capacity for growth as a leader.

His party's congressional record under the darkening skies of crisis proved, however, much less clear-cut than Willkie's own stand. In the fall of 1939, on repeal of the arms embargo, eight Republican senators had voted yea and fifteen nay, while in the House the tally stood twenty-one Republicans to a hundred and forty-three. In 1940, after Willkie's strong indorsement of selective service, eight Republican senators voted for this measure and ten against, fifty-two Representatives of his party for and a hundred and twelve against. Still later, after the election had come and gone, ten Republicans in the Senate approved lend-lease while seventeen opposed, and twenty-four in the House against a hundred and thirty-five. And as that summer waned, despite a personal appeal from Chief of Staff George C. Marshall not to wreck the new American army in an hour of peril, only seven Republican senators voted to renew selective service and thirteen to end it, while in the House their votes stood at twenty-one and a hundred and thirty-three respectively, so that this vital measure scraped through by a vote of two hundred and three to two hundred and two.

In looking with some astonishment upon the fledgling candidate they had hatched, the prevailingly isolationist Re-

publican old guard felt further lack of ease because Willkie
was unpredictable and apparently intractable to bossism. He
was still too green or idealistic to manipulate machine politics
for his own ends, as Roosevelt increasingly had learned to
do, in expedient if not always fastidious alliance with "Boss"
Hague in Jersey City, "Ed" Flynn and other Tammanyites in
New York and the Kelly-Nash outfit in Chicago. Willkie's
miscellaneous backers, however, included perforce all professional Roosevelt haters, many German-Americans and
Anglophobic Irish-Americans, the motley following of
Coughlin and Townsend and an overwhelming host of the
nation's daily papers, with disgruntled John L. Lewis bringing a minority flock of miners.* The outcome, though less
spectacular than in 1936, was decisive. Roosevelt won by
twenty-seven million ballots to his opponent's twenty-two
million, or 38 states and 449 electoral votes to 10 states and
82 votes. A postelection analysis showed that approximately
three million first voters had cast their ballots for Roosevelt,
only a million nine hundred thousand for Willkie.†

More important still, a *Fortune* poll disclosed that, by
comparison with surveys in the heat of the campaign, a
marked gain in national unity had occurred; few of the
calamity howlers of early November still regarded Roosevelt
as a menace.‡ Though the great debate over war and peace

---

* According to *Editor & Publisher*, Roosevelt received support from 40 per
cent of the press in 1932, 36 per cent in 1936 and less than 23 in 1940. See
I. F. Stone, "The Press Loses the Election," *Nation*, CLI, 467-468 (Nov. 16,
1940) ; and for a geographical survey, an editorial, "The Press v. the Public,"
New Republic, CIII, 405 (Sept. 23, 1940). After the 1944 election, beyond the
limits of this book, Secretary Ickes called attention to the fact that the percentage
reported by *Editor & Publisher* had shrunken to 17.7, indicating, he said,
"a progressively unhappy and dangerous decline in reader confidence." For
Lewis's rôle in the 1940 campaign, see Irving Bernstein, "John L. Lewis and
the Voting Behavior of the C.I.O.," *Public Opinion Quar.*, V (1941), 233-
249.

† American Institute of Public Opinion, *Public Opinion News Service*
(Princeton), Dec. 8, 1940.

‡ "Quarterly Survey XXXVI," *Fortune*, XXIII (Feb. 1941), 164. In his
annual message to Congress early in 1940, in appealing for unity the president

continued, vast numbers of dissidents now closed ranks in patriotic acceptance of the president's leadership. Indeed, many conservatives long critical of the New Deal swung heartily into line behind his international program. Between 1939 and 1941 Roosevelt passed by almost imperceptible degrees from being the tribune of the poor to the spokesman of a whole people in crisis.

The president's annual message to Congress on January 6, 1941, articulated a fighting faith in terms of "four essential human freedoms," namely, freedom of speech and worship and freedom from want and fear, as another signpost in the American march against fascism. That spring the United States seized all Axis shipping tied up in domestic ports, and took Greenland under military control in April and Iceland in July. In May the sinking of the freighter *Robin Moor* by German action led Roosevelt to proclaim an "unlimited national emergency" and, following a subsequent attack upon the destroyer *Greer*, he ordered the navy to "shoot on sight" Nazi submarines. On June 24, after Hitler invaded Russia and Prime Minister Winston Churchill promptly hailed as Britain's friends all foes of the Axis, American lend-lease was extended to a power whose totalitarianism was momentarily forgotten under the exigencies of war and admiration for its stout resistance to the common enemy.

In August the president met the prime minister at sea and drafted the Atlantic Charter setting forth joint principles reminiscent of Wilson's Fourteen Points, upon which they based their "hopes for a better future for the world." The principles included the denial of territorial aggrandizement, the right of all peoples to choose their forms of government,

had said, "Doctrines which set group against group, faith against faith, race against race, class against class, fanning the fires of hatred in men too despondent, too desperate to think for themselves, were used as rabble-rousing slogans on which dictators could rise to power." *Public Papers*, IX, 9. The opposition press was quick to remind Roosevelt that he himself had often called certain groups tories, economic royalists and other divisive names. But in the public eye his new rôle loomed steadily larger.

freedom of the seas, improved labor standards and social security everywhere, the fullest possible economic collaboration among nations and a "permanent system of general security." The global education of Americans was proceeding apace. In 1937, when a Gallup poll asked, "Do you think the United States should join a world organization with police power to maintain world peace?" only one out of four had given an affirmative answer; but by the autumn of 1941 about two in five agreed and the first few months of the next year saw the number rise to three out of five.

Lagging behind public opinion, officialdom in the summer of 1941 finally clamped an effectual embargo upon shipment of all *matériel* to Japan, now a declared member of the Axis and intent upon subjugating French Indo-China. The government also froze all Japanese assets in the United States. In November Tokyo sent one of its smoothest and most cynical diplomats, Saburo Kurusu, to peddle appeasement in Washington, while Japanese forces locked their stranglehold upon Indo-China and took up invasion stations around Thailand. Admittedly the hour was dark, with England's back to the wall and her shipping melting away daily under U-boat attack, Hitler's Field Marshal Erwin Rommel probing the approaches to Suez, the Nazis at the very gates of Moscow, and Japan preparing to overrun the "Greater East Asia" of her ambitions.

Only all-out participation by the world's ranking industrial-military power, and unity among groups in this greatest democracy, could stem the flood of encroaching disaster. Both the president and his people stood poised upon the brink of decision, but reluctance bred of earlier disillusion, isolationism and long debate seemed to arrest the final plunge. On December 6 Roosevelt addressed a personal appeal to Emperor Hirohito to preserve the threatened peace. The next day, shortly after sunrise, an armada of Japanese carrier-based aircraft—a hundred and five bombers and torpedo planes with attendant fighters—unexpectedly swarmed out of the blue over Hawaii. Blasting parked planes, hangars, fuel tanks and other installations on the main island, they concentrated upon Pearl Harbor, where the pride of the Pacific fleet lay at anchor. Long before the three-hour assault was over, the battleship *Arizona* sank a total loss; over three thousand sailors and soldiers were killed on decks, in engine rooms, oil-coated waters and burning barracks; and the *Oklahoma, California, Nevada* and *West Virginia* lay capsized or helpless, together with three destroyers, minor vessels and a large floating drydock. Three more battleships and three cruisers, though gravely wounded, were able to reply with brisk anti-aircraft fire, even though the destruction of a hundred and seventy-seven planes on the ground left the skies virtually clear to the invader. America had suffered the greatest humiliation in her military history—a sneak attack and disastrous defeat which instantly welded the nation into unity by the white heat of anger.

In Washington it was a Sabbath of unseasonable sunshine. Secretary Hull was preparing to receive the Japanese ambassador and the envoy Kurusu, his Tennessee temper already seething under their peculiarly dilatory tactics. In the oval study of the White House the president was finishing lunch on a tray, and as he chatted with Harry Hopkins before starting to beguile an hour over his stamp albums, the telephone rang. Secretary of Navy Frank Knox, holding in his hand a message to the fleet intercepted at Mare Island, said in level tones, "Mr. President, it looks like the Japanese have attacked Pearl Harbor . . . ." "No!" exclaimed the president incredulously. A few more words swept away all doubt. Anticipating the thought of millions of his countrymen, Hopkins murmured, "This is it."

Once more the quest for social justice had been engulfed in the urgency of another great war.

CHAPTER XV

CRITICAL ESSAY ON AUTHORITIES

PHYSICAL SURVIVALS

CONCERNING this series the Editor remarked some years ago that, "with so much basic research yet to be done, the task was somewhat like trying to write the story of Columbus while he was still sailing westward." Of the present volume this description is most indisputably true. Encumbered with documentary riches probably more extensive than for any other decade in American history, the writer remains uncomfortably aware of an enormous mass of undigested material awaiting future bibliographers, classifiers and monograph writers as well as the reservoir of diaries and reminiscences still unreleased.*

Save for the implicit threat of the atomic age, many characteristic physical survivals of this era give promise of long endurance. Notable examples are the Empire State Building, Rockefeller Center, the Museum of Modern Art and the George Washington and Triborough bridges in Manhattan; the mammoth low-cost housing projects in Brooklyn, Queens and the Bronx; the Washington triangle, including such structures as the Archives, Justice, Commerce, Internal Revenue, Labor, Post Office and Customs; Cincinnati's Union Station; Chicago's Merchandise Mart; Frank Lloyd Wright's ultramodern building for the S. C. Johnson wax company at Racine, Wisconsin; San Francisco's Golden Gate and

* In saving the present book from still greater shortcomings the author is indebted to Dr. Robert A. Millikan, Dr. Edwin P. Hubble, Professor H. J. Muller, Dr. Fiske Kimball, Professor W. W. Sweet, Dr. W. R. Valentiner, Mr. Charles W. Eliot II, Mr. Wendell Berge, Mrs. Howard Baker and Miss Julia Bennett for critical reading of certain portions; to Mr. Frederick L. Allen for free access to his extensive library of clippings, pamphlets and other ephemera; to Mr. Edward T. Canby for data concerning gramophone recordings; to Miss Gracia Manspeaker of the Huntington Library for help in the preparation of this manuscript; and to Professor Arthur M. Schlesinger, surviving editor of *A History of American Life*.

Bay bridges; and engineering triumphs like Hoover Dam, the TVA and Grand Coulee. Most of the pioneer streamlined trains were still in daily use when this book was written; developments in aviation are permanently represented in the Aircraft Building of the National Museum in Washington; and the adjacent Arts and Industries Building houses specimens of engineering innovation and industrial design. Elaborate technological exhibitions are in the New York Museum of Science and Industry, the Chicago Museum of Science and Industry and the Franklin Institute in Philadelphia. C. C. Lauritsen's million-volt X-ray tube of 1928 remains at the California Institute of Technology, and E. O. Lawrence's original glass cyclotron of 1930 at the University of California's Radiation Laboratory.

Pictorial material ranges from mural art under the New Deal—notably for the Justice Department, Treasury and Post Office in Washington—to the masses of photographs and films (frequently with sound recordings) in the National Archives originating with the CCC, PWA, NYA and WPA and showing their manifold activities. See *Guide to Material in the National Archives* (Wash., 1940). A panorama of the contemporary scene as viewed by artists appears in W. S. Hall, ed., *Eyes on America* (N. Y., 1939), reproducing over two hundred recent paintings. Also accessible are files of popular illustrated weeklies like *Life* (N. Y., 1936-   ) and *Look* (N. Y., 1937-   ); yearbooks like *American Annual of Photography* (N. Y. 1887-   ) and *U. S. Camera* (N. Y., 1935-   ); and such pictorial books as H. G. Alsberg, *America Fights the Depression: a Photographic Record of the CWA* (N. Y., 1934), Walker Evans, *American Photographs* (N. Y., 1938) and, in collaboration with James Agee, *Let Us Now Praise Famous Men* (Boston, 1941), Erskine Caldwell and Margaret Bourke-White, *You Have Seen Their Faces* (N. Y., 1937) and *Say, Is This the U. S. A.* (N. Y., 1941), Archibald MacLeish, *Land of the Free* (N. Y., 1938), and Dorothea Lange and P. S. Taylor, *An American Exodus* (N. Y., 1939). The *Guides* prepared by the Federal Writers' Project contain hundreds of excellent photographs of the American rural and urban landscape, public buildings and industrial installations as they looked in the thirties. Thomas Craven, ed., *Cartoon Cavalcade* (N. Y., 1943), offers a cross section of that art.

GENERAL WORKS

C. A. and Mary R. Beard, *America in Midpassage* (N. Y., 1939), though badly organized, C. A. Beard and G. H. E. Smith, *The Old Deal and the New* (N. Y., 1940), and Basil Rauch, *The History of the New Deal, 1933-1938* (N. Y., 1944), are helpful general accounts. The Committee on Recent Economic Changes, *Recent Economic Changes in the United States* (2 vols., N. Y., 1929), reported too early to offer more than background aid for this period; but the President's Research Committee on Social Trends, *Recent Social Trends in the United States* (2 vols., N. Y., 1933), is important, and from it stem monographs noted later. W. F. Ogburn, ed., *Social Changes in 1932* (Chicago, 1933), *Social Change and the New Deal* (Chicago, 1934) and *Social Changes during Depression and Recovery* (Chicago, 1935), are good annual surveys. A. C. Eurich and E. C. Wilson, *In 1936* (N. Y., 1937) and *In 1937* (N. Y., 1938), give a journalistic digest of two years' happenings. Also valuable for the mid-thirties are the thirteen *Research Bulletins on Social Aspects of the Depression* (N. Y., 1937) sponsored by the Social Science Research Council, mentioned individually later. Other highly useful treatments are Broadus Mitchell, *Depression Decade, 1929-1941* (Henry David and others, eds., *The Economic History of the United States*, IX, N. Y., 1947), and Horace Taylor and others, *Contemporary Problems in the United States* (N. Y., 1934-1935), revised as *Contemporary Economic Problems and Trends* (6th edn., 1938) and still later rewritten (with omission, however, of some significant material) as *Main Currents in Modern Economic Life* (7th edn., 1941).

E. K. Lindley, *The Roosevelt Revolution: First Phase* (N. Y., 1933) and *Half Way with Roosevelt* (N. Y., 1936), reflect the sympathetic observation of the president's favorite newspaperman; David Lawrence, *Beyond the New Deal* (N. Y., 1934), is hostile; and Eleanor L. Dulles, *Depression and Reconstruction* (Phila., 1936), and C. J. Enzler, *Some Social Aspects of the Depression* (Wash., 1939), are soberly detached. Two cultural studies, one of a particular community, are R. S. and Helen M. Lynd, *Middletown in Transition* (N. Y., 1937), and H. E. Stearns, ed., *America Now* (N. Y., 1938). Among impressionistic accounts of the Depression, M. A. Hallgren, *Seeds of Revolt* (N. Y., 1933), and Bruce Minton and John Stuart, *The Fat Years and the Lean* (N. Y., 1940), are leftist; and Gilbert Seldes, *The Years of the Locust* (Boston, 1933), and H. M. Robinson, *Fantastic Interim* (N. Y., 1943), colorful with little plan or purpose. The most satisfactory graphic accounts are J. N. Leonard, *Three Years Down* (N. Y., 1939), and F. L. Allen, *Since Yesterday* (N. Y., 1940).

Portions of C. J. Friedrich's *The New Belief in the Common Man* (Boston, 1942) discuss the evolution of the New Deal's basic philosophy, but the treatment is superficial. More scholarly are the relevant chapters in Merle Curti, *The Growth of American Thought* (N. Y., 1943).

Probably the most penetrating volume of overseas comment is *The New Deal* by the Editors of the London *Economist* (N. Y., 1937). B. P. Adams, ed., *You Americans* (N. Y., 1939), presents views by fifteen foreign correspondents. André Maurois, *En Amérique* (Paris, 1933) and *États-Unis 39* (Paris, 1939), report early and late impressions of the decade. Diego Rivera, *Portrait of America* (N. Y., 1934), presents, with reproductions of murals, propaganda rather than realistic reporting.

GOVERNMENT RECORDS

U. S. Superintendent of Documents, *Catalogue of the Public Documents of All Departments of the Government*, XX-XXV, cover the period 1929-1940, but do not include much mimeographed and multigraphed material issued by many federal agencies. L. F. Schmeckebier, *New Federal Organizations* (Wash., 1934) and *Government Publications and Their Use* (Wash., 1936), are general guides to the changing pattern of federal administration and its literature. These should be supplemented by J. K. Wilcox's compilations: *NRA, the New Deal for Business and Industry: a Bibliography* (Chicago, 1933); *Unemployment Relief Documents: Guide to the Official Publications and Releases of FERA and the 48 State Relief Agencies* (N. Y., 1936); *Guide to the Official Publications of the New Deal Administrations* (Chicago, 1934, with supplements 1936 and 1937); and *Public Documents . . . 1937* (Chicago, 1937). The last supplies a check list of publications on intermeshed federal and state administrations, invaluable for study of agencies like the FERA, WPA and NYA, along with such topics as state liquor control, state employment services, housing boards, old-age assistance, unemployment compensation, planning boards and interstate coöperation. The manuscript files of the multitudinous New Deal and defense agencies are in the National Archives.

The first decennial census in this era is summarized in *Abstract of the 15th Census* (Wash., 1933). Official surveys of the decade's basic economic problem include Bureau of the Census, *Unemployment 1930* (2 vols., Wash., 1931-1932); Federal Emergency Relief Association, *Unemployment Relief Census, October 1933: U. S. Summary* (Wash., 1934); and, as of November, 1937, *Final Report on Total and Partial Unemployment* (Census of Partial Employment, Unemployment and Occupations, 4 vols., Wash., 1938). The sixteenth census of 1940 offers notably full materials for a statistical study of American life in series like "Reports on Population" and "Reports on Housing." National Resources Planning Board, *Population Data from the 1940 Census* (Wash., 1943), should also be noted. For other federal publications of special concern to the social historian, see *Subject Index of Research Bulletins Issued by FERA and WPA, Division of Social Research* (Wash., 1937) and *Publications of the National Resources Planning Board: 1934-1943* (Wash., 1943).

PERSONAL MATERIAL

Both presidents of this epoch founded libraries containing archives of the first importance. At Stanford University Hoover added to his earlier collection of records on the First World War and his services in the commerce department his personal papers as chief executive, housing them in a steel and concrete tower, completed in 1941, as the Hoover Library of War, Revolution and Peace. Here also are the Ray Lyman Wilbur collection relating to child health, housing and costs of medical care, and the data gathered by such groups in the Hoover administration as the President's Research Committee on Social Trends, National Advisory Committee on Education and National Advisory Council on Radio in Education. Hoover's successor established in 1939 at Hyde Park, New York, the Franklin D. Roosevelt Library as a branch of the National Archives, its Dutch colonial building of local field stone completed in 1940. Among other things it includes Roosevelt's personal and official papers during the White House years 1933-1945, along with such memoranda as guest lists, about a hundred and fifty volumes of scrapbooks, "fan" mail and letters of criticism, and masses of photographic material personal and administrative. The private correspondence of Mrs. F. D. Roosevelt and the papers of Harry L. Hopkins as WPA chief are also deposited here.

Essential for Hoover's administration are his *State Papers and Other Public Writings* (W. S. Myers and W. H. Newton, eds., 2 vols., N. Y., 1934) and *The Hoover Administration* (N. Y., 1936), a documentary summary compiled by the same hands. Hoover's *Campaign Speeches of 1932* (N. Y., 1933), his *The Challenge to Liberty* (N. Y., 1934), *American Ideals versus the New Deal* (N. Y., 1936) and *Addresses upon the American Road* (N. Y., 1938) voice dissent from his successor's point of view. T. G. Joslin, *Hoover Off the Record* (N. Y., 1934), is a friendly narrative by an associate. Critical is R. G. Tugwell, *Mr. Hoover's Economic Policy* (N. Y., 1932). A useful book for the bridge between administrations is R. V. Peel and T. C. Donnelly, *The 1932 Campaign* (N. Y., 1935). Basic for the New Deal are the nine published volumes of Roosevelt's *Public Papers and Addresses* (S. I. Rosenman, ed., N. Y., 1938-1941). Early speeches with linkages of comment are published in Roosevelt's *Looking Forward* (N. Y., 1933) and *On Our Way* (N. Y., 1934); later ones in volumes like *Rendezvous with Destiny* (N. Y., 1944) and *Nothing to Fear* (Boston, 1946).

Among phonograph recordings commercially available are Roosevelt's First Inaugural (Union no. 201); speeches of both Hoover and Roosevelt in "Cavalcade of Presidents" (Victor PS no. 1); excerpts of Roosevelt addresses between 1933 and 1945 in "Voices of Victory" (WOR Recordings) and between 1941 and 1945 in "Historical Recordings" (no. 100). Collections in the Library of Congress, Harvard University and the New York University Film Service Library contain numerous noncommercial transcriptions, and a collection in the National Archives (RG 201) includes addresses by Roosevelt, Henry A. Wallace, Wendell L. Willkie and other public figures. The Hyde Park Library has some three hundred sound recordings by Roosevelt (dating from 1924) and his colleagues, besides about five hundred records of orchestral and vocal music made by various WPA groups, together with a few programs broadcast under the Rural Electrification Administration and by the Office of Coördinator of Inter-American Affairs. Also belonging to this Library, but on deposit in the National Archives, are nearly 300,000 feet of motion-picture film of Roosevelt and his associates, chiefly newsreel shots from 1928 onward.

The career of F. D. Roosevelt is set forth in pictures and cartoons in Don Wharton, ed., *The Roosevelt Omnibus* (N. Y., 1934), and biographically in Sara D. Roosevelt, *My Boy Franklin* (N. Y., 1933), Eleanor Roosevelt, *This Is My Story* (N. Y., 1939), E. K. Lindley, *Franklin D. Roosevelt: a Career in Progressive Democracy* (N. Y., 1931), Emil Ludwig, *Roosevelt: a Study in Fortune and Power* (N. Y., 1938), and Gerald Johnson, *Roosevelt: Dictator or Democrat?* (N. Y., 1941). Hostile are J. P. Warburg, *Hell Bent for Election* (N. Y., 1935), and J. T. Flynn, *Country Squire in the White House* (N. Y., 1940). Joseph Alsop and Robert Kintner, *Men around the President* (N. Y., 1939), describes the cabinet and brain trust toward the end of the second administration.

Among memoirs Raymond Moley, *After Seven Years* (N. Y., 1939), reflects disenchantment, and Frances Perkins, *The Roosevelt I Knew* (N. Y., 1946), approbation. H. A. Wallace, *New Frontiers* (N. Y., 1934), comments upon the first year of agriculture's New Deal; Frances Perkins, *People at Work* (N. Y., 1934), reviews the labor program; and H. L. Hopkins, *Spending to Save* (N. Y., 1936), presents a close-up of the FERA and WPA. In telling the story of the PWA and also of conservation, H. L. Ickes, *Back to Work* (N. Y., 1935) and *Autobiography of a Curmudgeon* (N. Y., 1943), are matched in pungency only by H. S. Johnson's narrative of the NRA, *The Blue Eagle from Egg to Earth* (N. Y., 1935). J. A. Farley writes spiritedly of politics in *Behind the Ballots* (N. Y., 1938), while D. C. Roper's account of the department of commerce in *Fifty Years of Public Life* (Durham, N. C., 1941) is colorless. The most copious document kept by a high official of the New Deal, Henry Morgenthau, jr.'s, diary, is as yet unpublished. I. H. Hoover, *Forty-Two Years in the White House* (Boston, 1934), touches upon both presidents of the era, as does E. W. Starling and Thomas Sugrue, *Starling of the White House* (N. Y., 1946). R. T. McIntire, *White House Physician* (N. Y., 1946), draws upon the medical memories of twelve years.

Recollections of observant journalists, often poised between idealism and cynicism, include Walter Duranty, *I Write as I Please* (N. Y., 1935), Vincent Sheean, *Personal History* (N. Y., 1935), Negley Farson, *Way of a Transgressor* (N. Y., 1936), and T. L. Stokes, *Chip Off My Shoulder* (Princeton, 1939). Among socially minded autobiographies, the range extends from H. H. Kroll, *I Was a Sharecropper* (Indianapolis, 1937), to M. H. Ross, *Death of a Yale Man* (N. Y., 1939), tracing the conversion of a young bond salesman into a prolabor advocate working for the NLRB. A fine series of thumbnail life stories, gathered by Federal Writers' Project interviewers from citizens in North Carolina, Tennessee and Georgia, is presented in *These Are Our Lives* (Chapel Hill, 1939). Specimens of autobiography by eccentric political figures are Huey Long, *Every Man a King* (New Orleans, 1933), and F. E. Townsend, *New Horizons* (Chicago, 1943).

THE PEOPLE

POPULATION: W. S. Thompson and P. K. Whelpton, *Population Trends in the United States* (*Recent Social Trends Monograph*, N. Y., 1933), a standard work, should be supplemented by the former's *Research Memorandum on Internal Migration in the Depression* (Social Sci. Research Coun., *Bull.*, no. 30, 1937). N. E. Himes, *Medical History of Contraception* (Balt., 1936), is also authoritative. Dorothy D. Bromley, "Birth Control and the Depression," *Harper's Mag.*, CLXIX (1934), 563-574, summarizes the results of a Milbank Foundation survey, and National Resources Committee, *Problems of a Changing Population* (Wash., 1938), reveals trends mirrored in vital statistics as well as in educational, social and cultural patterns. A convenient reading list on matters affecting the nation's people is American Social Problems Study Committee, *Guide for the Study of American Social Problems* (N. Y., 1942); also valuable here and for subjects cited below is the Russell Sage Foundation's *Social Work Year Book* (N. Y., 1929-   ).

MINORITY GROUPS: A classified bibliography is *The Negro,* compiled by the Division of School Libraries and revised and reprinted through the courtesy of the Julius Rosenwald Fund (State Dept. of Educ., Nashville, Tenn., 1941). C. S. Johnson, *The Negro in American Civilization* (N. Y., 1930), gives an analysis at the threshold of this era. For later developments and a masterly review of the whole problem, see Gunnar Myrdal and others, *An American Dilemma* (2 vols., N. Y., 1944), a study made between 1938 and 1942 for the Carnegie Corporation. The best historical treatment is J. H. Franklin, *From Slavery to Freedom* (N. Y., 1947). Roi Ottley, *New World A-Coming* (Boston, 1943), is a journalist's able account of Harlem in the Depression. Also useful are C. G. Woodson, *The Negro Professional Man and the Community* (Wash., 1934); C. S. Johnson, *Growing Up in the Black Belt* (Wash., 1941); E. F. Frazier, *The Negro Family in the United States* (Chicago, 1939); John Dollard, *Caste and Class in a Southern Town* (New Haven, 1937); and Illinois WPA, *The Cavalcade of the American Negro* (Chicago, 1940), a graphic view of this race's contribution to American life. The somber side is presented by A. F. Raper, *The Tragedy of Lynching* (Chapel Hill, 1933).

For other groups as well, see D. R. Young, *Research Memorandum on Minority Peoples in the Depression* (Social Sci. Research Coun., *Bull.*, no. 31, 1937); Carey McWilliams, *Brothers under the Skin* (Boston, 1943) and *Prejudice—Japanese-Americans: Symbol of Racial Intolerance* (Boston, 1944); Louis Adamic, *A Nation of Nations* (N. Y., 1945); and Wallace Stegner, *One Nation* (Boston, 1945), which offers a photographically documented account. For the political exiles of the thirties, see particularly M. R. Davie, *Refugees in America* (N. Y., 1947).

WOMEN AND THE FAMILY: A number of works illuminate the rôle of women, notably Sophonisba P. Breckinridge, *Women in the Twentieth Century* (N. Y., 1933), Lorine Pruette, ed., *Women Workers through the Depression* (N. Y., 1934), E. R. Groves, *The American Woman* (N. Y., 1937), and *U. S. Senate Hearings on Equal Rights for Men and Women* (75 Cong., 3 sess., S. J. Resolution 65, 1938). References on the family in the Depression are supplied by Mirra Komarovsky, "Selected Bibliography on the Family, 1935-1940," *Am. Sociological Rev.*, V,

558-565, and J. K. Folsom, *The Family and Democratic Society* (N. Y., 1943), 697-727. Specific accounts include M. F. Nimkoff, *The Family* (Boston, 1934); R. C. Angell, *The Family Encounters the Depression* (N. Y., 1936); S. A. Stouffer, P. F. Lazarsfeld and A. J. Jaffe, *Research Memorandum on the Family in the Depression* (Social Sci. Research Coun., *Bull.*, no. 29, 1937); Ruth S. Cavan and Katherine H. Ranck, *The Family and the Depression* (Chicago, 1938); and Mirra Komarovsky, *The Unemployed Man and His Family* (N. Y., 1940). E. A. Rundquist and R. F. Sletto, *Personality in the Depression* (Minneapolis, 1936), though obsessed with testing techniques, supplies useful data respecting the psychology of hard times and relief.

YOUTH: Louise A. Menefee and M. M. Chambers, comps., *American Youth: an Annotated Bibliography* (Wash., 1938), contains some 2500 items. For the background of youth's problems, see Thacher Winslow and F. P. Davidson, eds., *American Youth: an Enforced Reconnaissance* (Cambridge, 1940). Essential is *Youth and the Future* (Wash., 1942), the six-year general report of the American Youth Commission. Also useful are Howard Bell, *Youth Tell Their Story* (Wash., 1938), a digest of group opinion; WPA *Research Monographs* like B. L. Melvin and Elna N. Smith, *Rural Youth* (no. 15, Wash., 1938); and *Reports* of the White House Conferences on Children in 1930 and 1940. An indispensable summary is Bureau of the Census, *The Facts about Youth as Portrayed in the 1940 Census* (*Population*, ser. P-3, no. 19). For child labor, see Katharine du P. Lumpkin and Dorothy W. Douglas, *Child Workers in America* (N. Y., 1937); for federal relief, Kenneth Holland and F. E. Hill, *Youth in the CCC* (Wash., 1942), P. O. Johnson and O. L. Harvey, *The National Youth Administration* (Wash., 1938), and Betty and E. K. Lindley, *A New Deal for Youth* (N. Y., 1938); and for mores, Dorothy D. Bromley and Florence H. Britten, *Youth and Sex* (N. Y., 1938), and Maxine Davis, *The Lost Generation* (N. Y., 1936). For delinquency, juvenile and otherwise, consult Thorsten Sellin, *Research Memorandum on Crime in the Depression* (Social Sci. Research Coun., *Bull.*, no. 27, 1937), and, more specifically *Facts about Juvenile Delinquency* (Wash., 1935), with bibliography.

INDUSTRY AND COMMERCE

BUSINESS AND FINANCE: W. C. Mitchell, *Business Cycles* (N. Y., 1927), J. M. Clark, *Strategic Factors in Business Cycles* (N. Y., 1934), and G. V. Cox, *An Appraisal of American Business Forecasts* (Chicago, rev. edn., 1930), offer analyses of the patterns of prosperity and adversity. Valuable for conditions leading up to the New Deal are J. C. Bonbright and G. C. Means, *The Holding Company* (N. Y., 1932), A. A. Berle, jr., and G. C. Means, *The Modern Corporation and Private Property* (N. Y., 1933), and the searching inquiry into holding companies contained in the Federal Trade Commission's *Summary Report to the Senate,* Parts 72A and 73A, *Utility Corporations* (Wash., 1935). For the débâcle of 1929, see J. D. Magee, *Collapse and Recovery* (N. Y., 1934), and A. B. Adams, *National Economic Security* (Norman, Okla., 1936), an excellent general account. For the banking crisis early in 1933 C. C. Colt and N. S. Keith, *28 Days* (N. Y., 1933), C. B. Upham and Edwin Lamke, *Closed and Distressed Banks* (Wash., 1934), and J. F. T. O'Connor, *The Banking Crisis and Recovery under the Roosevelt Administration* (Chicago, 1938), are useful; a pro-Hoover account is Lawrence Sullivan, *Prelude to Panic* (Wash., 1936). A. D. Noyes, *The Market Place* (Boston, 1938), is sound but dull; F. L. Allen, *The Lords of Creation* (N. Y., 1935), draws a lively picture; while postmortems under Senate inquiry are marshaled by Ferdinand Pecora, *Wall Street under Oath* (N. Y., 1936). Brookings Institution studies like E. G. Nourse and others, *America's Capacity to Produce* (Wash., 1934), Maurice Leven, H. G. Moulton and C. A. Warburton, *America's Capacity to Consume* (1934), H. G. Moulton, *The Formation of Capital* (1935), the same author's *Income and Economic Progress* (1935) and, with others, *The Recovery Problem in the United States* (1936), are solid and important. For words of caution, however, note A. F. Burns, "The Brookings Inquiry into Income Distribution and Progress," *Quar. Journ. of Econs.,* L, 476-623, charging that "the diagnosis [*i.e.,* need for a price-reduction program to stimulate consumption and reduce overhead costs while increasing output] bears little relation to any of the findings." A popular summary of Brookings material, with oversimplifications, is Stuart Chase, *Idle Money, Idle Men* (N. Y., 1940). F. C. Mills, *Prices in Recession and Recovery* (N. Y., 1936), is scholarly.

NEW DEAL INNOVATIONS AND CONDITIONS: G. C. Johnson, *The Treasury and Monetary Policy, 1933-1938* (*Harvard Political Studies*, Cambridge, 1939), reviews fiscal developments. Discussions of business practices under the New Deal are A. R. Burns, *The Decline of Competition* (N. Y., 1936), and E. D. Kennedy, *Dividends to Pay* (N. Y., 1939). Broader in scope are J. M. Clark, *The Social Control of Business* (rev. edn., N. Y., 1939), L. S. Lyon, M. W. Watkins and Victor Abramson, *Government and Economic Life* (2 vols., Wash., 1939-1940), and Merle Fainsod and Lincoln Gordon, *Government and the American Economy* (N. Y., 1941). L. S. Lyon and others, *The National Recovery Administration* (Wash., 1935), M. F. Gallagher, *Government Rules Industry* (N. Y., 1934), and C. F. Roos, *NRA Economic Planning* (Bloomington, Ind., 1937), treat the New Deal's first experiment in the supervision of business. The retort of private enterprise to regulation is described by S. H. Walker and Paul Sklar, *Business Finds Its Voice* (N. Y., 1938). For analysis of the export problem, with primary attention to farm commodities, see A. E. Taylor, *The New Deal and Foreign Trade* (N. Y., 1935). In the wake of the 1937-1938 recession a joint congressional committee investigated monopolies, cartels, trade associations, investment-banking practices, patent controls and kindred symptoms of concentrated power—the first inquiry of this kind since the Industrial Commission of 1898—and its records (1938-1941), now in the National Archives, are a mine of material on Big Business prior to and during the New Deal. The most important are accessible as *Verbatim Records of the Proceedings of the Temporary National Economic Committee* (39 vols.). For further material upon cartels, consult T. W. Arnold, *The Bottlenecks of Business* (N. Y., 1940), D. C. Edwards, *Economic and Political Aspects of International Cartels* (Wash., 1944), and Wendell Berge, *Cartels: Challenge to a Free World* (Wash., 1944). E. M. Eriksson, *The Supreme Court and the New Deal* (Los Angeles, 1941), succinctly summarizes decisions touching the New Deal, with bibliography.

LABOR

Emanuel Stein and others, *Labor and the New Deal* (N. Y., 1934), and C. R. Daugherty, *Labor under the NRA* (Boston, 1934), trace labor's upsurge in the heyday of the Blue Eagle; R. R. R. Brooks, *When Labor Organizes* (New Haven, 1937) and *Unions of Their Own Choosing* (New Haven, 1939), carry the story to the sit-down strikes. Herbert Harris, *American Labor* (New Haven, 1938), though partial to the CIO, is less violently anti-A. F. of L. than Edward Levinson, *Labor on the March* (N. Y., 1938). Harold Seidman, *Labor Czars* (N. Y., 1938), discusses racketeering; Louis Adamic, *Dynamite* (rev. edn., N. Y., 1934), deals with class violence; while Clinch Calkins, *Spy Overhead* (N. Y., 1937), describes industrial espionage. S. H. Slichter, *Union Policies and Industrial Management* (Wash., 1941), is an impartial discussion. NRA mediation techniques are treated by L. L. Lorwin and Arthur Wubnig, *Labor Relations Boards* (Wash., 1935); later developments, by Joseph Rosenfarb, *The National Labor Policy and How It Works* (N. Y., 1940). For statistical information, consult M. Ada Beney, *Wages, Hours and Employment in the United States, 1914-1936* (Natl. Indus. Conf. Bd., *Studies,* no. 229, 1936). The growth of unionism in an unorganized industry is traced by H. J. Lahne, *The Cotton Mill Worker* (N. Y., 1944). For the rising demands of military production, see Twentieth Century Fund, *Labor and National Defense* (N. Y., 1941).

AGRICULTURE

The best introduction to the social and cultural aspects of agriculture is *Farmers in a Changing World,* the excellent *Yearbook for 1940* of the Department of Agriculture. Other general surveys include O. E. Baker, Ralph Borsodi and M. L. Wilson, *Agriculture in Modern Life* (N. Y., 1939), and C. T. Schmidt, *American Farmers in the World Crisis* (N. Y., 1941). Conditions at the beginning of the era are well set forth by E. de S. Brunner and J. H. Kolb, *Rural Social Trends* (*Recent Social Trends Monograph,* N. Y., 1933), and later by Brunner and Irving Lorge, *Rural Trends in Depression Years* (N. Y., 1937), and Dwight Sanderson, *Research Memorandum on Rural Life in the Depres-*

sion (Social Sci. Research Coun., *Bull.*, no. 34, 1937). Population shifts are treated in such WPA *Research Monographs* as C. E. Lively and Conrad Taeuber, *Rural Migration in the United States* (Wash., 1939), F. M. Vreeland and E. J. Fitzgerald, *Farm-City Migration and Industry's Labor Reserve* (Phila., 1937), and J. N. Webb, *The Migratory-Casual Worker* (Wash., 1937). For "Okies" and other orphans of the soil, see U. S. Department of Labor, *Migration of Workers* (2 vols., Wash., 1938), and Carey McWilliams, *Factories in the Field* (Boston, 1939).

The heart of the rural problem is addressed by the National Resources Committee's *Farm Tenancy*, a report of the President's Committee (Wash., 1937); C. C. Taylor, Helen W. Wheeler and E. L. Kirkpatrick, *Disadvantaged Classes in American Agriculture* (U. S. Dept. of Agr., *Social Research Report*, no. 8, 1938); and C. S. Johnson, W. W. Alexander and E. R. Embree, *The Collapse of Cotton Tenancy* (Chapel Hill, 1935). A wealth of observation appears in A. F. Raper, *Preface to Peasantry* (Chapel Hill, 1936) and, with I. de A. Reid, *Sharecroppers All* (Chapel Hill, 1941); and T. J. Woofter, jr., and Ellen Winston, *Seven Lean Years* (Chapel Hill, 1939). Detailed Brookings studies are J. S. Davis, *Wheat and the AAA* (Wash., 1935); H. B. Rowe, *Tobacco under the AAA* (1935); H. I. Richards, *Cotton and the AAA* (1936); and E. G. Nourse, J. S. Davis and J. D. Black, *Three Years of the AAA* (1937). U. S. Bureau of Agricultural Economics, *Technology on the Farm* (Wash., 1940), is the best survey of that subject.

RELIEF AND SECURITY

POVERTY AND UNEMPLOYMENT: A bibliography prepared by the University of Chicago's Public Administration Service, *Unemployment and Relief Documents* (Chicago, 1934), is helpful. The Red Cross report of the first major undertaking of this era is *Relief Work in the Drought of 1930-1931* (Wash., 1931). Josephine C. Brown, *Public Relief, 1929-1939* (N. Y., 1940), spans Old Deal and New. Summaries of New Deal policies are made by A. E. Burns and E. A. Williams, *A Survey of Relief and Security Programs* (WPA, Wash., 1938) and *Federal Work, Security, and Relief Programs* (WPA, Wash., 1941), and by Elias Huzar, *Federal Unemployment Relief Policies: the First Decade* (Ph.D.

thesis, Princeton Univ., 1938), digested in *Journal of Politics,* II, 321-335. Other important works are National Resources Planning Board, *Security, Work, and Relief Policies* (Wash., 1942); another NRPB publication, *Development of Resources and Stabilization of Employment* (1942); A. V. Macmahon, J. D. Millett and Gladys Ogden, *The Administration of Federal Work Relief* (Chicago, 1941), useful for the managerial side; and two Social Science Research Council *Memoranda:* F. S. Chapin and S. A. Queen, *Social Work in the Depression* (*Bull.,* no. 39, 1937), and R. C. and Mary K. White, *Social Aspects of Relief Policies in the Depression* (*Bull.,* no. 38, 1937). For the human side, with case histories, see E. W. Bakke's studies, *The Unemployed Worker* (New Haven, 1940) and *Citizens without Work* (New Haven, 1940); J. M. Williams, *Human Aspects of Unemployment and Relief* (Chapel Hill, 1933); Marie D. Lane and Francis Steegmuller, *America on Relief* (N. Y., 1938); C. C. Zimmerman and N. L. Whetten, *Rural Families on Relief* (WPA, Wash., 1938); and American Association of Social Workers, *This Business of Relief* (N. Y., 1936). For unemployment as a chronic problem, consult House Committee on Labor, *To Provide for a United States Unemployment Commission* (75 Cong., 1 sess., Hearings on H. R. 8180, 1937); and Corrington Gill, *Wasted Manpower* (N. Y., 1939).

NEW DEAL AGENCIES: The best general account of the Federal Emergency Relief Administration is E. A. Williams, *Federal Aid for Relief* (N. Y., 1939); the FERA's *Final Statistical Report,* directed by T. E. Whiting, was issued in 1942. The FERA's *Monthly Reports* (May, 1933-December, 1935) are basic for this agency as well as the temporary CWA. Louise V. Armstrong, *We Too Are the People* (Boston, 1938), vividly describes early days of FERA relief in a Michigan village. An admirable survey of its heir is D. S. Howard, *The WPA and Federal Relief Policy* (N. Y., 1943); useful for one facet is D. S. Campbell, F. H. Bair and O. L. Harvey, *Educational Activities of the WPA* (Wash., 1939); while J. C. Bevis and S. L. Payne, *Former Relief Cases in Private Employment* (WPA, Wash., 1939), rounds out the picture. *Inventory: an Appraisal of the Results of the WPA* (Wash., 1938), is typical of the agency's stocktaking. For the Civilian Conservation Corps, see Federal Security Agency, *The*

CCC at Work (Wash., 1941); the Corps' national weekly, *Happy Days* (started in 1933), which culled material from local camp papers; and *Bibliography: a List of References on the United States Civilian Conservation Corps,* issued by the director in 1939.

A competent dissertation with bibliography is J. F. Isakoff, *The Public Works Administration* (Urbana, Ill., 1938). To H. L. Ickes's books already mentioned should be added, in this connection, his *Accomplishments of the Federal Emergency Administration of Public Works, 1933-1936* (Wash., 1936). The *Record of PWA* is a summary issued in 1939. For the moot question of pump-priming, see A. D. Gayer, *Public Works in Prosperity and Depression* (N. Y., 1935), and J. K. Galbraith and G. G. Johnson, jr., *Economic Effects of the Federal Public Works Expenditures, 1933-1938* (NRPB, Wash., 1940). See later, under "Planning," for the TVA.

SOCIAL SECURITY: The basic problem is sketched by Abraham Epstein, *Insecurity, a Challenge to America* (N. Y., 1933). A concise factual presentation is Social Security Board, *Security in America* (Wash., 1937). The most authoritative treatment is P. H. Douglas, *Social Security in the United States* (rev. edn., N. Y., 1939), supplemented by Isabel G. Carter, ed., *Appraising the Social Security Program* (Am. Acad. of Polit. and Social Sci., *Annals,* CCII, 1939). The chief pressure bloc for old-age assistance is described in Twentieth Century Fund, *The Townsend Crusade* (N. Y., 1936).

PLANNING

THE CITY: A pre-Roosevelt appraisal is R. D. McKenzie, *The Metropolitan Community* (*Recent Social Trends Monograph,* N. Y., 1933); specific attention is given the New York area by R. L. Duffus, *Mastering a Metropolis* (N. Y., 1930). C. E. Ridley and O. F. Nolting, eds., *What the Depression Has Done to Cities* (Chicago, 1935), discusses municipal finance, health, housing, public libraries and other sufferers from hard times. National Resources Committee, *Status of City and County Planning in the United States* (Wash., 1937), Thomas Adams, *Outline of Town and City Planning* (N. Y., 1936), and Katherine McNamara, *Bibliography of Planning, 1928-1935* (Cambridge, 1936), indicate the new trends and accomplishments. Other significant works are W. F. Ogburn, *Social Characteristics of Cities* (Chicago, 1937); G. R. Leighton, *Five Cities* (N. Y., 1939), tracing their life cycle; Lewis Mumford, *The Culture of Cities* (N. Y., 1938), a brilliant presentation of planning; and the Urbanism Committee of the National Resources Committee, *Our Cities* (Wash., 1937), factual and stimulating.

HOUSING: No comprehensive account of Hoover's Home Loan Banks and Roosevelt's Home Owners' Loan Corporation and Federal Housing Administration has yet been compiled, but periodic reports are available. Monograph VIII of the Temporary National Economic Committee, *Toward More Housing* (Wash., 1940), contains valuable data, including the story of restrictions in the building trades. Arguments about public housing are aired in National Association of Housing Officials, *Summary of Hearings on the Wagner Housing Bill* (Chicago, 1936). The *Housing Officials' Yearbook* (Chicago, 1935-   ) of the National Association of Housing Officials is a valuable source. M. W. Straus and Talbot Wegg, *Housing Comes of Age* (N. Y., 1938), considers mainly PWA construction. Edith E. Wood, *Recent Trends in American Housing* (N. Y., 1931) and *Slums and Blighted Areas in the United States* (Federal Emergency Administration of Public Works, *Housing Bull.*, no. 1, 1935), are illuminating. Useful discussions are Henry Wright, *Housing Urban America* (N. Y., 1935), C. A. Perry, *Housing for the Machine Age* (N. Y., 1939), and Carol Aronovici, *Housing the Masses* (N. Y., 1939), with critical bibliography. James Ford and others, *Slums and Housing: with Special Reference to New York City* (2 vols., Cambridge, 1936), affords historical perspective and a wealth of detail. James and Katherine M. Ford, *The Modern House in America* (N. Y., 1940), briefly discusses new trends in house planning, serviceability and materials, with photographs.

THE REGION: Indispensable is National Resources Committee, *Regional Factors in National Planning and Development* (Wash., 1935); a brief account of steps taken is the same agency's brochure *National Planning* (Wash., 1938). Between 1936 and 1943 the National Resources Planning Board or antecedent agencies sired thirteen *Regional Planning Reports*, beginning with the Pacific Northwest and closing with Puerto Rico. Also valuable are the twenty-two Drainage Basin Committee *Reports*, issued in

1937. No student of industrial planning can afford to overlook the same agency's *Patterns of Resource Use* (Wash., 1938), *The Structure of the American Economy: Basic Characteristics* (1939), and *Industrial Location and National Resources* (1943). Among nonofficial publications H. W. Odum and H. E. Moore, *American Regionalism* (N. Y., 1938), is comprehensive; K. B. Lohmann, *Regional Planning* (Ann Arbor, 1936), synoptic; and Isaiah Bowman, *Geography in Relation to the Social Sciences* (N. Y., 1934), thoughtful.

Essential for the Southern "problem region" are Odum's *Southern Regions of the United States* (Chapel Hill, 1936), with bibliography; R. B. Vance, *Human Geography of the South* (Chapel Hill, 1935); W. C. Holley, Ellen Winston and T. J. Woofter, jr., *The Plantation South, 1934-1937* (WPA, Wash., 1940); Allison Davis, B. B. and M. R. Gardner, *Deep South* (Chicago, 1941); and National Emergency Council, *Report on Economic Conditions of the South* (Wash., 1938). Among subjective interpretations by Southerners, the best are W. J. Cash, *The Mind of the South* (N. Y., 1941), a well-considered historical approach, and Jonathan Daniels, *A Southerner Discovers the South* (N. Y., 1938). The principal experiment in regional planning is treated authoritatively in David Lilienthal, *TVA: Democracy on the March* (N. Y., 1944); an appendix lists important literature on the TVA, noting that a complete bibliography would run to over 3500 items. Among the more important are C. L. Hodge, *The Tennessee Valley Authority* (Wash., 1938), scholarly; Willson Whitman, *God's Valley* (N. Y., 1939), stressing human interest; C. H. Pritchett, *TVA: a Study in Public Administration* (Chapel Hill, 1943); and R. L. Duffus and others, *The Valley and Its People* (N. Y., 1944), presenting facts and pictures. For the controversial "yardstick" aspect of the TVA, see J. C. Bonbright, *Public Utilities and the National Power Policies* (N. Y., 1940).

CONSERVATION: Carter Goodrich and others, *Migration and Economic Opportunity* (Phila., 1936), surveys depressed and overexploited areas while pointing up the need for intelligent land use. Division of Information, Resettlement Administration, *The Resettlement Administration and Its Work* (Wash., 1935), discusses both suburban and rural projects. Conrad Taeuber and C.

C. Taylor, *The People of the Drought States* (WPA, Wash., 1937), is supplemented by vivid narratives like Caroline A. Henderson, "Letters from the Dust Bowl," *Atlantic Mo.*, CLVII (1936), 540-551, and R. D. Lusk, "Life and Death of 470 Acres," *Sat. Eve. Post*, CCXI, 5-6 ff. (Aug. 13, 1938). Excellent federal documents fraught with social implication are H. S. Person, *Little Waters* (Soil Conservation Service, Wash., 1935); H. H. Bennett, *Soil Conservation and Flood Control* (U. S. Dept. of Agr., *Miscel. Publ.*, no. 253, 1936); and for overgrazing, *The Western Range* (74 Cong., 2 sess., *Senate Doc.*, no. 199, 1936). P. B. Sears, *Deserts on the March* (Norman, Okla., 1935), and Stuart Chase, *Rich Land, Poor Land* (N. Y., 1936), are popular treatments; more technical is A. E. Parkins and J. R. Whitaker, eds., *Our National Resources and Their Conservation* (N. Y., 1936).

SCIENTIFIC RESEARCH

Lewis Mumford, *Technics and Civilization* (N. Y., 1936), and J. E. Thornton, ed., *Science and Social Change* (Wash., 1939), take a comprehensive sweep. More detailed in coverage from 1937 to 1942 is the three-volume *Science in Progress* (New Haven, 1939-1942) edited by G. A. Baitsell. Also important are Harold Ward, ed., *New Worlds in Science* (N. Y., 1941), and Bernard Jaffe, *Men of Science in America* (N. Y., 1944). *Research—a National Resource*, a three-volume series by the National Resources Committee, comprises *Relation of the Federal Government to Research* (Wash., 1938), *Industrial Research* (1940) and *Business Research* (1941). Under the same imprint, *Technological Trends and National Policy* (1937) and *Energy Resources and National Policy* (1939) are admirable surveys of technological and engineering progress.

G. W. Gray, *New World Picture* (Boston, 1936), is an introduction to physics and astronomy; E. P. Hubble, *The Observational Approach to Cosmology* (N. Y., 1937), a more advanced treatment of the latter. H. B. Lemon, *From Galileo to Cosmic Rays* (Chicago, 1934), G. R. Harrison, *Atoms in Action* (N. Y., 1939), and A. K. Solomon, *Why Smash Atoms?* (Cambridge, 1940), attractively broach the subject, while R. A. Millikan, *Electrons* (+ *and* —), *Protons, Photons, Neutrons, Mesotrons, and Cosmic Rays* (rev. edn., Chicago, 1947), is more technical. Basic knowledge in biology is reviewed by Richard Goldschmidt, *Ascaris* (N. Y., 1937); genetics is summarized by T. H. Morgan, *The Scientific Basis of Evolution* (N. Y., 1935); and physiology by W. B. Cannon, *The Wisdom of the Body* (rev. edn., N. Y., 1939). Henry Borsook, *Vitamins* (N. Y., 1940), is authoritative. Advances in medicine are recorded in Paul de Kruif, *The Fight for Life* (N. Y., 1938), somewhat marred by emotionalism.

HEALTH AND THE CONSUMER

MEDICAL CARE: S. D. Collins and Clark Tibbitts, *Research Memorandum on Social Aspects of Health in the Depression* (Social Sci. Research Coun., *Bull.*, no. 36, 1937), scans the problem raised by I. S. Falk, C. R. Rorem and Martha D. Ring in *The Costs of Medical Care* (Chicago, 1933) and the Wilbur Committee's *Medical Care for the American People: the Final Report* (Chicago, 1932). A progressive surgeon's reflections appear in Hugh Cabot, *The Doctor's Bill* (N. Y., 1935); another argues a more explicit solution in J. P. Warbasse, *Cooperative Medicine* (N. Y., 1936); and Henry Sigerist, *Medicine and Human Welfare* (New Haven, 1941), considers "social medicine." James Rorty, *American Medicine Mobilizes* (N. Y., 1939), describes the clash between the American Medical Association and sponsors of the Wagner health bill in 1938. See also the Library of Congress's important bibliography, *Health Insurance in the United States and Foreign Countries* (Wash., 1938). For public health, *Bulletins* of the U. S. Public Health Service and files of the Milbank Memorial Fund *Quarterly* (N. Y., 1923-) are rewarding.

SOCIAL ASPECTS OF CONSUMPTION: Other costs in addition to medical care are examined in National Resources Committee surveys: *Consumer Incomes in the United States: Their Distribution in 1935-1936* (Wash., 1938); *Consumer Expenditures in the United States: Estimates for 1935-1936* (1939); *Family Expenditures in the United States* (1941); and *The Consumer Spends His Income* (1939), a pamphlet digest of these findings. R. S. Vaile, *Research Memorandum on Social Aspects of Consumption in the Depression* (Social Sci. Research Coun., *Bull.*, no. 35, 1937), is useful, along with J. G. Brainerd, ed., *The Ultimate Consumer* (Am. Acad. of Polit. and Social Sci., *Annals*,

CLXXIII, 1934). For appraisal of the NRA Consumers' Advisory Board, see Persia C. Campbell, *Consumer Representation in the New Deal* (N. Y., 1940). Helen Sorenson, *The Consumer Movement* (N. Y., 1941), affords the best survey of its kind, while teaching of this subject is discussed in Stephens College Institute for Consumer Education, *Consumer Education for Life Problems* (Columbia, Mo., 1941). For coöperatives, consult B. B. Fowler, *Consumer Coöperation in America* (N. Y., 1936), and John Daniels, *Coöperation: an American Way* (N. Y., 1938).

RELIGION AND EDUCATION

S. C. Kincheloe, *Research Memorandum on Religion in the Depression* (Social Sci. Research Coun., *Bull.*, no. 33, 1937), and Hornell Hart, "Religion," *Am. Journ. of Sociology*, XLVII, 888-897, are general surveys. Extensive data are summarized by H. P. Douglass and E. de S. Brunner, *The Protestant Church as a Social Institution* (N. Y., 1935), while J. A. Ryan, *Seven Troubled Years, 1930-1936* (Ann Arbor, 1937), speaks for liberal Catholicism, and Marcus Bach, *They Have Found a Faith* (Indianapolis, 1946), describes the cultists.

In education the Joint Commission on the Emergency in Education, *The Schools and the Depression* (Wash., 1933), furnishes an early picture. Summaries of later developments are Educational Policies Commission of the National Education Association, *Research Memorandum on Education in the Depression* (Social Sci. Research Coun., *Bull.*, no. 28, 1937), and the Commission's *Education and Economic Well-Being in American Democracy* (Wash., 1940); also valuable is *What People Think about Youth and Education* (Natl. Educ. Assoc., *Bull.*, no. 17, 1940). For higher education, see the report of "Committee Y" of the American Association of University Professors, *Depression, Recovery and Higher Education* (N. Y., 1937); R. L. Duffus, *Democracy Enters College* (N. Y., 1936); and R. F. Butts, *The College Charts Its Course* (N. Y., 1939). The *Journal of Adult Education* (N. Y., 1929-1941), superseded by *Adult Education Journal* (N. Y., 1942-   ), offers abundant material on that topic, which is further enriched by two *Handbooks of Adult Education in the United States* edited by Dorothy Rowden (N. Y.,

1934, 1936), M. A. Cartwright, *Ten Years of Adult Education* (N. Y., 1935), and R. A. Beals and Leon Brody, comps., *The Literature of Adult Education* (N. Y., 1941).

THE CREATIVE ARTS

GENERAL: F. P. Keppel and R. L. Duffus, *The Arts in American Life* (*Recent Social Trends Monograph*, N. Y., 1933), presents a good background up to the early thirties. Jacob Baker, *Government Aid during the Depression to Professional, Technical and Other Service Workers* (Wash., 1936), is a survey by the WPA director of these manifold activities, and Grace Overmyer, *Government and the Arts* (N. Y., 1939), contributes a friendly review.

MUSIC: J. T. Howard's detailed and authoritative *Our American Music* (3d edn., N. Y., 1946), with a good bibliography, includes an account of the Federal Music Project, while Aaron Copland, *Our New Music* (N. Y., 1941), reflects a leading composer's enthusiasms.

PAINTING AND SCULPTURE: Martha C. Cheney, *Modern Art in America* (N. Y., 1939), is a good general survey. For the federal program, see *Public Works of Art Project* (Assistant Secretary of the Treasury, *Report to the FERA*, Wash., 1934), and Edward Bruce and Forbes Watson, *Mural Designs, 1934-1936* (*Art in Federal Buildings*, I, Wash., 1936). The Museum of Modern Art catalogue, *New Horizons in American Art* (N. Y., 1936), contains over a hundred plates of the best painting, sculpture and prints done under the WPA. The autobiography of George Biddle, father of the federal art program, *An American Artist's Story* (N. Y., 1939), relates its origin. Other autobiographies mirroring the social consciousness of the age are T. H. Benton, *An Artist in America* (N. Y., 1937), and Rockwell Kent, *This Is My Own* (N. Y., 1940).

ARCHITECTURE: Two Museum of Modern Art publications are useful: *Guide to Modern Architecture in the Northeast States* (N. Y., 1940) and Elizabeth Mock, ed., *Built in USA, 1932-1944* (N. Y., 1944). Poles apart are R. A. Cram, *My Life in Architecture* (Boston, 1936), by the chief exponent of the Gothic style, and F. L. Wright, *An Autobiography* (N. Y., 1932), by the champion of the moderns.

LETTERS: The third volume of V. L. Parrington's *Main Currents in American Thought* (N. Y., 1930), though left incomplete by his death in 1929, rounds out an important trilogy in the social interpretation of American literature and exercised a stimulating effect through the thirties. Alfred Kazin, *On Native Grounds* (N. Y., 1942), is easily the best book on the prose of this era; but good supplementary material occurs in Malcolm Cowley, ed., *After the Genteel Tradition* (N. Y., 1937), and Maxwell Geismar, *Writers in Crisis* (Boston, 1942). For the accomplishments of the FWA, see "Work of the Federal Writers' Project of WPA," *Publishers' Weekly*, CXXXV, Part I (1939), 1130-1135; Katharine Kellock, "The WPA Writers: Portraitists of the United States," *American Scholar*, IX (1940), 473-482; Mabel S. Ulrich, "Salvaging Culture for the WPA," *Harper's Mag.*, CLXXVIII (1939), 653-664; and Lewis Mumford, "Writers' Project," *New Republic*, XCII, 306-307 (Oct. 20, 1937). *American Stuff: an Anthology of Prose and Verse* (N. Y., 1937) represents "off-time" creative activity by FWP employees. A project undertaken at the close of this era for publication in 1948, *Literary History of the United States* (R. E. Spiller and others, eds., 2 vols. of text, 1 of bibliography), contains instructive material, including a chapter by Malcolm Cowley on the literary profession in the thirties, from which the present writer has benefited.

LEISURE AND RECREATION

GENERAL: F. R. Dulles, *America Learns to Play* (N. Y., 1940), has two chapters pertinent here, while J. R. Tunis, *Democracy in Sport* (N. Y., 1941), considers the social philosophy of games. J. F. Steiner, *Americans at Play* (*Recent Social Trends Monograph*, N. Y., 1933), gives mainly the pre-Depression picture; his *Research Memorandum on Recreation in the Depression* (Social Sci. Research Coun., *Bull.*, no. 32, 1937) extends the narrative. *Recreation* (N. Y., 1907-   ), the National Recreation Association monthly, devotes one issue annually (normally June) to a "Year Book" reviewing community recreation; the Association's *Park Recreation Areas in the United States: 1940* offers a survey of municipal and county park systems; under the same sponsorship appeared G. D. Butler, *Introduction to Community Recreation* (N. Y., 1940), containing a chapter on the Depression.

A spate of books on the uses of leisure flooded the early years of this decade; Gove Hambidge, *Time to Live* (N. Y., 1933), is typical. Touring, pleasure travel and related matters are considered by M. A. Willey and S. A. Rice, *Communication Agencies and Social Life* (*Recent Social Trends Monograph*, N. Y., 1933). G. A. Lundberg, Mirra Komarovsky and Mary A. McInerny, *Leisure: a Suburban Study* (N. Y., 1934), traces behavior patterns in New York's Westchester county.

READING: The most accessible pastime is viewed by Douglas Waples, *Research Memorandum on Reading Habits in the Depression* (Social Sci. Research Coun., *Bull.*, no. 37, 1937), bringing up to date a survey of group interests by Waples and R. W. Tyler, *What People Want to Read About* (Chicago, 1931). Annual lists in Alice P. Hackett, *Fifty Years of Best Sellers, 1895-1945* (N. Y., 1945), and files of *Publishers' Weekly* (N. Y., 1872-   ) are valuable. O. H. Cheney, *Economic Survey of the Book Industry, 1930-1931* (N. Y., 1931), and Jacob Loft, *The Printing Trades* (N. Y., 1944), cover terminal points in the era for that industry. R. L. Duffus, *Our Starving Libraries* (Boston, 1933), records the impact of hard times.

RADIO: P. F. Lazarsfeld, *Radio and the Printed Page* (N. Y., 1940), reflects the sociologist's view; Lazarsfeld and F. N. Stanton, eds., *Radio Research* (N. Y., 1941-   ), contains much social and cultural history, as do Hadley Cantril and G. W. Allport, *The Psychology of Radio* (N. Y., 1935), and H. S. Hettinger, ed., *New Horizons in Radio* (Am. Acad. of Polit. and Social Sci., *Annals*, CCXIII, 1941). See also annuals of the National Advisory Council on Radio in Education, *Radio in Education* (Chicago, 1931-1935). The pressure of commercialism rising in the thirties is surveyed in Llewellyn White, *The American Radio* (Commission on Freedom of the Press, *Publs.*, V, Chicago, 1947), and in Federal Communications Commission, *Public Service Responsibility of Broadcast Licensees* (Wash., 1946).

MOVIES: An ambitious "Film Index" was compiled under auspices of the Federal Writers' Project, canvassing some 25,000 books and articles relating to motion pictures; only one volume of a proposed three has been published: Harold Leonard, ed., *The Film as Art: a Bibliography* (N. Y., 1941). Among better studies of the movies are Lewis Jacobs, *The Rise of the American Film* (N. Y., 1939); L. C. Rosten, *Hollywood: the Movie Colony, the Movie Makers* (N. Y., 1941); and Ruth A. Inglis, *Freedom of the Movies* (Commission on Freedom of the Press, *Publs.*, IV, Chicago, 1947). For their social influence, see Edgar Dale, *The Content of Motion Pictures* (N. Y., 1935), and Margaret F. Thorp, *America at the Movies* (N. Y., 1940); for censorship, Raymond Moley, *The Hays Office* (Indianapolis, 1945).

POPULAR MUSIC: Dance bands find their celebrants in Benny Goodman and Irving Kolodin, *The Kingdom of Swing* (N. Y., 1939). The Decca Album Series, "Songs of Our Times," contains recordings of the song hits through this period, some fifteen to twenty-five for each year; four albums covering the years 1928-1931 have now appeared.

THE THEATER: Laudatory accounts of the Federal Theater are Willson Whitman, *Bread and Circuses* (N. Y., 1937), and Hallie Flanagan, *Arena* (N. Y., 1940). A more critical study, sponsored in 1942 by the American Council of Learned Societies, was directed by Dr. W. F. MacDonald of the Ohio State University; read in manuscript by the writer through the kindness of Dr. D. H. Daugherty, it will soon be accessible in print.

PUBLIC OPINION AND WORLD CRISIS

THE PUBLIC MIND: General works are H. L. Childs, *An Introduction to Public Opinion* (N. Y., 1940), and P. F. Lazarsfeld and others, *The People's Choice: How the Voter Makes Up His Mind in a Presidential Campaign* (Columbia Univ. Bur. of Applied Social Research, *Publ.*, no. B-3, 1944). For ways of testing the collective mind, consult George Gallup, *A Guide to Public Opinion Polls* (Princeton, 1944), and files of *Public Opinion Quarterly* (Princeton, 1937-   ). The chasm between old methods and new can be seen by comparing C. E. Robinson, *Straw Votes* (N. Y., 1932), with Hadley Cantril, *Gauging Public Opinion* (Princeton, 1944). For freedom of utterance, see Zechariah Chafee, jr., *Free Speech in the United States* (Cambridge, 1941), numerous pamphlets of the American Civil Liberties Union, M. L. Ernst, *The First Freedom* (N. Y., 1946), and Commission on Freedom of the Press, *A Free and Responsible Press* (Chicago, 1947). For propaganda H. D. Lasswell and others, *Propaganda and Promotional Activities, an Annotated Bibliography* (Minneapolis, 1935), provides a guide. Of especial interest are L. W. Doob, *Propaganda* (N. Y., 1935), and H. L. Childs, ed., *Pressure Groups and Propaganda* (Am. Acad. of Polit. and Social Sci., *Annals,* CLXXIX, 1935).

FOREIGN POLICY: Merle Curti, *Peace or War, the American Struggle: 1636-1936* (N. Y., 1936), surveys the whole peace movement, while W. E. Rappard, *The Quest for Peace* (Cambridge, 1940), analyzes neutrality and isolation over the preceding twenty years. W. S. Myers, *The Foreign Policy of Herbert Hoover, 1929-1933* (N. Y., 1940), is laudatory. A. W. Dulles and H. F. Armstrong, *Can America Stay Neutral?* (N. Y., 1939), probes weaknesses in the neutrality legislation of the thirties; the case for hemispheric defense and overseas isolation is argued by C. A. Beard, *A Foreign Policy for America* (N. Y., 1940); and a useful digest with bibliography is J. W. Walch, *Complete Handbook on American Isolation* (mimeographed, Portland, Me., 1939). Duncan Aikman, *The All-American Front* (N. Y., 1940), S. F. Bemis, *The Latin American Policy of the United States* (N. Y., 1943), and John MacCormac, *Canada: America's Problem* (N. Y., 1940), treat inter-American relations, while the Orient receives attention in T. A. Bisson, *American Policy in the Far East, 1931-1941* (N. Y., 1941), and Eleanor Tupper and G. E. McReynolds, *Japan in American Public Opinion* (N. Y., 1937). The diplomatic background and documents are supplied by Department of State, *Peace and War: United States Foreign Policy, 1931-1941* (Wash., 1943). Joseph Alsop and Robert Kintner, *American White Paper* (N. Y., 1940), offers a popular narrative strongly pro-Roosevelt, and Forrest Davis and E. K. Lindley, *How War Came* (N. Y., 1942), advances the story through Pearl Harbor. Social and cultural effects of the Second World War, on the eve of and after the nation's entry, are examined by W. F. Ogburn, ed., *American Society in Wartime* (Chicago, 1943).

APPENDIX

ADDITIONAL FOOTNOTES

Page Line

2   11   ". . . summer of 1929." H. D. Hill, "The Adoration of Groups," *Atlantic Mo.*, CXLIII (1929), 759-764.

3   31   ". . . jumped to 70,950." J. N. Leonard, *Three Years Down* (N. Y., 1939), 37.

4   7   ". . . was not clear." Scholarly evidences of this interest are W. C. Mitchell, *Business Cycles: the Problem and Its Setting* (N. Y., 1927), and J. M. Clark, *Strategic Factors in Business Cycles* (N. Y., 1934). In 1931 a Foundation for the Study of Cycles, Inc., was set up by Edward R. Dewey at Riverside, Connecticut, to study all types, from economic and social phenomena to fluctuations in crops and animal life.

4   25   ". . . in the summer of 1929." "Everybody Ought to Be Rich," interview in *Ladies' Home Journ.*, XLVI (Aug. 1929), 9.

5   16   ". . . than permanent investments." D. L. Dumond, *Roosevelt to Roosevelt* (N. Y., 1937), 299.

5   30   ". . . by a four-inch tail." For the origin and definition of holding companies, see H. U. Faulkner, *The Quest for Social Justice* (*A History of American Life*, XI), 28. The equity of the topmost Insull holding company in one operating company at the base of the pyramid was only one twentieth of one per cent of the bank investment of the operating company. See the Federal Trade Commission, *Summary Report on Utility Corporations* (70 Cong., 1 sess., *Senate Doc.*, no. 92, 1935), Pt. 72A, 858.

6   6   ". . . the motions of prosperity." J. D. Magee, *Collapse and Recovery* (N. Y., 1934), 137-138.

Page Line
6   24   ". . . three billion dollars." "Pickpockets, Inc.," *Nation*, CL, 465 (April 13, 1940).

6   33   ". . . ing." L. M. Hacker, *A Short History of the New Deal* (N. Y., 1934), 27.

7   2   ". . . and recklessly abused." E. F. Gay, "The Great Depression," *Foreign Affairs*, X (1932), 535.

7   26   ". . . the account was cleared." For the heyday of installment buying, see P. W. Slosson, *The Great Crusade and After* (*A History of American Life*, XII), 181-183. According to Bureau of the Census figures, in 1929 the volume of installment sales was about six and a half billion dollars; by 1935 it had subsided to two billion. Horace Taylor and others, *Main Currents in Modern Economic Life* (N. Y., 1941), II, 188.

8   19   ". . . in 1917-1918." See Slosson, *Great Crusade and After*, 199-204.

9   2   ". . . $20,000,000 annually." A. E. Burns and E. A. Williams, *A Survey of Relief and Security Programs* (WPA, Wash., 1938), 7.

9   7   ". . . scant publicity resulted." F. L. Allen, *The Lords of Creation* (N. Y., 1935), 308.

9   12   ". . . ing." E. G. Nourse and others, *America's Capacity to Produce* (Wash., 1934), 415, 429-430. A different computation, on the basis of serviceability rather than vendibility, made in Harold Loeb and others, *The Chart of Plenty* (N. Y., 1935), raises this percentage of nonutilization to forty-four per cent.

9   24   ". . . severity and duration." A. H. Hansen, "What Causes a Business Downturn?" *New Republic*, XCIII, 382 (Feb. 2, 1938). Stuart Chase, in his timely *Prosperity: Fact or Myth* (N. Y., 1929), 17—a book written on the eve of the great débâcle—termed it "a prosperity founded on forcing people to consume what they do not need, and often do not want."

10   2   ". . . larly." A. B. Adams, *National Economic Security* (Norman, Okla., 1936), 75.

Page Line

10   4   ". . . among the rich." Loeb and others, *Chart of Plenty*, 61.

10   22   ". . . one." Leven and others, *America's Capacity to Consume*, 54-55. Disparities seemed less sensational, however, when the nation's gross income from production was divided among the classes sharing it. Thus the 1929 national income from current production, totaling eighty billion dollars, exhibited such allotments as: employees' wages 42.2 per cent, salaries 18.7, investment profits 17.9, farmers 6.4 (p. 165).

10   30   ". . . 1922 and 1929." *Income and Economic Progress* (*Public Affairs Pamphlet*, no. 1, 1936), 20.

11   8   ". . . First World War." See Burns and Williams, *Survey of Relief and Security Programs*, 74, for the general productivity of labor. They observe that even during the Depression, from 1929 to 1935, production in general increased another 10 per cent.

11   22   ". . . to the consumer." Quoted by T. J. Wertenbaker, *Labor Costs and American Democracy* (Princeton, 1938), 12, in an extended discussion of this problem.

12   32   ". . . estimated forty billion." *American Year Book for 1929*, 297.

13   16   ". . . adversely affected." *Time*, XIV, 45 (Nov. 11, 1929).

14   28   ". . . had enjoyed in 1928." *New International Year Book for 1932*, 49; *for 1933*, 47. For mordant comment upon the Empire State Building, see Edmund Wilson, *The American Jitters* (N. Y., 1932), 132-136; and similarly for Rockefeller Center, M. R. Werner, "Radio City," *Atlantic Mo.*, CLI (1933), 468-476.

16   26   ". . . clients." Leonard, *Three Years Down*, 139.

17   8   ". . . passing trains." R. S. and Helen M. Lynd, *Middletown in Transition* (N. Y., 1937), 13-19.

Page Line

17   15   ". . . with forty-one." U. S. Department of Commerce, *National Income in the United States, 1929-1935* (Wash., 1936), 22. Diverse ways of computation led to diverse results. Thus R. F. Martin, *National Income in the United States, 1799-1938* (N. Y., 1939), 6-7, by reckoning "total realized net income" arrives at somewhat different figures. F. D. Roosevelt, *Public Papers and Addresses* (S. I. Rosenman, ed., N. Y., 1938-1941), VII, 233 (and throughout), sets the 1932 national income at the still lower figure of thirty-eight billion dollars. All in all, says A. H. Hansen, *After the War—Full Employment* (National Resources Planning Board, Wash., 1942), 5, "the idleness of the decade of the thirties was responsible for the loss of $200 billions of income."

17   19   ". . . and commodities." F. A. Shannon, *Economic History of the People of the United States* (N. Y., 1934), 856.

17   25   ". . . sustained." C. J. Enzler, *Some Social Aspects of the Depression* (Wash., 1939), 19, 171.

17   32   ". . . 60 per cent." S. S. Kuznets, *National Income, 1929-1932* (Natl. Bur. of Econ. Research, *Bull.*, no. 49, 1934). After allowance for lowered living costs, wage-earners who were still employed in 1933 had suffered a cut of only a quarter in their 1929 earnings. R. S. Vaile, *Research Memorandum on Social Aspects of Consumption in the Depression* (Social Sci. Research Coun., *Bull.*, no. 35, 1937), 16.

18   3   ". . . than in private." Walter Lippmann, *Interpretations: 1931-1932* (N. Y., 1932), 34.

18   6   ". . . $495 in 1933." Martin, *National Income*, 6-7.

18   9   ". . . next year." Horace Taylor and others, *Contemporary Problems in the United States* (rev. edn., N. Y., 1936-1937), II, 250 *n*.

18   25   ". . . ten dollars a month." Enzler, *Some Social Aspects of the Depression*, 15.

18   33   ". . . per cent." Maurice Leven, *The Income Structure of the United States* (Wash., 1938), 119-124,
who sees the professional groups suffering proportionately heavier losses from the Depression than did employed workers.

19   5   ". . . fully employed." W. S. Myers and W. H.
Newton, *The Hoover Administration* (N. Y., 1936),
36. For details, see Bureau of the Census, *Unemployment* (*U. S. Fifteenth Census, 1930*), I (unemployment by states and counties, in urban and rural areas),
and II (general report, unemployment by occupations
in April, 1930, and returns from special census of
January, 1931).

19   10   ". . . five million more." A chart of unemployment
estimates prepared by the Bureau of Research and Statistics of the Social Security Board is in American
Academy of Political and Social Science, *Annals*,
CCII, 9.

19   36   ". . . sick of apples." "New York in the Third
Winter," *Fortune*, V (Jan. 1932), 109; Leonard,
Three Years Down, 139-140; Clinch Calkins, *Some
Folks Won't Work* (N. Y., 1930), 122-123.

21   5   ". . . heroes of 1933." H. G. Moulton and others,
The Recovery Problem in the United States (Wash.,
1936), 28-29, and F. C. Mills, *Prices in Recession and
Recovery* (N. Y., 1936), 24-25.

21   30   ". . . the Canadian line." Roosevelt, *Public Papers*,
I, 764. For measures of retaliation, see E. C. Kirkland,
A History of American Economic Life (rev. edn.,
N. Y., 1939), 702-703. For Hoover's argument that
this tariff had nothing to do with the Depression, note
his Cleveland campaign speech of 1932, *State Papers*,
II, 337 ff.

22   8   ". . . of the depression." Lynds, *Middletown in
Transition*, 17, 428.

Page Line

22   13   ". . . marketing practices." See Slosson, *Great Crusade and After*, 188.

24   1   ". . . First World War." See Slosson, *Great Crusade and After*, 290 *n.*

25   21   ". . . youth and beauty." Lorine Pruette, *Women Workers through the Depression* (N. Y., 1934), 32, 86.

26   13   ". . . canned goods dwindled." R. S. Lynd in President's Research Committee, *Recent Social Trends in the United States* (N. Y., 1933), II, 907, and Bruce Melvin, "Rural Life," *Am. Journ. of Sociology*, XXXVII, 937-941.

27   9   ". . . refused to yield." See Table 15, "Consumers," President's Research Committee, *Recent Social Trends*, II, 899, 906-907.

27   18   ". . . by Childs restaurants." "New York in the Third Winter," *Fortune*, V (Jan. 1932), 41 ff.

27   24   ". . . an ash tray." R. S. Vaile, *Research Memorandum on Social Aspects of Consumption in the Depression* (Social Sci. Research Coun., *Bull.*, no. 35, 1937), 21; R. S. and Helen M. Lynd, *Middletown in Transition* (N. Y., 1937), 280.

27   25   ". . . close-up picture." Lynds, *Middletown in Transition*, 10-11.

28   4   ". . . ilies." W. F. Ogburn, "Our Times," *Am. Journ. of Sociology*, XLVII, 810.

28   12   ". . . the 1929 level." President's Research Committee, *Recent Social Trends*, II, 906, and tables, 897-898.

28   18   ". . . manship." J. B. Swinney, *Merchandising of Fashions* (N. Y., 1942), 362.

29   9   ". . . open-toed shoe." See Katherine Casey and Claire Sullivan, "Charting the Fashions," *Atlantic Mo.*, CXLV (1930), 799-807; "Cosmetics: the

American Woman Responds," and "Model Women," *Fortune,* II (Aug. 1930), 29-32, 89-91; F. L. Allen, *Since Yesterday* (N. Y., 1940), 136-137; "Skirts Are Getting Shorter," *Life,* VI, 59 (Feb. 27, 1939).

29 23 ". . . in the South." Table no. 1 in A. D. Morehouse, "The Real Property Inventory of 1934," *Survey of Current Business,* XIV, no. 11 (1934), 16-19.

29 25 ". . . as much." D. L. Dumond, *Roosevelt to Roosevelt* (N. Y., 1937), 422.

32 4 ". . . of the spirit." The three comments here quoted will be found respectively in J. M. Williams, *Human Aspects of Unemployment and Relief* (Chapel Hill, 1933), 113; Lynds, *Middletown in Transition,* 474; and "In the Wind," *Nation,* CXLVII, 590 (Dec. 3, 1938).

32 18 ". . . repressive anxiety." Mirra Komarovsky, *The Unemployed Man and His Family* (N. Y., 1940), 130-136.

33 1 ". . . average job holder." O. M. Hall, "Attitudes of Unemployed and Employed Engineers," *Journ. of Social Psychology,* VI, 224-251.

33 10 ". . . down." R. O. Beckman, "Mental Perils of Unemployment," *Occupations,* XII (1933), 28.

33 25 ". . . in the mid-thirties." Maxine Davis, *The Lost Generation: a Portrait of American Youth Today* (N. Y., 1936), 10.

33 30 ". . . try to get out." Unemployment Committee of the National Federation of Settlements, *Case Studies of Unemployment* (Phila., 1931), xxxii.

33 35 ". . . time-hallowed philosophy." O. M. Hall, "Attitudes and Unemployment: a Comparison of the Opinions and Attitudes of Employed and Unemployed Men," *Archives of Psychology,* CLXV, 24-25.

34 31 ". . . Townsend crusade demonstrated." See pp. 203-204.

Page   *Line*

35   31   ". . . do in Norway." California State Unemployment Commission, *Report and Recommendations* (Sacramento, 1933), 94-95.

36   7   ". . . it made women." E. A. Rundquist and R. F. Sletto, *Personality in the Depression: a Study in the Measurement of Attitudes* (Minneapolis, 1936), 370, who report that most of the jobless built some kind of rationalization against the encroaching sense of inferiority (397).

36   12   ". . . for his country." Hall, "Attitudes and Unemployment," 31-32.

36   18   ". . . leave me alone." California State Unemployment Commission, *Report*, 92.

36   23   ". . . the word 'revolution.' " W. J. Cash, *The Mind of the South* (N. Y., 1941), 363.

36   32   ". . . starve to death." Louise V. Armstrong, *We Too Are the People* (Boston, 1938), 30.

37   2   ". . . starve?" *N. Y. Times*, March 28, 1931, 1.

37   11   ". . . need of relief." W. S. Myers and W. H. Newton, *The Hoover Administration* (N. Y., 1936), 68. For the previous history of the bonus, see P. W. Slosson, *The Great Crusade and After* (*A History of American Life*, XII), 76-77.

38   14   ". . . the troubled waters." See the first-hand observations reported by E. K. Lindley, *The Roosevelt Revolution* (N. Y., 1933), 67.

39   6   ". . . the city." J. N. Leonard, *Three Years Down* (N. Y., 1939), 281.

39   13   ". . . was largely contributory." "Social Practice," *Survey*, LXX (1934), 291. M. A. Hallgren, *Seeds of Revolt* (N. Y., 1933), chap. i, presents additional evidence.

39   17   ". . . sixteen." Esther Jacobs, "Is Malnutrition Increasing?" *Am. Journ. of Public Health*, XXIII, 786.

Page Line

39   23   ". . . per cent by 1931." Williams, *Human Aspects
of Unemployment and Relief*, 54.

40   3   ". . . food and vegetables." Stuart Chase, *The Economy of Abundance* (N. Y., 1934), 127.

40   19   ". . . 14.2 in 1936." Leonard, *Three Years Down*,
113, and *World Almanac for 1940*, 514. Somewhat
different percentages appear in the *New International
Year Book for 1933*, 194, ascribed to Dr. Frederick L.
Hoffman, which, however, agree in ranking 1932 as
the zenith year since data began to be kept, save for the
panic year 1908, which slightly exceeded 1932.

40   24   ". . . poverty in itself." See Ruth S. Cavan, *Suicide*,
(Chicago, 1928), 270, 273; and for the Great Depression, L. I. Dublin and Bessie Bunzel, *To Be or
Not to Be: a Study of Suicide* (N. Y., 1933), esp.
chap. viii.

40   29   ". . . creased." As estimated by the Casket Manufac-
turers' Association of America, quoted by R. S. Lynd,
"The People as Consumers," in President's Research
Committee, *Recent Social Trends*, II, 910.

42   23   ". . . communities." Herbert Hoover, *The Challenge
to Liberty* (N. Y., 1934), 54-55.

43   19   ". . . in this decade." E. L. Bogart, "The Changing
Economic Functions of Government," Am. Acad. of
Polit. and Social Sci., *Annals*, CCVI, 1-5; H. G.
Moulton and others, *The Recovery Problem in the
United States* (Wash., 1936), 103-107.

45   8   ". . . of 'hooverizing.' " P. W. Slosson, *The Great
Crusade and After* (*A History of American Life*, XII),
58-59.

45   26   ". . . something for nothing." D. S. Howard, *The
WPA and Federal Relief Policy* (N. Y., 1943),
43-50, 830-834, who notes that the mores do not
raise this last objection to condemn inherited wealth or
lucky speculation.

Page Line
46   8   ". . . Colonel Arthur Woods." Herbert Hoover, *State Papers* (W. S. Myers, ed., N. Y., 1934), I, 405. "Give a Job" and "Spruce Up" were the favored slogans of this campaign.

46   14   ". . . matched since 1924." *Trends in Community Chest Giving* (Community Chests and Councils, Inc., *Bull.*, no. 87, 1936). Upon a comparative basis, private relief funds in 1929 had supplied 24 per cent of the total outlay for relief, but by 1934 they comprised a bare 3 per cent. A. E. Burns and E. A. Williams, *A Survey of Relief and Security Programs* (WPA, Wash., 1938), 12.

46   25   ". . . of the need." Joanna C. Colcord and others, *Emergency Work Relief: as Carried Out in Twenty-Six American Communities, 1930-1931* (N. Y., 1932).

46   31   ". . . Newton D. Baker." Baker's point of view in regard to relief as the potential sapper of pride and initiative is revealed by his article, "The Decay of Self-Reliance," *Atlantic Mo.*, CLIV (1934), 726-733.

47   22   ". . . made into clothing." For an impressionistic picture of relief work among the hill folk of Kentucky, see Edmund Wilson, *The American Jitters* (N. Y., 1932), chap. ix; a more factual account of Red Cross activity at this time is Grace Abbott, *From Relief to Social Security* (Chicago, 1941).

48   17   ". . . as embarrassed banks." For Hoover's statement concerning the purposes of the RFC, see his *State Papers*, II, 106-107; for his apologia for General Dawes late in the campaign of 1932, II, 442-446.

49   14   ". . . for the former." Letter to H. S. Crocker, May 21, 1932, and Hoover's press statement upon elimination of "pork-barrel features," in Hoover, *State Papers*, II, 191, 235-237.

49   27   ". . . of mortgage holders." E. K. Lindley, *Half Way with Roosevelt* (N. Y., 1936), 103; A. M. Schlesin-

Page Line

ger, *Political and Social Growth of the American People, 1865-1940* (N. Y., 1941), 532.

50 29   ". . . campaign of 1932." E. K. Lindley, *The Roosevelt Revolution* (N. Y., 1933), 3.

51 17   ". . . the common interest." Quoted by C. A. and Mary R. Beard, *America in Midpassage* (N. Y., 1939), 130, in a useful parallel analysis of the Democratic and Republican platforms in 1932.

51 28   ". . . away." W. S. Myers and W. H. Newton, *The Hoover Administration* (N. Y., 1936), 20; and Hoover, *State Papers*, II, 418, for his oft-quoted declaration of October 31, 1932, in New York City.

52 2   ". . . corn." Joslin, *Hoover Off the Record*, 315.

52 10   ". . . within easy reach." Roosevelt, *Public Papers*, I, 646.

52 27   ". . . the federal authority." Roosevelt, *Public Papers*, I, 799.

53 9   ". . . ter." Roosevelt, *Public Papers*, II, 518; Lindley, *Roosevelt Revolution*, 61.

54 18   ". . . poverty and fear." Hoover, *State Papers*, 477-478; Roosevelt, *Public Papers*, I, 862.

54 28   ". . . for human welfare." W. A. White, *Forty Years on Main Street* (N. Y., 1937), 151, quoting his editorial apropos of this and the succeeding presidential election.

55 2   ". . . its beneficent originality." "The Permanent New Deal," *Yale Rev.*, XXIV (1935), 652.

56 10   ". . . through the ranks." *Public Papers*, I, 772.

56 29   ". . . health and wages." Frances Perkins, *The Roosevelt I Knew* (N. Y., 1946), 30-31.

58 19   ". . . tivism." Commission on the Social Studies, *Conclusions and Recommendations* (N. Y., 1934), 13.

Page	Line	
59	8	". . . cattle, you know." Perkins, *Roosevelt I Knew*, 108.
59	19	". . . a managed currency." The background of Keynes's monetary theory is delineated in his *Treatise on Money* (London, 1930); his specific prescription for the Great Depression is set forth concisely in his Halley Stewart lecture in *The World's Economic Crisis and the Way of Escape* (N. Y., 1932), 57-75, and more fully in his *General Theory of Employment, Interest, and Money* (N. Y., 1936). For Roosevelt's cursory acquaintance with Keynes, see Perkins, *Roosevelt I Knew*, 225-226.
60	3	". . . land of opportunity." For Roosevelt's utterances on this point, see his *Public Papers*, IV, 17, 271.
60	13	". . . and individual capacities." Roosevelt, *Public Papers*, VII, xxix.
62	5	". . . exceeding two billion." W. S. Myers and W. H. Newton, *The Hoover Administration* (N. Y., 1936).
62	28	". . . ury." T. G. Joslin, *Hoover Off the Record* (N. Y., 1934), 360. For a contrary view, see "Balance Sheet of the New Deal," Special Supplement, *New Republic*, LXXXVII, 141 (June 10, 1936).
64	22	". . . mere monetary profit." F. D. Roosevelt, *Public Papers and Addresses* (S. I. Rosenman, ed., N. Y., 1938-1941), II, 12.
67	23	". . . fire started anyhow." Dixon Wecter, *The Hero in America* (N. Y., 1941), 455-456.
68	2	". . . investment advisers' law." A concise summary of the whole program is found in Roosevelt, *Public Papers*, IX, 334-336. In practice, the long interval required for legal appeal converted the "death sentence" in the act of 1935 into a reprieve until after the close of this era.
68	26	". . . competitive devaluation." For Roosevelt's explanation of his act, see *Public Papers*, II, 264-266. Its

Page Line

repercussions are described by Sumner Welles, *The Time for Decision* (N. Y., 1944), 53 ff.

69 11 ". . . confidence and stability." See R. S. Tucker, "Price Fluctuations and the Gold Supply," *Journ. of Polit. Economy*, XLII, 517-530.

69 17 ". . . at West Point." H. M. Bratter, "The Silver Episode," *Journ. of Polit. Economy*, XLVI, 609-652, 802-837.

70 28 ". . . completed the restoration." See Roosevelt, *Public Papers*, II, 49-54, for the summons to drastic economies; and 219-221, and III, 173-181, for later concessions.

71 8 ". . . of federal enforcement." For the earlier history of national prohibition, see P. W. Slosson, *The Great Crusade and After* (*A History of American Life*, XII), chap. iv. Results of the National Economic League poll on the questions of the hour are in T. W. Arnold, *The Folklore of Capitalism* (New Haven, 1937), 105-107.

71 25 ". . . rout of preacherdom." Elmer Davis, "How the Wets Won," *Current History*, XXXIX (1933), 276-284.

72 22 ". . . the municipalities sixteen." A. E. Burns and E. A. Williams, *A Survey of Relief and Security Programs* (WPA, Wash., 1938), 14.

73 21 ". . . than farm folk." "Quarterly Survey," *Fortune*, XVII (Jan. 1938), 83. For an early résumé of arguments, see S. C. Wallace, *The New Deal in Action* (N. Y., 1934), chap. xxxii.

74 2 ". . . less." This dormant agency of the First World War was revitalized under the Wagner-Peyser act of June 6, 1933.

74 7 ". . . in that year." A. E. Burns and E. A. Williams, *Federal Work, Security, and Relief Programs* (WPA, Wash., 1941), 39.

Page Line

74 12 ". . . ruary, 1934." Burns and Williams, *Survey of Relief and Security Programs*, 3.

75   2 ". . . quiry." L. P. Stryker, *Report to . . . the Aldermanic Committee to Investigate the Relief Administration in the City of New York* (N. Y., 1935); F. L. Allen, *Since Yesterday* (N. Y., 1940), 177. A short history of the CWA is given by Harry L. Hopkins, *Spending to Save* (N. Y., 1936). The record of its integrity, in the handling of huge sums, was remarkably good. M. S. Stewart, *This Question of Relief* (*Public Affairs Pamphlet*, no. 8, 1936), 26, notes that out of 70,000 CWA administrators, only 22 were convicted of serious irregularities.

75 13 ". . . clothier, also benefited." Louise V. Armstrong, *We Too Are the People* (Boston, 1938), 162.

75 26 ". . . ten per cent." Armstrong, *We Too Are the People*, 280; E. A. Williams, *Federal Aid for Relief* (N. Y., 1939), 233.

76 29 ". . . of the PWA." H. L. Ickes, *Autobiography of a Curmudgeon* (N. Y., 1943), 295. The vast proliferation of federal agencies under the New Deal—"alphabet soup," as Al Smith called it derisively—may appear baffling without a convenient guide such as that supplied by Horace Taylor and others, *Contemporary Problems in the United States* (N. Y., 1936-1937), I, 484-489.

77 14 ". . . upon private business." A. D. Gayer, *Public Works in Prosperity and Depression* (Natl. Bur. of Econ. Research, *Publs.*, no. 29, 1935), 89-125.

77 19 ". . . thirty-four thousand projects." H. L. Ickes, *Back to Work: the Story of PWA* (N. Y., 1935), 49, 199; *World Almanac for 1944*, 599.

78   1 ". . . at any price." *America Builds: the Record of PWA* (PWA, Wash., 1939), 227-230.

78   7 ". . . years' normal growth." *America Builds*, 143-144.

Page Line

78   19   ". . . this activity ceased." Ickes, *Autobiography*, 287-295.

79   13   ". . . *Looking Backward*." See A. M. Schlesinger, *The Rise of the City* (*A History of American Life*, X), 262.

80   4   ". . . the right questions." Editors of the London *Economist, The New Deal: an Analysis and Appraisal* (N. Y., 1937), 149.

82   26   ". . . the American Congress." F. D. Roosevelt, *Public Papers and Addresses* (S. I. Rosenman, ed., N. Y., 1938-1941), II, 246, 252.

84   22   ". . . thirteen million unemployed." J. M. Clark, *Social Control of Business* (N. Y., 1939), 435.

85   3   ". . . road to recovery." *N. Y. Times*, Jan. 19, 1934.

86   15   ". . . in local affairs." U. S. *v.* Schechter Poultry Corp. *et al.*, 55 S. Ct., 844 (1935); for Roosevelt's comment, see *Public Papers*, IV, 221.

86   30   ". . . speeded the effort." L. S. Lyon and others, *The National Recovery Administration* (Wash., 1935), 873.

87   6   ". . . in many instances." See Lyon, *National Recovery Administration*, 18-24, and Horace Taylor and others, *Main Currents in Modern Economic Life* (N. Y., 1941), I, 312-315.

87   21   ". . . preserving free enterprise." D. R. Richberg, *Government and Business Tomorrow* (N. Y., 1943), 19.

87   25   ". . . the corporative state." A. R. Burns, *The Decline of Competition* (N. Y., 1936), 519.

88   11   ". . . their youth." Dorothy B. Bromley, "Newspapers and Child Labor," *Nation*, CXL, 131 (Jan. 30, 1935).

88   20   ". . . to satisfy nobody." However, Section 7A of the NRA law encouraged the spread of carriers' unions

Page Line

whose members, themselves over sixteen years of age, took up the cudgels against child labor. A. M. Lee, *The Daily Newspaper in America* (N. Y., 1937), 297-300.

88   33   ". . . the New Deal." Isabelle Keating, "Reporters Become of Age," *Harper's Mag.*, CLXX (1935), 601-612. The Dean S. Jennings case, involving an editorial worker discharged for his Guild activities, was adjudicated late in 1934 by the National Labor Relations Board in the plaintiff's favor (no. 195). He was ordered reinstated, but this was never done.

89   11   ". . . candidacy." F. L. Mott, "Newspapers in Presidential Campaigns," *Public Opinion Quar.*, VIII (1944-1945), 357, 362, gives the figure in the 1936 campaign as about 60 per cent of the party press; other estimates run as high as 85 per cent.

89   17   ". . . against the editorials." Bruce Bliven, "Public Opinion," Harold Stearns, ed., *America Now* (N. Y., 1938), 250, citing a survey made by the editors of the *New Republic*. The declining prestige of editorials is discussed by Virginius Dabney, "What's Wrong with Newspaper Editorials?" *Sat. Rev. of Lit.*, XXVIII, 8 (Feb. 24, 1945).

89   30   ". . . of autocratic power." *American Liberty League: a Statement of Its Principles and Purposes* (Wash., n. d.), 2.

90   21   ". . . a dire need." See R. L. Dewey, "The Transportation Act of 1940," *Am. Econ. Rev.*, XXXI, 15-26. For continuance of discriminatory freight rates, a particular grievance to South and West, see *Regionalized Freight Rates: Barrier to National Productiveness* (78 Cong., 1 sess., *House Doc.*, no. 137, 1943).

92   14   ". . . means of production." Duncan Aikman, "America Talks Debt," *Harper's Mag.*, CLXXIV (1936), 91-97; "Expenditures, 1930-1940," Taylor

and others, *Main Currents in Modern Economic Life*, II, 228-231.

93 14 ". . . in 1939." See Taylor and others, *Main Currents in Modern Economic Life*, II, 242, who on pp. 223 and 228 cite figures for the rise in the total cost of government, from eleven billion dollars in 1929 to seventeen by 1938.

93 28 ". . . from Congress." D. D. McKean, "Soaking the Poor," *New Republic*, LXXXIV, 121-123 (Sept. 11, 1935); R. M. Haig and others, *The Sales Tax in the American States* (N. Y., 1934). Carl Shoup, "The Sales Tax," Am. Acad. of Polit. and Social Sci., *Annals*, CLXXXIII, 104-110, calls it the most significant development in American taxation since the First World War, with an annual yield of $400,000,000.

93 34 ". . . stipulated conditions." For state and local control as well as the social effects of repeal, see L. V. Harrison and Elizabeth Raine, *After Repeal* (N. Y., 1936).

94 17 ". . . of national prohibition." "Quarterly Survey," *Fortune*, XVII (Jan. 1938), 86. See also Paul Studenski, *Liquor Consumption among the American Youth* (N. Y., 1937), 11-12, and J. A. Hawes, *Twenty Years among the Twenty-Year-Olds* (N. Y., 1929), 112.

94 22 ". . . and its philosophy." See H. U. Faulkner, *The Quest for Social Justice* (A History of American Life, XI), 77-78.

94 28 ". . . visions." J. H. Foth, "Workmen's Accident Compensation," J. T. Adams, ed., *Dictionary of American History* (N. Y., 1940), V, 485.

95 19 ". . . continuing employment." Roosevelt, *Public Papers*, VII, 392.

96 4 ". . . recovery." Roosevelt, *Public Papers*, III, 454.

96 31 ". . . the other A's." *These Are Our Lives*, 15.

Page Line

97   24   ". . . or five dollars." D. S. Howard, *The WPA and Federal Relief Policy* (N. Y., 1943), 55; A. E. Burns and E. A. Williams, *A Survey of Relief and Security Programs* (WPA, Wash., 1938), 1-2; Taylor and others, *Main Currents in Modern Economic Life*, II, 312.

98   10   ". . . thirty million persons." Howard, *WPA*, 30-32.

98   25   ". . . WPA innovations." Stanley High, "A Kind Word for the South," *Sat. Eve. Post*, CCX, 14 ff. (Jan. 8, 1938). Howard, *WPA*, 126-129, and the pamphlet *Questions and Answers on the WPA* (WPA, Wash., 1939), 7-8, offer summaries of its achievement.

99   6   ". . . American communities." Congressman Clifton A. Woodrum, for example, chief executioner of the WPA Theater, declared that some other aspects of the program were "almost like the accomplishments of King Solomon." *Congressional Record*, LXXXVI, pt. vi, 6251 (May 16, 1940).

99   28   ". . . blandishment indeed." R. S. and Helen M. Lynd, *Middletown in Transition* (N. Y., 1937), 122.

100   7   ". . . and other supplies." See a Southern storekeeper's statement in *These Are Our Lives*, 287, a volume published under the WPA's own Federal Writers' Project, but showing apparently great fidelity of reportage.

100 30   ". . . pointingly small." Statistics and conclusions from J. K. Galbraith and G. G. Johnson, jr., *Economic Effects of the Federal Public Works Expenditures, 1933-1938* (NRPB, Wash., 1940), 108-109, who note that federal expenditures rose from less than 2 per cent of the total construction in predepression days to 35 per cent under the New Deal.

101 29   ". . . Germany and Italy." See Walter Lippmann, "The Providential State," *Atlantic Mo.*, CLVIII (1936), 403-412.

Page *Line*

102   2   ". . . it ever was." Lynds, *Middletown in Transition*, 408-409.

102   15   ". . . of the Constitution." S. H. Walker and Paul Sklar, *Business Finds Its Voice* (N. Y., 1938). For indoctrination on the other side, see E. P. Herring, "Official Publicity and the New Deal," Am. Acad. of Polit. and Social Sci., *Annals*, CLXXIX, 167-175, and Elisha Hanson, "Official Propaganda and the New Deal," same vol., 176-186.

102   19   ". . . —stop Roosevelt." *N. Y. Times*, June 12, 1936.

103   8   ". . . of working conditions." Morehead *v.* New York *ex rel.* Tipaldo, 298 U.S., 587 (June 1, 1936.)

103   15   ". . . economic royalists." Roosevelt, *Public Papers*, V, 236.

103   33   ". . . met their master." Roosevelt, *Public Papers*, V, 568-569.

104   11   ". . . the Democratic fund." Louise Overacker, "Campaign Funds in the Presidential Election of 1936," *Am. Polit. Sci. Rev.*, XXXI, 473-498.

104   19   ". . . -seven per cent." On a percentage basis this was slightly less than the margin of Harding's triumph in 1920, although Roosevelt's total volume of 27,478,-945 votes and all electoral votes save eight made the winner of 1936 far more impressive. See E. E. Robinson, *The Presidential Vote, 1936* (Stanford Univ., 1940), 1-2. Robinson's earlier study, *The Presidential Vote, 1896-1932* (Stanford Univ., 1934), 30, notes that in his first election Roosevelt captured the old areas of progressivist support which Theodore Roosevelt had gained in 1912 and La Follette in 1924.

105   4   ". . . it upon another." C. B. Swisher, *American Constitutional Development* (Boston, 1943), chap. xxxvi.

Page Line
106   14   ". . . five to four." Joseph Alsop and Turner Cat-
           ledge, *The 168 Days* (N. Y., 1938), and Roosevelt,
           Public Papers, VI, 35-66 and *passim.* Volume IV of
           Public Papers, embracing the year 1935, is significantly
           entitled "The Court Disapproves," V (1936) "The
           People Approve" and VI (1937) "The Constitution
           Prevails." Foes of the president no doubt construed
           this last title in their own way.

106   23   ". . . won a war." Roosevelt, *Public Papers*, VII,
           393. For the aftermath of this fight, see M. W. Childs,
           "The Supreme Court Today," *Harper's Mag.*,
           CLXXVI (1938), 581-588.

106   27   ". . . with private facilities." Alabama Power Com-
           pany *v.* Ickes, 302 U. S., 364 (1938).

107   13   ". . . complacency or hope." For the causes of labor's
           earlier losses, see F. C. Mills, *Economic Tendencies in
           the United States* (Natl. Bur. of Econ. Research,
           Publs., no. 21, 1932), 481, and Emanuel Stein and
           others, *Labor and the New Deal* (N. Y., 1934), 9.

108   7   ". . . of his employment." The Court decision was
           that of Texas & New Orleans R. R. Co. *v.* Brother-
           hood of Railway and Steamship Clerks, 281 U. S.,
           548 (1930); for the Norris-La Guardia act, see *U. S.
           Statutes at Large*, XLVII, 70. The latter left loopholes
           respecting the action of state courts. See R. R. R.
           Brooks, *Unions of Their Own Choosing* (New Haven,
           1939), 34-36. For previous use and abuse of injunc-
           tions, see H. U. Faulkner, *The Quest for Social Justice*
           (*A History of American Life*, XI), 62-64, and P. W.
           Slosson, *The Great Crusade and After* (same ser.,
           XII), 67.

109   5   ". . . wholly unaffected." Leo Wolman, *Wages and
           Hours under the Codes of Fair Competition* (N. Y.,
           1935), 8, reckons the reduction achieved by the NRA
           at five hours. M. Ada Beney, *Wages, Hours, and Em-
           ployment in the United States, 1914-1936* (Natl.

Indus. Conf. Bd., *Studies*, no. 229, 1936), finds that between 1929 and 1936 the work week of the average male worker fell from 48.3 hours to 39.4, that of the average female from 44.2 to 35.2. The unskilled laborer's week was pared about two hours more than that of the skilled and semiskilled, to reach a floor approximately the same by 1936. Concerning regional differences, see the same author's *Differentials in Industrial Wages and Hours in the United States* (Natl. Indus. Conf. Bd., *Studies*, no. 238, 1938), 31.

109 27 ". . . this organization." L. L. Lorwin and Arthur Wubnig, *Labor Relations Boards* (Wash., 1935), 45 ff. According to John L. Lewis, "Adapting Union Methods," Am. Acad. of Polit. and Social Sci., *Annals*, CLXXXIV, 180, over 300,000 workers were drawn into company unions in 1933-1935.

110 18 ". . . not mutually exclusive." See Leo Wolman, "Labor Unions and the Labor Policy," *Yale Rev.*, XXXVI (1947), 231-241. "The spreading of disparaging rumors about the labor organizations or union leaders, issuing antiunion pamphlets, or directly denouncing the union to employees, for instance, are violations of the Act." National Labor Relations Board, *7th Annual Report* (1942), 43.

110 23 ". . . workers were averted." F. D. Roosevelt, *Public Papers and Addresses* (S. I. Rosenman, ed., N. Y., 1938-1941), VII, 375-376.

111 16 ". . . Labor Relations Board." A strongly prolabor account of the Minneapolis strike, in a sociological matrix, is C. R. Walker, *American City* (N. Y., 1937). For a journalistic report of San Francisco's general strike, see *Time*, XXIV, no. 4, 10-11, no. 5, 13 (July 23 and 30, 1934); for background and aftermath, F. M. Kleiler, "Maritime Labor Grows Up," *Survey Graphic*, XXVIII (1939), 18-22. For the textile strike, see H. J. Lahne, *The Cotton Mill Worker* (N. Y., 1944), chap. xiv.

Page   Line

111   24   ". . . for private detectives." Edward Levinson, *Labor on the March* (N. Y., 1938), 150; Clinch Calkins, *Spy Overhead, the Story of Industrial Espionage* (N. Y., 1937). In applying the Wagner act the NLRB sought with considerable success to outlaw espionage.

113   19   ". . . of its ends." Marjorie R. Clark, "Recent History of Labor Organization," Am. Acad. of Polit. and Social Sci., *Annals*, CLXXXIV, 161-168; R. R. R. Brooks, *When Labor Organizes* (New Haven, 1937), 300-302; Robert Bendiner, "C. I. O., from Committee to Congress," *Nation*, CXLVII, 590-593 (Dec. 3, 1938). Frances Perkins, *The Roosevelt I Knew* (N. Y., 1946), 126-127, states that Lewis's proposal of himself as vice-presidential running mate in 1940 and Roosevelt's rejection of the offer caused the final rift in their relations.

114   7   ". . . year." Levinson, *Labor on the March*, 57. For the history of this type of strike, see Louis Stark, "Sit-Down," *Survey Graphic*, XXVI (1937), 316-320. Its employment in 1906 by the I. W. W., though effectual, had given it a prejudicial taint of syndicalism, and it failed to catch on. Herbert Harris, *American Labor* (New Haven, 1938), 292.

114   29   ". . . 484,711 workers." Harris, *American Labor*, 288. See also A. C. Eurich and E. C. Wilson, *In 1937* (N. Y., 1938), pt. i, chap. ii, and J. A. Fitch, "Steel and the CIO," *Survey Graphic*, XXVI (1937), 186-191.

115   23   ". . . a healthy symptom." Roosevelt, *Public Papers*, VI, 272. For figures, see *Statistical Abstract of the United States for 1943*, 157.

116   11   ". . . however, was small." For a strongly leftist view, see Selden Rodman, "Lasser and the Workers' Alliance," *Nation*, CXLVII, 242-244 (Sept. 10, 1938); a more impartial picture is E. W. Bakke, *Citizens without Work* (New Haven, 1940), 75-78.

Page   Line

116   19   ". . . peanized." A book like Lewis Corey's *Crisis of the Middle Class* (N. Y., 1935) sought to analyze the new polarization of class consciousness in America in terms of the relative friendliness of the "old" middle class of small merchants and manufacturers toward the aspiring workers, in contrast to the split middle class now gravitating toward either proletarian or capitalist extremes.

116   32   ". . . among the farmers." Brooks, *When Labor Organizes*, 243. For the Grange, see Allan Nevins, *The Emergence of Modern America* (*A History of American Life*, VIII), 169-171.

117   23   ". . . of national defense." D. R. Richberg, *Government and Business Tomorrow* (N. Y., 1943), 52-53.

117   36   ". . . tions." *N. Y. Times*, March 25, 1932; Harold Seidman, *Labor Czars* (N. Y., 1938), 116.

118   8   ". . . in local politics." Vorse, *Labor's New Millions*, 278-279.

118   15   ". . . industry." Seidman, *Labor Czars*, chap. xv. A more indulgent account of the same activities is Brooks, *Unions of Their Own Choosing*, chap. vii.

119   6   ". . . of the House." Perkins, *Roosevelt I Knew*, 261, who also supplies comments upon the lackluster attitude of organized labor, 258.

119   12   ". . . try." Roosevelt, *Public Papers*, VII, 392.

119   19   ". . . neighborhood." Public Law 846, 74th Congress.

119   29   ". . . cents." Public Law 718, 75th Congress.

119   31   ". . . for interstate commerce." For earlier federal efforts to regulate child labor, see Slosson, *Great Crusade and After*, 175-176.

120   7   ". . . roughly, 2,000,000." *World Almanac for 1944*, 613.

Page   Line

120   21   ". . . all-time high." W. F. Ogburn, "Our Times," *Am. Journ. of Sociology*, XLVII, 808. Whereas in September, 1940, the A. F. of L. still estimated the unemployed at 8,544,000 and the National Industrial Conference Board at 6,696,000, within the next year over three million more nonagricultural workers had jobs than in 1940 and four million more than in November, 1929. R. E. Montgomery, "Labor," same vol., 932.

120   27   ". . . 1941." B. M. Rich, *The Presidents and Civil Disorder* (Wash., 1941), chap. xi.

121   10   ". . . the New Deal." Roosevelt, *Public Papers*, VIII, 490-506.

121   18   ". . . needs, long neglected." Roosevelt, *Public Papers*, VIII, 6.

121   33   ". . . land for everybody." Roosevelt, *Public Papers*, VIII, 65-66.

123   9   ". . . ables on relief." Urbanism Committee of the National Resources Committee, *Our Cities* (Wash., 1937), vii.

123   16   ". . . form." See H. U. Faulkner, *The Quest for Social Justice* (*A History of American Life*, XI), 93-104.

123   27   ". . . American way." For the high proportion of foreign-born, see Urbanism Committee, *Our Cities*, 9.

124   27   ". . . saved from eviction." For a summary of HOLC accomplishments, see F. D. Roosevelt, *Public Papers and Addresses* (S. I. Rosenman, ed., N. Y., 1938-1941), II, 236-237, and for data concerning foreclosures, Carol Aronovici, *Housing the Masses* (N. Y., 1939), 114. According to J. H. Fahey, HOLC chairman, when the agency "is finally liquidated in 1948 . . . it will show a net profit of some $11,000,000." The HOLC, he stated, had foreclosed on fewer than 200,000 loans, largely between 1937 and 1940: after

the latter date the war boom greatly helped rapid retirement of such indebtednesses. *Time*, XLVII, 82
(April 22, 1946).

125   32   ". . . thousand dwelling units." Housing Committee,
Twentieth Century Fund, *American Housing: Prob-
lems and Prospects* (N. Y., 1944), 277. For a con-
spectus of PWA housing, see M. W. Straus and Talbot
Wegg, *Housing Comes of Age* (N. Y., 1938), and
H. L. Ickes, *Back to Work: the Story of PWA* (N. Y.,
1935), chap. ix, the former noting (31) that joint
surveys in the mid-thirties by the departments of commerce and agriculture found that, in the urban zone,
one dwelling in six was unsafe and unfit for habitation, one in six overcrowded; in rural areas, one in two
needed major repairs or else was hopelessly unfit, while
only one in twenty met the "American Standard."

126   12   ". . . hundred rental projects." For a convenient
summary of the FHA and related aspects of federal
housing assistance, see Horace Taylor and others, *Main
Currents in Modern Economic Life* (N. Y., 1941),
II, 352-354.

126   17   ". . . this program." Loula D. Lasker, "Three Years
of Public Housing," *Survey Graphic*, XXVI (1937),
78 ff., who gives a résumé of the real-property inventory undertaken in sixty-four cities by the department
of commerce and published in 1934—showing that
only 37 per cent of all dwellings needed no structural
repairs, while at the other pole no less than 25 per cent
had no bathing facilities and 17.1 per cent no private
indoor toilet.

126   28   ". . . million population." Basil Rauch, *The History
of the New Deal, 1933-1938* (N. Y., 1944), 291-
292.

127   5   ". . . ravages of tuberculosis." Roi Ottley, *New
World A-Coming* (N. Y., 1943), 85. For a graphic
account of Negro health problems, see Thomas Parran,

Page   Line

M.D., "No Defense for Any of Us," *Survey Graphic*, XXVII (1938), 197-202.

127   12   ". . . lic welfare agency." Gunnar Myrdal, *An American Dilemma* (N. Y., 1944), I, 350.

127   17   ". . . each family housed." In an article written by Straus for the *American Year Book for 1939*, 582-583, he observes that this cost compares favorably with the annual federal expenditure of $1049 to maintain one CCC worker, $732 for each WPA laborer and $111 to pay one farmer's agricultural benefits. M. J. Pusey, "Reclaiming Our Slums," *Yale Rev.*, XXVIII (1939), 724-748, is critical of the program's financing.

127   27   ". . . than fifteen hundred." U. S. Housing Administration, *Annual Report for 1941*, 76-77.

128   2   ". . . million units short." *New International Year Book for 1940*, 34. Statistics for the following year, cited below, are drawn from the same annual for 1941, 29.

128   18   ". . . a thousand units." C. T. Larson, "Packaged Houses," *Survey Graphic*, XXVI (1937), 377-382.

128   34   ". . . dismissed as 'frills.' " P. W. Slosson, *The Great Crusade and After* (*A History of American Life*, XII), 408, describes their earlier heyday. For the subsequent decline, see C. E. Ridley and O. F. Nolting, eds., *What the Depression Has Done to Cities* (Chicago, 1935), 11.

129   6   ". . . well." Urbanism Committee, *Our Cities*, 46, and H. W. Odum and H. E. Moore, *American Regionalism* (N. Y., 1938), 112. Four hundred county planning boards were almost wholly a development of the New Deal era. National Resources Committee, *Regional Planning* (Wash., 1938), 7.

129   14   ". . . billion dollars annually." J. A. Miller, "They're All Afraid to Mention It," *Rev. of Revs.*,

XCII (1936), 54-56. For a more detailed picture, see R. D. McKenzie, *The Metropolitan Community* (N. Y., 1933), chap. xx.

130 15 ". . . of the Union." R. D. McKenzie, "Metropolitan Communities," President's Research Committee, *Recent Social Trends in the United States* (N. Y., 1933), I, 492-496. For statistics on decentralization, see B. L. Melvin, "Stake in the Land," *Rev. of Revs.*, XCIV (1936), 48-50.

130 23 ". . . on the periphery." *N. Y. Times*, Jan. 16, 1942.

130 32 ". . . fourteen per cent." W. F. Ogburn, "Our Times," *Am. Journ. of Sociology*, XLVII, 810. E. de S. Brunner and T. L. Smith, "Village Growth and Decline," *Rural Sociology*, IX, 103-115, note the net loss between 1930 and 1940 of 145 "villages" through passage into the "town" category, and also increase in the number of "market towns."

131 22 ". . . momentarily into jeopardy." For a factual account, with layouts, see "Greenbelt Towns," *Architectural Record*, LXXX, 215-234. In the Bound Brook case the U. S. Court of Appeals on May 18, 1936, ruled that the federal government had no right to engage directly in housing or resettlement since housing projects lie outside the constitutional conception of "the general welfare." Franklin Township in Somerset County, N. J., *et al. v.* Tugwell, 85 Fed. Rep., ser. 2, 208. Professor Tugwell wrote to the author, January 22, 1947: ". . . the Bound Brook decision merely prevented the building of that particular project. . . . My recollection is that it was not appealed but was merely ignored in other jurisdictions."

132 3 ". . . of the drought." Dwight Sanderson, *Research Memorandum on Rural Life in the Depression* (Social Sci. Research Coun., *Bull.*, no. 34, 1937), 80; E. de S. Brunner and Irving Lorge, *Rural Trends in De-*

Page *Line*

pression *Years* (N. Y., 1937), 67-69. A graphic documentary account is R. B. Vance, *How the Other Half Is Housed: a Pictorial Record of Sub-Minimum Farm Housing in the South* (Chapel Hill, 1936).

132 19 ". . . forty thousand persons." Roosevelt, *Public Papers,* IV, 143-155; R. G. Tugwell, "Changing Acres," *Current History,* XLIV (1936), 57-63; W. W. Alexander, "Rural Resettlement," *Southern Rev.,* I (1936), 528-539.

133 2 ". . . in the 1930's." The maximum number at any one time befell in January, 1935, when nearly two million families, comprising almost nine million individuals, were on federal rolls. T. J. Woofter, jr., and Ellen Winston, *Seven Lean Years* (Chapel Hill, 1939), 12; WPA, *Research Bulletin,* ser. 3, no. 1, 4.

133 11 ". . . the other way." U. S. Department of Agriculture, *Yearbook for 1935,* 674; *for 1940,* 390. The quickened interest in rural self-sufficiency was reflected in books like Ralph Borsodi, *Flight from the City: the Story of a New Way to Security* (N. Y., 1933).

133 19 ". . . years before." W. S. Thompson, *Research Memorandum on Internal Migration in the Depression* (Social Sci. Research Coun., *Bull.,* no. 30, 1937), 22-25, 32. He suggests, however, that the 1935 agricultural census was more apt to count suburbanites as farmers than the decennial tally of 1930. The drift, though clear, is therefore susceptible of exaggeration. For regional disparities, see R. G. Tugwell, "National Significance of Recent Trends in Farm Population," *Social Forces,* XIV (1935), 1-7.

133 23 ". . . of the twenties." Dept. of Agr., *Yearbook for 1940,* 841-842, where the net migration from the farm, *i.e.,* not offset by the contrary flow, is estimated to average 351,000 yearly during 1934-1938.

134 5 ". . . to larger communities." Within the entire age group of from twenty to twenty-four years in the na-

Page Line

tion 58.3 per cent in 1940 were urban, 20.1 rural nonfarm and 21.6 farm folk. Bureau of the Census, *Facts about Youth as Portrayed in the 1940 Census* (*Population*, ser. P-3, no. 19), 2. Of course, this continued the trend of the previous decade. Tugwell in the article cited above remarks that "of the youngsters between 15 and 20 years of age living on farms in 1920, four out of every ten had moved away by 1930."

134 10 ". . . suckers." Committee on Population Problems, National Resources Committee, *Problems of a Changing Population* (Wash., 1938), 111.

135 9 ". . . criticism." The summary of types of tenant farming is drawn from the report of the National Resources Committee, *Farm Tenancy* (Wash., 1937), 48-49. For details of daily life, see T. J. Woofter, jr., and others, *Landlord and Tenant on the Cotton Plantation* (WPA, *Research Monograph*, no. 5, 1936).

135 11 ". . . days." See Allan Nevins, *The Emergence of Modern America* (*A History of American Life*, VIII), 18-20.

135 18 ". . . thence to ownership." C. C. Taylor, Helen W. Wheeler and E. L. Kirkpatrick, *Disadvantaged Classes in American Agriculture* (Dept. of Agr., *Social Research Report*, no. 8, 1938), 55-56.

135 22 ". . . and bankruptcy sales." Estimates of the Bureau of Agricultural Economics, as of the year ending March 15, in Dept. of Agr., *Yearbook for 1935*, 687. Taxes alone, amounting to some 266 per cent of their prewar rates in the corn belt, seemed an intolerable burden. Mary H. Vorse, "Rebellion in the Corn Belt," *Harper's Mag.*, CLXVI (1932), 3.

135 28 ". . . until he fainted." For the Iowa mob and Judge C. C. Bradley, see *N. Y. Times*, April 28, 1933.

Page	Line	

136   6   ". . . a century earlier." R. B. Vance, *Farmers without Land* (*Public Affairs Pamphlet*, no. 12, 1937), 3; National Resources Committee, *Farm Tenancy*, iv.

136   31   ". . . humblest farm workers." See Howard Kester, *Revolt among the Sharecroppers* (N. Y., 1936), and editorial in the *Nation*, CXLVIII, 79 (Jan. 21, 1939).

138   10   ". . . seven in 1933." See Slosson, *Great Crusade and After*, 193-194. For an explicit bill of grievances, see W. G. Stuart, "A Dirt Farmer Speaks His Mind," *Atlantic Mo.*, CXLV (1930), 309-318.

138   33   ". . . fifty years before." Dept. of Agr., *Agricultural Statistics for 1940*, 544-545, and *Yearbook for 1939*, 128, *for 1940*, 6.

139   25   ". . . ministration." C. T. Schmidt, *American Farmers in the World Crisis* (N. Y., 1941), 118-119.

139   31   ". . . Cross." Am. Acad. of Polit. and Social Sci., *Annals*, CLV, pt. i, is devoted to "Organized Commodity Markets"; see esp. 56-73. For a friendly account of the Board, see J. D. Black, "Social Implications of the Restriction of Agricultural Output," *Am. Econ. Rev.*, XXI, Supplement, 114-124; for a hostile one, C. P. Howland, "The Failure of Farm Board Stabilization," *Yale Rev.*, XXI (1932), 503-519.

140   1   ". . . disheartening." Taylor, Wheeler and Kirkpatrick, *Disadvantaged Classes*, 3.

140   14   ". . . program a chance." Vorse, "Rebellion in the Corn Belt," 1-10; Clifton Hicks, "Upheaval in the Corn Belt," *Harper's Mag.*, CLXIX (1934), 621-632; M. A. Hallgren, *Seeds of Revolt* (N. Y., 1933), chap. viii.

140   23   ". . . spring of 1933." In the beginning the emergency farm credit act of 1933 assumed federal responsibility for the interest alone of bonds issued, but under the act of 1934 setting up the Federal Farm Mort-

Page *Line*

gage Corporation the principal was also guaranteed. Roosevelt, *Public Papers,* II, 84-90, 183; III, 27-28.

140   35   ". . . behind this program." E. G. Nourse, J. S. Davis and J. D. Black, *Three Years of the Agricultural Adjustment Administration* (N. Y., 1937), 23.

142   7   ". . . desperate remedies." See H. A. Wallace, *New Frontiers* (N. Y., 1934), 174-181, for comment on this program. Factual summaries are in E. K. Lindley, *The Roosevelt Revolution* (N. Y., 1933), 243-244, and C. T. Schmidt, *American Farmers in the World Crisis* (N. Y., 1941), 129.

142   20   ". . . for such purposes." It was set up in October, 1933, to assist the AAA in removing farm surpluses and the FERA in supplying food and clothing to the destitute. After 1935, because of the growing stress upon its liaison with agriculture instead of relief, its name was changed to the Federal Surplus Commodities Corporation. Nourse, Davis and Black, *Three Years of the AAA,* 197, 199; Roosevelt, *Public Papers,* III, 296; E. K. Lindley, *Half Way with Roosevelt* (N. Y., 1936), 194.

142   31   ". . . only regional." *American Year Book for 1940,* 474; *New Republic,* XCIX, 86 (May 31, 1939).

143   8   ". . . by two sociologists." Brunner and Lorge, *Rural Trends,* 48-51.

143   33   ". . . maybe they're right." Quoted by R. L. Neuberger, "Some Like Roosevelt," *Nation,* CXLVII, 7-8 (July 2, 1938).

144   8   ". . . services." J. S. Davis, *On Agricultural Policy, 1926-1938* (Stanford Univ., 1939), 465-466.

144   33   ". . . in the program." *American Year Book for 1940,* 469. For a summary of farm legislation 1936-1938, see Roosevelt, *Public Papers,* V, 95-102, and VII, 88-97. For an adverse opinion of the ever-normal granary as "unnecessary" famine insurance in this day

Page   Line

of quick transportation and as illusory in its concept of parity prices, see J. S. Davis, *Wheat and the AAA* (Wash., 1935), 441.

145   4   ". . . reduce cutthroat competition." Nourse, Davis and Black, *Three Years of the AAA*, 443, concludes that "it had a positive recovery effect of substantial magnitude, though not as great as was anticipated."

145   9   ". . . in two seasons." Nourse, Davis and Black, *Three Years of the AAA*, 300-301, revising somewhat lower figures given by H. I. Richards, *Cotton and the AAA* (Wash., 1936), 290. The value of the tobacco crop rose from $107,821,000 in 1932 to $240,937,000 in 1934. H. B. Rowe, *Tobacco under the AAA* (Wash., 1935), 251.

145   12   ". . . per cent respectively." Nourse, Davis and Black, *Three Years of the AAA*, 286.

145   19   ". . . that in 1919." See Roosevelt, *Public Papers*, VII, 94-96, for a review of the benefits claimed for the AAA.

145   34   ". . . the government." W. C. Holley, Ellen Winston and T. J. Woofter, jr., *The Plantation South, 1934-1937* (WPA, Wash., 1940), 40, 44, based upon a sampling of 246 Southern plantations. See also Arthur Raper, *Preface to Peasantry* (Chapel Hill, 1936), 245.

146   3   ". . . tale." C. S. Johnson, E. R. Embree and W. W. Alexander, *The Collapse of Farm Tenancy* (Chapel Hill, 1935), 50; the quotation is from Brunner and Lorge, *Rural Trends*, 48.

146   7   ". . . o' my renters." Dorothea Lange and P. S. Taylor, *An American Exodus* (N. Y., 1939), 80. These investigators were told in Arkansas: "Some of the landowners would rather work the cotton land themselves and get all the government money. So they cut down to what they can work themselves, and the farming people are rented out. They go to town on relief" (150). On the displacement of workers by tractors,

drought and other causes, see testimony of Paul S.
Taylor in Temporary National Economic Committee,
Verbatim Record of the Proceedings (Wash., 1938-
1941), XIII, 489-502 (April 24, 1940).

146   19   ". . . could have done." For comment on these changing attitudes, see a quotation from Carl C. Taylor,
chief of the division of farm population and rural
life, in Sanderson, *Research Memorandum on Rural
Life,* 144.

146   26   ". . . and of thinking." Bureau of Agricultural Eco-
nomics, *Technology on the Farm* (Wash., 1940), 9;
C. C. Taylor, "Rural Life," *Am. Journ. of Sociology,*
XLVII, 844.

147   7   ". . . those who survived." Virginius Dabney, *Below the Potomac* (N. Y., 1942), 76; G. C. Stoney,
"No Room in Green Pastures," *Survey Graphic,* XXX
(1941), 14-20.

147   14   ". . . was so picked." "Technology Overtakes the
Hired Man," *Sat. Eve. Post,* CCX, 22 (Jan. 15,
1938).

147   21   ". . . laborers were available." Virginia Cocalis, "The
Man with the Machine," *Survey Graphic,* XXVIII
(1939), 475-477, and Dale Kramer, "Eviction by
Machinery," *Nation,* CLII, 497-499 (April 26,
1941).

147   29   ". . . income of $1798." National Resources Com-
mittee, *Technological Trends,* 107.

148   7   ". . . of ten agriculturalists." J. M. Carmody, "Rural
Electrification in the United States," *Am. Acad. of
Polit. and Social Sci., Annals,* CCI, 82-88.

148   20   ". . . of the total." Slosson, *Great Crusade and After,*
195; R. T. Beall, "Rural Electrification," Dept. of
Agr., *Yearbook for 1940,* 802. Shortly before the
REA began operation in 1935, the number stood at
743,000, or 10.9 per cent.

Page Line
148   26   "... sumption." By 1940, to meet production needs, 1,600,000 fewer farm workers were required than in 1929. Dept. of Agr., *Yearbook for 1940*, 880.

148   36   "... cent." T. W. Schultz, "Economic Effects of Agricultural Programs," *Am. Econ. Rev.*, XXX, 127-164.

149   25   "... into Big Business." After the need for emergency loans was largely past, the FCA lent additional sums for the purchase of more land, equipment, improvements and erection of buildings. See Roosevelt, *Public Papers*, II, 183. By 1939 this agency had so advanced about $8.2 billion and gone far toward eliminating the private financing of agriculture. Taylor and others, *Main Currents in Modern Economic Life*, II, 56.

150   27   "... America promised well." C. G. Wrenn and D. L. Harley, *Time on Their Hands* (Wash., 1941), 148-149.

151   10   "... by bread alone." Brunner and Lorge, *Rural Trends*, 284.

151   18   "... for the future." *How Permanent Is the Farm Program?* (mimeographed pamphlet of the Dept. of Agr., 1939, an address before the American Farm Bureau Federation, Dec. 5, 1939). From the Republican camp about this time issued sentiments almost identical: "Until the national economy as a whole is brought to a full and balanced recovery ... the necessity of some form of direct subsidy to agriculture to secure effective parity and to control the impact of surpluses upon farm prices must be recognized." *A Program for a Dynamic America* (Republican Program Committee, *Report*, Feb. 16, 1940), 43.

151   23   "... Social Security Board." Ralph Turner in Dept. of Agr., *Yearbook for 1940*, 1023.

152   24   "... control." For the vetoed McNary-Haugen bill, see Slosson, *Great Crusade and After*, 212. Concern-

Page Line

ing the farmer's changing psychology, see C. C. Munz, "Will the Farmer Vote for Willkie?" *Nation*, CLI, 186-188 (Sept. 7, 1940); and for a broader background, P. H. Johnstone, "Old Ideals versus New Ideals in Farm Life," Dept. of Agr., *Yearbook for 1940*, esp. 145-147.

154   9   ". . . the natural milieu." For various definitions, see H. W. Odum and H. E. Moore, *American Regionalism* (N. Y., 1938), 2, 276, and Lewis Mumford, *The Culture of Cities* (N. Y., 1938), 305, 367.

154   28   ". . . in the background." National Resources Committee, *Regional Planning* (Wash., 1938), 5-6; F. D. Roosevelt, *Public Papers and Addresses* (S. I. Rosenman, ed., N. Y., 1938-1941), VI, 499.

155   11   ". . . states." See R. L. Duffus, *Mastering a Metropolis* (N. Y., 1930), and in greater detail the official eight-volume *Regional Survey of New York and Its Environs* (N. Y., 1927-1931).

155   20   ". . . tively late." Odum and Moore, *American Regionalism*, 202-206.

156   10   ". . . timber and water." Odum and Moore, *American Regionalism*, 194-199.

157   17   ". . . and Robert Toombs." Allen Tate, "Regionalism and Sectionalism," *New Republic*, LXIX, 158-161 (Dec. 23, 1931); Donald Davidson, *The Attack on Leviathan: Regionalism and Nationalism in the United States* (Chapel Hill, 1938); J. C. Ransom, "The "Aesthetics of Regionalism," *Am. Rev.*, II (1934), 290-310.

157   22   ". . . and reciprocating." F. J. Turner, *The Significance of Sections in American History* (N. Y., 1932), 51.

158   3   ". . . and social inadequacy." Donald Davidson, "Where Regionalism and Sectionalism Meet," *Social*

Page Line

Forces, XIII (1934), 23-31; H. W. Odum, *Southern Regions of the United States* (Chapel Hill, 1936), 13, 227. For the status of Southern sectionalism in the previous decade, see P. W. Slosson, *The Great Crusade and After* (*A History of American Life*, XII), chap. ix, esp. 251-253.

159 33 ". . . for opportunities elsewhere." Jonathan Daniels, "Georgians Discover Georgia," *Survey Graphic*, XXVIII (1939), 199-203.

160 11 ". . . in her long history." Roosevelt, *Public Papers*, VII, 421, 471-475.

161 2 ". . . the United States." Odum and Moore, *American Regionalism*, 543; National Emergency Council, *Report on Economic Conditions of the South* (Wash., 1938), 22.

161 7 ". . . in the country." National Emergency Council, *Report on Economic Conditions*, 6-7, 32.

161 23 ". . . for the nation." For the backwardness of education, see National Emergency Council, *Report on Economic Conditions*, 25-28; and for conditions in the Georgia highlands, W. H. Gaumnitz and Katherine M. Cook, *Education in the Southern Mountains* (U. S. Dept. of Educ., *Bull.*, no. 26, 1937), 27 ff. Yet, with the exception of Georgia, the Southern states averaged an expenditure of 4.4 per cent of the total annual income of their people for education as compared with a national average of 3.8. According to her means, therefore, the South was making a brave effort. C. W. Dabney, *Universal Education in the South* (Chapel Hill, 1936), II, 495.

161 27 ". . . seven national magazines." W. C. Holley, Ellen Winston and T. J. Woofter, jr., *The Plantation South, 1934-1937* (WPA, Wash., 1940), 69.

162 13 ". . . of the Negro." A. F. Raper and I. de A. Reid, *Sharecroppers All* (Chapel Hill, 1941), 255.

Page   Line

162   24   ". . . blacks were dismissed." Allison Davis and B. B. and M. R. Gardner, *Deep South* (Chicago, 1941), 425-429. For the high incidence of unemployment among Southern Negroes, see Gunnar Myrdal, *An American Dilemma* (N. Y., 1944), I, 289.

162   30   ". . . grew more equitable." C. S. Johnson, "The Negro," *Am. Journ. of Sociology*, XLVII, 855, and *The Negro College Graduate* (Chapel Hill, 1938), 371.

163   7   ". . . on marketing quotas." A. F. Raper, *Preface to Peasantry* (Chapel Hill, 1936), 243; *Negro Year Book for 1937-1938*, 24.

163   10   ". . . vote." Myrdal, *American Dilemma*, I, 488-489.

163   16   ". . . the poor white." Kentucky, on the marches of the Deep South, also lacked a poll tax. The effect of its removal was often striking. Whereas South Carolina under this tax reported only 14.1-per-cent participation in elections by persons of voting age, tax-free North Carolina showed 50 per cent. G. C. Stoney, "Suffrage in the South," *Survey Graphic*, XXIX (1940), 5.

163   22   ". . . community standards high." Raper, *Preface to Peasantry*, 312-323, 346.

163   27   ". . . the Southern Negro." Gaines *v.* Canada, Registrar of the University of Missouri *et al.*, 305 U. S., 337.

163   35   ". . . as a quarter." Myrdal, *American Dilemma*, I, 295, and II, 1231, gives estimates admittedly rough.

164   13   ". . . by public funds." Myrdal, *American Dilemma*, I, 197; *Negro Year Book for 1937-1938*, 19. Stanley High, "Black Omen," *Sat. Eve. Post*, CCX, 5 (May 21, 1938), states that in Chicago, Cleveland and St. Louis they made up from forty to fifty per cent of the jobless.

Page	Line	
165	2	". . . workers for white." Myrdal, *American Dilemma*, I, 207.
166	10	". . . white population . . . ." "The Negro," *Am. Journ. of Sociology*, XLVII, 864. For similar pronouncements by a Southern white, see Odum, *Southern Regions*, 485.
166	23	". . . ical contention." See Slosson, *Great Crusade and After*, 76.
167	12	". . . to go ahead." In proposing creation of the TVA to Congress, the president envisaged it as "a corporation clothed with the power of Government but possessed of the flexibility and initiative of a private enterprise." Roosevelt, *Public Papers*, II, 122-123.
168	9	". . . from industrial accidents." E. L. Bishop, "The Health and Safety Services of the Tennessee Valley Authority," *Public Personnel Rev.*, IV (1943), 9-16; TVA Health and Safety Department, *Malaria and Its Control in the Tennessee Valley* (Chattanooga, 1942). The model labor-management relations of this agency are discussed by Judson King, *The TVA Labor Relations Policy at Work* (Wash., 1940).
168	19	". . . first conservation department." John Chancellor, *The Library in the TVA Adult Education Program* (Chicago, 1937); TVA, *Recreation Development of the Tennessee River System* (76 Cong., 3 sess., House Doc., no. 565, 1940).
170	3	". . . provoked hot debate." Roosevelt, *Public Papers*, III, 354.
171	10	". . . from TVA competition." Ashwander *v.* Tennessee Valley Authority *et al.*, 297 U. S., 288 (1936); and Tennessee Electric Power Co. *et al.*, *v.* Tennessee Valley Authority *et al.*, 386 U. S., 118 (1939).
172	1	". . . of regional planning." See Odum and Moore, *American Regionalism*, chap. iv, and National Resources Committee, *Drainage Basin Problems and Programs* (Wash., 1936).

Page   *Line*

172   11   ". . . of the TVA." Roosevelt, *Public Papers*, VI, 252-258. In regard to the nation's mightiest watercourse, the Mississippi River Commission was already operating in respect to such vital matters as flood control and navigation. See *Regional Planning*, issued by the National Resources Committee in thirteen parts, each dealing with a separate region; and for a synopsis, the brochure *Regional Planning*.

172   27   ". . . gressor nations." Roosevelt, *Public Papers*, VI, 387-411.

172   30   ". . . under the first." See H. U. Faulkner, *The Quest for Social Justice* (*A History of American Life*, XI), 3-4.

174   11   ". . . to stand on." *Land of the Free* (N. Y., 1938), 51 ff.

174   22   ". . . were chronic wanderers." J. N. Webb and Malcolm Brown, *Migrant Families* (WPA, Wash., 1938), xiv, xxv-xxviii, 100. With inauguration of the WPA this program closed in the autumn of 1935. For criticisms, see W. F. Ogburn, ed., *Social Changes during Depression and Recovery* (Chicago, 1935), 779.

175   6   ". . . per cent respectively." See J. N. Webb, *The Transient Unemployed* (WPA, *Research Monograph*, no. 3, 1935), 75-78, and *U. S. Sixteenth Census* (1940), Preliminary Release, ser. P-5a, no. 16.

175   24   ". . . come seeking employment." Carey McWilliams, *Ill Fares the Land* (Boston, 1942), 30, and *Southern California Country* (N. Y., 1946), 137.

175   34   ". . . enforced a truce." McWilliams, *Ill Fares the Land*, 16, and *Factories in the Field* (Boston, 1939), chap. xiii.

176   7   ". . . fringes, by 1939." See Great Plains Committee, *The Future of the Great Plains* (Wash., 1936), and U. S. Department of Agriculture, *Yearbook for 1940*, 437.

Page	Line	
176	35	". . . are concerned with." Quoted in Odum and Moore, *American Regionalism*, 257. For further reflections upon the dangers of bureaucracy in regionalism, see 107, and C. E. Merriam, "Planning Agencies in America," *Am. Polit. Sci. Rev.*, XXIX, 197-211.
177	16	". . . power." Lilienthal, *TVA*, chaps. xiv-xv.
178	15	". . . the American family." See P. W. Slosson, *The Great Crusade and After* (*A History of American Life*, XII), 145-147.
178	20	". . . previous decade." *American Year Book for 1940*, 603.
178	29	". . . gets into print." For comment on Norris's novel, see Harry Hansen in *N. Y. World*, Aug. 14, 1930.
179	10	". . . indorsed birth control." *N. Y. Times*, June 3, 1931.
179	19	". . . Catholic practice." See S. A. Stouffer, "Trends in the Fertility of Catholics and Non-Catholics," *Am. Journ. of Sociology*, XLI, 143-166; N. E. Himes, "A Decade of Progress in Birth Control," Am. Acad. of Polit. and Social Sci., *Annals*, CCXII, 93.
179	31	". . . of their indorsement." For mail-order catalogues, see D. L. Cohn, *The Good Old Days* (N. Y., 1940), 254. A summary of polls is in Abraham Stone and Harriet Pilpel, "The Social and Legal Status of Contraception," *N. C. Law Rev.*, XX, 212-225.
180	2	". . . societies following suit." The federal decision is U. S. *v.* One Package, 86 Fed. Rep., ser. 2, 737. See also R. H. Shryock, "Freedom and Interference in Medicine," Am. Acad. of Polit. and Social Sci., *Annals*, CC, 41.
180	21	". . . alleviation of poverty." G. M. Cooper, F. M. Pratt and M. J. Hagood, "Four Years of Contraception as a Public Health Service in North Carolina," *Am. Journ. of Public Health*, XXXI, 1248; Regine K.

Page   Line

Stix, "Birth Control in a Midwestern City," Milbank Memorial Fund, *Quar.,* XVII (1939), 69-71.

180   36   ". . . in elementary schoolrooms." National Resources Committee, *Problems of a Changing Population* (Wash., 1938), 136-137; H. P. Fairchild, "When the Population Levels Off," *Harper's Mag.,* CLXXVI (1938), 596.

181   16   ". . . on relief." *Security or the Dole? (Public Affairs Pamphlet,* no. 4, 1936), 7; Social Security Board, *Social Security in America* (Wash., 1937), 244. At the latter date state and local governments were spending, in all, $37,500,000 annually to aid needy children.

181   19   ". . . for crippled children." P. H. Douglas, *Social Security in the United States* (N. Y., 1939), chap. vii.

181   26   ". . . 1934 and 1938." Katharine F. Lenroot, "Child Welfare, 1930-1940," Am. Acad. of Polit. and Social Sci., *Annals,* CCXII, 2-3.

181   33   ". . . -five and nineteen." Bureau of the Census, *The Facts about Youth as Portrayed in the 1940 Census (Population,* ser. P-3, no. 19), 3.

182   12   ". . . sufferers." E. K. Lindley, *The Roosevelt Revolution* (N. Y., 1933), 234; F. D. Roosevelt, *Public Papers and Addresses* (S. I. Rosenman, ed., N. Y., 1938-1941), IV, 284; Katharine du P. Lumpkin and Dorothy W. Douglas, *Child Workers in America* (N. Y., 1937), 59, 82 and *passim;* National Emergency Council, *Report on Economic Conditions of the South* (Wash., 1938), 41-44.

182   27   ". . . in 1924." See Slosson, *Great Crusade and After,* 176.

183   2   ". . . in June, 1939." Beulah Amidon, "Children Wanted," *Survey Graphic,* XXVI (1937), 10-15; R. G. Fuller, "Child Labor—Continued," Am. Acad. of Polit. and Social Sci., *Annals,* CCXII, 146-152.

Page   Line
183   20   ". . . the labor force." H. M. Bell, *Youth Tell Their Story* (Wash., 1938), 143-152, based upon a survey of 13,528 Maryland young people. Nettie P. McGill and Ellen N. Matthews, *The Youth of New York City* (N. Y., 1940), 160, found in the metropolis that a third had never had a job. For American Youth Commission estimates, see National Resources Committee, *Problems of a Changing Population*, 199; and for the quotation, Bureau of the Census, *Facts about Youth*, 3.

183   29   ". . . thousand." J. N. Leonard, *Three Years Down* (N. Y., 1939), 191, 272-273; J. N. Webb, *The Transient Unemployed* (WPA, *Research Monograph*, no. 3, 1935), 16; Towne Nylander, "Wandering Youth?" *Sociology and Social Research*, XVII, 560-568.

184   7   ". . . or petty crime." G. E. Outland, *Boy Transiency in America* (Santa Barbara, Calif., 1939), 39, 101-102, based mainly on FERA Transient Service records. For the migration of rural youth, see B. L. Melvin, *Rural Youth on Relief* (WPA, Wash., 1937), and T. J. Woofter, jr., and Ellen Winston, *Seven Lean Years* (Chapel Hill, 1939), chap. v.

184   15   ". . . away from home." Vernon Jones, "Relation of Economic Depression to Delinquency, Crime and Drunkenness in Massachusetts," *Journ. of Social Psychology*, XXXII, 279; J. M. Williams, *Human Aspects of Unemployment and Relief* (Chapel Hill, 1933), chap. viii. The crime rate generally declined in the thirties under hard times and prohibition repeal save for offenses against property. Robbery rose to a notable peak in 1932 and again in the recession of 1937. Thorsten Sellin, "Crime," *Am. Journ. of Sociology*, XLVII, 898-906.

184   21   ". . . during the decade." *New International Year Book for 1939*, 641-643. For correlation with relief,

Page *Line*

see *American City,* LIII (1938), 101. Some general conclusions are drawn from J. H. S. Bossard, ed., *Children in a Depression Decade* (Am. Acad. of Polit. and Social Sci., *Annals,* CCXII, 1940).

185 8 ". . . lawbreaking." For the cult of the FBI, see J. E. Hoover, "Every Scout a Future G-Man," *Liberty,* XVII, 53-55 (Feb. 24, 1940).

185 31 ". . . against *Nature.*" William James, *Memories and Studies* (N. Y., 1911), 290.

186 13 ". . . their 'teens." Holland and Hill, *Youth in the CCC,* 127.

186 22 ". . . and self-confidence." Howard Rowland, "Can the CCC Blaze a New Trail?" *Survey Graphic,* XXVI (1937), 321-325; Helen M. Walker, *The CCC through the Eyes of 272 Boys* (Cleveland, 1938).

187 2 ". . . billion trees planted." For the cost, see H. C. Lanpher, "The CCC," *Social Service Rev.,* X (1936), 623-636; for a résumé of accomplishments, Federal Security Agency, *The CCC at Work: a Story of 2,500,000 Young Men* (Wash., 1941).

187 16 ". . . school-administered projects." F. E. Hill, *The School in the Camps* (N. Y., 1935); H. W. Oxley, *CCC Camp Education: Guidance and Recreational Phases* (Office of Educ., *Bull.,* no. 19, 1937).

187 30 ". . . out-of-school projects." P. O. Johnson and O. L. Harvey, *The National Youth Administration* (Wash., 1938), 16. Betty and E. K. Lindley, *A New Deal for Youth: the Story of the NYA* (N. Y., 1938), 23, discusses costs.

188 11 ". . . boys and girls." Lindleys, *New Deal for Youth,* 157-158.

188 24 ". . . into boondoggling." For thoughtful criticism of the NYA, see Marie D. Lane and Francis Steegmuller, *America on Relief* (N. Y., 1938), 154, and

Page   Line

Maxine Davis, *The Lost Generation* (N. Y., 1936),
250-251.

188   30   ". . . the trend continued." Davis, *Lost Generation*,
124.

189   7   ". . . existence." "The Nation's Biggest Business,"
editorial in *Survey Graphic*, XXVIII (1939), 583.

189   18   ". . . schools were closed." On tax delinquency and
unpaid teachers, see National Conference on the
Financing of Education, *Report* (Wash., 1933), chap.
v; anon., "Spasmodic Diary of a Chicago School-
Teacher," *Atlantic Mo.*, CLII (1933), 513-526; and
Merle Curti, *The Social Ideas of American Educators*
(N. Y., 1935), 576.

190   11   ". . . -bodied literate adults." Dorothy Rowden, ed.,
Handbook of Adult Education in the United States
(N. Y., 1936), 28-53. Other innovations included
the so-called unemployed retraining schools, craft projects, farm camps and similar groups devised to train
or refresh jobless youth. D. L. Harley, *Youth—Finding Jobs* (Office of Educ., *Bull.*, no. 18-V, 1936).

190   15   ". . . by the WPA." D. S. Howard, *The WPA and
Federal Relief Policy* (N. Y., 1943), 127-128, describes later developments. Excluding relief classes, the
total of adults enrolled in organized educational activity in the mid-thirties was estimated at fourteen
million, as against eleven in the mid-twenties. While
university-extension, agricultural-extension and vocational courses grew, private correspondence schools,
chautauquas and lyceums dwindled. M. H. Cartwright,
Ten Years of Adult Education (N. Y., 1935), 60.
During the season 1933-1934 the original Chautauqua, largely forgotten by the age of movies and radio,
fell into the hands of a "friendly receivership," but
was put back on its feet in 1936 by a group of sponsors with sentimental loyalties. Rebecca Richmond,
Chautauqua: an American Place (N. Y., 1943), 151-
161.

Page Line

190 19 ". . . an occasional skyscraper." See Slosson, *Great Crusade and After*, 334-335.

191 3 ". . . and 1933-1934." American Association of University Professors, *Bulletin*, XXIII, 119.

191 11 ". . . teachers." "The Young College Instructor and the Depression," Am. Assoc. of Univ. Professors, *Bull.*, XXII, 507-509. Walter Kotschnig, *Unemployment in the Learned Professions* (London, 1937), 154.

191 26 ". . . the increases continued." Am. Assoc. of Univ. Professors, *Bull.*, XXIII, 120; Davis, *Lost Generation*, 123.

192 3 ". . . degrees, were challenged." For the earlier reform tendencies, see Slosson, *Great Crusade and After*, 339-341.

193 5 ". . . to totalitarians abroad." R. M. Hutchins, *No Friendly Voice* (Chicago, 1936) and *The Higher Learning in America* (New Haven, 1936); H. D. Gideonse, *The Higher Learning in a Democracy* (N. Y., 1937).

193 32 ". . . confirmed his findings." For the evidence, see Davis, *Lost Generation*, 46-47, and Bell, *Youth Tell Their Story*, 216-228. For comment on the conservative side, see H. W. Dodds, "What Youth Seeks Today Is Security," *Vital Speeches*, III, 583-584 (July 15, 1937). For youth's attitudes on war and peace, see later in the present volume, chap. xiv.

194 4 ". . . in the mid-thirties." F. C. Palm, *The Middle Classes—Then and Now* (N. Y., 1936), 382. For similar reports, see Alzada Comstock, "The College Girl: 1933 Model," *Current History*, XXXIX (1933), 180-184, and C. F. Gauss, "Youth Moves toward New Standards," *Scribner's*, XCVII (1935), 91-95.

Page   Line

194   11   ". . . pretty nearly anywhere." Quoted by F. L.
Allen, *Since Yesterday* (N. Y., 1940), 157. For
thoughtful comment on this attitude, see a quotation
from Aubrey Williams in McGill and Matthews,
Youth of New York City, xi, and a speech at the
National Conference on Social Work by Sidney Hol-
lander, *N. Y. Times*, June 21, 1939.

194   18   ". . . of the world." For a summary of polls on
Roosevelt's popularity, see Dixon Wecter, *The Hero
in America* (N. Y., 1941), 469. Concerning the forecast of youth's ordeal by war, see Thacher Winslow
and F. P. Davidson, eds., *American Youth: an Enforced Reconnaissance* (Cambridge, 1940), 39.

194   28   ". . . creed or politics." See American Youth Congress, *Youngville, U. S. A.* (N. Y., 1937), 33-34.
For a specimen attack upon the AYC as procommu-
nist, see an article by Archie Roosevelt and Murray
Plavner in *Liberty*, XVII, 13-14 (April 27, 1940),
and a reply by Mrs. F. D. Roosevelt, same vol., 6-8
(June 22, 1940). Under increasing tensions of the
Second World War pro-Soviet leadership in the AYC
grew steadily more apparent, and Mrs. Roosevelt later
became estranged.

194   36   ". . . axes to grind." L. D. Coffman, "The Exploitation of Youth," *Educational Record*, XVII (1936),
95-105.

195   17   ". . . displayed greater accord." T. F. Neblett,
"Youth Movements in the United States," Am. Acad.
of Polit. and Social Sci., *Annals.*, CXCIV, 141-151;
"One Year of Student Unionism," *Student Advocate*,
II (Feb. 1937), 11-13; American Student Union, 4th
National Convention, *Report of Proceedings* (Dec. 27
to 30, 1938), 9, 69.

195   23   ". . . Martin Dies." For characteristic appeals to the
public, see Martin Dies, "More Snakes Than I Can
Kill" and "The Reds in Hollywood," *Liberty*, XVII,
42-46, 47-50 (Feb. 10, 17, 1940).

Page	Line	
196	19	". . . legion." About four years later, under auspices of the National Education Association, the query "Should youth discuss controversial topics?" was agreed to by nearly three out of four. *What People Think about Youth and Education* (Natl. Educ. Assoc., *Bull.*, XVII, no. 5, 1940), 197. See also Am. Acad. of Polit. and Social Sci., *Annals*, CC, and H. K. Beale, *Are American Teachers Free?* (N. Y., 1936), esp. 117-123, 155-156, for oath laws. In his *History of Freedom of Teaching in American Schools* (N. Y., 1941), 264, Beale declares that, despite pressure to conform, "many more teachers do hold unorthodox views today than ever before."
196	33	". . . in the decade." Slosson, *Great Crusade and After*, 148-150; Caroline F. Ware, *Greenwich Village, 1920-1930* (Boston, 1935), 238.
197	7	". . . make." McGill and Matthews, *Youth of New York City*, 30-32.
197	15	". . . for true love." Bromley and Britten, *Youth and Sex*, 4-6, who note that the mothers of this college generation, surveyed by Katharine B. Davis, *Factors in the Sex Life of Twenty-Two Hundred Women* (N. Y., 1929), reported only 7 per cent as having had premarital relations, and that only 19 per cent of the still unmarried ones were tolerant of such practices.
197	16	". . . cheap, vulgar, immoral." Davis, *Lost Generation*, 83-90, and I. S. Wile, ed., *The Sex Life of the Unmarried Adult* (N. Y., 1934), 136.
197	21	". . . hoped for children." "Youth in College," *Fortune*, XIII (June 1936), 156.
197	27	". . . but a wife." Walter Morris, *American in Search of a Way* (N. Y., 1942), 220.
198	6	". . . ade." Bureau of the Census, *Marriage and Divorce Statistics, U. S.: 1887-1937* (Vital Statistics, Special Reports. IX, no. 60. 1940), 819.

Page Line
198   12   ". . . the next year." Joanna C. Colcord, "Family Desertion and Non-Support," E. R. A. Seligman, ed., *Encyclopaedia of the Social Sciences* (N. Y., 1930-1935), VI, 79; S. A. Stouffer and L. M. Spencer, "Marriage and Divorce in Recent Years," Am. Acad. of Polit. and Social Sci., *Annals*, CLXXXVIII, 67-69; *World Almanac for 1946*, 524.

198   22   ". . . 1929 and 1933." S. A. Stouffer and others, *Research Memorandum on the Family in the Depression* (Social Sci. Research Coun., *Bull.*, no. 29, 1937), 183-184; Bascom Johnson and P. M. Kinzie, "Prostitution in the United States," *Journ. of Social Hygiene*, XIX (1933), 467-491.

198   36   ". . . marriages per thousand." The year 1942, beyond the chronology of this book, attained a still higher rate of 13.25, but then it fell to 11.77 in 1943 and 10.96 in 1944. *World Almanac for 1947, 774.*

199   12   ". . . ty-six." For the long-term lag in marriages, see M. S. Stewart, *Youth in the World of Today* (*Public Affairs Pamphlet*, no. 22, 1938), 30; for stricter requirements of social hygiene, M. F. Nimkoff, "The Family," *Am. Journ. of Sociology*, XLVII, 869-870.

199   25   ". . . world's dark uncertainties." For a depression-dated analysis of this attitude, see J. H. Preston, "Love among the Ruins," *Harper's Mag.*, CLXIX (1934), 182-189; for one reflecting the prewar psychology, J. K. Folsom, *The Family and Democratic Society* (N. Y., 1943), 481.

200   12   ". . . of the earth." Ewan Clague and Anne E. Geddes, "Why We Need a Social Security Program," Am. Acad. of Polit. and Social Sci., *Annals*, CCII, 19. For statistics, see M. S. Stewart, *Pensions after Sixty* (*Public Affairs Pamphlet*, no. 46, 1940), 5; National Resources Committee, *Problems of a Changing Population* (Wash., 1938), 25, 32; and *American Year Book for 1940*, 845, 600, which notes that between

Page   Line

1930 and 1940 the number of persons sixty-five and older increased by 35 per cent.

200   18   ". . . quit their jobs." P. H. Douglas, *Social Security in the United States* (rev. edn., N. Y., 1939), 5 *n.*

201   13   ". . . assumed these responsibilities." Douglas, *Social Security*, 5; Abraham Epstein, *The Challenge of the Aged* (N. Y., 1928), 50.

201   26   ". . . relatives or friends." Alvin Rosenman, "Old-Age Assistance," Am. Acad. of Polit. and Social Sci., *Annals*, CCII, 54; *Security or the Dole?* (*Public Affairs Pamphlet*, no. 4, 1936), 4.

201   34   ". . . were now mandatory." Douglas, *Social Security*, 7.

202   6   ". . . for such purposes." Waller Wynne, jr., *Five Years of Rural Relief* (WPA, Wash., 1938), xii.

202   24   ". . . at forty-five." Oliver Carlson, *A Mirror for Californians* (Indianapolis, 1941), 290—also a useful source for the EPIC campaign described next—and Carey McWilliams, *Southern California Country*, (N. Y., 1946), 295-296.

203   13   ". . . in backwater communities." McWilliams, *Southern California*, 296-299. In his novel *Co-op* (N. Y., 1936) Sinclair later set forth fictionally his scheme of coöperatives for the unemployed. Near the close of this era, his own shift in interest reflecting that of millions more, the novelist launched his "Lanny Budd" series, a leftist interpretation of global history from the start of the First World War to outbreak of the Second.

205   3   ". . . movement rapidly ebbed." Raymond Clapper, "Middle-Age Money-Go-Round," *Survey Graphic*, XXVII (1938), 533-537; Max Knepper, "Scrambled Eggs in California," *Current History*, LI (1939), 58-60, 64; and Winston and Marian Moore, *Out of the Frying Pan* (Los Angeles, 1939).

Page	Line	
205	10	". . . dollars an acre." *N. Y. Times,* Nov. 8, 1939.

207 6 ". . . popular influence waned." R. G. Swing, *Forerunners of American Fascism* (N. Y., 1935), 51-52, and A. M. and Elizabeth B. Lee, *The Fine Art of Propaganda: a Study of Father Coughlin's Speeches* (N. Y., 1939).

207 20 ". . . August 14, 1935." Public Law 271, 74th Congress.

209 23 ". . . partially employed." Early in 1938 the president estimated that three million persons had lost jobs in private employment during the past quarter-year. F. D. Roosevelt, *Public Papers and Addresses* (S. I. Rosenman, ed., N. Y., 1938-1941), VII, 83, 336.

210 1 ". . . of 1932-1933." Roosevelt, *Public Papers,* VII, 395. For a graphic picture of the recession, see A. C. Eurich and E. C. Wilson, *In 1937* (N. Y., 1938), chap. iv.

210 5 ". . . social-security act." "Another Trial for 'Pump-Priming,'" *Congressional Digest,* XVII, nos. 6-7, 1652 ff.

211 8 ". . . back to sin!" Eurich and Wilson, *In 1937,* 201.

211 10 ". . . established one." See A. M. Schlesinger, *The Rise of the City* (*A History of American Life,* X), 339-344.

211 14 ". . . of human welfare." H. P. Douglass and E. de S. Brunner, *The Protestant Church as a Social Institution* (N. Y., 1935), summarizes its conclusions.

211 21 ". . . security." A. E. Holt, "Organized Religion as a Pressure Group," Am. Acad. of Polit. and Social Sci., *Annals,* CLXXIX, 42-49.

211 27 ". . . a third socialism." *World Tomorrow,* XVII (1934), 231.

Page Line

212 2 ". . . like the Y. M. C. A." J. M. Williams, *Human Aspects of Unemployment and Relief* (Chapel Hill, 1933), chap. xiii.

212 12 ". . . church employment agencies." S. C. Kincheloe, *Research Memorandum on Religion in the Depression* (Social Sci. Research Coun., *Bull.*, no. 33, 1937), 106-107; information to the author from the late Heber J. Grant, president of the Church of Latter Day Saints. Good Catholic liaison with the jobless was observed by E. W. Bakke, *Citizens without Work* (New Haven, 1940), 24.

212 14 ". . . in their history." C. J. Dutton, "America's Bankrupt Churches," *Current History*, XXXIX (1933), 57-62.

212 20 ". . . 1930 and 1934." B. Y. Landis, "The Church and Religious Activity," W. F. Ogburn, ed., *Social Changes during Depression and Recovery* (Chicago, 1935), 780-787.

212 33 ". . . of American life." See, for example, the Reverend Francis X. Talbot, "Catholicism in America," in Harold Stearns, ed., *America Now* (N. Y., 1938), 536-540.

213 21 ". . . of social forces." E. de S. Brunner and Irving Lorge, *Rural Trends in Depression Years* (N. Y., 1937), chap. xii.

213 26 ". . . exceeded their parents." Hornell Hart, "Religion," *Am. Journ. of Sociology*, XLVII, 891, and in President's Research Committee, *Recent Social Trends in the United States* (N. Y., 1933), I, 402.

213 32 ". . . tence." "Why No Revival?" *Christian Century*, LII, pt. 2, 1168-1170 (Sept. 18, 1935).

214 1 ". . . of their lives." See, for example, Hugh Hartshorne, ed., *From School to College* (New Haven, 1939), 254; H. M. Bell, *Youth Tell Their Story* (Wash., 1938), 205; and "Youth in College," *Fortune*, XIII (June 1936), 155.

Page *Line*

214   7   ". . . scientists and psychologists." J. H. Leuba, "Religious Beliefs of American Scientists," *Harper's Mag.*, CLXIX (1934), 291-301.

216   9   ". . . trampled underfoot." Claris E. Silcox and G. M. Fisher, *Catholics, Jews, and Protestants* (N. Y., 1934).

216   16   ". . . wars." J. M. Versteeg, "A New Holiness Movement," *Christian Century*, LII, 109-111 (Jan. 23, 1935); H. M. Robinson, *Fantastic Interim* (N. Y., 1943), 292; editorial in the *Nation*, CXLIX, 135 (Aug. 5, 1939).

216   28   ". . . years before." See C. R. Fish, *The Rise of the Common Man* (*A History of American Life*, VI), 187-190. An account of Rutherford appears in *Current Biography for 1940*, 702-705.

217   3   ". . . civil-liberty suits." H. R. Southworth, "Jehovah's 50,000 Witnesses," *Nation*, CLI, 110-112 (Aug. 10, 1940); and a pictorial account of their activities in *Life*, IX, 20-21 (Aug. 12, 1940). The Court in 1940 ruled that the requirement that public-school teachers and pupils salute the flag was constitutional, but that state acts penalizing a sect for public solicitation of funds were not. Cantwell *v.* Connecticut, 310 U. S., 296. Later decisions, however, amplified and modified this decision. For a general account, see H. H. Stroup, *The Jehovah's Witnesses* (N. Y., 1945).

217   32   ". . . the sedition statutes." McWilliams, *Southern California*, 262-266, discusses both the Ballard and the Bell cults.

219   4   ". . . in 1933." J. F. Steiner, *Research Memorandum on Recreation in the Depression* (Social Sci. Research Coun., *Bull.*, no. 32, 1937), 45.

219   11   ". . . the same eclipse." For shrinking athletic-club memberships, see Steiner, *Recreation in the Depression*, 83, and F. L. Allen, *Since Yesterday* (N. Y., 1940),

Page Line

148. Social clubs with light dues and overhead—women's clubs, civic and luncheon clubs—survived more easily. Charles W. Ferguson in his *Fifty Million Brothers: a Panorama of American Lodges and Clubs* (N. Y., 1937) has a kind word for Rotary, chambers of commerce and other groups which in the previous decade would have stirred naught save derision in the young intellectual.

219 20 ". . . million to nine." As reckoned by Postmaster-General James A. Farley, *Behind the Ballots* (N. Y., 1938), 257-258.

219 26 ". . . million in all." *Fortune*, V (Jan. 1932), 46.

220 24 ". . . outcome of games." President's Research Committee, *Recent Social Trends in the United States* (N. Y., 1933), II, 909, 929.

220 29 ". . . indebtedness." See P. W. Slosson, *The Great Crusade and After* (*A History of American Life*, XII), 274-275.

221 26 ". . . began to flag." *Information Please Almanac for 1947*, 847.

222 13 ". . . the growing generation." For typical surveys of needs, see Ruth E. Eckert and T. O. Marshall, *When Youth Leave School* (N. Y., 1938), 311; C. G. Wrenn and D. L. Hartley, *Time on Their Hands* (Wash., 1941), 5; and National Recreation Association, *The Leisure Hours of 5,000 People* (N. Y., 1934), 1-2.

222 24 ". . . of CCC labor." Fanning Hearon, "The Recreation Renaissance," *Recreation*, XXIX (1935), 289-293, 324-325.

223 8 ". . . million in 1935." W. W. Pangburn, "Play and Recreation," Am. Acad. of Polit. and Social Sci., *Annals*, CCXII, 123; E. K. Lindley, *Half Way with Roosevelt* (N. Y., 1936), 143.

Page	Line	

223 12 ". . . million." F. D. Roosevelt, *Public Papers and Addresses* (S. I. Rosenman, ed., N. Y., 1938-1941), VII, 554.

223 16 ". . . chain of trails." Justin Cline, "Youth Hostels: America," *Nation's Schools*, XX (1937), 14-18.

224 1 ". . . centers increased tenfold." National Recreation Association, *Municipal and County Parks in the United States: 1940* (N. Y., 1940), viii, 14.

224 7 ". . . and the like." J. R. Tunis, *Democracy in Sport* (N. Y., 1941), 35; G. D. Butler, *Introduction to Community Recreation* (N. Y., 1940), 73-74.

224 18 ". . . and amateur drama." Federal Works Agency, *Report on Progress of the WPA Program* (Wash., 1939), 92. A considerable number of these recreational facilities were for Negroes or both races. The number of archery ranges and shuffleboard courts doubled between 1935 and 1939. *Recreation*, XXXIV (1940-1941), 137. A year later more than half a million teams were playing softball. Its vogue doubtless owed much to the new temper of American sport—more casual, friendly, less grimly competitive. Arthur Noren, "Softball—the New American Fever," *Recreation*, XXXIV, 735-736, 745.

224 33 ". . . and sun bathing." For federal spending estimates, see Wrenn and Harley, *Time on Their Hands*, 48; and for New York City developments, Hubert Herring, "Robert Moses and His Parks," *Harper's Mag.*, CLXXVI (1937), 26-37.

225 15 ". . . slacks." Census of Manufactures news release, Sept. 5, 1935.

225 17 ". . . thronging the highways." Butler, *Community Recreation*, 44; J. F. Steiner in President's Research Committee, *Recent Social Trends*, II, 922.

226 8 ". . . steamer." Konrad Bercovici, "Gypsy in a Trailer," *Harper's Mag.*, CLXXIV (1937), 621-626, and CLXXV (1937), 67-75.

Page Line

226 20 ". . . the year before." P. G. Hoffman and N. M. Clark, "The White Line Isn't Enough," *Sat. Eve. Post*, CCX, 12-13 (March 26, 1938); *World Almanac for 1943*, 507; John Bainbridge, *Little Wonder* (N. Y., 1946), 56-58.

226 31 ". . . billion in 1941." *World Almanac for 1943*, 505.

226 33 ". . . the Depression struck." See Slosson, *Great Crusade and After*, 231-233.

227 3 ". . . by the R.F.C." L. M. Hacker, *American Problems of Today* (N. Y., 1938), 253-254.

227 20 ". . . fourth." G. E. Barber, "The Air-Conditioning Equipment Industry," *Harvard Business Rev.*, XI, 356; R. S. Vaile, *Research Memorandum on Social Aspects of Consumption in the Depression* (Social Sci. Research Coun., *Bull.*, no. 35, 1937), 36; G. R. Harrison, *Atoms in Action* (N. Y., 1939), 298.

228 8 ". . . in 1941 alone." J. F. Steiner, *Americans at Play* (N. Y., 1933), 58; Keith Hutchinson, "Aircraft Preferred," *Nation*, CXLIX, 579-580 (Nov. 25, 1939); *International Year Book for 1941*, 7. For earlier developments, see Slosson, *Great Crusade and After*, 397-405.

228 24 ". . . act in 1935." H. L. Smith, *Airways* (N. Y., 1942), chaps. xx-xxii.

228 33 ". . . freight." *World Almanac for 1942*, 279-280.

229 3 ". . . a hundred thousand." *International Year Book for 1940*, 6; for *1941*, 6.

229 18 ". . . sight." For early depression figures, see the *Brookmire Analyst*, June 9, 1930, 4. Later ones appear in Steiner, *Recreation in the Depression*, 95; Vaile, *Social Aspects of Consumption in the Depression*, 24; and P. F. Peter, "The American Listener in 1940," Am. Acad. of Polit. and Social Sci., *Annals*, CCXIII, 1-2.

Page Line
229   23   ". . . habits of listeners." P. F. Lazarsfeld, *Radio and the Printed Page* (N. Y., 1940), 302-329.

229   26   ". . . in daily use." As shown by a joint survey of the two leading chains in 1938, cited by Peter, "American Listener in 1940," 3.

230   4   ". . . stations." Llewellyn White, *The American Radio* (Commission on Freedom of the Press, *Publs.*, V, Chicago, 1947), 20-22.

230   12   ". . . doubled." K. G. Bartlett, "Trends in Radio Programs," Am. Acad. of Polit. and Social Sci., *Annals*, CCXIII, 16-17.

230   27   ". . . of military decision." Dixon Wecter, "Hearing Is Believing," *Atlantic Mo.*, CLXXVI (1945), 61.

230   31   ". . . -presidency in 1920." *N. Y. Times*, Dec. 6, 1936.

231   2   ". . . the unseen audience." For helpful comment on these matters the writer is indebted to Edward T. Canby, gramophone editor of the *Saturday Review of Literature*.

231   20   ". . . car in panic." Hadley Cantril, *The Invasion from Mars* (Princeton, 1940).

231   35   ". . . unpopular listening hours." Peter, "American Listener in 1940," 6; P. F. Lazarsfeld, "The Daily Newspaper and Its Competitors," Am. Acad. of Polit. and Social Sci., *Annals*, CCIX, 40; White, *American Radio*, 54-65.

232   11   ". . . papers." T. R. Carskadon, "The Press-Radio War," *New Republic*, LXXXVI, 132-135 (March 11, 1936); T. C. Streibert and Fulton Lewis, jr., "Radio as a News Medium," Am. Acad. of Polit. and Social Sci., *Annals*, CCXIII, 59.

232   19   ". . . 1934) eighty-three." White, *American Radio*, 20-22.

233   2   ". . . pression." Douglas Waples, *Research Memorandum on Social Aspects of Reading in the Depres-*

Page Line

        sion (Social Sci. Research Coun., *Bull.*, no. 37, 1937), 187; H. A. and B. W. Overstreet, *Town Meeting Comes to Town* (N. Y., 1938).

234   7   ". . . popular." Dickson Skinner, "Music Goes into Mass Production," *Harper's Mag.*, CLXXVIII (1939), 484-490.

234   26   ". . . rhythmic style." See Slosson, *Great Crusade and After*, 281-283.

235   16   ". . . over the nation." "Whoa-ho-ho-ho-ho!" *Time*, XXVII, 32 *n.* (Jan. 20, 1936). Dance-band leaders like Goodman, Tommy Dorsey, Harry James and "Count" Basie found their leading impresario in a young New York enthusiast named John Henry Hammond. See Irving Kolodin, "Number One Swing Man," *Harper's Mag.*, CLXXIX (1939), 431-440.

236   7   ". . . amusement." See Slosson, *Great Crusade and After*, 393.

236   12   ". . . began to flow." Lewis Jacobs, *The Rise of the American Film: a Critical History* (N. Y., 1939), 423.

236   16   ". . . family." L. C. Rosten, *Hollywood: the Movie Colony—the Movie Makers* (N. Y., 1941), 3. Hollywood's scale of affluence was little affected by the Great Depression; with envy or disapproval the citizen continued to read of $7500-a-week actresses and $100,000-a-year directors (73).

237   12   ". . . fects." Typical studies are Edgar Dale, *The Content of Motion Pictures* (N. Y., 1935), Ruth C. Peterson and L. L. Thurstone, *Motion Pictures and the Social Attitudes of Children* (N. Y., 1933), and other monographs written under the Payne Fund. A more philosophical essay upon the theme is Mortimer Adler, *Art and Prudence* (N. Y., 1937).

237   24   ". . . of the 1920's." Ruth A. Inglis, *Freedom of the Movies* (Commission on Freedom of the Press, *Publs.*, IV, Chicago, 1947), 4, 8-11.

Page Line

238 29 ". . . scored its point." See Raymond Moley, *The Hays Office* (Indianapolis, 1945), chap. vi, and Inglis, *Freedom of the Movies,* 120-125.

239 5 ". . . actor Charlie Chaplin." For the earlier career of the century's most famous comic, see Slosson, *Great Crusade and After,* 395.

240 3 ". . . social justice." Outside the ambit of Hollywood, the several excellent documentaries by Pare Lorentz on soil conservation and his dramatic story of obstetrics in Chicago's slums, "The Fight for Life" (1940), were produced by the United States Film Service, financed out of WPA and PWA funds, but terminated by Congress in 1940.

241 17 ". . . prosperous." E. R. Beach, "Double Features in Motion-Picture Exhibitions," *Harvard Business Rev.,* X, 505-515.

241 31 ". . . before." Inglis, *Freedom of the Movies,* 47-50.

242 3 ". . . of the drawing." In Denver an almost penniless hitchhiker and his wife won a $20,000 "Cinderella house." Forbes Parkhill, "Bank Night Tonight," *Sat. Eve. Post,* CCX, 20-21 (Dec. 4, 1937).

243 2 ". . . a billion dollars." Samuel Lubell, "Ten Billion Nickels," *Sat. Eve. Post,* CCXI, 12-13 (May 13, 1939).

243 13 ". . . annually in wagers." "The Numbers," *Time,* XXIX, 42-43 (Jan. 4, 1937).

243 30 ". . . risk-taking nature." "America Gambling," *Life,* VI, 45-53 (Feb. 6, 1939), in a pictorial review of Herbert Asbury's *Sucker's Progress: an Informal History of Gambling in America from the Colonies to Canfield* (N. Y., 1938).

244 3 ". . . two read books." Merle Curti, *The Growth of American Thought* (N. Y., 1943), 702.

244 19 ". . . subjects." R. L. Duffus, *Our Starving Libraries* (Boston, 1933), 2, 52-53, 117, 131; "The Public

Page *Line*

Library in the Depression," *Library Quar.*, II (1932), 321-343.

244 26 ". . . soever." Duffus, *Our Starving Libraries*, 27-28; C. J. Enzler, *Some Social Aspects of the Depression* (Wash., 1939), 120-121.

245 9 ". . . -one million copies." Douglas Waples, "Communications," *Am. Journ. of Sociology*, XLVII, 910.

245 18 ". . . 600 in 1930." Paul Neurath, "One-Publisher Communities," *Journalism Quar.*, XXI (1944), 230-242; B. N. Garnett, "Changes in the Basic Newspaper Pattern," Am. Acad. of Polit. and Social Sci., *Annals*, CCXIX, 57; C. E. Rogers, "The Rôle of the Weekly Newspaper," same vol., 151-157; M. L. Ernst, *The First Freedom* (N. Y., 1946), 291.

245 30 ". . . publicity & communication." Jacob Loft, *The Printing Trades* (N. Y., 1944), 28-31. For a sweeping review of the problem, see Ernst, *First Freedom*, who remarks that the disappearance of a thousand newspapers from modern America is no less ominous than the dominion by four radio networks of programs broadcast by two thirds of all stations, or the control by five movie companies of seventy per cent of the cinema traffic. See also Commission on Freedom of the Press, *A Free and Responsible Press* (Chicago, 1947).

246 1 ". . . kind of newspaper." A. M. Lee, *The Daily Newspaper in America* (N. Y., 1937), 276; Nettie P. McGill and Ellen N. Matthews, *The Youth of New York City* (N. Y., 1940), 282.

246 12 ". . . comics and pictures." F. L. Mott, "Trends in Newspaper Content," Am. Acad. of Polit. and Social Sci., *Annals*, CCXIX, 63.

246 20 ". . . them to adults." W. M. Marston, "Why 100,-000,000 Americans Read Comics," *Am. Scholar*, XIII (1943-1944), 35-44, who dates the start of this transition from "funny papers" to "adventure comics" about 1930.

Page *Line*

246 30 ". . . henceforth widely adopted." "$30,000,000 Worth of Teletype," *Fortune*, V (March 1932), 40-43 ff.

247 14 ". . . resided in numbers." A popular account is Charles Fisher, *The Columnists* (N. Y., 1944).

248 1 ". . . other periodicals." J. J. Firebaugh, "Vocabulary of *Time* Magazine," *Am. Speech*, XV (1940), 232-242.

248 14 ". . . sixteen million." For a sardonic commentary, see J. L. Brown, "Picture Magazines and Morons," *Am. Mercury*, XLV (1938), 404-408.

248 22 ". . . best-seller ranks." F. L. Allen, *Since Yesterday* (N. Y., 1940), 263-264.

248 25 ". . . abolishing that ordeal." *Fortune*, XIII (June 1936), 101.

249 2 ". . . novels." Alfred Kazin, *On Native Grounds* (N. Y., 1942), 493-499, observes that "nothing in this new literature, indeed, stands out so clearly as its attempt to use and even to imitate the camera."

249 17 ". . . 1935 onward." Douglas Waples, *Research Memorandum on Social Aspects of Reading in the Depression* (Social Sci. Research Coun., *Bull.*, no. 37, 1937), 60-61, 75-76.

249 21 ". . . and political debate." Elizabeth B. Schlesinger, "They Say Women Are Emancipated," *New Republic*, LXXVII, 125-127 (Dec. 13, 1933), and "The Women's Magazines," same mag., CXIV, 345-347 (March 11, 1946).

250 21 ". . . *Omnibook* also popularized." John Bainbridge, *Little Wonder; or, The Reader's Digest and How It Grew* (N. Y., 1946).

250 25 ". . . flow gradually resumed." Waples, *Social Aspects of Reading in the Depression*, 60.

Page Line

250 29 ". . . bookshops." C. T. Wheeler, "Dollar Books—a Pricing Experiment," *Harvard Business Rev.*, X, 341-437.

251 5 ". . . of book clubs." For the earlier period, see P. W. Slosson, *The Great Crusade and After* (*A History of American Life*, XII), 423-424.

251 31 ". . . 1929 and 1939." Waples, "Communications," 908 and table; Ernst, *First Freedom*, 294.

254 17 ". . . of Soviet ideology." For glimpses of the League in its heyday, see Henry Hart, ed., *American Writers' Congress* (N. Y., 1935), and Malcolm Cowley, "Notes on a Writers' Congress," *New Republic*, XCIX, 192 (June 21, 1939); for the subsequent upset, Granville Hicks, "On Leaving the Communist Party," same mag., C, 244-245 (Oct. 4, 1939).

260 25 ". . . Treasury." Federal Works Agency, *Questions and Answers on the WPA* (Wash., 1939), 22; "Work of the Federal Writers' Project of WPA," *Publishers' Weekly*, CXXXV, pt. i, 1130-1135 (March 18, 1939).

261 8 ". . . den clarity." Katharine Kellock, "The WPA Writers: Portraitists of the United States," *Am. Scholar*, IX (1940), 475.

261 25 ". . . degree redressed." R. C. Binkley, "The Cultural Program of the WPA," *Harvard Educational Rev.*, IX, 156-174; Federal Works Agency, *Questions and Answers*, 22.

261 32 ". . . Hollywood casting bureaus." Hallie Flanagan, *Arena* (N. Y., 1940), 14.

262 24 ". . . million people annually." Albert McCleery and Carl Glick, *Curtains Going Up* (N. Y., 1939); Marjorie Patten, *The Arts Workshop of Rural America* (N. Y., 1937).

264 8 ". . . in this country." Quoted in the *Congressional Record*, LXXXIV, pt. viii, 8100 (June 28, 1939).

Page Line

264 20 ". . . the project closed." During its lifetime the Federal Theater produced 1813 plays, with an average of 1077 performances monthly. Federal Works Agency, *Questions and Answers*, 22. For the Dies report and the closing phase, see Flanagan, *Arena*, 347-363.

266 18 ". . . of this era." F. P. Keppel and R. L. Duffus, *The Arts in American Life* (N. Y., 1933), 168. The total number of commercial concerts fell from about 3750 in 1929-1930 to 2600 in 1932-1933, then climbed back to normal by 1936-1937. J. T. Howard, "Better Days for Music," *Harper's Mag.*, CLXXIV (1937), 483-491.

266 25 ". . . private lessons." "Federal Music Project," Oscar Thompson, ed., *International Cyclopedia of Music and Musicians* (N. Y., 1939); Federal Works Agency, *Questions and Answers*, 22.

266 34 ". . . the past ten." Harold Stearns, ed., *America Now* (N. Y., 1938), 68. See also J. T. Howard, *Our American Music* (3d edn., N. Y., 1946), 690-691.

267 25 ". . . soon." A useful account of early developments is Edward Bruce, "Art and Democracy," *Atlantic Mo.*, CLVI (1935), 149-152.

267 32 ". . . of Rockefeller Center." For poetic comment on the Rivera incident, see Archibald MacLeish, *Frescoes for Mr. Rockefeller's City* (N. Y., 1933).

268 12 ". . . color and texture." Constance Rourke, "Index of American Design," *Magazine of Art*, XXX (1937), 207-211 ff.

268 17 ". . . and doctrinaire canvases." Moreover, as the former director, Holger Cahill, wrote retrospectively, the regional emphasis "in many instances became lost in hometown enthusiasms that ran to the sentimental-picturesque." "In Our Time," *Magazine of Art*, XXXIX (1946), 310. See also F. H. Taylor, "The

Page *Line*

American Artist: 1935," *Atlantic Mo.*, CLVII (1936), 182-188.

269 31 ". . . building and endowment." E. A. Jewell, "Mellon's Gift," *Magazine of Art*, XXX (1937), 78-83.

270 13 ". . . Chicago's Field Museum." Her world-wide quest is related in *Heads and Tales* (N. Y., 1936).

272 11 ". . . during the year." The conclusions rested upon a careful sample survey of a third of a million families and individuals living alone. National Resources Committee, *The Consumer Spends His Income* (Wash., 1939), 4-7. The 14 per cent of consumer units with incomes under $500 spent nearly 52 per cent more than they earned (14). The figures cited later are also drawn from this digest.

273 16 ". . . a bare $9." Committee on the Costs of Medical Care, *Medical Care for the American People* (Chicago, 1932); I. S. Falk, C. R. Rorem and Martha D. Ring, *The Costs of Medical Care* (Chicago, 1933).

273 28 ". . . centers or clinics." U. S. Bureau of Agricultural Economics, *Technology on the Farm* (Wash., 1940), 209; Helen Hall and Paul Kellogg, "The Unserved Millions," *Survey Graphic*, XXVII (1938), 436-441.

274 2 ". . . American Medical Association." For the conservative point of view, see Morris Fishbein, "Sickness Insurance and Sickness Costs," *Hygeia*, XII (1934), 1070-1076.

274 13 ". . . full-time employed." G. St. J. Perrott and S. D. Collins, *Relation of Sickness to Income and Income Changes in Ten Surveyed Communities* (*U. S. Public Health Report*, L, no. 18, May 3, 1935); Edgar Sydenstricker, "Health and the Depression," Milbank Memorial Fund, *Quar. Bull.*, XI (1933), 273-280.

274 26 ". . . and sometimes refused." Daisy Worcester, "Public Health and Private Doctors," *Survey Graphic*, XXIII (1934), 148-155; President's Research Com-

Page *Line*

mittee, *Recent Social Trends in the United States* (N. Y., 1933), II, 910.

275 16 ". . . cians." S. D. Collins and Clark Tibbitts, *Research Memorandum on Social Aspects of Health in the Depression* (Social Sci. Research Coun., *Bull.*, no. 36, 1937), 169; U. S. Department of Agriculture, *Yearbook for 1940*, 875.

275 32 ". . . right." This speech and a summary of findings by the National Health Survey of 1937-1938—confirming higher illness rates among the unemployed and poorly employed—are in James Rorty, *American Medicine Mobilizes* (N. Y., 1939), chap. i.

276 15 ". . . subscribers." C.-E. A. Winslow, "Medical Care for the Nation," *Yale Rev.*, XXVII (1939), 504; Collins and Tibbitts, *Social Aspects of Health in the Depression*, 169. For early developments, including employers' insurance systems, see Pierce Williams, *The Purchase of Medical Care through Fixed Periodic Payment* (Natl. Bur. of Econ. Research, *Publs.*, no. 20, 1932); for later ones, I. S. Falk, *Security against Sickness* (N. Y., 1936).

276 33 ". . . organizations at work." Avis D. Carlson, "And Now a Co-op Hospital," *Survey Graphic*, XXVI (1937), 470-473; John Daniels, *Cooperation: an American Way* (N. Y., 1938), 330-337.

276 36 ". . . in the twenties." See P. W. Slosson, *The Great Crusade and After* (*A History of American Life*, XII), 212-213.

277 17 ". . . million members." Horace Taylor and others, *Main Currents in Modern Economic Life* (N. Y., 1941), II, 207; R. H. Elsworth, *Statistics of Farmers' Cooperative Business Organizations* (Farm Credit Administration, Wash., 1936), 120. Interest in the cooperative principle was sufficiently widespread for Roosevelt to send a fact-finding committee, headed by

Page Line

Jacob Baker, to study European systems in 1936. See its report, *Coöperative Enterprise in Europe* (1937).

277　25　". . . and inferior materials." See Slosson, *Great Crusade and After*, 362-371, and Helen Sorenson, *The Consumer Movement* (N. Y., 1941), 9-10.

278　4　". . . its best advertisers." Elizabeth E. Hoyt, *Consumption in Our Society* (N. Y., 1938), 117.

278　16　". . . distrust and comparison." Kenneth Dameron, "The Consumer Movement," *Harvard Business Rev.*, XVII, 271-289.

279　3　". . . combined mailing lists." Early developments are sketched in President's Research Committee, *Recent Social Trends*, chap. xvii, and by Edith Ayers, "Private Organizations Working for the Consumer," Am. Acad. of Polit. and Social Sci., *Annals*, CLXXIII, 158-165; for later aspects Sorenson, *Consumer Movement*, gives a comprehensive picture.

279　9　". . . the *Consumers' Guide*." Persia C. Campbell, *Consumer Representation in the New Deal* (N. Y., 1940).

279　24　". . . and labels." Basil Rauch, *The History of the New Deal, 1933-1938* (N. Y., 1944), 308. For the earlier law, see H. U. Faulkner, *The Quest for Social Justice* (*A History of American Life*, XI), 237-238.

279　35　". . . setting the pace." Bernard Jaffe, *Men of Science in America* (N. Y., 1944), 544.

280　24　". . . were other innovations." For the development of plastics, see William Haynes, *This Chemical Age* (N. Y., 1942).

281　4　". . . nation's annual output." G. W. Gray, *The Advancing Front of Science* (N. Y., 1937), 161.

281　32　". . . forty simultaneous conversations." G. R. Harrison, *Atoms in Action* (N. Y., 1939), 60.

Page *Line*
282 16 ". . . hundred million pounds." "Birdseye Frosted Foods," *Fortune*, X (Oct. 1934), 135-137; "Quick-Frozen Foods," same mag., XIX (June 1939), 61-65 ff.; J. P. Ferris and R. B. Taylor, "Immersion Quick Freezing, Its Application to Rural Processing Industry," *Mechanical Engineering*, LXI (1939), 437-442.

282 22 ". . . annually by 1930." Jaffe, *Men of Science in America*, 462. For the earlier developments, see Slosson, *Great Crusade and After*, 380-381.

282 35 ". . . in checking haemorrhage." W. J. Dann, "Nicotinic Acid and Vitamin B₂," *Science*, LXXXVI, 616-617 (Dec. 31, 1937); E. A. Doisy and others, "Vitamin K," same mag., XCI, 58-62 (Jan. 19, 1940).

283 20 ". . . dollars annually." Editorial in *New Republic*, XCVII, 272 (Jan. 11, 1939).

283 35 ". . . efficacy against anemia." R. O. Cummings, *The American and His Food* (Chicago, 1940), chaps. xii-xiv.

284 6 ". . . 1937 onward." John Pfeiffer, "Sulfanilamide," *Harper's Mag.*, CLXXVIII (1939), 386-396.

284 36 ". . . brain tumors." B. M. Newman, "Electrical Rhythms of the Human Brain," *Scientific American*, CLIX (1938), 186-188, 236-238.

285 18 ". . . and wet seasons." A. E. Douglass, *Tree Rings and Chronology* (Univ. of Arizona, *Bull.*, VIII, no. 4, 1937).

286 7 ". . . radically new traits." H. J. Muller, "Heritable Variations, Their Production by X Rays and Their Relation to Evolution," Smithsonian Institution, *Ann. Rep. for 1929*, 345-362. For background, note his *Out of the Night: a Biologist's View of the Future* (N. Y., 1935).

Page Line

286   28   "... nearly three quarters." President and Treasurer of the Carnegie Corporation, *Report for the Year Ended September 30, 1941* (N. Y., 1941), 40.

286   34   "... Mrs. Felix Fuld." See "Organization and Purpose," Institute for Advanced Study, *Bull.*, no. 1, 1930.

287   28   "... began." Jaffe, *Men of Science*, 486-489.

288   7   "... snug and deterministic." For relativity, see Slosson, *Great Crusade and After*, 374.

288   26   "... probably much less." For an authoritative summary of these developments, see R. A. Millikan, *Electrons (+ and —), Protons, Photons, Neutrons, Mesotrons, and Cosmic Rays* (rev. edn., Chicago, 1947), 360-406.

289   4   "... makes 'heavy water.'" Jaffe, *Men of Science*, 520.

289   14   "... a Nobel Prize." Gray, *Advancing Front of Science*, 103-105.

289   36   "... to be smashed." E. O. Lawrence, "Atoms Old and New," G. A. Baitsell, ed., *Science in Progress* (New Haven, 1939), I, i. Merle A. Tuve at the Carnegie Institution's Department of Research in Terrestial Magnetism was another pioneer in atom smashing.

290   15   "... nium." The state of atomic research on the eve of the Second World War is well set forth by A. K. Solomon, *Why Smash Atoms?* (Cambridge, 1940).

290   23   "... August 5, 1945." J. P. Baxter, 3d, *Scientists against Time* (Boston, 1946), chaps. xxvii-xxviii.

290   32   "... beauty." Jaffe, *Men of Science*, 554.

291   7   "... to all mankind." J. E. Thornton, ed., *Science and Social Change* (Wash., 1939), 512.

292   1   "... half times actuality." Harold Loeb and others, *The Chart of Plenty* (N. Y., 1935), xiii, 148. This book, though useful, should be accepted with caution

Page Line

by reason of its sketchy methods and lush generalizations.

292 16 ". . . sionate and intelligent." National Resources Committee, *Technological Trends and National Policy* (Wash., 1937), 87; Thornton, ed., *Science and Social Change*, 295; S. M. and Laura Rosen, *Technology and Society* (N. Y., 1941), 457. For Roosevelt's comment on this problem, see his *Public Papers and Addresses* (S. I. Rosenman, ed., N. Y., 1938-1941), VIII, 285.

292 36 ". . . of visitors." *New International Year Book for 1933*, 135. For the exposition of 1893, see A. M. Schlesinger, *The Rise of the City* (*A History of American Life*, X), 283-286.

296 24 ". . . and the safe." R. S. and Helen M. Lynd, *Middletown in Transition* (N. Y., 1937), 419. For a sensitive analysis of such fears and worries, see Avis D. Carlson, "Courage for Tomorrow," *Harper's Mag.*, CLXXVIII (1939), 466-473.

297 11 ". . . an earlier day." Well expressed in Elton Mayo's analysis of industrial maladjustments in *Social Problems of an Industrial Society* (Cambridge, 1945), chap. i.

299 29 ". . . against foreign enmity." F. D. Roosevelt, *Public Papers and Addresses* (S. I. Rosenman, ed., N. Y., 1938-1941), VIII, 5-7.

300 32 ". . . permission to migrate." Louis Adamic, *America and the Refugees* (*Public Affairs Pamphlet*, no. 29, 1939), 13. Jews were admitted not under a quota of their own, but that of the country of birth, which decidedly favored their entry under pressures of persecution. *American Year Book for 1940*, 593-594. For development of the quota system, see P. W. Slosson, *The Great Crusade and After* (*A History of American Life*, XII), 299-302.

301 9 ". . . since 1820-1830." *World Almanac for 1947*, 780.

Page Line
301   18   ". . . of their adoption." Harold Fields, *The Refugee in the United States* (N. Y., 1938), 119, 125-140, and Malcolm Cowley, "Exiles of the Arts," *New Republic*, XCIX, 105-106 (May 31, 1939). M. R. Davie, *Refugees in America* (N. Y., 1947), is the fullest account.

302   15   ". . . caldron of intolerance." Arthur Derounian (John Roy Carlson, *pseud.*), *Under Cover* (N. Y., 1943), *passim*.

302   26   ". . . it is true." "Good Will to Men," *Atlantic Mo.*, CLXII (1938), 733-740. See also "Jews in America," *Fortune*, XIII (Feb. 1936), 79-85 ff.; and A. J. Smith, "Christian Terror: Anti-Semitism in New York City," *Christian Century*, LVI, 1017-1019 (Aug. 23, 1939). In 1938 the publishers Simon & Schuster withdrew from sale Jerome Weidman's novels because they showed Jews in an unfavorable light. *American Year Book for 1938,* 799.

305   1   ". . . conference in London." Herbert Hoover, *State Papers* (W. S. Myers, ed., N. Y., 1934), I, 233, also II, 22, 337. At the time this was no partisan issue. W. S. Myers and W. H. Newton, *The Hoover Administration* (N. Y., 1936), 294, note Roosevelt's telegram to Hoover on December 19, 1932, calling the president's disarmament policy "clear and satisfactory." Nevertheless, as an old navy man, Roosevelt in power soon began to foster warship building.

305   5   ". . . intervention in 1917." War Policies Commission, *Hearings before the Commission Appointed under the Authority of Public Resolution No. 98* (71 Cong., 2 sess., 1931).

306   3   ". . . victim." Allan Nevins and L. M. Hacker, eds., *The United States and Its Place in World Affairs* (Boston, 1943), 390-395.

306   23   ". . . War and Fascism." Dorothy Thompson, "Who Wants Peace?" *Survey Graphic*, XXVI (1937), 57-62 ff.

Page	Line	

307 2 ". . . fensive war." *World Tomorrow*, XVII (1934), 226-230. The story of clergymen in the First World War is told in a manner characteristic of the thirties by Ray H. Abrams, *Preachers Present Arms* (N. Y., 1933); the sequel of their growing reluctance is traced by Walter Van Kirk, *Religion Renounces War* (Chicago, 1934).

307 18 ". . . objectors." See H. M. Bell, *Youth Tell Their Story* (Wash., 1938), 246-249; Maxine Davis, *The Lost Generation* (N. Y., 1936), 99-101; and for first-hand statements, World Youth Congress, *Youth Demands a Peaceful World* (N. Y., 1938).

307 28 ". . . a narrow margin." Harvey Wish, *Contemporary America* (N. Y., 1945), 566.

308 24 ". . . the American temper." *Propaganda Analysis*, March, 1938, 1. For merchandisers' protests against Japan, see "The Boycott Is Winning," *Nation*, CXLVI, 33 (Jan. 8, 1938).

309 14 ". . . or his conscience." Roosevelt, *Public Papers*, VIII, 460-464. The impossibility he recognized was one which Woodrow Wilson had requested in exhorting his countrymen in 1914 to be "impartial in thought as well as in action." Wilson, *Public Papers* (N. Y., 1927), III, 157-159. Attitudes on the brink of this second war—hazy but intense, under the conviction that "something ought to be done," yet with a pervasive sense of escapism—are well analyzed by R. L. Neuberger, "What the Home Folks Say about Events Abroad," *Harper's Mag.*, CLXXIX (1939), 407-412. In this same issue, 337-351, occurs also a characteristic article by Charles A. Beard, "Giddy Minds and Foreign Quarrels."

309 24 ". . . sharpened its expression." A useful account of Roosevelt's leadership in the light of the Gallup polls is given by Hadley Cantril, "Public Opinion in Flux," *Am. Acad. of Polit. and Social Sci., Annals*, CCXX,

Page   Line

136-152, somewhat expanded in the same author's *Gauging Public Opinion* (Princeton, 1944).

311   14   ". . . ability to pay." Nevins and Hacker, *United States and Its Place in World Affairs*, 467-468.

311   29   ". . . war in Europe." D. S. Howard, *The WPA and Federal Relief Policy* (N. Y., 1943), 133; *American Year Book for 1940*, 638-641.

312   11   ". . . break with precedent." C. W. Stein, *The Third-Term Tradition* (N. Y., 1943), 333-339.

312   34   ". . . hundred and two." For a tabulation of these votes, see editorial, "Mr. Roosevelt's First Speech," *N. Y. Times*, Oct. 7, 1944.

314   12   ". . . march against fascism." Roosevelt, *Public Papers*, IX, 672.

315   4   ". . . security." Sumner Welles, *Where Are We Heading?* (N. Y., 1946), 4-17.

316   31   ". . . 'This is it.' " Forrest Davis and E. K. Lindley, *How War Came: an American White Paper* (N. Y., 1942), 3-6.

317   4   ". . . still sailing westward." In W. E. Lingelbach, ed., *Approaches to American Social History* (N. Y., 1937), 84.

INDEX

415